RECONSTRUCTING PARENTAGE

Reconstructing Parentage is a comprehensive investigation into what makes someone a parent. Drawing on liberal-egalitarian philosophy, the book argues that the community must ensure children's basic rights, including their right to a parent. In light of parenthood's political foundation, no adult could have a natural right or duty to parent based in genetics, procreation, caregiving, or intentions. Nevertheless, by scrutinizing existing law, the book uncovers a limited role for each intuitive basis of parentage and reassembles them into a pluralistic system of parentage law. *Reconstructing Parentage* offers a timely and thought-provoking analysis of a complex and contentious issue in modern society.

Gregg Strauss is Professor of Law at the University of Virginia School of Law, where he is Codirector of the Family Law Center.

Reconstructing Parentage

GREGG STRAUSS
University of Virginia

CAMBRIDGE
UNIVERSITY PRESS

CAMBRIDGE
UNIVERSITY PRESS

Shaftesbury Road, Cambridge CB2 8EA, United Kingdom

One Liberty Plaza, 20th Floor, New York, NY 10006, USA

477 Williamstown Road, Port Melbourne, VIC 3207, Australia

314–321, 3rd Floor, Plot 3, Splendor Forum, Jasola District Centre,
New Delhi – 110025, India

103 Penang Road, #05–06/07, Visioncrest Commercial, Singapore 238467

Cambridge University Press is part of Cambridge University Press & Assessment,
a department of the University of Cambridge.

We share the University's mission to contribute to society through the pursuit of education, learning and research at the highest international levels of excellence.

www.cambridge.org
Information on this title: www.cambridge.org/9781009485418

DOI: 10.1017/9781009485449

When citing this work, please include a reference to the DOI 10.1017/9781009485449

First published 2025

A catalogue record for this publication is available from the British Library

A Cataloging-in-Publication data record for this book is available from the Library of Congress

ISBN 978-1-009-48541-8 Hardback
ISBN 978-1-009-48546-3 Paperback

For Laura, Nathan, and Carter, who have taught me everything I know about parenting.

Contents

Acknowledgments

Without the unreserved support of the University of Virginia (UVA) School of Law, from research leave to a manuscript workshop, this book would not exist. Thank you to all my UVA colleagues, who generously gave their time to provide invaluable comments and guidance. Special thanks to Naomi Cahn, Kim Ferzan, and Debbie Hellman for being steadfast sources of discernment as I found my way through the arguments in this book. Thank you to the generous participants at the manuscript workshop, Katherine Baker, Brian Bix, Maxine Eichner, Jennifer Hendricks, Robin Kar, David O'Brien, and Emily Stolzenberg, for your invaluable suggestions. Thanks to Al Levin, my research assistant, for helping me reach the finish line. To my family law colleagues, especially participants in the Family Law Scholars and Teachers Conference, your kindness and insight are a constant source of inspiration. Thank you to my mentors, Larry Solum and Michael Moore, who set me on the law and philosophy path.

Thank you to my extraordinary parents, Debbie and Dale, for sacrificing so much to provide us a wonderful home. And finally, thank you to my wife, Laura, for your boundless patience and support through this lengthy process. Without you, this book and my career would still be a passing dream.

Portions of Chapter 4 are revised versions of material published in Gregg Strauss, *What Role Remains for De Facto Parenthood?*, 46 *Florida State University Law Review* 909 (2018).

Portions of Chapter 5 are revised versions of material published in Gregg Strauss, *Parentage Agreements Are Not Contracts*, 90 *Fordham Law Review* 6 (2021).

Introduction

"Who is this child's parent?" Few questions need a definitive answer more, yet the law of parentage is drifting in the other direction. Some American states now recognize as many as eleven routes to parentage. When the parentage rules conflict, states typically hide behind judicial discretion. Some statutes direct the family court to apply whichever rule rests on "weightier policy," without identifying the relevant policies. Others instruct courts to assign parenthood however serves the best interest of the child, leaving the judge to balance a host of controversial values. Parentage law is calling out for normative guidance.

The evolution of family forms has fractured commonsense norms of parentage, and moral and legal theory have been unable to reunite the pieces. Courts and scholars recognize four fundamental grounds for parenthood – genetics, causation, caregiving, and agreements – but neither courts nor academics identify convincing moral principles to justify inferring parenthood from these factual bases. Each justifies limited rights or duties, but we have no theory to explain how to combine them into a coherent system for assigning the full bundle of parenthood.

Reconstructing Parentage rebuilds a justified system of rules out of contemporary parentage law. The first step is to reorient our perspective on parenthood. Parenthood is not, in the first instance, a personal relationship between a child and an adult. The grounds of parenthood cannot justify parental rights and duties directly because parenthood is a political office. To meet children's basic rights, society must ensure that some caregivers have exclusive authority to guide each child's life. All children have a right to a parent. Some adults have priority to fill this role, but not because they have a natural right or duty. Instead, parentage law finds principles that allow adults to enter the parental role consistent with equal respect for the child and other adults. Guided by liberal-egalitarian political philosophy, each ground of parentage can be shaped to fulfill a limited role. This book reconstructs a pluralistic theory of parentage law that returns order to the many conflicting principles of parentage recognized in existing law, legal theory, and moral philosophy.

I PERVASIVE UNCERTAINTY ABOUT PARENTAGE

Outside family law circles, people often express surprise that it can be challenging to identify a child's parents. Everyone recognizes the complexity of assisted reproductive technology, but most people remain blissfully confident about "ordinary" cases – probably because our cultural imagination is still captured by a midcentury picture of a husband and wife raising their shared genetic children together. Marriage still plays an outsized role in parentage, but it has no intrinsic importance for the law or morality of parentage. The façade of certainty behind marital parenthood cracks easily under the pressure of a handful of mundane and real cases.

The marital paradigm is a tad naïve, even for heterosexual couples. Who should be the father when a married woman conceives a child in an affair? This trite story still confounds parentage law and morality. Pamela Fischer conceived Alicia during an affair with her business partner, Richard Zollino.[1] Pamela wanted to preserve her family with her husband Eric and their older daughter, so she ended the affair. Richard never spoke up but could not hide his interest. When he started attending Alicia's extracurricular activities, Eric became suspicious and sought a paternity test. After raising Alicia for fifteen years, Eric divorced Pamela and sued Richard for the cost of raising the child. The state trial court and supreme court divided, as have many courts, about whether men in Eric and Richard's situation should have a duty to raise and support a child.

In the paradigm case of marital parenthood, a husband is the genetic father of the child conceived with his wife. They plan to raise the child together, and he helps care for the child. Adultery cases illustrate how easily those four factual bases of parenthood – genetics, causation, agreements, and caregiving – might separate. The states have not settled on a consistent approach to conflicts between marital and genetic fathers. Some maintain categorical priority for intact marital families; others allow any genetic fathers to seek parenthood; and many vacillate when a marital father, like Eric, has raised the child.

In contemporary life, a marital paradigm is more than naïve. It is quixotic. For the last fifteen years, around 40 percent of children have been born to unmarried parents.[2] While most nonmarital parents are in a romantic relationship at the time of the birth, they often break up relatively quickly. These children typically live exclusively with their birth mothers, seeing their genetic fathers sporadically, if at all.[3] When unmarried mothers enter new cohabiting relationships, the child will often develop relationships with nonmarital or marital stepparents. Any plausible vision of parenthood must account for these stepparent relationships.

1 Fischer v. Zollino, A.3d 270, 274 (Conn. 2012).

2 Joyce A. Martin et al., *Births: Final Data for 2019* (National Vital Statistics Reports Vol. 70, No. 2, Mar. 23, 2021), www.cdc.gov/nchs/data/nvsr/nvsr70/nvsr70-02-508.pdf.

3 Clare Huntington, *Postmarital Family Law: A Legal Structure for Nonmarital Families*, 67 STAN. L. REV. 167, 188–89 (2015).

Even this broader lens obscures another common childhood experience, one that challenges the tendency to equate parenthood with conjugal partnerships. For the first three years of her life, Anna lived with her mother, Beth.[4] Her father, Charles, was a Marine stationed across the country, where he lived with his wife and two children. When Anna was almost four, her paternal grandmother, Rhonda, received emergency custody because Beth was homeless and abusing drugs. After a year, the adults entered a settlement that made Rhonda the "residential and legal custodian." Beth would receive weekly supervised visits with Anna, which would increase to overnight stays if she sustained a residence, drug treatment, and employment – conditions imposed by the child welfare agency. Charles would see Anna as often as he could arrange it with Rhonda.

Beth maintained her relationship with Anna but met none of the conditions. In the next round of litigation, Rhonda sought permanent custody. Charles would ordinarily have been entitled to custody, but the settlement counted as a waiver of his parental priority, so the judge had authority to select whichever custodian he believed best for Anna. Charles was a good father to his other children and maintained a close relationship with Anna through daily calls. However, the judge worried that a long-distance move would disrupt her life and other relationships, impairing her mental health and development. Rhonda had provided Anna with a home, supplied mental health care, and enrolled her in preschool and enriching activities like gymnastics. Anna's years with her grandmother were the only stable years of her life. The court's judgment made Rhonda a coequal parent for all legal purposes except in name.

Most people think parents should be entitled to seek help caring for their children in times of crisis without losing their parental rights, but once a child develops psychological attachments with a long-term custodial caregiver, their relationship starts to look like parenthood. Should a guardian or stepparent gradually become a legal parent, and does it matter why the parent sought help, what precisely they agreed, or how the child understands the relationship?

When familiar stories like marital infidelity and guardianships still confound our legal and moral intuitions about parentage, it is no wonder that we flounder in the face of innovative reproductive technology. The uncertainty in these assisted reproduction cases might seem to reflect the novelty of the technology, but many of its problems are simply extensions of the same basic conflicts among the four bases of parentage.

Consider gestational surrogacy. Suppose two men decide they want to raise a child, and their female friend agrees to carry an embryo created from a donor egg and the sperm of one of the men. Only one of the males can be a genetic parent, but both are parents by agreement. Both men are also causal parents because the

[4] *In re* A.L., No. 18-C000209, 2021 WL 2072170 (Ohio Ct. App. May 24, 2021) (names abbreviated for anonymity reasons, which I have replaced with hypothetical names).

genetic father would not have taken this path without his partner's encouragement. They are not the only causal parents, however. The egg donor and surrogate are as well. Only the agreement keeps the donors from parentage. Surrogacy cases focus on genetics, causation, and agreements, but caregiving often plays an implicit role. If the intended fathers break up during the pregnancy, many courts will impose child support on the nonbiological father because he helped his partner conceive. Should his causal role through the agreement also be sufficient to give him parental *rights* before he does anything to care for the child?

Once we recognize how parentage agreements deliberately disentangle genetics, causation, and caregiving, even more questions arise. If adults can agree to share parenthood, can they agree to tailor parental rights and duties? Some adoptive or intended parents agree to give visitation rights to birth parents or gamete donors. Two friends on opposite coasts may agree to coparent a child without living together.[5] Maybe three or more adults could agree to coparent. Common sense morality has become a shaky foundation for parentage, and the law has lost its footing as well.

II THE LAW OF PARENTAGE: A QUICK PRIMER

As family forms evolved over the last century, the routes to legal parenthood proliferated. Some US states now recognize as many as eleven parentage doctrines. Each state maintains its own parentage law, primarily passed through statutes but often supplemented by common law. Significant variation exists across states, but the diversity is cabined by federal law and influential model acts. State parentage is shaped by constitutional law and norms regarding parental rights, marital rights, and sex equality, as well as federal statutes regarding child support.[6] This section offers an overview of American parentage law for unfamiliar readers. Subsequent chapters explain each doctrine in detail, with particular attention to the law's internal justification.

In all states, gestational parents are presumed legal parents at birth. Unmarried genetic fathers are not. If birth parents are on amicable terms, they can sign a voluntary acknowledgment of paternity at the hospital. Otherwise, one of them will need to file a paternity petition. If the petition is timely, genetic ties are usually sufficient to establish parentage for purposes of child support and visitation. While state law sets the specific procedures, all states must allow paternity petitions because the Constitution protects genetic fathers' opportunity to become parents. Most states

5 Martha M. Ertman, Love's Promises: How Formal and Informal Contracts Shape All Kinds of Families (2016).

6 Douglas NeJaime, *The Constitution of Parenthood*, 72 Stan. L. Rev. 261 (2020). The United States Supreme Court's interventions are sporadic, and its opinions fracture on the same fault lines as state law, so I am skeptical of calls for the Court or federal constitutional law to settle parentage disputes. *E.g.*, Jeffrey A. Parness, *Federal Constitutional Childcare Parents*, 90 St. John's L. Rev. 965 (2016); Michael J. Higdon, *Constitutional Parenthood*, 103 Iowa L. Rev. 1483, 1525 (2018).

now extend similar rights and duties to mere genetic mothers who have shared their eggs with their partners for in vitro fertilization.

Someone who helps raise a child has several routes to parentage. The birth mother's spouse will be a presumed parent until someone rebuts their parentage in court. Her unmarried cohabitant becomes a presumed parent if they live with the child for a significant time and hold themselves out as a parent. The parties can typically rebut these presumptions during infancy using genetic evidence, but a paternity challenge for an older child may be barred by equitable estoppel or by a statute of limitations of two or four years. These equitable and statutory limits protect nonbiological functional parents. Around a third of states have gone further in this direction, adopting de facto parenthood. Anyone can become a parent if a legal parent allows them to fulfill parental roles long enough for the child to develop parental bonds.

All states also have tools to create nonbiological parenthood prospectively. A child with no legal parents may be adopted into a new family. Adoptive parents, unlike biological ones, must submit to an investigation by social workers, after which a court will decide whether the adoption is in the child's best interests. If a child has just one legal parent, the parent may consent to second-parent adoption by a spouse or nonmarital partner. Many states also have more streamlined tools enabling a birth mother to share parenthood with a partner. When a married woman conceives a child with donor gametes, many states treat the spouse as a legal parent if he consents to the procedure. In a handful of states, a birth mother can also agree to share parentage at birth with an intended parent by signing an acknowledgment of parentage. Finally, around half of the states recognize gestational surrogacy agreements. Some surrogacy statutes treat intended parents, rather than the gestational parent, as parents at birth, while others offer expedited adoption with no screening.

That makes eleven parentage tests: a gestational presumption, voluntary acknowledgments of paternity, voluntary acknowledgments of parentage, genetic parentage petitions, a residential presumption, a marital presumption, parentage by estoppel, de facto parentage, adoption, preconception agreements, and surrogacy agreements. Although states multiplied the routes to parentage, few developed helpful guidance for resolving competing parentage claims. Some states have pairwise orderings for a few rules, mostly to choose between genetic or marital fathers or to arrange donor conception. When the unranked doctrines conflict, as they often do, family courts are told either to pick the presumption "which on the facts is founded on the weightier considerations of policy and logic"[7] or to "adjudicate parentage in the best interests of the child."[8] Such ad hoc discretionary standards risk giving free rein

7 Unif. Parentage Act § 4(b) (Unif. Law Comm'n 1973) [hereinafter UPA 1973].
8 Unif. Parentage Act § 613 (Unif. Law Comm'n 2017) [hereinafter UPA 2017].

to judicial prejudices. Even at best, judges must rely on their personal judgment about what kinds of parenting and childhood are valuable.

Parentage disputes cannot be resolved without normative principles. Each legal doctrine reflects some combination of the four factual bases of parentage: genetics, causation, caregiving, and agreements. What weight each should carry depends on the moral or prudential reasons that justify inferring parental rights or duties from those facts. Sometimes, parentage law is explicit about its moral premises, but courts and legislators rarely interrogate their normative commitments closely, much less explain how they relate to one another. The law lacks a cohesive normative theory that could return order to its many legal rules.

III LEGAL AND MORAL THEORIES OF PARENTAGE

With positive law tied in knots, one might hope normative theory could help straighten things out. Unfortunately, family law scholars seem stuck in interminable debates over whether to allocate legal parenthood based on genetics, gestation, function, or intentions. Part of the problem is that lawyers use "function" and "intent" in ways that are deeply ambiguous and partially overlapping. I untangle these concepts in subsequent chapters, but I generally avoid using these traditional labels unless necessary.

Another impediment is that legal scholarship often operates pragmatically without seeking deep or wide justifications. Specific rules become targets for reform because they generate unjust outcomes in salient cases. Such conflicts are common because parentage rules are an imperfect proxy for conflicting grounds and rationales. For example, among heterosexual couples the marital presumption is an accurate proxy for genetics, causation, caregiving, and agreements. Should the marital presumption also apply to same-sex spouses, when their marriage is still a good proxy for the last three grounds even if the spouses cannot both be genetic parents? Lawyers who want to protect lesbian and gay parents disparage the need for genetic ties, accentuate caregiving and agreements, and thus conclude that equality requires extending the presumption. Such pragmatic reforms have made parentage law more just. At the same time, they avoid explaining how the grounds relate to one another. Even as some LGBTQ+ advocates are belittling genetics to expand the marital presumption, others are championing the right of same-sex couples to use surrogacy to create genetic families. The result is a fragmented regime.

More theoretically ambitious legal scholars select and defend a single ground, insisting that only one theory can provide determinate, consistent, and just rules. Agreements and caregiving receive the most support among lawyers, although often under terms like "intention," "contract," "consent," and "function." Few family law scholars support genetic theories, despite the central role of genetics in positive law and in public discourse. A handful of prominent legal scholars are pluralists, but their primary normative justification is the advancement of equality for LGBTQ+

and functional parents.[9] Again, while I will agree with many of their conclusions, the reasoning is backward. Before determining whether equality demands new categories of legal parents, we must articulate the normative premises that justify legal parenthood in the first place.

That task might naturally fall to moral philosophy. Unlike family law scholars focused on parental rights, most ethicists begin with a theory of parental duties. Three theories predominate. The oldest is causal parenthood. Parents incur a duty to care for a child because their voluntary procreative acts create a child who will suffer without care. The causal theory is less common among family law scholars, but it is deeply ingrained in child support law. The other two leading philosophical theories share a label, "voluntarism." One focuses on voluntary caregiving. When an adult voluntarily performs custodial caregiving, knowing it will cause the child to form psychological attachments, this adult is obligated to continue raising the child to avoid harming the child. The last prominent theory makes a stronger voluntarist claim: adults must accept parental duties. Some consent expressly through adoption or signing an acknowledgment of parentage. Others consent tacitly by performing an act that social conventions treat as consent to parental duties, such as taking a child from the hospital or marrying the birth parent.

Despite their disagreement about the source of parental duties, most ethicists accept a broadly fiduciary theory of parental rights. Adults hold authority only as necessary to fulfill their parental duties to the child. Once we identify who holds parental duties, limited parental authority follows. The competing theory of parental rights is a labor theory. Adults acquire a right to parent a child because they perform valuable work caring for the child and, in the process, develop an interest in sustaining the relationship. This theory primarily justifies parenthood for caregivers but might also justify initial rights for birth parents because of their work of gestation and childbirth.

I will argue in Chapters 2 through 6 that none of these legal or moral theories is individually sufficient to justify parental duties or rights, much less to justify an assignment of the entire bundle. Many ethicists and lawyers want to tame parentage.[10] They want to trim it to one primary ground and one primary moral principle. Other grounds must either be discarded as mistaken, reinterpreted as derivative proxies for the favored principle, or treated as a second-best rule for

9 Libby Adler, *Inconceivable: Status, Contract, and the Search for a Legal Basis for Gay & Lesbian Parenthood*, 123 PENN ST. L. REV. 1, 20 (2018); Douglas NeJaime, *The Nature of Parenthood*, 126 YALE L.J. 2260 (2016).

10 Kolers and Bayne argue for a pluralistic account but without developing the structure to make it possible. Tim Bayne & Avery Kolers, *Toward a Pluralist Account of Parenthood*, 17 BIOETHICS 221 (2003). Fuscaldo offers an account of causal parentage that she contends would be consistent with pluralist accounts. Giuliana Fuscaldo, *Genetic Ties: Are They Morally Binding?*, 20 BIOETHICS 64 (2006). More legal scholars are openly pluralistic, likely because they face the reality of family conflict and the range of legal parentage rules. *See, e.g.*, Ayelet Blecher-Prigat, *Conceiving Parents*, 41 HARV. WOMEN'S L.J. 119 (2018); NeJaime, *supra* note 9.

nonideal cases when the favored parent is unavailable. Even legal scholars, despite their ingrained pragmatism, often hope for a monistic theory. For example, advocates of "functional" parentage insist that a child's real parent is whoever cares for the child. Genetic ties are irrelevant. The marital presumption is a derivative rule to protect the relationship between the child and a spouse likely to raise the child. The law offers adoption, donor waivers, and preconception agreements *because* these tools encourage caregiving.

Many ethicists also expect monistic theories of parentage to have a particular structure: (1) the parent–child relationship is a descriptive kind, either natural or social; and (2) parental duties and rights are entailed by general moral principles that apply to all instances of the kind.[11] Consider the causal theory. Parents are procreators, the people whose voluntary acts cause a child to exist. Children will suffer without a caregiver to raise them, and whenever an agent's conduct causes a risk of injury to others, the agent has an affirmative duty to take reasonable steps to prevent it. Thus, procreators have a duty to raise their children to prevent them from suffering. Labor theories of parental rights have a similar structure. A child's "real" parent is the person who performs the valuable work of raising a child. Whenever an agent invests work in a morally permissible project, they acquire a defeasible claim against other people's interference. Hence, caregivers have a claim to continue raising the child. Even skeptics about parental rights assume a similar reductive justificatory structure. They simply reject all attempts at reduction. If parental rights cannot be derived from a descriptive kind plus a generally applicable moral principle, then no one can have a right to become a parent.[12]

Parsimony and reduction are epistemic virtues, but we should resist their pull in parentage theory. Some moral phenomena are complicated. The people we call "parents" stand in many distinct moral and descriptive relations with "their" children. Each child has two genetic parents and a gestational mother, each of whom should have a liberty to raise the child. Most biological parents are also causal parents with a duty to ensure the child receives the material and emotional care they need for an adequate life. Hopefully, someone does provide this material and emotional care, but the child's caregiver need not be a biological or causal parent. Once the child forms attachments with their caregiver, the caregiver has a duty to

[11] Some pluralistic theories have the same structure. Michael Austin argues that moral parental duties can arise through consent, causation, or custody, and anyone with parental duties has the prima facie right against interference with their ability to fulfill the duties, which the state "encodes" in law. MICHAEL W. AUSTIN, CONCEPTIONS OF PARENTHOOD: ETHICS AND THE FAMILY 59–60 (2016). I reject the claims that parental duties (or rights) can be grounded in private acts that the law simply enforces. What we need is something more like Archard's two-level theory. He justifies parenthood as an institution first and then offers instrumental reasons for assigning parenthood to adults. David Archard, *The Obligations and Responsibilities of Parenthood*, *in* PROCREATION AND PARENTHOOD: THE ETHICS OF BEARING AND REARING CHILDREN 103 (David Archard & David Benatar eds., 2010). My theory has a similar two-level structure but with a deontological justification for both parenthood and the rules for its assignment.

[12] James G. Dwyer, *Deflating Parental Rights*, 40 L. & PHIL. 387 (2021).

continue caring for the child or, if they must end the relationship, to manage the transition to prevent psychological harm. Procreation and caregiving thus generate duties to the child, but the duties cannot justify a parental status that is unified, exclusive, and permanent. Moreover, neither is necessary for parental rights and duties. An adult can also become a parent through adoption or a parentage agreement before they perform any caregiving, and these adults are full, coequal parents, not second-best backups.

I want to maintain the intuition – reflected in parentage law – that adults can acquire moral duties and rights of parenthood from multiple distinct relations. Parenthood is not reducible to one moral principle supervening on one natural relation. What, then, explains the unity of parenthood? And can there be any hope of bringing order to the many criteria for parentage?

IV RECONCEIVING PARENTAGE

To rebuild the structure underlying parentage law, we need to reorient our understanding of parenthood. In a somewhat revisionist fashion, I will use "parenthood" to refer to the bundle of parental rights and duties and "parentage" to refer to the rules for determining who holds these parental rights and duties.

A *Parenthood as a Political Office*

Western cultures view parenthood as a quintessentially personal relationship. Parenthood is one of our most intimate relationships, central to our identity. Many people – including justices of the US Supreme Court – also think parenthood does not depend on law for its existence.[13] Parents would be obligated to raise their children even if they lived alone on the proverbial deserted island. This image makes it tempting to suppose parental duties and rights must arise from some natural relation like genetics or caregiving. Legal rights and duties track these preexisting interpersonal moral relations, with pragmatic accommodations.

Despite its broad appeal, this approach is backward. Parenthood is a form of political authority. A parent sets the path of their child's life by controlling their physical location, education, religion, relationships, chores, and curfews. Modern parenting norms are gentler, but parents still control their children's lives with coercion. How can anyone rightfully wield authority to shape another's life without denying their equal dignity? No one can have a personal moral right to this type of authority over another person. That does not mean we should infer no one can permissibly parent children. Instead, we should stop expecting to reduce parental rights or duties to ordinary moral principles that govern our other interpersonal relationships.

[13] Smith v. Org. of Foster Fams. for Equal. & Reform, 431 U.S. 816, 839 (1977).

To understand parentage, we must reverse our moral analysis. Begin instead with political rights and duties. To ensure justice for children, the community must ensure that someone fulfills parental responsibilities for each child.[14] Parenthood is a political office. Whoever occupies the parental office must meet the child's need for intimate caregiving and authoritative guidance. That political relationship generates further, more nuanced personal moral relations. Parents owe their children much more than adequate care and guidance. However, their intimate relationship with their child presupposes, rather than justifies, their parental duties. Parenthood cannot be derived from a relationship between the adult and child independent of a political community.

Accordingly, I begin my pluralist theory of parentage in Chapter 1 by developing a liberal-egalitarian theory of parenthood. Drawing on ideas from John Rawls and Immanuel Kant, I argue that legal parenthood is necessary to reconcile child-rearing authority and responsibility with equal respect for children and their caregivers.

A community treats its members as equals only if it ensures that they receive a fair share of primary goods. Primary goods are goods like nutrition, shelter, and basic income that are valuable for the pursuit of any reasonable conception of a good life. Children are also entitled to relational goods.[15] Each child needs a stable relationship with an intimate caregiver to flourish in childhood and develop into a thriving adult. A child also needs their caregiver to wield practical authority over their lives. Children have a right to guidance. Among adults, this authority would be inimical to equality. A community treats its adult citizens as equals only if they are free to pursue lives that they judge as valuable. Equal respect for children requires a different tack. Children lack their own values,[16] so each child needs an adult to make comprehensive judgments about how they should translate their primary goods into a flourishing life. Someone must judge where a child should live, what they should eat, what activities they should pursue, and with whom they should develop relationships. Public officials cannot legitimately make such judgments; this authority must fall to a private caregiver. Somewhat paradoxically, a community treats its members as equals only if it ensures that some private person exercises authority over each child's life.

This extraordinary political power must be circumscribed to render it consistent with the child's status as an equal member of society, now and in the future. The classic liberal strategy for reconciling citizens' equal liberty with nonconsensual political authority is to limit the power of the offices and the rules for acquiring that power.

[14] Others have made this claim, although typically focusing on children's needs. *See, e.g.*, Joseph Millum, The Moral Foundations of Parenthood 111–14 (2018).

[15] Harry Brighouse & Adam Swift, Family Values: The Ethics of Parent–Child Relationships (2014); Millum, *supra* note 14, at 31–34, 115–16.

[16] Tamar Schapiro, *What Is a Child?*, 109 Ethics 715 (1999).

Political authority must be limited and structured to ensure officeholders serve their public function. The state must define and protect children's basic rights. Children need an adult to supply the specific values that will guide their lives, but only the community can legitimately decide what all children need to live their own, full lives as equal members. In Chapter 1, I offer a few tentative thoughts about how best to divide authority between children, parents, and the state regarding education and medical care. However, the book's primary focus is on the structure of parenthood.

The law must shape authority over children so that whoever holds it can make substitute judgments to guide a child's life. That authority must be relatively broad and exclusive. If the state divided authority over children by subject area, such as between a physician, teacher, and caregiver, no one would have the authority to make the overarching judgments necessary to give coherence to the child's life. Moreover, a large group of adults cannot share authority over a child, as in a commune. The group's collective decisions will often not qualify as judgments at all. One adult also cannot be responsible for a large group of children, as in an orphanage. An orphanage director cannot act solely on behalf of one child without violating their duty to others. The community must give a small number of adults broad authority over the lives of a small number of children. In other words, children are entitled to parental authority.

After Chapter 1 defends this liberal-egalitarian theory of parenthood as an institution, the rest of the book explains how specific adults obtain parental authority over specific children. The community must identify principles for assigning parenthood that respect the equal status of the child, the parent, and other adults. In other words, it needs parentage law. Recognizing parenthood as a political office reveals two deep moral challenges for parentage law.

The first is to find reasons for assigning parenthood that respect children as equal members of society throughout their lives. Similar principles will constrain parental rights and the rules for acquiring them. For example, even if someone believes raising their genetic child is essential to their salvation, this adult's interests cannot justify a claim to dictate the child's life without treating the child as a subordinate. That does not mean parentage law must be defined with an exclusive focus on children's interests. A child is not entitled to the best available parent, any more than they are entitled to the best life. When articulating a system of equal respect, children's interests cannot have categorical priority over adult interests. Childrearing is central to many reasonable conceptions of the good life, including many that value genetic heritage. A political theory of parentage must explain how adults can have a fair opportunity to pursue parenthood consistent with equal respect for the child.

Perhaps more surprisingly, parenthood also threatens the equal status of adults. Parental duties are demanding. A parent must reorient their lives to serve their child's ends. In addition to being emotionally and financially costly, parental duties sit uneasily with the liberal notion that each person should have equal liberty to pursue their own ends. Imagine if officials conscripted someone to raise a child because this person could offer the best life for the child. They are using the conscript to serve the child and the state. A community must find respectful rules for assigning child-rearing duties. Moreover, even the rights of parenthood can be perilous. A parent commits to raising a child for a long time, which is risky without assurance that you cannot be supplanted as the child's parent. Nevertheless, at least two people are needed to create a child, and adults often raise a child together. The second challenge for parentage law is to explain how any adult obtains parental duties and rights without denying equal respect to other adult citizens.

Both challenges would be easier to meet if parenthood could be reduced to personal, enforceable moral rights and duties. If each child had a right to be parented by a specific adult who had a correlative duty to parent them, then parental law could respect adults and children by dutifully replicating personal morality. Unfortunately, the traditional bases of parentage are ill-suited for such a role. No moral principles justify inferring the full suite of parental duties or rights from any traditional ground of parentage, whether genetics, causation, caregiving, or agreement. There is an inevitable gap between these personal duties and political parenthood. Chapters 2 through 5 catalog the limits of existing moral theories, but there is also a general reason to doubt any univocal theory. Communities rely on parents to meet children's distributive rights. It would be miraculous if each child's rights as a citizen correlated perfectly with duties that an individual has through a personal relationship.

Fortunately, once we recognize parenthood as a political office, we can reconceive the relationship between parental rights or duties and the grounds of parentage. We do not need to find grounds that justify assigning parental rights or duties to a specific adult. Parenthood – the bundle of rights and duties held by a parent – is justified by its political function to meet the child's basic right to caregiving and guidance. Parentage – the principles that determine which adults have parental rights and duties for each child – only needs principles for assigning the parental office in ways that demonstrate equal respect for the child, parent or parents, and other adults.

B *Reconstructing Parentage Law*

How should we develop just rules for identifying parents? Fortunately, we need not start from scratch. As family structures have changed over the last seventy years, courts and legislators have debated who has the duty and right to raise children. Although public officials rarely reason from a comprehensive perspective, they often bring broadly liberal and egalitarian commitments to specific parentage disputes. The law of parentage reflects a host of insights – vastly more than any theorist could hope to glean directly from first principles.

Accordingly, I begin with the law of parentage in the United States.[17] My goal is to unearth the sound principles that underlie existing doctrines and explain how to realign them into a just system of parentage law. This project requires honing many doctrines and jettisoning a few others. Given the numerous jurisdictions, rules, and principles in American family law, rebuilding a consistent parentage system requires more revision of legal doctrines and principles than strictly "interpretive" legal theories might countenance. Nevertheless, with the guidance of a liberal-egalitarian theory of parenthood, we can reconstruct American parentage law into an ordered and justified set of rules for identifying parents.

Chapters 2 through 5 assess the basic grounds of parentage: genetics, causation, caregiving, and agreements. Each of these chapters follows the same tripartite structure. The first part begins with the existing law. I explain the legal rules that recognize a ground of parentage, paying particular attention to the law's reasons for inferring parental rights or duties from this ground. The second part turns to moral theory, arguing that no principles of personal morality justify inferring full parental rights or duties from this ground. I criticize moral theories of parentage on their terms, but my aim is not to "win" by stacking up objections. The lesson is never merely critical. I appraise the limits *and* insights of existing theories to reveal the role each ground should play in a pluralistic political theory. Accordingly, the third part turns to the political theory of parentage. It reveals how a liberal-egalitarian theory can preserve the insights of courts, legislators, lawyers, and ethicists about each ground of parentage. Once properly delimited, each ground can serve a specific function in the assignment of political parenthood.

Over the course of these four chapters, a pluralistic parentage regime unfolds that can meet the two moral challenges for parentage law. Chapter 6 reassembles those pieces into a structured, pluralist theory of parentage law. The remainder of this introduction sketches that final picture. This summary presupposes some legal and philosophical knowledge, but the coming chapters will explain each doctrine and principle in detail. My goal here is to indicate how the pieces of parental law can be reassembled into an ordered whole. The guiding moral principle is that all citizens should have equal liberty to build families, as long as their familial projects show equal respect for the child and other adults. This principle will justify a claim to parental liberty for biological and nonbiological parents, but parentage law should begin, as it currently does, with biology.

Genetic and gestational parents have a conditional liberty right to raise their progeny. A liberal state cannot design parentage law to facilitate a contested vision of valuable families like procreative parenthood (2.II.C). Nevertheless, many reasonable citizens value genetic heritage and should be able to pursue genetically related

[17] I do not believe American law offers the only justified system of parentage. On the contrary, comparative study of parentage law offers many additional insights. Unfortunately, comparative law is outside my area of expertise, and fifty states already offer substantial differences to manage.

families, so long as their procreative and parenting rights are consistent with equal respect for the child and other adults.

To respect children's right to a parent, the right of biological parents to raise their progeny must be conditional on timely commitment and adequate fulfillment of parental roles (2.III.B.1). Moreover, to ensure distributive justice for children, the community must offset the luck of the parental lottery (2.III.B.2). While no child is entitled to the best available parent, a citizen's life prospects should not be fixed by random differences in parental resources or abilities. This demand of distributive justice should be met by increasing public assistance for families, rather than by monitoring or licensing of parents, which shifts the distributive injustice to adults.

The law must also shape genetic parents' rights to ensure equal respect for gestational parents. A genetic parent's right *not* to reproduce must end after insemination or embryo transfer; any further control violates the gestational parent's right to bodily integrity (3.III.C). Nevertheless, the genetic parent should retain their conditional parental liberty because the gestational parent does not immediately acquire exclusive parental authority.

Gestational parents should have their own conditional liberty right to raise the child. If they plan to raise the child, their work of gestation and childbirth demonstrates commitment sufficient to satisfy any public concern for the child's right to a parent. Gestational parents should be, as they are, presumed legal parents unless they waive their parental liberty. The gestational parent does not, however, have a claim to *exclusive* parenthood based on gestational work. An adult may hold exclusive authority to shape a child's life only once they are meeting the child's right to care and guidance, because only then does the child have a reciprocal interest in the exclusive relationship (3.III.A–B).

Accordingly, a genetic parent may retain their conditional liberty to pursue parenthood alongside a gestational parent. Yet, unlike a gestational parent, genetic parents must do something more to demonstrate commitment to parenting (2.III.B). They may coparent alongside the gestational parent, relying on the marital or residential presumption. They can also commit expressly after the birth by signing a voluntary acknowledgment of paternity or maternity, if the gestational parent agrees. States must also allow genetic parents to file parentage petitions so they can commit and obtain joint custody unliterally. Otherwise, the law would empower gestational parents to decide whether the genetic parent may have familial liberty (4.III.C). The genetic parent's willingness and ability to coparent cooperatively should affect the extent of their custody, not their right to it (6.II.B.1).

Existing laws about the rights of biological parents are roughly correct, but many prevalent ideas about parental duties are poorly grounded. Genetic ties do not justify any parental duties, even financial ones (1.II.B). As courts recognize, most genetic parents are also causal parents, which gives them some special duties toward the child. Anyone whose voluntary actions help create a child has a duty to ensure the child receives the care needed for an adequate life. However, causal duties are not parental duties. Most causal parents are not required to raise the child personally and may not even have the liberty to do so (2.II.B).

Nevertheless, causal parents have duties to other adults that justify some financial support obligations. Causal parents (including nonbiological parents) may have duties to assist one another (3.II.A.4), especially if they create a child as part of a shared preconception plan (5.III.D). In addition, under a luck-egalitarian theory of justice, the individuals whose voluntary acts create a child may justly bear part of the social cost of raising the child (2.III.A). Unfortunately, American child support law exceeds the limits of distributive justice (2.III.B). It extracts child support from people who are not even causal parents, such as male rape victims. It also perpetuates distributive injustice by penalizing already impoverished parents and using adults' private duties to obscure the community's failure to meet children's distributive needs.

The same derived liberty principles that justify biological parentage rules can also justify parental liberties for nonbiological parents. A state that allowed only biological parenthood would deny equal familial liberty to citizens who want nonbiological families (5.III.A). Moreover, parenthood is an office that carries social respect, so all citizens are entitled to a fair opportunity to become parents regardless of gender, sexuality, or reproductive ability. Liberal-egalitarian communities must have parentage laws that enable citizens to pursue nonbiological parenthood in ways consistent with equal respect for the child and biological parents.

Family law has developed the necessary tools. When a child has no parents, legal adoption allows an unrelated adult to create parental duties and rights through an express commitment. Law is necessary to create this power because no one has, as a matter of interpersonal morality, the power to create rights or duties simply by a unilateral act of will (5.II; 5.III.B). When a child has only one parent, the law should also empower the parent to share parenthood. Parenthood includes the authority to shape one's family life, such as choosing to cohabit and share childcare. It should also include a power to share parenthood prospectively through second-parent adoption (5.III.C). Without this legal power, two adults can pursue a coparenting project only by accepting mutual subordination. At any time, the legal parent may withdraw their partner's privilege to parent, and the partner may withdraw the support that the legal parent relied upon to pursue their parenting project.

The power to share parenthood should be extended to agreements before conception or at birth. Any gestational or genetic parent should have authority to share parenthood with a partner if the other biological parent waives their liberty to raise the child (5.III.C.3; 5.III.D). These rules empower the biological parent, who has a liberty to raise the child and plans to do so, to commit to sharing parenthood with a nonbiological parent. This delegated power bypasses adoption screening, but states have few legitimate reasons to second-guess a biological parent's decision to pursue family with their partners (5.III.C.3.a). States do have adequate public reasons to regulate some parentage agreements. Liberal-egalitarian communities may have comprehensive surrogacy regulations to prevent exploitation of surrogates and support gender equality (5.III.E). Moreover, adoption or parentage agreements must confer parenthood only as a predefined status. Individual adults have no contractual authority to tailor parental rights or duties that the community has set based on its collective judgments about children's primary goods (5.II.C).

Nevertheless, biological parents and their partners should generally be free to decide who will raise the child. Once they begin raising the child, their caregiving builds the relational attachments that justify full parental rights for the child and adult (4.III.B). As the child develops attachments, their right to a parent becomes a right to *this* parent. Once an adult with a liberty to parent commits to parenthood, other citizens and the state should respect their project to raise the child, so long as their decisions fall within reasonable parental discretion.

Child-rearing alone, however, cannot justify parenthood. An existing legal parent should be able to seek caregiving assistance from daycares, relatives, cohabitants, or friends without risk of losing their exclusive parental rights (4.II.B.3). As a default, states should trust a parent to judge what other adult relationships are good for their child. Nevertheless, parental discretion over a child's relationships, like all parental discretion, must be circumscribed by law. A parent cannot be allowed to deprive a child of relational attachments necessary for their well-being. All states need a legal tool like third-party visitation to test parents' relational decisions, albeit with narrow standing rules and deferential substantive review.

In two situations, child-rearing can justify parenthood because the legal parent has forfeited their right to exclusive authority. The first is abandonment. Parents in crisis should be able to entrust their children to third-party custodians. However, a parent who leaves a child for too long forfeits their exclusive authority, allowing a court to award custody or parenthood to the custodian who fulfilled parental roles (4.III.D). The second situation is coresidential child-rearing. A community may decide that a legal parent forfeits their exclusive authority through long-term shared child-rearing, after which the nonparent obtains parental rights and duties.

The law can protect parental caregiving relationships in several ways. The first is through the residential and marital presumptions. States presume that a legal parent consents to child-rearing by a cohabitant or spouse, and the rebuttal timelines reflect a legislative judgment about when children develop parental bonds (4.III.D). Before this time, the spouse or cohabitant has only a conditional liberty to raise the child, so whether someone can rebut the presumption should depend on whether the spouse or cohabitant's caregiving liberty rests on presumed genetic ties or presumed agreement of the gestational parent (6.II.D). States may also develop de facto parent doctrines to apply whenever someone raises a child with the legal parents' consent and a judge concludes the child developed parental attachments (4.III). Courts must carefully craft substantive and procedural standards for de facto parenthood to prevent it from replacing the rules of abandonment and presumptions with unguided judicial discretion.

* * *

The jumbled puzzle of parentage law is awaiting assembly. The resulting pluralistic system will not be simple. Its doctrines will interlock in complex ways, and the underlying moral principles often need articulation. Nevertheless, once reconstructed, parentage law can render determinate judgments in most cases, minimize resort to unbridled judicial discretion, and satisfy the demands of liberal-egalitarian justice.

1

Political Parenthood

In February 1970, Madeline Smith, a registered foster parent, took in Eric and Danielle Gandy, who were then four and two years old.[1] After four years in her care, both children regarded Smith as their mother. Danielle had never seen their biological mother. Eric no longer remembered her. Unfortunately, a social worker became worried that Smith's arthritis limited her ability to supervise older children, so the foster agency removed the children to another foster home.

Smith sued New York, alleging the state deprived her of familial liberty without due process by "abruptly and summarily" removing the children from her care. Existing precedent established that parents have a constitutional right to care, custody, and control of their children. Smith argued that after four years of intimate caregiving she had forged a psychological family with Eric and Danielle that deserved similar constitutional protection.[2] The United States Supreme Court disagreed. Although it technically held only that the agency satisfied due process by holding an informal preremoval conference, the opinion's reasoning throws cold water on the idea of constitutional rights for foster families.[3]

The Justices conceded that foster and legal parents fulfill similar familial functions. The "importance of the familial relationship, to the individual and to the society, stems from the emotional attachments that derive from the intimacy of daily association, and from the role it plays in promoting a way of life through the instruction of children." In long-term foster placements, "it is natural that the foster family should hold the same place in the emotional life of the foster child, and fulfill the same socializing functions, as a natural family." However, constitutional parental rights protect an "interest in family privacy [that] has its source … not in state law, but in

1 Org. of Foster Fams. for Equal. & Reform v. Dumpson, 418 F. Supp. 277, 280 (S.D.N.Y. 1976).

2 *Id.* at 281; Smith v. Org. of Foster Fams. for Equal. & Reform, 431 U.S. 816, 839 (1977).

3 *Smith*, 431 U.S. at 847. The Court expressly declines to hold that foster parents have no fundamental liberty interest in their relationship, but the opinion is often mistakenly read as standing for that conclusion. *E.g.*, Removal of child from foster home, 3 N.Y. Fam. Ct. Law & Prac. § 15:15. *See* Douglas NeJaime, *The Constitution of Parenthood*, 72 Stan. L. Rev. 261, 312–13 (2020) (noting discrepancy in dicta and in lower court rulings against foster parents).

intrinsic human rights."[4] In Smith's foster care case, "the State seeks to interfere, not with a relationship having its origins entirely apart from the power of the State, but rather with a foster family which has its source in state law and contractual arrangements."[5] The "emotional ties" in foster families "have their origins in an arrangement in which the State has been a partner from the outset," which "argue[s] against any but the most limited constitutional 'liberty' in the foster family."

Many people find the Court's underlying idea – that the parent–child relationship precedes the state or law – intuitive.[6] Social and legal norms shape parenthood, of course, but the core of the parent–child relationship seems independent of any social or legal convention. Even many scholars who oppose the Court's genetic vision of parenthood accept this deeper premise, disagreeing only about the relationship that grounds parenthood. Instead, adults become parents because they are gestational carriers, intentional parents, or functional caregivers. Parental rights and duties can then be justified by applying general moral principles to parent–child relationships that exist independent of political or legal authority.

Despite its intuitive appeal, this perspective is backwards. A hint of the problem appears in the reasoning of *Smith* itself. Parenthood is not only about care; it is also about socialization. Parents direct children's lives and enforce their directions with coercion. No individual can have a personal moral right to such dominion over another person's life. Nevertheless, every community gives some adults special authority to raise children. Social norms identify the adult who has this authority over each child and direct others not to interfere with their childrearing. This allocation of authority creates the space in which the child and their caregiver form their intimate relationship.[7] Therefore, the community is a partner from the outset in *all* parental relationships.

Parenthood is a relationship of political authority. Any attempt to ground parental rights or duties directly in some natural or functional relationship between the adult and child is bound to fail. This does not entail, however, that parenthood is a mere creature of positive law that states may reallocate however they wish. It is a common mistake to suppose human rights must all be moral rights that individuals could have outside of law. On the contrary, many human rights are claims to legal structures, because law is sometimes necessary to secure a person's status as an equal member of the community. This is particularly common in two situations: when one person exercises moral authority over another and when one person is obligated to serve another's ends. Relations like these create forms of subordination. Parenthood has both features. A parent wields authority over a child, and the parent has a duty to serve the child's ends. Parenthood's moral relations threaten the equal status of the child and the parent.

4 *Smith*, 431 U.S. at 845.

5 *Id.* at 844.

6 Hawkins v. Grese, 809 S.E.2d 441, 443 (Va. Ct. App. 2018) (relying on *Smith* to deny that state law's failure to recognize de facto parenthood violated the constitution).

7 Frances E. Olsen, *The Myth of State Intervention in the Family*, *in* Justice, Politics, and the Family (2014).

This chapter argues that a legal structure like parenthood is necessary to reconcile childrearing authority and duties with equal respect for children and caregivers. Drawing on the political philosophy of Immanuel Kant and John Rawls, I argue that liberal-egalitarian justice requires the community to adopt parenthood as a political office. Part I explains the distinction between personal and political morality, setting the stage by noting many similarities between parenthood and paradigmatic political rights and duties. Part II provides the sustained argument that parenthood is political. The community can ensure justice for children only by giving a small number of intimate caregivers broad control over the lives of a small group of children. Every child has a political right to a parent or parents.

The next four chapters apply this political conception of parenthood to parentage law and theory. Those chapters demonstrate that parental rights and duties cannot be inferred from natural or functional kinds like genetics, causation, caregiving, or agreements. Instead, as this chapter argues, parenthood can be justified only by demands of justice. Once we recognize this separation between the justification of parenthood and the rules for assigning it, a political conception of parenthood can realign the insights of existing parentage law into an ordered, pluralistic system. To begin that jurisprudential task, we must understand the sense in which parenthood is political and why liberal-egalitarian justice demands parenthood.

I PARENTHOOD AS A POLITICAL OFFICE

This part explains what I mean by saying parenthood is "political" rather than "personal." I hope it can defuse some intuitive resistance to the idea of political parenthood, as well as head off the misunderstanding that I intend to revive a traditional public/private distinction.

As a general matter, I divide the class of moral duties and rights into two broad categories: personal and political.[8] Personal rights and duties are grounded in respect for others *as persons*. Personal morality includes negative and positive duties, such as to not lie or to help others in need. Violations of either can demonstrate a failure to respect others as persons. These personal duties are universal, but our actions and relationships lend them determinacy and directedness. For example,

[8] The moral universe can be divided in other ways. Rawls distinguished natural duties independent of any of our actions from obligations incurred through voluntary acts. John Rawls, A Theory of Justice 97–98 (1999). Millum, a parentage theorist, distinguishes natural duties from artificial ones that depend on social conventions. Joseph Millum, The Moral Foundations of Parenthood 87 (2018). My personal/political distinction comports with Kant's distinction between virtue and right, although not in a strictly textual manner. Kantian philosophers use "juridical" to refer to duties of right, but I find readers outside philosophy associate that term with "jurisprudence" in the sense of focused on an area of doctrinal law; like First Amendment jurisprudence. My concern is with political morality as a subset of *moral* rights and duties. Political morality often requires creating positive law, but the moral necessity of law requires an additional argument.

some relationships generate concerns about exploitation, such as between ministers and parishioners or between charitable donors and recipients.[9] Other relationships may identify the people to whom we owe a special duty of benevolent assistance, such as our friends or neighbors.

Political rights and duties, in contrast, are grounded in respect for other people *as equal members of a community*.[10] Examples include a right to distributive justice and political representation. Because collective relations mediate these political rights and duties, they are not owed by any one person to another. For example, a society's economic institutions shape the lives of its members, which will fail to treat them with equal respect unless each member has a claim to a fair share of resources that the institutions generate. Yet no individual has a duty to ensure the justice of the market institutions sustained by our collective activities. Justice is not simply an aggregate of bilateral duties. Sections A and B will explore this example and others, which should help crystallize this distinction between personal and political morality.

This book is an extended argument that parenthood is a political office. Section A begins this process by offering reasons to suspend the widespread intuition that parental rights and duties arise from personal relationships between an adult and a child. The full proof that parenthood is political rather than personal must await the next four chapters, which argue no principles of personal morality derive parental rights or duties from the four basic parentage grounds.

Even an entire book cannot fully defend my assumption that some moral relations are irreducibly political. Nevertheless, Section B illustrates that this premise is plausible by describing three classes of political rights and duties and explaining the features that make them irreducibly political. Along the way, it points out features that each class shares with parenthood. Part II builds off those insights to present a direct argument that parenthood is political.

A *Intuitive Resistance to Political Parenthood*

The idea that the contours of family are political rather natural should be uncontroversial.[11] In feminist scholarship, it is nearly axiomatic. Catherine MacKinnon argues that the social norms and legal rules of family were shaped to oppress women and exploit their sexual, reproductive, caregiving, and domestic

9 Barbara Herman, *Being Helped and Being Grateful: Imperfect Duties, the Ethics of Possession, and the Unity of Morality*, 109 J. Phil. 391 (2012).

10 I refer to community members, rather than persons or individuals, because political duties are associational duties that arise only in a community. Although "citizens" is the more common term in liberal theory, I have found readers assume that using "citizen" implies political obligations are owed only to fully participant members of a state, as opposed to noncitizen immigrants. I operate with a rough notion of community without prejudging its boundaries, because I believe only legitimate, deliberative institutions can fix the scope of political obligations.

11 Martha Fineman, The Autonomy Myth: A Theory of Dependency 150–51 (2004); Martha C. Nussbaum, *The Future of Feminist Liberalism*, 74 Proceedings and Addresses of the American Philosophical Association 47, 199 (2000).

labor.[12] Anita Allen and Martha Fineman argue that Western nations sustain themselves by using a sexualized marital family to coerce women into providing caregiving labor necessary to meet the needs of children and the elderly.[13] The modern family does not reflect a prepolitical arrangement dictated by nature free of legal intervention. It is an inextricable piece of our political and economic structures.

Despite aspersions by its critics, many liberal philosophers also recognize the family as a political institution shaped by social and legal coercion. Rawls was insufficiently attuned to family life,[14] but earlier liberals were more attentive, and subsequent liberals corrected Rawls's omission. Harriet Taylor Mill and John Stuart Mill argued that society uses women to meet caregiving needs by inculcating gender norms in children that constrain women's life prospects.[15] This tradition is carried forward by liberal-egalitarian theorists of the family like Martha Nussbaum and David Archard, among many others.[16] Maxine Eichner articulates what I take as the current liberal-egalitarian consensus.[17] Any just society must ensure care for its dependent members, including children and the elderly. Most societies rely on families to provide dependent care. Accordingly, the state structures labor markets and welfare institutions around some vision of a "normal" family (in a mixed statistical and prescriptive sense).[18] The family is an inextricable part of "the basic structure," so justice demands the community ensure that it organizes family life in ways consistent with the equal status of children, the elderly, and their caregivers.[19]

12 Catharine A. MacKinnon, Toward a Feminist Theory of the State 76–80 (1989).

13 Anita L. Allen, Uneasy Access: Privacy for Women in a Free Society (1988); Martha Fineman, The Neutered Mother, The Sexual Family, and Other Twentieth Century Tragedies (1995).

14 *See, e.g.*, Fineman, *supra* note 11, at 214–17, 232–37 (arguing Rawls underappreciated how "background conditions" of the social contract consist of an integrated set of workplace expectations, gendered family responsibilities, and privatization of citizen support).

15 John Stuart Mill, The Subjection of Women (1869).

16 David Archard, Children: Rights and Childhood 177 (2014).

17 Maxine Eichner, The Supportive State: Families, Government, and America's Political Ideals 81 (2010).

18 *Id.* at 82–84.

19 In later work, Rawls concedes to Okin that familial institutions are part of the basic structure but still insists that law should not regulate how family members relate to one another. John Rawls, *Idea of Public Reason Revisited, in* Political Liberalism, § 5, 468–73 (expanded ed. 2005). It should regulate entry and exit and prevent abuse and neglect; otherwise, it should allow citizens to shape their family life by comprehensive values and trust families to care for one another based on affection. Rawls's critics rightly point out that he failed to reconcile these positions. Eichner, for instance, argues that Rawls accepts a strong public/private distinction because his commitment to liberal neutrality reinforced his earlier assumption that families can fulfill a prepolitical function without state influence. Eichner, *supra* note 17, at 24–26. Unlike some critics, I doubt Rawls's mistake has deep ties to the structure of justice as fairness. Representatives in the original position must design the basic structure knowing citizens live their entire lives within it, which means the developmental goods of family must be subject to principles of justice. Rawls is not arguing the family is immune from justice, but that justice requires not directly regulating intimate life to allow intact families to act on nonpolitical values like love. This conclusion is consistent with views, like Fineman's, that protect autonomy for caregivers. Unfortunately, because Rawls had no theory of private law, he could not explain how law

Even liberals who readily admit that marriage and family structures are political may still find it counterintuitive to treat parenthood as inherently political. Parenthood is one of our most intimate relationships. Parental duties have political ramifications, but the duties seem to arise directly from the personal relationship between a parent and child without mediation by the state. A parent would seem to have a duty to love and raise their child on the proverbial deserted island. Parental duties also seem inapt for a political relation. Parents ought to love their children, and this type of partiality seems inappropriate in political relationships.

I accept that procreators and caregivers can incur personal duties to children that do not depend on political norms. Those personal duties, however, fall far short of the full-fledged rights and duties of parenthood. Demonstrating this requires a detailed analysis of the moral principles applicable to each personal relationship between a child and an adult – genetic, causal, caregiving, and agreements. The next four chapters argue that these relationships cannot justify full parental duties or rights. In the remainder of this section, I hope to loosen the "parenthood is personal" intuition by accentuating how anomalous parental rights and duties would be among the class of personal rights and duties. Section B will present three features common to political rights and duties, each of which is shared by parenthood.

Parents claim extraordinarily broad moral authority over their children's lives. They claim a moral power to create duties for children and a privilege to enforce them with coercion. A parent may choose their teen's curfew and ground them for coming home late. Parents set rules for homework, chores, activities, and even friendships. Furthermore, most parents believe they have the liberty to use this power without others' interference. If your daughter is playing at a friend's house as her curfew approaches, her friend's parents cannot give her permission to stay late. They lack the power to alter your daughter's curfew; if they purport to do so, they wrongly interfere with your parenting. The state can modify these parental rights by setting rules for curfew, employment, schooling, or healthcare.[20] Yet, even against the state, parents assert a right to guide children's daily lives, activities, religion, and educational priorities. Last, children cannot easily exit this relationship of parental power, if at all. If a child leaves home without parental permission, the state will return the "runaway" child. In some states, they can even charge the child with a crime.[21] Older youth can seek emancipation, but financial hardship makes it rarely feasible.

When else may one person exercise such dominion over another's life? Employment is the only remotely comparable private relation. Employers issue

can prescind from direct enforcement of equality norms inside families and still ensure that familial relations are consistent with equality.

20 Hutchins v. D.C., 188 F.3d 531, 545 (D.C. Cir. 1999) (parents had no constitutional right to grant children free rein to move about unaccompanied after state-imposed curfew).

21 Twenty-six states require an officer to return a runaway child to their guardian, which is galling because most children run away from home to escape abuse or threats from a caregiver. Jordan Enciso, *Leaving Home: How Running Away Impacts the Lives of Juveniles and Society as a Whole*, 19 Fla. Coastal L. Rev. 143, 148–49, 158–59 (2018).

directives to employees backed by a threat of termination. Employment, however, is a limited-scope relationship premised on consent and subject to state regulation. When an employer wields authority over significant aspects of an employee's life, such as for domestic employees, their relationship becomes troubling for reasons similar to parenthood. Yet even a domestic employee can end the employer's power by quitting. The closest analogs to parental authority are relations of political authority like citizenship. Legislators have the power to impose new duties on citizens; officers enforce legal duties with coercion; and citizens may lack the legal right or practical ability to exit the polity. Given the breadth of parental authority, it is worth considering whether parenthood is also inherently political.

Parents' moral duties are also extraordinarily demanding. Many countries demand parents meet most of their child's developmental needs until the age of majority. The law may only police neglect, but a parent's responsibility is not merely to ensure their child receives a tolerable life. Parents should ensure their child flourishes. To do so, parents must reorient a large portion of their lives to serve the child's well-being. Few duties impose as extensively on individual liberty. The breadth and stringency of parental duties are rivaled only by state conscription for military or civil service – classic political obligations. The parent's duties to meet their child's needs also have a curious tie to collective obligations. A large share of what a child needs is not a function of anything their parents did. Over the last fifty years, childhood has become more protracted and expensive as children need more education for economic self-sufficiency. The community created this burden of extended childhood, yet much of that burden has fallen upon their parents – parents who did nothing different from adults in previous generations.

To be clear, I am not denying that parent–child relationships involve personal duties grounded in respect for and love of the child as an individual. They do. No relationship is more intimate than parenthood. A parent and their child share their love, lives, and dreams. The intimate parental relationship is replete with moral nuance, most of which I do not discuss in this book. Nevertheless, the uniqueness of parental authority and duties offers a good reason to suspend the intuition that the intimate relationship can justify the duties or authority. Instead, an adult can develop this intimate relationship only because they already have political rights and duties over the child. A political conception of parenthood specifies the range of liberty for families to form these intimate relationships. I defend such a political conception of parenthood in Part II.

B *Three Classes of Political Relations*

This book cannot fully defend its second, admittedly controversial, assumption that some moral rights and duties are inherently political in the sense that they cannot be reduced to duties that we owe directly to one another as persons. Instead, I hope to motivate the idea that some moral duties are irreducibly political by describing three types of duties and rights that make necessary reference to collective political relations. Parenthood shares features with all three. The parallels identified in this section are fleshed out in Part II of this chapter and in the next four chapters.

1 Parental Duties and Rights Are Demands of Distributive Justice

One class of political rights consists of rights *held by individuals as community members, with correlative duties held by the community as a collective.* Entitlements of distributive justice exemplify this category. Comparing charity and justice can help clarify this class.

Everyone has an affirmative duty of charity to help others in need. We have this duty simply because other people have intrinsic value. We owe charity to everyone, not just members of our community. No one, however, has a claim to our charity. If we had a perfect duty to help anyone in need, then once anyone chooses an end, everyone else would be obligated to assist them to achieve it. Everyone's life would become a mere means to serve others' ends. Any supposed right to charity is inconsistent with equal dignity. That does not mean that we can have no duty of charity. Instead, charity is what Kant calls an "imperfect" duty. We must make it our end to help some people in need sometimes, but we have the discretion to judge how to balance charity against our other duties and our pursuit of other valuable ends.[22]

Distributive justice, in contrast, is a matter of strict rights. Each community member has a claim to a fair share of resources generated by the community's collective efforts. But who holds the correlative duty to ensure they receive their just entitlement? Other individuals cannot hold it. Suppose each American is entitled to a basic income of $12,000. An impoverished person cannot demand their basic income from any passing pedestrian. Allowing the burden to fall on such an arbitrary basis would fail to treat the pedestrian as an equal. The entire community shares this duty. Yet it is equally silly to think each impoverished American has a claim on every other American for 0.0036 cents, a 334 millionth share of a $12,000 basic income.

The problem here is not pragmatic, as if pedestrians need to calculate a moderate donation that will reduce the injustice they encounter without undermining their own goals. Treating justice as a personal duty disrespects the obligors. Like a supposed right to charity, it turns each citizen into a means to justice for others. It also disrespects the recipients. One private citizen cannot ensure another's status as an equal, even in principle. If Jeff Bezos paid a basic income to each needy person, his massive act of charity would not create a just society. It would create a relationship of dependence that undermined equal citizenship.

Only a collective commitment to ensure distributive entitlements can satisfy the demands of justice in a way that respects the equality of all community members. No

22 For a fuller discussion of imperfect duties, see Gregg Strauss, *Why the State Cannot Abolish Marriage: A Partial Defense of Legal Marriage*, 90 IND. L.J. 1261, 1301–02 (2015).

individual is responsible for the social, economic, and political institutions that shape all our lives. Our collective actions sustain these institutions, which is permissible only if we, as a collective, sustain political institutions that protect each member's entitlements as an equal in the community.

In Part II, I will argue that every child has a right to a parent as a matter of distributive justice. Children need intimate caregivers to meet their material and psychological needs, and they need these caregivers to have the legal power to direct their lives. The community can only meet its distributive obligations to children by ensuring each child has a parent.[23] The right to a parent does not rest on the child's needs *as a person*, like the duty of charity. Relying on charities to care for orphans renders them dependent on others' goodwill to meet basic needs, which fails to treat them as equal members of the community. Moreover, children's right to a parent does not correlate with a duty held by some specific person. A child who washes up on our shores in a basket has a right to a parent. The bystander who finds the child should save them, but this bystander's personal duty is limited. A state that forced the bystander to raise the child for eighteen years would treat the conscript as a means to serve the welfare of the child and the state. The community that sustains its basic economic and family structures is responsible for ensuring each child has a parent willing to fulfill this role.[24]

2 Parenthood Is a Political *Office*

The second class of political rights and duties concerns *offices that may be created only by a political community*. Examples include the office of voter, judge, or legislator. An office is a set of powers and duties that can be held by any number of partially fungible occupants, along with rules to identify the person who holds the office.[25] Many offices include the moral authority to alter others' rights and duties. Legislators, for example, claim the authority to set ends for the community as a collective. No one could have a personal claim to authority to set ends for others. Nevertheless, in a community, justice demands offices with precisely this moral authority.

Judicial offices are a paradigmatic example. When two people sincerely disagree about their rights and are unable to compromise, neither can demand the other acquiesce to their judgment. The only way to resolve the conflict while respecting

23 Katharine K. Baker, *Quacking like a Duck: Functional Parenthood Doctrine and Same-Sex Parent*, 92 Chi.-Kent L. Rev. 135, 129 (2017).

24 Harry Brighouse & Adam Swift, Family Values: The Ethics of Parent-Child Relationships 82–84 (2016). Brighouse and Swift conclude "adults have a duty to parent children," but when they explicate the duty, it sounds more political than personal. Even if no adult has a duty to parent the child, the child still has a claim to a parent that is "best understood as the right that adults get together and establish an institutional mechanism for assigning the relevant (perfect) duties to" parent the child. In other words, a child's claim to a parent is a claim against the community to a system of parentage law that will help find the child a parent.

25 Scott J. Shapiro, Legality 75–77, 166–67 (2013).

both parties as equals is to appoint a third person to adjudicate the dispute using settled principles. Again, the problem is not simply pragmatic in that we need third parties to reduce conflict among irrational or egoistic actors. In the face of reasonable disagreement, each person has only two options: assert authority to judge for the other person or submit to the other person's judgment. They disrespect the other person or themselves. Moral equality is impossible unless the community creates adjudicative institutions.

The community must also define rules for determining who holds the judicial office. No one is personally entitled to hold this authority by virtue of their personal interests. Nevertheless, many individuals can have an interest in pursuing the office. A judgeship is an esteemed social role. Some people believe there is intrinsic value in fulfilling this function to articulate principles of justice on behalf of the community. Consequently, the office must be open to any citizen who fulfills the relevant criteria determined by the community. Once an individual satisfies all those legal criteria, the individual's interests may justify a personal claim to occupy the office. Clarity about this right to an office is crucial to understanding the relationship between parental authority and the right to be a parent.

Suppose the United States Senate refuses, for no reason, to seat a duly elected senator. This refusal is wrong because it flouts their constitutional duty, defies the will of the people, and violates the rights of the senator-elect. The senator-elect's right to the office differs from more familiar "power-rights." Each person has a right to contract, for instance, because our interest in autonomy justifies a power to change our moral relations with others. The right to a political office is different. The senators' interests do not justify their office or affect the content of their rights and duties. A legitimate state requires a representative body with legislative authority, which justifies senators' powers. The Constitution defines their precise contours. Senators must wield their authority only by making judgments about what serves the country and their constituents. Nevertheless, once a senator-elect meets the specified criteria, they can acquire a right to the office grounded in their own interests. Serving as a senator might be the crowning achievement of a person's life. Denying them this right wrongs them personally, in addition to undermining the institution.[26]

Parenthood is a similar kind of political office.[27] Part II will argue that distributive justice determines the scope of parental rights and duties. Parents have the powers

26 A liberal political theory must add this nuance to the common assumption that "liberals believe that rights to control the life of another person must be justified" only by appeal to that person's consent or interests, never by "the interests of the person doing the controlling." Anca Gheaus, *The Best Available Parent*, 131 ETHICS 431, 435 (2021).

27 Shapiro argues that parenthood is not an office for two reasons: (1) parental rights decrease over time and (2) parental turnover is not expected, whereas offices have stable rights and anticipate more than one occupant. SHAPIRO, *supra* note 25, at 210. Neither condition, however, is essential to the concept of an office. An office's powers may be contingent on facts that change over time. All offices need some "impersonality," in the sense that different individuals could serve as the officeholder, but offices can vary in the degree of fungibility and expected turnover.

and obligations necessary to ensure the child's fair share of primary goods is translated into a valuable life. The functions of parenthood include meeting the child's generic and relational needs (Part II, Section A) and directing the child's life (Part II, Section B). A parent must provide substitute judgment about what constitutes a valuable childhood and adult life. No individual could have a *personal* right to such authority over another person. Nevertheless, it is a morally necessary function, so every community must define an office of parenthood and set conditions for acquiring the office for a particular child.

What does this mean for the right to be a parent? A biological parent may be interested in raising their progeny, and a custodial caregiver may be interested in continuing their parental project. As I argue in the next four chapters, the community should protect these interests by giving genetic parents, gestational parents, caregivers, and intended parents the right to become legal parents, so long as they (like the senator-elect) meet the legal conditions for the office and fulfill its obligations. Adults' interests can shape the rules for assigning parenthood, but they cannot justify parental authority or duties, and they cannot shape their content. Parenthood is justified and defined by its political function to ensure equal respect for children.

3 Parenthood Is Private Authority That Requires Political Specification and Control

The final class of political rights and duties are *held between individual members because they are necessary for equal liberty*. The classic examples are property and contract rights. I have argued elsewhere that marriage falls into this category.[28] Private law seems "personal" insofar as it governs relations between individuals and its primary value is autonomy, but it is political in its justification, source, and content. This section explains these three political aspects, drawing heavily on recent interpretation of Kant's private law theory by Arthur Ripstein and Helga Varden.[29] Some of the Kantian methods for reconciling private law with equal respect become helpful in Part II.C to reconcile parental authority with equal respect.

According to Kant, private rights are necessary to ensure everyone has equal liberty to pursue their ends. The clearest example is property. We live in a shared physical world. A person may pursue their ends only if they have the moral power to acquire rights to exclude others from some objects. I have a liberty to be a potter only if I have the privilege to use clay. I must also have the power to place others under a duty not to use clay that I stockpiled; otherwise, others can use it for their ends the moment I put it down. Self-respect requires me to assume I have this privilege and

[28] Gregg Strauss, *The Positive Right to Marry*, 102 VA. L. REV. 1691, 1746–60 (2016).

[29] ARTHUR RIPSTEIN, FORCE AND FREEDOM: KANT'S LEGAL AND POLITICAL PHILOSOPHY 91–106 (2010); Helga Varden, *Kant's Non-Voluntarist Conception of Political Obligations: Why Justice Is Impossible in the State of Nature*, 13 KANTIAN REV. 1 (2008).

this power to acquire property. Otherwise, I treat my liberty as subordinate to others' choices. Unfortunately, everyone else should reason similarly from their perspective. When my neighbor wants to build a brick house, how can they accept that my choice to use clay for pottery gives them a duty not to use it? That would mean their liberty to build a house is subject to my choice. None of us can pursue our ends without assuming that we can acquire rights over others concerning objects, but if anyone has such unilateral authority, no one has equal liberty.[30]

Private law offers a way out of this dilemma. The reconciliation proceeds in two steps, beginning with an argument for the moral necessity of legitimate law and moving to arguments for the moral necessity of private law with particular content.

Suppose we had a set of universal rules of property acquisition and ownership. Anyone who acquired property would be exercising the same powers as anyone else. We would have formal equal liberty. But where could we get the rules? If we act on our own judgment about the correct rules, the dilemma of unilateral authority recurs at a higher level of abstraction. Suppose I endorse a Lockean principle that one can acquire property rights by performing labor on unowned resources if as much and as good remains in the commons. I conclude that I have an exclusive right to clay that I dug from nearby because there are other clay sources. My neighbor may reach a different yet equally sincere and reasonable judgment. Maybe the other clay is harder to reach or is inferior for bricks, or maybe they endorse a left-libertarian principle that we each have an equal right to common stock. If I persist in acting on my judgment, I presume that I have authority to judge which principle governs our relations and how it applies to our specific case. My neighbor cannot acquiesce in my conduct without failing to respect themselves as a person of equal moral status entitled to act on their own judgment.[31]

Legitimate property *law* is the first step to enable equal respect. If a public authority selects a system of rules for everyone in the community and empowers third parties to judge how those rules apply in particular cases, then no member of the community is subject to the unilateral choice of any other. Suppose our community adopted a capture rule. Now when I stockpile clay, I am exercising a public power that was authorized by the community on behalf of us both. We each have a right to demand the community establish such a regime of private law that will enable us to respect one another's equal liberty, as well as duty to establish and support these institutions.[32]

However, legitimate private law is necessary but insufficient. Private law itself threatens equal liberty unless it is subject to three kinds of restrictions to reconcile it with equal respect. First, private law doctrines must be circumscribed to avoid undermining equal liberty in their own domain. Property law, for example, must

30 Varden, *supra* note 29, at 13; Kyla Ebels-Duggan, *Kant's Political Philosophy: Kant's Political Philosophy*, 7 Phil. Compass 896, 898 (2012).

31 Varden, *supra* note 29, at 14–17.

32 *Id.* at 17–18, 25; Ripstein, *supra* note 29, at 157.

recognize easements by necessity. If someone could acquire exclusive rights to all land surrounding their neighbor, then property law would give them authority to decide how their neighbors can access that land for their projects. Second, law must prohibit citizens from using private law to perpetuate forms of structural subordination that undermine equal liberty. Restrictive covenants are a legitimate way for private owners to promote community, but the law must prohibit racial covenants that maintain segregation. Last, the law must include public rights that prevent individually innocent claims from aggregating in ways that undermine equal liberty. For example, Christopher Essert argues that universal ownership of land undermines equal liberty without a coexisting right to housing. When individuals or the state owns all land, anyone without a home has no liberty to sleep, cook, or urinate – even to *simply be* anywhere – without another's permission.[33]

These three limits are not imposed on the pristine private law, distorting its commitment to liberty in favor of public welfare. Private law and its restrictions both arise from the same commitment to equal liberty. Citizens have equal liberty to pursue their own ends only if a legitimate public authority issues and adjudicates private law in ways that comply with these limitations.

Like private law, parenthood is a form of morally necessary private authority fraught with the risk of subordination. Every child is entitled to some private caregiver with authority to direct their life, but this very authority threatens the child's equal status.[34] Many of the solutions for this tension are akin to those in private law. First, no individual adult can unilaterally claim authority over a child. A public authority must specify parental rights and the grounds for acquiring them, ensuring that parenthood and parentage respect the equal dignity of the child. Second, the community must enforce limits on parental authority so that a parent does not use their legal power to compromise a child's equal status. Finally, the community must offset the systemic effects of its parenthood regime that contribute to systemic inequality. Differences in parental resources or abilities may affect children's life prospects, so the community must offset these effects with public caregiving support and public education. The law should also take affirmative steps to counter gendered differences in caregiving that perpetuate gender inequality.

* * *

Parents and children share a deeply intimate relationship, but parenthood's extraordinary duties and authority are irreducibly political. We have seen that to ensure justice for children (I.B.1), the community must create an office of parenthood (I. B.2) that is defined and limited by law in ways that respect the equal dignity of the

33 Christopher Essert, *Property and Homelessness*, 44 Phil. & Pub. Aff. 266 (2016). Similar arguments can justify a right to poverty relief: a state cannot allow property rights to create an economic system in which some people are dependent on others' charity as the only way to pursue their own lives. Ripstein, *supra* note 29, at 279–81.

34 Anca Gheaus, *Child-Rearing with Minimal Domination: A Republican Account*, 69 Pol. Stud. 748 (2021).

child and parent (I.B.3). Just as no theory of justice dictates a full property regime, it will not dictate all the contours of parenthood. Citizens can reasonably disagree about how best to reconcile children's rights and parents' powers and how to reconcile parenthood with distributive justice. Only public officials exercising legitimate authority can specify a full regime of parenthood. Nevertheless, abstract moral arguments are sufficient to justify the general rights and duties of parenthood. Part II turns to this task.

II POLITICAL CONCEPTION OF PARENTHOOD

This part argues that parenthood is a political office essential to distributive justice. Each child is entitled to an adequate parent, just as they are entitled to adequate nutrition, shelter, and education. The community has a duty to identify parents, delegate authority to them, and support them as they satisfy the distributive rights of child citizens.

The political justification for parenthood has three parts. Section A argues that each child is entitled to an intimate caregiver, drawing on arguments from feminists like Susan Miller Okin and Martha Fineman and liberals like Harry Brighouse and Adam Swift. However, a right to a caregiver is not yet a right to a parent. A "parent" is an individual with a duty to ensure a child's generic and relational needs are met and the discretionary authority to decide how to do so. Section B argues that each child is entitled to this kind of parental *authority*. It presents an original argument that a just community must empower a small number of intimate caregivers with broad control over the lives of a small group of children. In other words, justice requires parents. Section C considers additional limitations necessary to reconcile parental authority with equal respect for children and parental duties with equal respect for adults.

A *Distributive Right to Caregiving*

This book assumes, rather than defends, a liberal-egalitarian theory of justice. Nevertheless, it is necessary to recount some foundations of this conception of justice to see how applying it to children generates a right to a parent. This section sketches core principles of justice for children and explains how they justify a right to intimate caregiving.

1 Distributive Justice

Humans cannot avoid living together in communities. We are born, live, and die in a world where our lives are molded by others' choices and the community's social, economic, and political institutions. This mutual influence is not lamentable. Without it, we would not have a distinctly human existence. Yet this influence raises moral problems. How can the community shape our lives yet still treat each of us as our own person with equal dignity?

John Rawls articulated the basic answer: A community treats its members as equals only if its basic institutions enable each person to pursue a life that they judge valuable from their perspective. Equal respect, in this sense, grounds liberal rights and distributive justice.

Liberal rights protect each person's authority to live by their own judgment. A community treats its members as equals only if it allows them to judge for themselves what ends are valuable and how to pursue them, so long as their actions are consistent with equal liberty for everyone else.[35] This principle justifies fundamental liberties like the right to bodily integrity and freedom of expression, as well as legal rights to private property and contract for reasons explained in 1.I.B.3. Notice that liberal rights need not be justified by the overriding value of choice or negative liberty. That is a regrettably common caricature of liberalism. Liberal rights ensure everyone has equal entitlement to live by their judgment about what constitutes a valuable life.

Distributive justice ensures that each community member has a reasonable opportunity to realize those values. Each member is entitled to a fair share of primary goods and capacities needed to pursue a valuable life in their community. Rawls called these "primary" goods because they are valuable regardless of the full conception of the good a citizen accepts. Primary goods include material resources like goods and services, but the category is much more capacious. As Martha Nussbaum and Amartya Sen argue, humans also need capacities to translate goods into valuable lives.[36] Moreover, it is not enough for society to meet members' basic needs. Because the fundamental social, economic, and legal institutions shape everyone's lives, each member is entitled to a fair share of the resources generated by those institutions. A community does not treat members as equals if it sustains basic institutions that systematically advantage some individuals without offsetting benefits to the least well-off.

While a community must ensure distributive justice, it must also respect adults' decisions about how to use their goods to pursue a life they judge valuable. Even if expert bureaucratic directives would on balance result in more preference satisfaction, such paternalistic interventions deny equal respect by presuming to settle our ends for us. The ultimate value of any primary good can be assessed only by unrestricted judgments about the good life.[37] This role for values is evident in well-defined belief systems. Spiritual groups from Hasidic Judaism to New Age countercultures care deeply about how their members use apparently generic goods like food or education. What is true for members of these groups is true for everyone, even people who do not identify with a defined ethical or religious tradition.[38] Our

35 Rawls, *supra* note 8, at 56.

36 Martha C. Nussbaum, Women and Human Development: The Capabilities Approach 70 (2001).

37 John Rawls, Justice as Fairness: A Restatement 57 (2001).

38 Rawls's emphasis on "comprehensive doctrines" unfortunately intellectualized and reified the idea, leading Rawls to shift his focus from individual judgments to consensus among idealized religious or philosophical systems. John Rawls, *Reply to Habermas*, *in* Political Liberalism, 387–89 (expanded ed. 2005).

lives reflect our judgments about what is valuable, whether that is religious virtue, family life, creative expression, intellectual achievement, athletic excellence, or aesthetic experience. The state cannot legitimately dictate how we use our primary goods, because the state cannot purport to set ends for us while still regarding us as equals.

It is also essential to note that justice is not opposed to material inequality per se, much less to any given pattern of wealth at a snapshot in time. America's wealth inequality is unjust because of its differential effect on people's ability to pursue lives that they can judge valuable. Property rights – and other liberal rights – create forms of social, economic, and legal power that must be regulated so all members may pursue their ends as equals. Focusing on one snapshot in time is also inappropriate because basic institutions structure our entire lives. As Rawls said, principles of justice govern those who live their "complete life" within an ongoing society.[39] A just community must consider how its institutions shape our lives from birth to death.

2 Distributive Justice for Children: Goods and Caregivers

What does a community owe its members who, at this moment, are children? As Martha Fineman emphasizes, all human lives begin and end in periods of dependency where we cannot meet our own needs, and any of us might have been or become subject to disabilities.[40] Equal respect demands the community meet the needs of all its dependent members, including children.[41] A just community must ensure that each child has a fair share of primary goods they need to experience a valuable childhood and to develop into an adult capable of pursuing a life they judge valuable.[42]

Moreover, although human development follows biological paths, childhood dependency is also not a simple natural fact caused exclusively by children's development.[43] Childhood is a status shaped by contingent social norms. Children are molded from birth to participate in their community. Toddlers learn the local language and are inculcated with customs of sociability. Families and

39 John Rawls, Political Liberalism 18 (2005). *See also* Eichner, *supra* note 17, at 52–55.

40 Fineman, *supra* note 11.

41 Christie Hartley, *Disability and Justice*, 6 Phil. Compass 120 (2011). The point is not that the state should even out the effects of luck because children, elderly persons, or persons with atypical abilities are not responsible for their situation. This kind of "luck egalitarian" arguments begin with an intuition like, "There but for the grace of god goes I." A better intuition to start with is, "There I have been; there I will be." In our deliberative perspective as designers of just social institutions, we are all potentially children, elderly, and at risk of not having the abilities valued in our market economy. No one could, consistent with rightful self-respect, design a system in which they may become fully dependent with inadequate means of subsistence.

42 Brighouse & Swift, *supra* note 24, at 62–65.

43 Paula S. Fass, *Is There a Story in the History of Childhood?*, *in* The Routledge History of Childhood in the Western World 1 (Paula S. Fass ed., 2013). *See* Olsen, *supra* note 7; Archard, *supra* note 16, at 43–45, 48–49.

schools raise children to participate in the community by teaching them its relevant skills, whether that be caregiving, farming, weaving, reading, mathematics, or computing. Youth is the longest for affluent children in post-industrial democracies, where full participation in labor markets requires extensive education. We restrict children's market labor and mandate secondary education. Children live in a world of coerced dependency, which generates a special claim on the community to ensure their current and developmental needs.

What are children's needs? And is parenthood necessary to meet them? Recent philosophical literature divides children's primary goods into two rough categories: generic and relational goods.[44] Any just society must meet both types of needs, but it seems possible to do so without parents in our modern sense.

First, children need generic goods like food, clothing, shelter, play, and education. Such childhood goods are generic in two senses. They are useful regardless of one's conceptions of a good life. They can also be provided in multiple ways.[45] The United States relies primarily on parents to supply children with food and shelter and to ensure young children have adequate opportunities for play and education. Other nations provide more generous public subsidies directly to children. A community can provide food, housing, daycare, or preschooling to children directly without using parents as intermediaries. Historically, parents held primary responsibility for their children's education, but states turned to public schooling as market economies demanded widespread skills that few parents could teach. Just as states unbundled education from parenthood, they could unbundle other generic goods. A community could collectivize cooking and daycare, as in communes or Israeli kibbutzim. Collective provision of generic goods has practical drawbacks, but it also enables a community to ensure children receive the goods they deserve.

Second, children need relational goods. Feminists, care theorists, liberal egalitarians, and natural law theorists agree that children are entitled to sustained relationships with affectionate adult caregivers who meet their physical, emotional, and intellectual needs.[46] Children need people to care for them who care about them.[47]

44 Elizabeth Brake, *Willing Parents: A Voluntarist Account of Parental Role Obligations*, *in* PROCREATION AND PARENTHOOD: THE ETHICS OF BEARING AND REARING CHILDREN 151 (David Archard & David Benatar eds., 2010); S. MATTHEW LIAO, THE RIGHT TO BE LOVED (2015); Simon Keller, *Four Theories of Filial Duty*, 56 PHIL. Q. 254, 266–68 (2006) (distinguishing "generic" from "special" goods that a parent or a child can receive from no one [or almost no one] else).

45 Some primary goods may be specific to childhood, such as a greater ability for immersive imaginative play made possible by brain development. Colin Macleod, *Agency, Authority and the Vulnerability of Children*, *in* THE NATURE OF CHILDREN'S WELL-BEING: THEORY AND PRACTICE 53, 60–61 (Alexander Bagattini & Colin Macleod eds., 2015).

46 EVA FEDER KITTAY, LOVE'S LABOR: ESSAYS ON WOMEN, EQUALITY AND DEPENDENCY (2d ed. 2019); Pamela Laufer-Ukeles, *The Relational Rights of Children*, 48 CONN. L. REV. 741, 764–66, 780–82 (2015); Brake, *supra* note 44 at 174; BRIGHOUSE & SWIFT, *supra* note 24, at 71–73, 77, 118; LIAO, *supra* note 44; NANCY E. DOWD, REDEFINING FATHERHOOD 157 (2000) (describing children's need for "nurturing").

47 This is not my phrase, but I cannot find its source. It is consistent with the above positions.

Psychologists believe that consistent, affectionate, and attuned caregiving aids infant development, which can have enduring effects on social and academic competence.[48] An affectionate and consistent adult presence may help young children learn to regulate their emotions, develop a sense of agency and responsibility, and build confidence.[49] Even older children still need caregivers who can help guide them as they learn to exercise their growing capacities, safeguarding their future welfare against the effects of a child's immature judgment and diminished conative control.[50] The community is obligated to help ensure children receive their primary goods, yet these relational goods can be supplied only by another individual within an ongoing relationship.

Such caregiving relationships are both valuable now and necessary for the child to develop their capacities. In this respect (and others), children have dual interests as citizens. They have an interest in developing their capacities for future experience and judgment, including religious, aesthetic, ethical, and political matters. Children have an interest in developing their agency, as Feinberg famously argued.[51] However, children are not merely incomplete adults. As Anca Gheaus notes, children's different capacities may foster distinctive experiences with intrinsic value, such as imaginative play, flexible learning, penetrating wonder, or engrossing emotions.[52] However we specify the list of primary goods for children, the community must ensure children receive the primary goods essential to their current and future well-being.[53]

But even the relational goods need not be supplied by parents.[54] A child's need for intimate caregiving relationships could be met within different family structures,

[48] K. Lee Raby et al., *The Enduring Predictive Significance of Early Maternal Sensitivity: Social and Academic Competence Through Age 32 Years*, 86 Child Dev. 695, 704–05 (2015).

[49] Brighouse & Swift, *supra* note 24, at 72.

[50] *Id.* at 63.

[51] Joel Feinberg, *The Child's Right to an Open Future*, *in* Whose Child? Children's Rights, Parental Authority, and State Power 124 (William Aiken & Hugh LaFollette eds., 1980).

[52] Fass, *supra* note 43; Macleod, *supra* note 45; Anca Gheaus, *The "Intrinsic Goods of Childhood" and the Just Society*, *in* The Nature of Children's Well-Being: Theory and Practice 35, 41–42 (Alexander Bagattini & Colin Macleod eds., 2015).

[53] Eichner argues relational goods cannot be added to the list of Rawlsian primary goods. Eichner, *supra* note 17, at 22–23. However, I see no reason why political liberalism cannot include a more expansive set of caregiving goods, in much the same way that Eichner later argues public reason can justify active support for caregiving. *Id.* at 50. For efforts to incorporate caregiving in a Rawlsian framework, see Christie Hartley & Lori Watson, Equal Citizenship and Public Reason: A Feminist Political Liberalism (2018); Amy R. Baehr, *Political Constructivism and Justice in Caregiving*, *in* Caring for Liberalism: Dependency and Liberal Political Theory 187 (Asha Bhandary & Amy R. Baehr eds., 2020).

[54] Sarah Blaffer Hrdy, Mothers and Others: The Evolutionary Origins of Mutual Understanding (2009). Family law scholars typically argue children's relational interests justify constitutional rights to family integrity. *E.g.*, Shanta Trivedi, *My Family Belongs to Me: A Child's Constitutional Right to Family Integrity*, 56 Harv. C.R.-C.L. L. Rev. 267 (2021). However, the same interests might instead justify facilitating nonparental relationships. Gheaus argues young children have a right to nonparental care because it prevents domination by their parents and limits the risk of harm from imperfect parenting. Gheaus, *supra* note 34 at 755; Anca Gheaus, *Arguments for Nonparental Care for Children*, 37 Soc. Theory & Prac. 483, 499–501 (2011).

such as through kinship caregiving within extended families or by members of a communal caregiving group.

Brighouse and Swift contend, to the contrary, that only parental relationships can "reliably" meet children's "weighty developmental interests."[55] Every child needs someone who (1) demonstrates love through highly attentive provision of their needs over long periods of time, (2) serves as a central "disciplinary" model from whom the child will learn self-control and moral empathy through identification, and (3) is experienced by the child as exercising discretion based on their own judgment. A child can sustain this level of intimacy and identification only with "very few" adults. Thus, children's interests justify a right to a parent. Communal groups can meet their children's developmental needs only by delegating intimacy and discretion to a few adults, effectively recreating a parental relationship.[56]

I am unpersuaded that only parents can adequately meet children's relational needs. Although they draw on developmental psychology, Swift and Brighouse presuppose a conception of childhood, family, and agency remarkably reminiscent of middle-class, Western European families. Not all families or societies have the resources – or feel the need – to raise children with such highly individualized caregiving. Fortunately, child development does not require it. Children enjoy happy childhoods living in the shared custody of separated parents, sometimes with stepparents. Children thrive in communities that rely on extended families or communal caregiving. Even in Western societies, daycare and preschooling are a form of compensated communal caregiving. Wealthy families may rely on live-in nannies or send older children to boarding schools. Families can meet children's developmental needs while dividing physical and emotional care. Children have a right to an intimate caregiver, but this is not yet a right to a parent. The community could meet children's needs adequately without giving one caregiver broad authority over the child's generic and relational goods.

B *Distributive Right to Parenthood*

Even if parents are not strictly necessary, parenthood might still be an efficient way to satisfy children's generic and relational needs. Liberals often justify parenthood instrumentally in this fashion. Section 1 argues that the instrumental arguments are plausible but too speculative and contingent to be the whole story. Section 2.a argues that children have a right to private practical authority. Practical authority is itself a primary good for children, not a mere means to supply generic or relational goods. Section 2.b argues that this practical authority can be consistent with equal respect for the child only if structured like parenthood: bundled authority held by a few caregivers over a small number of children.

55 Brighouse & Swift, *supra* note 24, at 70–75.

56 *Id.* at 74–75.

1 Instrumental Arguments for Parenthood

The United States Supreme Court argues that the law protects parental authority because parents are most likely to have the knowledge, experience, and desire to do what is best for their child.[57] Similar instrumental theories are defended by law professors like Emily Buss, Elizabeth Scott, and Clare Huntington and philosophers like Brighouse, Swift, and Joseph Millum. Three types of instrumental arguments suggest that giving authority to parents facilitates child welfare.

First, bundling generic and relational goods can be efficient. The adult who lives with a child can meet their generic needs and, in the process, fulfill their relational needs.[58] Someone must feed the child, maintain their home, and read to them. Anyone could perform these tasks in principle, but it seems efficient if the same person who cooks and reads for a child has the authority to decide what to cook and read. Perhaps more importantly, caregiving tasks help form the emotional bonds constitutive of relational goods. Providing generic goods is a way for the adult to demonstrate they care for the child's well-being, which helps build the psychological attachments necessary for child development. A public authority that frequently intervened to monitor day-to-day decisions might undermine this bonding process.[59]

Second, caregivers may judge more accurately what is best for their child. Children need adequate nutrition, sleep, and enrichment, but someone must decide whether each child should eat meat, when they should go to bed, and whether they should spend time on sports or gaming. Scholars and courts argue that parents should make such choices because "[g]ood parents are likely to know their child and her particular situation better than other people."[60] A caregiver develops relationship-specific information about the child's preferences, state of mind, and developmental needs, which they can use to make tailored judgments. In contrast, legislators must use statistics to adopt general rules that necessarily ignore details about each child. Bureaucrats could investigate and make tailored judgments, but this process would be costly and inaccurate, and an official would have less time for each decision than a dedicated parent.

On the other hand, sometimes the state has the comparative epistemic advantage. Officials can marshal scientific expertise to collect and analyze empirical data. Institutions can leverage the epistemic advantages of multimember bodies. The state will likely reach more reliable general conclusions about matters that affect the welfare of all children similarly, such as the benefits of education or vaccination. The approach most likely to facilitate child welfare is a division of authority over children: officials determine what children need in general, while caregivers guide the child's everyday life.

57 Parham v. J.R., 442 U.S. 584, 602 (1979).

58 Clare Huntington & Elizabeth S. Scott, *Conceptualizing Legal Childhood in the Twenty-First Century*, 118 MICH. L. REV. 1371, 1415 (2019).

59 *Id.*

60 *Id.* at 1416 (citing Emily Buss, among others); MILLUM, *supra* note 8 at 55.

The third instrumental argument is that parents have stronger incentives to promote their child's well-being than other decision-makers.[61] Interest-alignment arguments typically begin with a sociobiological just-so story. Like all animals, humans naturally favor their progeny; hence, a genetic or gestational parent will care more for their child, on average, than a stranger or public official. Social conventions can then reinforce or redirect biological caregiving instincts. As adults fulfill caregiver responsibilities, they develop attachments to the child. These attachments can be built upon biological ties but can also arise from caregiving alone. The law further cultivates and harnesses these attachments by supporting parental authority. Scott and Scott argue that parental rights serve as nonmonetary incentives.[62] Allowing parents to decide how to raise children increases the parents' satisfaction with the role, enhancing their identification with the child and the quality of care. The law should be wary of interventions that might disrupt these attachments. When evolutionary, cultural, and legal incentives align parents' incentives with their children's welfare, the law can reasonably trust parents to do what is best for their children.

These instrumental arguments are a promising start, but instrumental rationality cannot be the entire story. Each of the instrumental arguments has significant weaknesses.

Chapter 3 will criticize sociobiological arguments for interest alignment in detail. In short, genetic incentives are too weak to justify parenthood. Genetic parents have an evolutionary incentive to facilitate the reproductive success of their progeny, but that is not an incentive to do what is best for each child or even what is best for one's children on average. Evolution is more discerning. Furthermore, human evolution favored incentives for collective caregiving by siblings, grandmothers, relatives, and friends, which can supplement or replace parental caregiving.[63] The law has little reason to blindly trust biological parents' evolutionary incentives more than the incentives of other caregivers.

Second, the epistemic argument is implausible for many classes of parents. Its weaknesses are acute as a justification for the initial assignment of parenthood. Few first-time parents are skilled caregivers. Gestational parents have some special knowledge about their newborns but no unique information about what is best for the child going forward.[64] That kind of knowledge develops only over time as the

61 Stephen G. Gilles, *On Educating Children: A Parentalist Manifesto*, 63 U. CHI. L. REV. 937, 953–56 (1996). For a critical analysis of the sociological justification, see David J. Herring, *Evolutionary Perspectives on Child Welfare Law*, *in* THE EVOLUTION OF VIOLENCE 53 (Todd K. Shackelford & Ranald D. Hansen eds., 2014).

62 Elizabeth S. Scott & Robert E. Scott, *Parents As Fiduciaries*, 81 VA. L. REV. 2401 (1995).

63 HRDY, *supra* note 54.

64 Jessica Feinberg, *Parent Zero*, 55 U.C. DAVIS L. REV. 2271, 2305–07 (2021) (discussing "gestating parent knows best" theory). It may be conceptually incoherent to ask which birth parent will best facilitate the child's interests, because the choice of caregiver affects what interests the child develops, raising a variant of Parfit's nonidentity problem. *See, e.g.*, I. Glenn Cohen, *Regulating Reproduction: The Problem with Best Interests*, 96 MINN. L. REV. 423, 437 (2011).

child grows and develops their own character, skills, and interests. A trained nurse would have immediate expertise and develop the same relationship-specific knowledge about this child. Even parents of older children are unlikely to have significant epistemic advantages when making crucial decisions affecting their welfare. As our children age, we are perpetually winging it. Few parents study child development in any detail. Few of us know more than physicians about whether veganism is healthy for children, more than psychologists about how often children should play video games, or more than teachers about what play activities build children's cognitive skills. Any epistemic argument for parenthood presumes that questions like these have correct answers, yet it entrusts these factual propositions to parents.

Last, the efficiency argument for bundling generic and relational goods with parental authority rests on empirical premises that are speculative, culturally contingent, and potentially discriminatory. Whether it is efficient for parents to supply generic goods depends on their costs, including the opportunity costs. Household labor has high opportunity costs, which is why wealthy parents often rely on paid domestic labor. The efficiency argument also leans heavily on the psychological premise that material care builds relational bonds. While it seems likely that bedtime rituals and sick care build relational attachments, the causal connection between cooking and attachment is more attenuated. And cleaning? And *paying* for food or housing? Feminist theory also gives us good reason to be skeptical about intuitions regarding the alleged connections between domestic labor and relational intimacy. Our familial institutions were shaped by social norms about "motherly love" that help sustain the gendered division of caregiving burdens – imposing the full cost of care on women.

Because these instrumental arguments take for granted existing cultural norms, they are curiously conservative for consequentialist arguments. Why not consider means to change family norms? We often have good reasons to violate family privacy norms in order to change parenting practices. Even if banning corporal punishment feels intrusive to some parents, changing child discipline norms might improve child welfare and, in the long run, feel less intrusive to parents once they have assimilated to the new norms. Similarly, state efforts to directly support children may seem intrusive only because we take a specific vision of family for granted: a nuclear family with heavily privatized dependency and extensive parental discretion. The state could nudge social norms toward the separation of care from financial responsibility, household management, and decisional authority. American states could provide direct financial assistance. They could encourage parents to share more authority with experts like teachers or doctors, improving educational or medical decision-making. Communal living might even increase efficiency through the shared provision of meals, housing, and domestic chores. Instrumentalists must consider these reforms and experiments, balancing the marginal benefit to children against the marginal reduction in parental satisfaction. The outcome of any such balance is difficult to predict with certainty.

If parental authority is merely an instrumental means to facilitate child welfare, then our faith in parental authority should be shaken by the bundling, epistemic, and interest-alignment arguments. If not, part of the justification for parenthood must lie elsewhere.

2 Children's Right to a Parent

Parenthood is not simply a means to supply children with goods. Each child is entitled to have at least one private person with the legal obligation and authority to guide the child's life on the child's behalf, and the community is obligated to ensure each child has such a parent.[65] Parental authority is necessary for equal respect, despite their apparent conflict. The argument for the right to a parent proceeds in two parts. Subsection a argues that because children lack the capacity to make or act on their own judgment about how to live, a community treats its children as equals only if it appoints a practical authority to direct their lives. This subsection is indebted to Tamar Schapiro, although it translates her Kantian theory of agency into a political conception of childhood that can form the legitimate basis for a liberal legal regime.[66] Subsection b argues that practical authority over children must be structured like parenthood, with broad authority held by a handful of caregivers over a small group of children.

To forestall misunderstanding, I do not offer a full theory of parent–child relationships. My political justification of parenthood has implications for parent–child–state conflicts, and I gesture toward them as necessary, but I do not explore in detail the scope of parental or state authority. Instead, my goal is to explain why and how the state may *ever* empower parents with authority to shape a child's life consistent with the equal dignity of the child.

A PRIVATE PRACTICAL AUTHORITY AS A PRIMARY GOOD FOR CHILDREN. Recall from II.A that liberal rights are necessary to respect each person's authority to guide

65 This section distinguishes the guidance and caregiving functions for analytical precision, but in practice most decisions that require guidance are also caregiving activities. Accordingly, I hope this analytical division need not replicate the gendered divide between maternal and paternal roles. Thanks to Jennifer Hendricks for alerting me to this apparent implication.

66 Tamar Schapiro, *What Is a Child?*, 109 ETHICS 715 (1999). Shapiro developed a Kantian theory of childhood to reconcile adult authority with respect for children. We must treat other agents as ends in themselves out of respect for their capacity to act on the basis of the universal moral law. However, children lack this ability. Their conduct is often caused by external influences or by internal impulses. Consequently, a child's choices are not attributable to the child as a person in a way deserving of blame or respect. Adults should not blame young children for their wrongful acts because their choices do not emanate from their will; instead, we should redirect their actions and reshape their motives through education or inducements. Similarly, adults are not required to respect children's preferences. Children's choices do not yet reflect value judgments attributable to them as persons. Instead, adults should act paternalistically toward children to help them develop the capacity to form and to act upon their own moral judgments.

their life by their own judgments. A person is entitled to liberal rights so long as they have two capacities: to judge what is valuable and to act on their value judgments. Once someone has these capacities, no one else can purport to dictate what this person must do without presupposing their own moral superiority. A community that does not give determinative weight to its members' judgments about their lives denies their equality.[67]

The community must not treat children's choices as determinative, because children are still developing these two moral capacities.[68] Young children lack the cognitive ability to judge ends or means. A toddler's choices do not reflect value judgments in any meaningful sense. Older children, like preteens, have the cognitive ability to make value judgments but not the conative control to act on them reliably. A just community must not allow children's uninformed or impulsive decisions to definitively shape their lives. Suppose, for instance, a parent was obligated to allow their six-year-old child to choose whether to go hiking or play video games. Or suppose the state had to respect a ten-year-old's choice whether to continue their education. Childhood decisions can determine what goods and capacities a person realizes over the course of their life. An immature child may forgo experiences that are intrinsically valuable or essential to future development. A state that treated children's choices or preferences about such matters as determinative would fail to respect them as equal citizens entitled to a life that they can deem valuable by their own judgment.[69]

Instead, the community must ensure someone exercises practical authority on behalf of each child. This practical authority must make value judgments for the child and direct their life to realize those values. I do not mean to imply that adults should ignore children. One cannot make judgments on a child's behalf without considering their predispositions, experiences, preferences, and beliefs. Even if children do not yet have their own settled values, they are not fungible blank slates. Making judgments from a child's perspective requires listening to the child more, not less. Furthermore, overruling a child's choices may hinder the supposed good to

67 RAWLS, *supra* note 39, at 29–35, 107–08.

68 Schapiro, *supra* note 66. Archard identifies three elements comprising "rational autonomy" – rationality, maturity, and independence – although his analysis reveals each category is multifaceted, scalar, and does not draw a categorical divide between adults and children. ARCHARD, *supra* note 16, at 88–91.

69 This account is similar to instrumentalist justifications for paternalism. Noggle, for example, argues that states need parents to protect the welfare of children and society because children lack stable preferences and demonstrate insufficient concern for their future selves. Robert Noggle, *Special Agents: Children's Autonomy and Parental Authority*, *in* THE MORAL AND POLITICAL STATUS OF CHILDREN 97 (David Archard & Colin Macleod eds., 2002); *See also* NORVIN RICHARDS, THE ETHICS OF PARENTHOOD 132 (2010); LAURA MARTHA PURDY, IN THEIR BEST INTEREST? THE CASE AGAINST EQUAL RIGHTS FOR CHILDREN (1992) (arguing parents must have authority to direct children's lives so children develop into adults who can lead worthwhile lives). However, as Archard argues, such instrumental arguments presuppose a relatively determinate answer about what traits are best for each child to develop. ARCHARD, *supra* note 16, at 72–79. That is precisely what the liberal state cannot provide. All that a liberal state can, and must, supply are primary goods and capacities necessary for children to develop into adults capable of exercising the two moral powers of citizenship.

be achieved and deny the child opportunities to develop their capacities. A practical authority must consider these current and developmental concerns.[70] Nevertheless, the fundamental point remains. Respect for children as equal members of the community requires appointing someone to exercise substitute judgment for each child, rather than treating children's choices as determinative.

As older children develop judgment and control of their actions, their choices become more attributable to them, which justifies greater responsibility and respect from the community. At what age must a minor's decisions about their life be treated as determinative? When can a child act on their own judgments, such that others must respect the child's decisions on where they worship, what they learn about, how they spend their leisure time, or who should hold political office? Should the state adopt a bright-line age of majority or assess competence with individualized tests?[71]

As I indicated above, these are natural follow-up questions, but I cannot answer them here. Sound answers require a specification of each liberal right and the capacities that it presupposes. Different capacities are needed to participate in religious practices, form contracts, consent to sex, choose an educational path, and vote in elections. Many capacities are scalar without natural thresholds. Human development follows general patterns, but capacities can develop at a different pace in different children. None magically switch on at a birthday. Caregivers for preteens and teenagers constantly face difficult judgments about what to allow their children to decide for themselves. Moreover, the community's family and educational institutions affect whether and how quickly children learn cognitive and volitional skills. Childhood is a political construction superimposed on statistical facts about human development within certain social institutions. Only a legitimate political authority can judge what capacities its members need to acquire full equal membership, including liberal autonomy rights.

For simplicity, I will assume that children do not develop their own judgment and control sufficient for self-determination rights until at least their preteen years.

[70] ARCHARD, *supra* note 16, at 120–22.

[71] Critics use similar questions to argue that capacity-based justifications of parenthood are over- or underinclusive. Some adults score lower on cognitive and volitional tests than some children. Either these adults should be subject to paternalistic intervention or children should be free of them. Samantha Godwin, *Children's Capacities and Paternalism*, 24 J. ETHICS 307 (2020); JAMES G. DWYER, THE RELATIONSHIP RIGHTS OF CHILDREN 150–52 (2006); James G. Dwyer, *Deflating Parental Rights*, 40 L. & PHIL. 387 (2021). Archard offers a concise response to objections of arbitrariness: society must draw some lines and good practical reasons exist for age-based categorizations rather than individualized decisions. ARCHARD, *supra* note 16, at 82–85. I agree with Archard's practical arguments but would also reject the liberationists' premise that political morality requires equal treatment of adults and children with the same capacities. This premise ignores the developmental justification of parental authority. Children are subject to parental authority so they can be equal participants over their life course. Once a citizen develops basic capacities for self-governance, no public reasons consistent with equal respect justify further control of their life (short of self-harm). When a citizen never develops the relevant capacities or loses them due to injury or illness, the community must accommodate the adult's existing capacities to facilitate their participation as equal members as much as possible.

I regard this line as conservative; others might push it earlier. During this period of childhood, every community member is entitled to have some adult exercise judgment on their behalf.

The next question is, Who should exercise practical authority over children? Should it be a legislature, judge, community, extended family, parent, teacher, or someone else?

It is tempting to insist that the state must allocate authority over children to whoever will best promote their welfare. Each child is their own person. If someone must exercise authority over a child, the state should choose whoever will best facilitate this child's current and future welfare. Ana Gheaus calls this the "best available caregiver" theory.[72] This approach could be ad hoc or rule-based. Mary Byrn and Jenni Ives argue that genetic parents or intended parents are most likely to be the best caregivers for a child.[73] According to the 2017 Uniform Parentage Act, whenever a child has competing parentage claims, judges should choose whichever adult best promotes the child's interests. Others might argue that parenthood itself can be justified only insofar as it serves children's interests. The United Nations Convention on the Rights of the Child, for example, insists that: "In all actions concerning children, whether undertaken by public or private social welfare institutions, courts of law, administrative authorities or legislative bodies, the best interests of the child shall be the primary consideration."[74]

This instrumental best-interests approach, whether ad hoc or rule-based, cannot fulfill the function of practical authority for children. The problem is easiest to see in epistemic arguments for parenthood. Some courts argue that parents have rightful authority because they know what is best for their children. How could a parent know whether their infant child will have a better life growing up in a city rather than a suburb? Or with a hypercompetitive drive rather than lighthearted contentment? Many scholars object that the best-interests approach to such questions presupposes an unrealistic amount of information. That is true, but there is a deeper problem that is not merely epistemic.

A person's interests are fixed relative to their values or ends. Because a child does not yet have their own values or ends, there is no answer about which home or character best serves this child's interests. Parents cannot claim superior information about such matters because – in a fundamental sense – there is nothing to know. Until a child follows some path long enough to develop her own values or ends, it is impossible to specify which option best facilitates their well-being.[75] Infants have no

[72] Anca Gheaus, *Children's Vulnerability and Legitimate Authority over Children*, 35 J. Applied Phil. 60 (2018).

[73] Mary Patricia Byrn & Jenni Vainik Ives, *Which Came First the Parent or the Child*, 62 Rutgers L. Rev. 305, 332–42 (2009).

[74] Convention on the Rights of the Child, Nov. 20, 1989, 1577 U.N.T.S. 3, art. 3.1 (1989).

[75] Feinberg identified a similar "paradox": a parent seeks to raise a child to provide a life that is good for the child, yet what is good for the child depends on their propensities and skills, and the parent's decisions about how to raise the child shape their propensities and skills. Feinberg, *supra* note 51, at 124–53, 146–48.

settled relationships, characters, values, or ends that could determine which caregiver will provide a better life. A best-interest-of-the-child principle is nearly incoherent as a method for identifying a specific caregiver for infants, selecting a default category of caregivers, or designing a society's caregiving institutions.

Of course, every community must have a general conception of child welfare to be in a position to design institutions for children. As described above, I favor a childhood version of Rawls's primary goods supplemented by capability theory. Children need to eat healthy food, get vaccinations, experience play, build friendships, and receive education. These primary goods are not specified by reference to any particular conception of a valuable life, but instead by what all citizens need to live a life that they can judge valuable by their own standards. Yet a society that only met children's basic needs would not be just. Each child must translate primary goods into a valuable life. Should a child subsist on chicken nuggets and carrots, or should they experience a variety of foods? How much food frustration should a child endure so that the child develops taste? Such questions can only be answered by reference to intrinsic values relating to health and pleasure. Value judgments like this are a pervasive aspect of childrearing. Someone must raise the child as a complete person with virtues like courage, grace, compassion, and sociability. A child needs an authority to judge what comprehensive values should direct their lives and to help them regulate their conduct so as to realize those values.

This function generates the first limit on who may wield practical authority over children. As Justice Powell wrote, a democracy must refrain from "affirmative sponsorship of particular ethical, religious, or political beliefs," and "[t]hus, it is cardinal with us that the custody, care and nurture of the child reside first in the parents, whose primary function and freedom include preparation for obligations the state can neither supply nor hinder."[76] Powell moved too quickly to parental authority, and his primary concern was religious upbringing, but his general point remains accurate. Raising a child requires selecting among theories of the good life. Public officials cannot legitimately dictate how a child should translate primary goods into a flourishing life. The community can ensure justice for children only by appointing some private person to exercise practical authority over a child's life.

Feinberg purports to have found a way out, arguing the paradox relies on overstatements about the malleability of propensities. Even young children have a certain "rudimentary character consisting of temperamental proclivities and a genetically fixed potential for the acquisition of various talents and skills," and parents can build on these baseline traits to make rough judgments about what is good for the child. If a child dislikes painting or shows little propensity for it, then band camp is better for them than art camp. Unfortunately, Feinberg's "solution" understates the value problem. The conclusion of his example rests on premises about the comparative value of art and music and of perseverance over one's baseline proclivities.

76 Bellotti v. Baird, 443 U.S. 622, 638 (1979) (J. Powell, plurality).

B FROM PRACTICAL AUTHORITY TO CAREGIVER AUTHORITY TO PARENTAL AUTHORITY. The argument so far has established the necessity of private practical authority over children, but it does not yet favor parenthood over other arrangements. Authority over children might fall to a family matriarch, a kibbutz, an orphanage director, or a teacher. It might also be divided among domain-specific experts, like caregivers, teachers, and physicians. The justification of parenthood must answer three more questions. Why should one authority make most decisions for a child? Why should one adult or small group hold this authority over only a small group of children? Why should this authority be the same person who fulfills the child's need for intimate caregiving?

i **Practical Authority Requires Bundling** Practical authority over children should remain substantially bundled because of the nature of the decisions made on their behalf. Many everyday decisions involve multiple values, and those values can cross many areas of a child's life. Whoever decides what a child eats must also judge how the child will balance the virtues of health, pleasure, and environmental concern. Whoever decides how a child spends their time must also judge how the child will balance the value of education, athletics, aesthetics, and spirituality.

The integration of values is most evident in traditions where spiritual values pervade everyday life. A new age devotee may believe that respect for life unites their commitment to veganism, yoga, environmentalism, and social justice volunteering. Few modern Americans expect their lives to be univocal to this extent, but our everyday decisions still need to be guided by relatively consistent judgments. When a caregiver tells their eleven-year-old to stop reading at 8:00 pm because the child has a basketball game the next day, this directive reflects the caregiver's judgment about the value of intellectual virtue, athleticism, and long-term health. To guide the child's life, someone needs practical authority to settle a range of value judgments related to a range of decisions.

What is the appropriate level of bundling? Pragmatic concerns place some limits on disaggregation. Even if physicians would make better dietary decisions, assigning this authority to a doctor will create conflicts with a caregiver's meal planning. Many scholars advocate giving associational rights to nonparents, but the time spent in visitation and the influence that nonparents exercise during that time are nontrivial impositions on parents' ability to guide their child's life.[77] Repeat conflicts might create instability in adult-child relationships, and the law has good reason to

[77] Gheaus advocates for nonparental associational rights to break the monopoly of parental authority. Gheaus, *supra* note 34. Other proposals for "nonexclusive parenthood" do not threaten parental exclusivity because they focus on protecting the attachments that children form during periods of nonparental custody when the univocality of parental authority is already compromised. Katharine T. Bartlett, *Rethinking Parenthood as an Exclusive Status: The Need for Legal Alternatives When the Premise of the Nuclear Family Has Failed*, 70 VA. L. REV. 879, 944–48 (1984).

reinforce "the meaning of parenthood as an enduring commitment."[78] However, the justification for bundling is not simply instrumental or expressive.

A community cannot meet its duty to its children if it splits authority between too many domain-specific authorities with limited duties. The boundaries around areas of the child's life are too porous. Should a teacher or caregiver decide how a child allocates evenings between homework, extracurriculars, church, and relaxation? Must a Native American child remain silent during an anthem celebrating a nation that spans from "sea to shining sea" as a result of land stolen from their ancestors? The community must ensure someone is responsible for judging what serves a child's well-being as a complete person, not merely isolated judgments about their physical, psychological, intellectual, moral, or spiritual health. All children need someone with the duty to make the substitute value judgments that give relative coherence to their lives.

I do not mean to imply that Western society, much less the United States, has identified a uniquely correct allocation of authority to guide children's lives. The issue permits a range of reasonable answers. Nevertheless, each child needs someone with broad authority and obligation to judge how the child will use primary goods to flourish as a person.

ii **Practical Authority Requires Modest Exclusivity** Having identified the reasons for bundling authority over many decisions, we can now turn to the reasons for limiting the number of adults who can wield this authority and the number of children subject to their authority. These two numerosity limits bring us closer to the ordinary notion of parentage.

A practical authority can exercise substitute judgment only for *small groups of children at a time*. Each child needs someone to judge on their behalf how they should live. This authority can treat a child as a person with equal dignity whose life matters for the child only if they strive to make substitute value judgments from the child's perspective as an individual.[79] Someone in charge of a large group of children cannot make judgments for each child as an individual.

The problem is most evident in orphanages. Even if the director is an ideally loving person, they cannot adopt the perspective of any single child to set and pursue this child's ends for the child's own sake. Special partiality for one child would violate the director's duty to the rest. Such conflicts are a common trope in orphan stories. Even in a well-run orphanage, children never feel loved as individuals. A director who falls in love with one child risks betraying the rest. Instead, the director must allocate resources fairly across all the orphans based on impersonal principles. Because of these distributive obligations, orphanages cannot wield

78 Ayelet Blecher-Prigat, *Conceiving Parents*, 41 HARV. WOMEN'S L.J. 119 (2018), at 133–35.

79 This does not presuppose a unique correct answer for each child, which would conflict with a premise of my general argument for authority. Instead, the focus here is on the perspective from which the authority must make the judgment. Thanks to Megan Boone for helping me clarify this position.

authority over children's lives in a way that respects each child as an equal person entitled to their own life.[80]

Of course, no caregiver can avoid distributional decisions entirely. There is no bright line between an orphanage with fifty children, a foster home with ten, and a parent with four. Sometimes a parent must make decisions for one sibling that affect the rest. A parent may send their child with a disability to a private tutor, even if this expense limits resources available for the siblings' education. Even a parent with only one child must make distributional decisions, sometimes favoring their own ends over the child's welfare. A parent may choose to relocate for their career, even if the new city has marginally worse schools. Nevertheless, an adult with authority over only a few children can adopt each child's perspective to make most judgments on the child's behalf. As the number of children under their care increases, it becomes more difficult to make decisions from the perspective of one child. Most decisions become distributive ones. When an orphanage is responsible for fifty children, its director will make most decisions for a child only as an abstraction, as one member of a community.

The function of substitute judgment also constrains the number of adults who can share authority over each child.[81] More than two adults can raise a child, but not many more. The possibility of three or more parents is a hot topic in family law. Even advocates of alternative families admit that caregiving groups face practical problems because of the increased likelihood of conflict. Of course, decision procedures exist to alleviate the practical problems. A group could aspire to unanimity and then use settlement mechanisms to resolve disagreements. They might fall back on majority voting or select a default decision-maker. Each procedure has benefits and drawbacks, but these practical concerns are not definitive.[82]

The moral problems might be. Each child deserves someone to guide their life with substitute value judgments. Some group decision procedures fulfill this function poorly, if at all. As List and Petit explored in *Group Agency*, some decision procedures do not satisfy the minimal conditions on rationality and preference

80 Of course, orphanages have other problems. They have a terrible history of physical abuse and neglect of children's generic needs, perhaps caused by incentives built into institutional structures. Even if orphanages could be reformed to avoid their blatant faults, they might also be incapable of supplying the relational goods of childhood. Brighouse, Swift, and Brake argue that institutional orphanages are too impersonal to provide the kind of loving care that children need on an individual level.

81 Other ethicists worry that large parental groups (more than four) may be unable to supply the relational intimacy necessary for child flourishing. Samantha Brennan & Bill Cameron, *How Many Parents Can a Child Have? Philosophical Reflections on the "Three Parent Case,"* 54 DIALOGUE: CANADIAN PHIL. REV. 45 (2015).

82 June Carbone & Naomi Cahn, *Parents, Babies, and More Parents*, 92 CHI.-KENT L. REV. 9, 46–51 (2017) (discussing arrangements for three or more parents and concluding that courts should typically assign a primary parent). Jacobs argues the law can recognize more than two parents by disaggregating parental rights, but her proposal either runs afoul of the need to bundle authority or applies the title "parent" to secondary relational rights. Melanie B. Jacobs, *Why Just Two? Disaggregating Traditional Parental Rights and Responsibilities to Recognize Multiple Parents*, 9 J.L. & FAM. STUD. 309 (2007).

aggregation to qualify as rendering a *judgment*.[83] For example, a majoritarian vote may often represent overlapping conclusions based on inconsistent judgments about what is best for the child. Admittedly, no decision procedure is perfect. Two parents must often compromise, but they can at least strive to deliberate in ways that can represent a shared judgment. Even a sole caregiver will not always make rational decisions – just as individuals do not when trying to direct their own lives. The community need not supply each child with a perfect decision-making process, but it must arrange some authority *capable* of reaching judgments. This precludes allowing a large group of caregivers to share equal decisional authority over a child. Without drawing precise numbers, I would doubt that a group of five adults could be equal parents without falling into default hierarchies.[84]

Each child has a right to substitute judgment, but neither orphanage directors nor collective groups can provide substitute judgment on behalf of each child as an individual. The community should vest authority over each child with one adult or a small group of adults, who should have authority over only a small group of children. These numerosity limits bring us one step closer to modern parenthood, but we are still not all the way there.

iii **Practical Authority over Children Should Fall to Intimate Caregivers** Why should this authority fall to caregivers? One might argue that the ideal practical authority for children would combine a psychologist's knowledge with a judge's wisdom and a parent's love. Competitive salaries might give each child a virtuous authority figure – a Mary Poppins. This expert could adjudicate conflicts among other adult experts in a child's life, such as caregivers, teachers, and physicians. Why not delegate authority over children to paid experts? The reason authority should fall to caregivers combines the fiduciary duty of a practical authority with care theorists' account of children's relational needs.

Whoever wields authority over a child's life has a duty of loyalty to make substitute judgments on the child's behalf. Because the child does not exist for anyone else's benefit, this adult must adopt the child's perspective when making decisions for them. An intimate caregiver is most likely to maintain this perspective. Care theorists argue that each child needs a sustained relationship with one affectionate caregiver.[85] This caregiver already needs authority to decide daily matters, like when the child eats and sleeps. Children need to recognize that this caregiver who

83 Christian List & Philip Pettit, Group Agency: The Possibility, Design, and Status of Corporate Agents chs. 3–4 (2011).

84 The problems of decisional complexity created by too many parents cannot be cabined to separated parents sharing custody, which merely highlights the structural problem of distributed legal authority. *Contra* Naomi Cahn & June Carbone, *Custody and Visitation in Families with Three (or More) Parents*, 56 Fam. Ct. Rev. 399 (2018).

85 Kittay and Fineman ground their theories in a comprehensive theory of human nature, arguing that children require mothers. Kittay, *supra* note 46; Fineman, *supra* note 13. Although I reject the gendered implications of tying relational goods to motherhood, the fundamental insight remains. *See also* Brake, *supra* note 44.

meets their daily needs also cares for them as a person. Moreover, many of the relevant decisions relate to caregiving tasks for young children, like how much time a child spends at home, in daycare, at playdates, or in church. Caregivers – who already exercise authority over their daily lives, meet their relational needs, and likely care for them as individuals – should also have the authority to direct their lives generally.

One might object that we delegate children's other relational needs to experts. For example, education is also plausibly a relational good. The community must educate each child, but quality education requires long-term relationships with teachers that children trust. The community fulfills its collective duty to educate children by hiring teachers. If paid teachers can meet children's relational needs, why not hire expert caregivers? Treating parental duties to children as identical to contractual obligations in labor markets would create tension with their fiduciary duties. The problem is not with payment per se. I do not want to revive the discredited notion that financial motives are incompatible with other-regarding care or activities of intrinsic worth.[86] Money is consistent with care. Ideal teachers care for their students, nurses for their patients, and lawyers for their clients. All occupations blend instrumental and intrinsic motivations, including genuine love. I also support public compensation for parents. Parents fulfill the community's obligations. We compensate others who hold political offices that fulfill our collective duties, such as teachers, police, soldiers, or judges. Nevertheless, there is something to the intuition that parental duties require exceptional loyalty.

Parents wield a type and degree of discretion unique in law, which requires a unique fiduciary duty. Admittedly, other people wield discretion over children. Teachers can judge the best methods to ensure their pupils learn. However, teachers have little discretion over the *ends* of education. Education is a primary good. Someone must judge what kind and degree of education children need to thrive in the community's basic institutions. That requires settling disagreements about the relative importance of physical education, fine arts, liberal arts, or science instruction. No private person may settle such disputes. Parents and teachers should have input, but only public officials with authority to act on behalf of the community may legitimately decide what education children need to become equal members of society.

In contrast, parents often exercise similar authority over a child's life. They do not merely have discretion over means; they have broad discretion over a wide range of the child's ends. To arrange the child's life, a caregiver must decide to what extent a child will pursue athletic, academic, artistic, or gaming excellence. They must decide what health means for the child: balancing physical health against pleasure, and experiences against physical risks. Many of these decisions intersect spiritual

[86] Katharine Silbaugh, *Turning Labor into Love: Housework and the Law*, 91 Nw. U. L. Rev. 1, 26–27 (1996).

judgments. Teachers may choose means to a state-defined education, but caregivers may choose ends for most domains of a child's life. Caregivers wield authority over the child as a whole person. This authority is qualitatively distinct.

As I argued above, a person can rightfully exercise practical authority over a child only if they exercise substitute judgment on behalf of the child. They must adopt the child's perspective to judge how the child should pursue ends as their own person.[87] Because caregiving tends to foster attachment with the child, caregivers are most likely to develop and sustain concern for the child as their own person. The likelihood that caregivers will form intimate ties offers a good reason, albeit not conclusive, to bundle authority over a child's life with the caregiving role.

The state cannot legally oblige caregivers to share the child's ends. Benevolent, reciprocal love is the core of most comprehensive theories about the value of family and childrearing. However, the state cannot demand or coerce the subjective adoption of ends.[88] This limit on legal authority is one reason public support for parenting is consistent with parents' legal duties. Financial incentives do not prevent one from exercising substitute judgment on another's behalf. It would be difficult to reconcile devotion to another's life with *purely* financial motivations, but human motives are often overdetermined. Monetary incentives need not crowd out other-regarding incentives. Public child support payments should not be set so high as to create this risk. Given parenthood's nonfinancial burdens and opportunity costs, I suspect that only very high salaries could induce mercenary parenting, but that is admittedly an empirical question.

* * *

We have seen that distributive justice requires the community to ensure that some private authority has the responsibility and the authority to judge how each child translates their primary goods into a flourishing life (B.2.b.i). To make substitute judgments on behalf of each child, this practical authority must be one adult or small group of adults responsible for a small number of children (B.2.b.ii). The adults most likely to sustain this duty of loyalty to a child are their intimate caregivers (B.2.b.iii). In other words, distributive justice requires a parent.

87 Dwyer, *supra* note 71, at 150–52. My political theory of parenthood shares the core fiduciary theory intuition that parents enjoy authority to fulfill their duty to the child, and this authority requires them to exercise substitute judgment on the child's behalf. Yet, the source of the duties may differ. Some fiduciary accounts assume parents have a right to authority to fulfill duties that the parent owes directly to the child. I reject this picture of law as enforcing preexisting personal duties. Lionel Smith offers the most extensive recent defense of a fiduciary theory, but his concern is with the structure of the relationship and says little about the source of the duties. Lionel Smith, *Parenthood Is a Fiduciary Relationship*, 70 U. Toronto L.J. 395 (2020). Scott and Scott defend their fiduciary theory from a welfarist perspective. Scott & Scott, *supra* note 62.

88 Some scholars argue that a duty to love is incoherent because love is not amenable to will. Brighouse & Swift, *supra* note 24, at 21. I think the problem is moral; coercion designed to force someone to adopt an end denies them equal dignity.

C Reconciling Parenthood with Equal Dignity for the Child and Adult

Children's right to a parent goes a long way toward reconciling parenthood with equal dignity for children, but the reconciliation is incomplete. Even if the institution of parenthood is generally justified, parental authority and duties contain the seeds of subordination. For reasons similar to those discussed regarding private law in I.B.3, the law must impose internal and external limits on the parental office to ensure that it remains consistent with equal dignity for the child and the parent. Communities have many reasonable ways to specify parenthood, just as they have many reasonable ways to specify property law. Abstract moral theory cannot specify a unique regime of parental rights and duties, but it can yield general limits on parenthood's substantive content. It also imposes limits on the rules for acquiring parenthood. This section sketches some broad implications for parenthood, focusing on elements that mirror constraints on parentage in subsequent chapters.

1 Internal Limits on Parental Rights

The first limit is a corollary of the child's right to a parent: the parent must be willing and able to fulfill the parental office adequately. Children have a claim *against* being raised by inadequate parents. Parents' constitutional rights are, as the United States Supreme Court has explained repeatedly, always coupled with their duties.[89] A community may not allow anyone to exercise authority over a child if the person is unwilling or unable to guide the child's life with reasonable judgments.[90] Since the child cannot assert their entitlements, officials must have the authority to ensure that each child has a "fit" parent who supplies their material and relational primary goods.

The appropriate method to ensure parental adequacy is up for debate. In the United States, the official default rule leaves biological parents to raise their children on their own, unless someone reports suspicions of neglect or abuse, in which case social workers initiate investigations and potential removal to a foster family. Some philosophers believe such *inter se* supervision is insufficient to protect children's welfare. Hugh LaFollette famously argued that no one should be allowed to take custody of a child without affirmatively demonstrating their parental abilities.[91] Recent progressive scholarship is highly critical of the American child protection system, arguing that it punishes impoverished families

[89] Jeffrey Shulman, The Constitutional Parent: Rights, Responsibilities, and the Enfranchisement of the Child 79–84 (2014).

[90] *In re* J.B.S., 237 A.3d 131, 144 (D.C. 2020) (a court should not afford "any special weight or deference to an unfit parent's preference in choosing between competing adoption petitioners"). Archard, *supra* note 16, at 178–81.

[91] Hugh LaFollette, *Licensing Parents Revisited*, 27 J. Applied Phil. 327 (2010); Hugh Lafollette, *Licensing Parents*, 9 Phil. & Pub. Aff. 182 (1980). In 2.III.B.3, I argue that ex ante licensing is not necessary to respect children.

by using removal as a substitute for public welfare and relies on methods of reporting and investigation that are systemically racist.[92] Rather than policing and blaming families, it insists the law should promote quality parenting by offering families affirmative support on a systemic basis.[93]

Nevertheless, the community has a duty to ensure parental adequacy, which it can fulfill only if it has authority to define and enforce limits on parental conduct. Rules defining the boundaries of reasonable parenting are akin to the internal doctrines of private law (like easements by necessity) that prevent morally necessary forms of legal authority from undermining their function. The community can determine that some conduct, like corporal punishment, is not justified by any plausible child welfare arguments given available scientific evidence.[94] Other conduct might be motivated, in a sense, by concern for the child but still inconsistent with the parent's fiduciary function. For example, the law may not allow a parent to withhold necessary medical treatments from a child, even if the parent honestly believes it is necessary for salvation.[95] This parent has chosen to foreclose most conceptions of a valuable life for the child in service of a single value. No one can purport to make such a judgment on behalf of the child. The parent cannot assert that their daughter shares these religious values because the child lacks their own values – that is the only reason *anyone* can decide for the child. The parent's purported trade-off treats the child as someone who exists to serve the parent's values rather than as a distinct person with equal dignity entitled to live a full life according to their own values.

Many problematic cases involve conflicts between primary goods and religious values, but the potential conflicts include secular values. For example, a parent must judge whether the benefits of a sport justify some physical risks, but the law must set age limits for dangerous activities like motocross and skydiving. Adults have the right to decide whether a thrill is worth risking their health or their lives, but the state cannot allow parents to make similar judgments about the risk to their child's future. A community that did not limit dangerous activities for children would not ensure that each child has a fair opportunity over the course of their life to pursue their own ends rather than their parent's chosen ends.

For similar reasons, the community must require education. An adult may decide for themselves whether to forgo college for an acting career, because the state must respect their authority to pursue their own life. Parents cannot make similar judgments on behalf of their high school children. In this respect, the US Supreme

92 Dorothy Roberts, Torn Apart: How the Child Welfare System Destroys Black Families – and How Abolition Can Build a Safer World 66–82 (2022).

93 Eichner, *supra* note 17; Cynthia Godsoe, *Parsing Parenthood*, 17 Lewis & Clark L. Rev. 113, 156–60 (2013).

94 Cynthia Godsoe, *Redefining Parental Rights: The Case of Corporal Punishment*, 32 Const. Comment. 281, 299–304 (2017).

95 Prince v. Massachusetts, 321 U.S. 158, 166–67 (1944); Phillips v. City of New York, 775 F.3d 538, 543 (2d Cir. 2015); Matter of McCauley, 565 N.E.2d 411, 414 (Mass. 1991).

Court's decision in *Wisconsin v. Yoder* is mistaken.[96] The Court held that Amish parents had a right to deny their children a high school education because the parents believed that only vocational skills were needed to flourish in their traditional farming community. Limiting the children's education reduced the likelihood that they would challenge their parents' Amish values and, if they did, increased the difficulty of transitioning into secular American life. These Amish parents used their children to sustain their agrarian way of life. No individual can have the authority to limit another person's life in this way. Only a political community can legitimately decide what capabilities members need to participate as equals in its social, economic, and political life. Wisconsin's citizens, acting through their legislature, expressed their collective judgment that all children needed a high school education. *Yoder* wrongly reallocated this authority to the Amish parents as private persons.[97]

The Court's famous paean to the Amish was irrelevant. These parents did not represent the Amish community and, regardless, the Amish are not a political unit entitled to political authority over their members. Any political theory must decide which community has legitimate authority to define and protect political equality. Is a child's political status defined by membership in the Amish community or as a citizen of the United States? Similar questions arise concerning Native American children and the Indian Child Welfare Act.[98] I cannot defend a particular theory of the bounds of political community here. Instead, I assume children have political rights as citizens of the United States and their state of residency, not their religious communities. That does not mean the Amish community is a "voluntary association." Members of the Amish community may conclude that their religious obligations bind them without consent. Nevertheless, the Amish community has no authority to coercively control the lives of adults who reach a contrary judgment – or prospectively prevent children from judging these matters for themselves.

One might worry that this liberal objection generalizes. If parents cannot constrain their children's lives in service of religious values, then parents should not use any comprehensive values to guide their children's lives. Michael Clayton, a Rawlsian political liberal, argues that parents may not legitimately "enroll" their children in the parents' comprehensive doctrines, which precludes even encouraging the child to accept their ethical or religious beliefs or participate in their practices.[99] He grounds this conclusion in an argument from Rawls's original position. A representative must design institutions to govern their life as a whole. They would not authorize parents to inculcate a comprehensive value system into a child, knowing that the child might later, as an adult, judge those values to be fundamentally mistaken. Even if they do not fully reject the parent's values and

96 406 U.S. 205 (1972).

97 SHULMAN, *supra* note 89, at 115–17.

98 Emily Stolzenberg, *Tribes, States, and Sovereigns' Interest in Children*, 102 N.C. L. REV. 1093 (2024).

99 MATTHEW CLAYTON, JUSTICE AND LEGITIMACY IN UPBRINGING ch. 3 (2006).

beliefs, they might still come to "resent the fact that [their] life will always have a particular history marked by [] interests and abilities [that] have been to some extent chosen by [their] parents."[100] Once we recognize that parenthood is a public office of coercive authority, parents should be subject to the liberal principle of legitimacy and the ideal of public reason. A parent may use comprehensive values only if instrumentally necessary to develop the child's capacities for a sense of justice and the good.

Clayton's theory comes close to the "caricature of ideal liberal parents . . . striving to avoid the creation of any particular personality in their children."[101] The problem, as a theoretical matter, begins because his notion of retrospective regret distorts reasoning from the original position. Behind the veil of ignorance, representatives must not know their own conception of the good, but they must know the psychological and social conditions for realizing the two moral capacities to develop and follow a conception of the good. Everyone's interests and abilities are shaped by their parents, peers, teachers, and culture in ways they do not choose. No one has a life free of "particular history." Our life influences increase the difficulty of revising our values, but without some such influences we would never become a person at all.[102] A child cannot develop moral agency by studying values at a safely detached distance, the way a professor studies Greek and Christian theories of virtue. A child develops the capacity to pursue a conception of the good only by pursuing a conception of the good under the guidance of parents, friends, and teachers. And these adults cannot guide the child's life only by public reasons. The child is unlikely to ever value athleticism or camaraderie if adults can encourage them to play sports only insofar as necessary to cultivate a sense of fair play. Moreover, as Bou-Habib and Olsaretti argue, parents dedicated to ignoring comprehensive values might undersupply intrinsically valuable childhood goods like play or prevent the child from developing intrinsically valuable nonpolitical character traits like humor.[103] A child needs their life to be guided by some adult's comprehensive values. This guidance will shape the child's interests and values, but that influence is not a regrettable side effect that a liberal society should seek to minimize. On the contrary, every child has a political right to comprehensive moral guidance.

Viewing their lives as a whole, representatives in the original position should recognize that, as children, they are entitled to a caregiver who will use comprehensive value judgments to provide them with a flourishing childhood and help develop their capacity to form their own conception of the good. A parent does not disrespect their child by encouraging them to participate in the parent's comprehensive

100 *Id.* at 99, 105.

101 Archard, *supra* note 16, at 77.

102 Robert Noggle, *A Chip off the Old Block: The Ethics of Shaping Children to Be Like Their Parents*, *in* Procreation, Parenthood, and Educational Rights 94 (Jaime Ahlberg & Michael Cholbi eds., 2017).

103 Paul Bou-Habib & Serena Olsaretti, *Autonomy and Children's Well-Being*, *in* The Nature of Children's Well-Being 25 (Alexander Bagattini & Colin Macleod eds., 2014).

traditions, whether grounded in religion, philosophy, or pop culture. The law must ensure that every child has an adequate parent who will guide the child's life by their conception of the good, yet always with a recognition that the child is their own person who eventually will come to make their own judgments.[104]

2 External Limits to Redress Parenthood's Distributional Effects on Children

The legal limits discussed so far – parental adequacy and state definition and protection of primary goods – reconcile the equality of individual children with the authority of their parents. The law must also reconcile equal citizenship with the systemic consequences of private parental authority. Even when a child has adequate parents, the child may still object if a parentage regime creates or perpetuates distributive injustice. The law regarding parents needs analogs for redistributive taxation and the ban on racial covenants (see I.B.3).

Parenthood has distributional effects. The assignment of parents can alter a child's lifetime well-being.[105] Inequalities in parental education, economic resources, social status, or parenting abilities can affect children's life prospects. The distribution of parents is as much a matter of luck as is the distribution of scarce talents with market value. Accordingly, the community does not treat its members as equals if the parentage lottery determines the child's share of the collective resources. The community must offset distributive inequalities created by parenthood. Current American law falls far short of any plausible liberal-egalitarian ideal. Redressing the parentage lottery requires, I would surmise, universal preschooling and public subsidies for caregivers along the lines suggested by advocates of the supportive state like Fineman or Eichner.[106]

In addition, parenthood can generate additional injustices through unjust legal rules or questionable conduct by social actors. Because parenthood is a role that carries social esteem, the law must ensure its parentage rules do not become a means to create and sustain social hierarchy. The United States long violated this principle by using marriage, legitimacy, and biological parentage to maintain racial apartheid. As recently as twenty years ago, same-sex couples in most states could not become joint parents – and the goal of many opponents of marriage equality was to withhold public validation from same-sex families. I argue in Chapter 6 that equality for

104 Reasonable disagreement will exist about the line between legitimate parental guidance and education for political autonomy, but that does not mean it is impossible for the community to draw reasonable lines. *Contra* SHULMAN, *supra* note 89, at 145–54.

105 CLAYTON, *supra* note 99, at 61; BRIGHOUSE & SWIFT, *supra* note 24, at 31.

106 EICHNER, *supra* note 17, at 61–69, 81–84. The collective duty to ensure each child receives adequate care is sufficient to justify public subsidies for caregivers. Subsidies might also be justified because perpetuating a community across generations is a public good in the economic sense of being nonexcludable and nonrivalrous, such that without subsidies we would have too little procreation and child-rearing. Serena Olsaretti, *Children as Public Goods?*, 41 PHIL. & PUB. AFF. 226 (2013).

lesbian and gay couples requires states to adopt parentage rules that empower intentional parents to establish parenthood before the birth of a child.

Other laws use parentage more subtly to reinforce inequalities around race, class, or disability. Although the US Constitution bans hereditary titles, many institutions maintain hereditary privileges that perpetuate racial and economic subordination, such as legacy admissions to elite universities.[107] Dorothy Roberts has argued that America's *laissez-faire* approach to assisted reproductive technology (ART) allows the fertility industry to profit by reinforcing essentialist notions of race and disability.[108] A liberal-egalitarian state should regulate sources of persistent inequality tied to its parenthood law. Like the ban on racial covenants that I discussed in I.B.3, such regulations are better seen not as public policy intrusions into the family but instead as emerging from the same commitment to equal respect for children that requires parenthood in the first place.

Even if regulations prevent blatant discrimination and distributive injustice, some parental choices that seem neutral or admirable still have distributional effects. A person's lifetime economic success often depends on traits or preferences developed under parental guidance, such as resilience or a love of science. Can a community committed to equal respect allow the parentage lottery to shape our lives in this manner? This question might be developed into a full-fledged objection from either the perspective of the child or the parent.

First, one might argue that it is *unfair to a child* if other kids' parents have greater parenting skills or inculcate traits more likely to facilitate success. It is tempting to say these inequalities are consistent with equal respect for the "disadvantaged" child only if this child received the best parent willing to take on the role.[109] In ethics, this is now known as the "best-available parent" principle. Anca Gheaus argues that any authority over another person must be founded on their consent or justified exclusively by their interests, which entails that children are entitled to the parent most likely to facilitate their interests.[110] Writing in children's law, James Dwyer argues that neglect law gives parents too much protection, often sacrificing the child's welfare to protect the parent's desire to raise them. Generalizing this objection, he argues that any time the state considers adult interests when designing rules for children, it treats children as mere means to serve adults' ends.[111] Consequently, Dwyer rejects any right to be a parent and is skeptical of reforms to neglect or foster law designed primarily to promote adult equality.[112] The mantra for this perspective is that children's law must focus exclusively on children's interests.

107 Michael J. Sandel, The Tyranny of Merit: What's Become of the Common Good? (2020).

108 *E.g.*, Dorothy E. Roberts, *Race, Gender, and Genetic Technologies: A New Reproductive Dystopia?*, 34 Signs 783, 789–96 (2009).

109 Peter Vallentyne, *Rights and Duties of Childbearing*, 11 Wm. & Mary Bill Rts. J. 991 (2002).

110 Gheaus, *supra* note 26, at 435, 444–45.

111 Dwyer, *supra* note 71, at 151.

112 *Id.* at 192–95; Dwyer, *supra* note 71 at 393.

This perspective rests on an inflated sense of children's entitlements. Although the law often wrongfully disregards children's interests, we should avoid swinging too far in the other direction. Children are *only* equal members of society. Like all citizens, children are entitled only to a fair share of primary goods over the course of their lives. A state cannot justly give children's interests lexical priority.[113] The state must consider adult interests even for laws that affect children's lives. For example, public schools had to consider teachers' welfare when deciding how to reopen during the COVID-19 pandemic. States must look for ways to prevent neglect without blaming indigent parents for their poverty in ways that sustain systemic racism. When designing the basic structure, a community must make trade-offs in ways that treat all citizens as equals.

Each child is entitled to a parent, but they are not entitled to an ideal parent or even the best available parent – notwithstanding the guilt cultivated by modern parenting culture. As with other primary goods, children are entitled to an adequate or good enough parent. A community treats its children with equal respect so long as it ensures parents provide sufficient care and guidance for the child to have a childhood with valuable experiences and develop into an adult who can flourish on their own terms.[114] Standards of "good enough" parenting must be fixed by collective judgments about children's distributive rights as part of a comprehensive scheme of justice that considers the interests of all citizens – including parents.

Law can even protect parental rights for reasons grounded in respect for adults, just as it can with other political offices (1.I.B.2). The law may respect an adult's project to raise their genetic child (2.II.A), a child they gestated (4.III.C), a child they helped create through ART (5.III.D), or a child for whom they have long served as a custodial caregiver (4.III.B). These are parental rights in the sense that these adults have a liberty to raise a child because it is necessary to respect the adults' familial projects. Nevertheless, the liberty right to raise a child does not treat the child as if

113 Gheaus argues parentage principles cannot consider adult interests because any authority relationship is justified only if the subordinate consents or the relationship serves their interests. Gheaus, *supra* note 26, at 435. By beginning her analysis with individual interests and interpersonal moral relationships, Gheaus slips too easily into a duty to maximize children's interests that paints as disrespectful trade-offs that are inevitable features of distributive justice. *See id.* at 446–49. The mistake becomes evident when Gheaus argues that denying a child the best parent so that an adequate parent can have the opportunity to raise a child is disrespectful in the same way that it is disrespectful to deprive a patient of the best surgeon so that an adequate surgeon can have the opportunity to practice medicine. I accept the situations are morally equivalent but regard the latter as an inevitable result of a just health care system with equal opportunity in employment.

114 Clayton rejects a similar argument for exclusively "child-centered" theories of parenthood. CLAYTON, *supra* note 99, at 54–66. Brighouse and Swift also conclude children have a right only to "good enough" parents, but the conclusion seems ad hoc given their interest-based theory of children's rights, according to which parents "have just those rights . . . that it is in their children's interests for them to have." BRIGHOUSE & SWIFT, *supra* note 24, at 94–95, 121. With this picture, it is difficult to avoid Gheaus's inference that a legal system violates children's rights if it allows a merely competent parent to raise a child when a better parent was available – or at least unless the parentage rules are designed on average to identify the best available parent.

they existed for the adult's benefit, insofar as the adult's liberty to parent is conditional on supplying the child's primary goods of adequate care and guidance.[115] The adult's claim is to fulfill the child's right to a parent.

The second distributive objection to parenthood starts instead *from the parent's moral duties*. Brighouse and Swift worry that parenting contributes to intergenerational inequality. Ordinary aspects of good parenting, like reading bedtime stories or sending a child to summer camp, confer comparative advantages on the children who receive them.[116] May a parent confer advantages on their child when they know it contributes to the persistence of inequality? Although Brighouse and Swift worry that parental partiality violates the parent's duty of justice, they ultimately conclude that parents must be allowed to benefit their children insofar as necessary to enable the child's goods crucial to human flourishing. Parents have a right to benefit their children in ways necessary to promote relational goods, such as reading bedtime stories, but no general permission to benefit their children in ways that might disrupt equality, such as by giving them bequests or sending them to expensive private schools.

I believe the parental partiality worry is overstated. A just state must allow all citizens to pursue their own ends. No citizen – adult or child – has a strict duty to sacrifice their well-being to facilitate distributive justice. Securing justice is the responsibility of the community as a collective. It does this by passing general laws that enable private and public rights. As individuals, we have an individual duty to help establish and maintain just institutions, but this duty must be imperfect for the same reasons as the personal duty of charity (1.I.B.1). If it were wrong to engage in any act that increased inequality, no one would have liberty to pursue their own ends. An adult does not violate their duty of justice by taking college classes, even if their new skills give them a competitive advantage. Similarly, a parent does not violate their duty of justice by sending their child to a private school, even if the child receives an educational advantage. On the contrary, parents *must* be partial. A parent's obligation is to adopt *the child's perspective* to judge how the child will flourish now and in the future. Partiality for one's child is no more problematic than partiality for one's own ends.

That does not mean parents may ignore reasons of justice when deciding how to raise their children – any more than each person can ignore reasons of justice in their own life. Parents must consider their child's imperfect duty of justice when deciding how to pursue the child's own ends. This is a difficult judgment to make, whether done for oneself or on behalf of one's child. Whatever one concludes as

115 Austin argues parents have a fundamental interest in making discretionary judgments about how to fulfill their duty to the child. Michael W. Austin, Conceptions of Parenthood: Ethics and The Family 74, 81–83 (2016). A parent's discretion enables them to make "a unique and personal contribution" by guiding how the child will "experience meaning and satisfaction in life, psychological well-being, and relational intimacy," which is in turn a source of meaning and satisfaction for the parent.

116 Brighouse & Swift, *supra* note 24, at 31–33, 127–30.

a personal matter, none of this means that the community cannot promote distributive justice by limiting private schools or parental bequests. These are classic problems of distributive justice, not questions about the private obligations of individual parents, and they pose no special challenge to the justice of the institution of parenthood.

3 Limits on Parental Duties

In addition to reconciling parenthood with equal respect for children, the community must ensure its regime of parenthood respects parents as well. Parenthood substantially limits a parent's liberty. The threat to adult liberty is apparent if we imagine a state assigning parenthood arbitrarily. Imagine that someone found a baby in a basket washed up on shore, and the community decides that this bystander alone must bear the cost of raising the child. This community uses the bystander to meet its collective duty to the child. Men who contest child support by arguing their sperm was stolen allege a similar unfairness. Equal respect for adults requires a fair basis for assigning parenthood.

The difficulty is not limited to involuntary parenthood. Parental duties themselves can become troubling, even when the adult expressly chooses to be a parent. Parents incur a duty to reorient their lives to serve their children's ends, and such an open-ended duty threatens the parents' equal liberty. Their liberty is now subject to the vagaries of the child's future development and choices. Suppose a teenager crashes their car, resulting in a severe disability. Does the adult's initial choice to become a parent really justify the added burdens created by a state that fails to provide adequate medical and disability support? Furthermore, adults cannot choose the content of their parental duties. The community fixes parental duties to ensure children will become equals within institutions chosen by the community. As mentioned above, parental duties have expanded considerably in the last hundred years.

If the community defines parental duties and imposes them on parents, how can parenthood be reconciled with the status *of the adult* as an equal member of society? The next four chapters will identify principles for acquiring parenthood that help reconcile parental duties with parents' equal status. For example, Chapter 2 argues that imposing parental duties solely based on genetic ties violates equal respect; however, Chapter 3 concludes that the state may impose some financial support obligations on anyone whose voluntary conduct caused a child to exist.

Just parentage principles are necessary but insufficient to reconcile parenthood with parental equality. This section concludes this chapter by identifying ways that the law structures parenthood itself to reduce the tension between parental duties and parental equality.

Children are entitled to parents who act on their behalf, making practical judgments about what will be a valuable life for them. While parental duties involve burdensome self-sacrifice, we should not overstate parents' fiduciary duties. In particular, we should be wary of the analogy to other legal fiduciary duties. Law often states the fiduciary duty of loyalty in categorical terms. A trust fiduciary, for example, has an "absolute" duty of loyalty to make decisions considering only the beneficiary's interests.[117] Applying such doctrines directly to parents would be a mistake.

Parents cannot, and must not, make decisions with a monomaniacal focus on a child's interests. No child is entitled to that level of care. As a matter of justice, each person's rights must be consistent with equal rights for others. No child has a right to demand that a parent focus *entirely* on the child's ends, irrespective of the parent's ends. Such a parental duty would subordinate the parent to the child. Children have no more right to claim the lives of adults than vice versa. Children have a right to have someone to guide their lives, not a right to a servant. Similarly, the state cannot demand that parents accept self-sacrifice as a condition for raising a child. Parents may consider their own well-being when making decisions that affect their family.

A nuanced description of parental obligations will limit the conflicts between the interests of a parent and their child. The parental function is to make value judgments on the child's behalf, and every reasonable conception of the good includes other-regarding values. A parent should not adopt an unreasonably egoistic theory of value when acting on their child's behalf. They must consider how promoting their child's ends will affect them, siblings, friends, neighbors, and communities.[118] They must forgo pursuing their child's ends to respect others' rights. They may forgo a measure of welfare for their child to advance the welfare of others or society. Such decisions do not treat the child as a mere means to serve others if they reflect a reasonable judgment about the good from the child's perspective.

Internal limits on parental duties can reduce but not eliminate conflicts between parenthood and equal liberty. Parental responsibilities remain a substantive burden. As Alstott argues, society demands adults enter a long-term commitment to give priority to their child's interests.[119] The financial and opportunity costs may relegate parents to a subordinate role in society. Against our background of gender injustice in the workplace and in caregiving norms, this subordination falls mostly on women. A liberal-egalitarian state must offer families public support to protect parents' equal status and take active steps to encourage gender equality in parenting, including revised workplace policies and legal support for coparenting.[120]

[117] Restatement (Third) of Trusts § 78 cmt. b (2007).

[118] The congruence argument (a child flourishes whenever their parents, siblings, neighbors, or community flourish) is generally implausible and capable of being assessed only within a full theory of the good life for children, families, and communities.

[119] Anne Alstott, No Exit: What Parents Owe Their Children and What Society Owes Parents 50 (2004); Clayton, *supra* note 99, at 61.

[120] Dowd, *supra* note 46, at 220–27. However, I believe Dowd's insistence on gender-specific interventions will reinforce, rather than combat, those norms. *Id.* at 229–31.

CONCLUSION

Parental responsibilities arise from demands of justice. A community treats its members as equals only if it ensures that each child has a caregiver with the authority to judge how the child should use primary goods to flourish as a child and become a thriving adult. The child's right to a parent is not contingent on what some adults did to create the child or to prepare to raise them. It rests on the child's status as an equal community member, and the public holds the correlative duty to ensure that all children have parents. A legitimate public authority must also define and constrain parental rights and duties in order to ensure these relations remain consistent with equal respect for the child and the adult. In other words, parenthood is a political office.[121]

What distinguishes parenthood from Madeline Smith's relationship with Eric and Danielle Grady is not that this foster family originated in state power. All parental rights and duties are inescapably entwined with political authority. The question, then, is how the parental office is acquired for a specific child. Smith alleged that she acquired parental rights by caring for Eric and Danielle and forming emotional bonds. If caregiving is sufficient, many stepparents and relative caregivers also acquire parental rights. Other citizens may insist that parenthood arises instead from genetics, causation, or intentions. The next four chapters demonstrate that no existing moral theories justify inferring parental rights and duties directly from any of these grounds.

Nevertheless, this failure should not cast doubt on the legitimacy of parental authority. Once we recognize parenthood as a political office, we can abandon the quest to find some natural or social relation between a child and an adult that justifies parental rights and duties. The rights and duties of parents are determined by the child's needs as an equal citizen. The law simply needs principles for acquiring this parental office that ensure equal respect for the child, the parent, and other adults. As I also show in the next four chapters, each of the four classic grounds can still play a specific role in this liberal parentage regime.

[121] Because any liberal-egalitarian political community must identify which family forms are capable of fulfilling the functions necessary to ensure justice for children, I believe Ristroph and Murray are mistaken to adopt a presumption in favor of "disestablishing the family," but I agree with their conclusions that the Supreme Court has allowed states to misuse this authority to squelch reasonable disagreement about family life based on nonpublic, ideological values. Alice Ristroph & Melissa Murray, *Disestablishing the Family*, 119 YALE L.J. 1236, 1260–63, 1267–71 (2009).

2

Parentage by Genetics

When A.P. and her husband Y.Z. had difficulty conceiving a child, they hired a fertility clinic to create embryos from her eggs and Y.Z.'s sperm and to implant them in A.P.[1] The in vitro fertilization worked. A.P. learned she was pregnant with twins. The birth brought an unwelcome shock. The twins were not their genetic children. A.P. and Y.Z. were of Asian descent; the infants were not.[2] The fertility clinic inadvertently implanted embryos created from two other clients, the Manukyans and another anonymous couple. In the ensuing custody dispute, the family court concluded that the genetic parent's claims trumped A.P.'s claim as the twin's gestational mother and Y.Z.'s claim as their intended father.[3]

Fertility mix-up cases are rare. When they do happen, genetic parents typically win,[4] even though genetic theories of parenthood find little sympathy among academics. Chapters 4 and 5 turn to the more favored gestational and intentional theories, but first we must consider whether and why the Manukyan's genetic ties might give them a claim to parenthood. We must be careful to avoid the naturalistic fallacy in this context.[5] An inescapable gap separates the empirical fact of genetic parentage from the normative rights and duties of parenthood.[6] Yet, we would also be remiss to ignore the widespread intuition – shared by parentage law – that genetic parents should have special rights and duties concerning their progeny. Since the

1 Complaint, A.P. v. CHA Health Systems, Inc., Case No. 1:2019cv03826 (E.D.N.Y. July 1, 2019).

2 Raizel Liebler, *Are You My Parent? Are You My Child? The Role of Genetics and Race in Defining Relationships after Reproductive Technological Mistakes*, 5 DePaul J. Health Care L. 15 (2002); Cynthia R. Mabry, *Who Is My Real Father? The Delicate Task of Identifying a Father and Parenting Children Created from an In Vitro Mix-Up*, 18 Nat'l Black L.J. 1 (2004).

3 Sarah Zhang, *IVF Mix-Ups Have Broken the Definition of Parenthood*, The Atlantic (Jul. 11, 2019), www.theatlantic.com/science/archive/2019/07/ivf-embryo-mix-up-parenthood/593725/ (last visited Mar. 8, 2024).

4 Leslie Bender, *To Err Is Human – ART Mix-Ups: A Labor-Based, Relational Proposal*, 9 J. Gender Race & Just. 443 (2005).

5 Daniel Callahan, *Bioethics and Fatherhood*, 1992 Utah L. Rev. 735, 738–39. J. David Velleman, *Family History*, 34 Phil. Papers 357, 370–71 (2005).

6 Courts sometimes fall into this trap, simply asserting that "the parent–child relationship finds its source not in a legislative act, but in the facts of life itself" that "arise[] from the conception and birth of children." J.R. v. Utah, 261 F. Supp. 2d 1268, 1286 (D. Utah 2002).

advent of DNA testing, genetic conceptions of paternity have become so pervasive that it is difficult to articulate the normative premises justifying the inference that genetic ties might ground parenthood.

That is the task set for this chapter. Part I explains the myriad ways in which genetic ties remain central to parentage law. Genetic parents have constitutional parental rights so long as they commit to parenthood. Genetic ties are often treated as sufficient for child support duties for a nonmarital birth parent, yet the birth parents may decide together to place the child for adoption, and sperm or egg donors may waive their rights and avoid duties entirely. Part II argues that no principles of personal morality can justify treating genetic ties as necessary or sufficient for parental duties or rights. Nevertheless, Part III argues that the political conception of parentage should recognize a derived liberty right for genetic parents to pursue legal parenthood, conditioned on timely commitment and supported by redistributive policies to support families.

I GENETICS IN PARENTAGE LAW

Genetic parentage remains central to US state and federal parentage law, both statutory and constitutional. This part explores the legal significance of genetic parentage and the justifications that the law proffers for its centrality.

A *The History of Genetics in American Law*

Given the salience of genetics in contemporary culture, it can be difficult to appreciate that the law disfavored mere biological parents for most of our history. "Blood ties" have long been central to Western understandings of kinship, but biological parentage was rarely sufficient for legal rights or duties. Under the common law in England and early America, a child born to unmarried parents had no legal parents.[7] Unmarried biological parents had no legal rights and few duties. Custody of an "illegitimate child" fell to the birth mother. However, if she was poor and in need of public support, state officials might place the young child with another family instead. These unmarried mothers had no right to sue the father for financial support.[8] Nonsupport was a criminal offense, but it could be prosecuted only by public officials as a way to reimburse almshouses[9] and punish extramarital

7 Leslie Joan Harris, *The Basis for Legal Parentage and the Clash Between Custody and Child Support*, 42 IND. L. REV.611, 615 (2009).

8 Neville Brown, *Family Maintenance and Its Enforcement in the United States*, 13 INT'L L. & COMP. L. Q. 139, 165–66 (1964); Harris, *supra* note 7, at 617.

9 Brown, *supra* note 8, at 165–66; Elizabeth D. Katz, *Criminal Law in a Civil Guise: The Evolution of Family Courts and Support Laws*, 86 U. CHI. L. REV. 1241, 1256–57 (2019) (describing transition from poor law that focused on reimbursement of almshouses to revised poor law that gave mothers a right to support).

sex.[10] Interestingly, the support duty was not limited to parents. The local poor relief agency could also sue any close relatives, from grandparents to siblings.[11]

Although insufficient for parenthood, blood ties did determine a child's status as a free or enslaved person. As Dorothy Roberts has shown, white Americans sustained the racial caste system with an "invented hereditary trait of race" that made selective use of biology.[12] Children inherited their enslaved status from their birth mothers. An enslaved mother could have no parental rights, because her child was regarded as the property of her enslaver. To justify intergenerational enslavement, whites invented strategic myths about physical and intellectual differences tied to heritable races, but the heritability fictions needed to be selective because the child of an enslaved mother could have half, three-quarters, or more European ancestry. The myth became that a "Black parent automatically passed down a whole set of inferior traits," which meant that "the meaning of the genetic tie in American law and culture was infused with the paramount objective of keeping the white bloodline free from Black contamination."[13] Similar anxieties about racial purity underwrote selectively enforced laws against interracial fornication and marriage. These laws primarily targeted white women, who might confer free status on "mulatto" children who could challenge the dichotomous racial hierarchy.[14] Similar statutes persisted through Jim Crow. The law's construction of racialized families continues to affect norms of family identification.[15]

In the late nineteenth and early twentieth centuries, many states reformed nonsupport laws to allow custodial mothers to sue fathers for child support.[16] Although genetic fathers were now civilly liable for nonsupport, few states treated nonmarital fathers as equal parents. The sexual revolution of the 1960s brought some legal changes, but it was the Supreme Court that lit the match on a family law revolution in the 1970s. In a series of "illegitimacy cases," the Court forced states to treat children born to married and unmarried parents the same in nearly all respects, including inheritance, wrongful death damages, and child support.[17] A parallel line

10 Katharine K. Baker, *The DNA Default and Its Discontents: Establishing Modern Parenthood*, 96 B. U. L. Rev. 2037, 2045 (2016). Courts officially replaced the punishment rationale with the rationale that causal parents have a duty to support their children. McLain v. Meadows, 44 Cal. App. 402, 403 (1919).

11 Brown, *supra* note 8, at 168.

12 Dorothy E. Roberts, *The Genetic Tie*, 62 U. Chi. L. Rev. 209, 229 (1995) (citing Neil Gotanda, *A Critique of "Our Constitution is Color-Blind,"* 44 Stan. L. Rev. 1, 32 [1991]).

13 *Id.* at 230.

14 A. Leon Higginbotham Jr. & Barbara K. Kopytoff, *Racial Purity and Interracial Sex in the Law of Colonial and Antebellum Virginia*, 77 Geo. L.J. 1967, 1997 (1988).

15 Angela Onwuachi-Willig, According to Our Hearts: *Rhinelander v. Rhinelander* and the Law of the Multiracial Family 179–84 (2013).

16 Brown, *supra* note 8, at 167.

17 Levy v. Louisiana, 391 U.S. 68 (1968); Weber v. Aetna Casualty & Surety Co., 406 U.S. 164 (1972); Gomez v. Perez, 409 U.S. 535 (1973).

of "unmarried father" cases (discussed at length below) established federal constitutional rights for genetic fathers.[18]

Federal welfare reform in the late 1980s and early 1990s further entrenched genetic notions of paternity.[19] Congress created a system of interstate welfare enforcement to help states recoup welfare payments. To participate in the system, states must give birth parents a form to establish paternity in the hospital and admit genetic evidence in paternity actions.[20] Increased access to fertility treatments and genetic ancestry tests have also helped cement genetic ideas of parentage in the public consciousness.[21] Sections B and C review the law that emerged from this family law revolution, beginning with the duties of genetic parents.

B *Legal Duties of Genetic Parents*

In a paternity suit related to child support, genetic evidence is often dispositive. If unmarried individuals conceive the child through sexual intercourse, genetic paternity is typically the only relevant issue (unless the child also has a competing marital father). A suit for child support may be brought at any time during the child's minority.[22] If a presumed marital father seeks to avoid parental duties for an infant, disproving his genetic paternity is sufficient. Sometimes that is enough even for older children.[23]

Nevertheless, many exceptions demonstrate that genetic parentage is not sufficient for legal parental duties. A genetic parent owes no child support if a court terminates their parental rights in preparation for adoption. A genetic parent has no duties if a marital or residential parent remains a presumed parent or becomes an adjudicated parent. Last, a genetic parent has no duties if they donate sperm or eggs at a clinic and, sometimes, if they donate sperm for private artificial insemination. Gamete donation must be nonsexual, however. If a male and female conceive

18 Joanna L. Grossman, *Legitimacy, Parentage, and the Plight of Unmarried Mothers*, 74 SMU L. Rev. 277, 288 (2021); David D. Meyer, *Family Ties: Solving the Constitutional Dilemma of the Faultless Father*, 41 Ariz. L. Rev. 753, 758 (1999).

19 Jana Singer, *Marriage, Biology, and Paternity: The Case for Revitalizing the Marital Presumption*, 65 Md. L. Rev. 246, 253 (2006). *See generally* Jane C. Murphy, *Legal Images of Fatherhood: Welfare Reform, Child Support Enforcement, and Fatherless Children*, 81 Notre Dame L. Rev. 325 (2005).

20 42 U.S.C. § 666(C)(1). *See* Leslie Joan Harris, *The New Illegitimacy: Revisiting Why Parentage Should Not Depend on Marriage*, 20 Am. U. J. Gender Soc. Pol'y & L. 467, 475–76 (2011); Baker, *supra* note 10, at 2048–49.

21 Harris, *supra* note 7, at 619–21 (describing the social and ideological forces).

22 Clark v. Jeter, 486 U.S. 456, 464 (1988).

23 Ashburn v. Rogers, 803 S.E.2d 469, 473 (S.C. Ct. App. 2017) (adjudicated father disestablished paternity after sixteen years, arguing it would not affect child's interests as they had no relationship); Alisha C. v. Jeremy C., 808 N.W.2d 875, 885 (Neb. 2012) (statute empowers putative father with genetic proof to disestablish paternity at any time, even after adjudication of parentage); Taylor v. Taylor, Nos. CH03-926, 2004 WL 1462261 (Va. Cir. June 3, 2004) (adjudicated marital father disestablished paternity of twelve-year-old).

a child through intercourse, and only one of them wants to raise the child, the other still has parental duties regardless of the adults' preconception plan.[24]

What reasons do courts offer to support this regime of genetic child support? Sadly, very few. Most courts assert dogmatically that genetic parents have a social and moral duty to the child and the state.[25] They can often cite a long string of old precedents, but the line typically peters out in unadorned assertions of "natural right and justice."[26] Some courts falsely ascribe their position to the common law.[27]

When courts do offer a normative justification, they stick to three arguments. First, through the 1960s, many state courts justified paternity actions as punishment for nonmarital sex.[28] For reasons of constitutional law and political morality, this argument no longer merits consideration.[29]

The most common argument is that biological parents, not taxpayers, should bear the cost of raising children.[30] This privatization rationale was the driving force when Congress ramped up child welfare enforcement.[31] This congressional push involved overt racial, gender, and marital discrimination. Even as they sought to valorize white stay-at-home moms, welfare reformers demonized African American mothers as "welfare queens" exploiting the public to finance their choice to have children they could not support because they lacked husbands. They also directed their ire at "deadbeat dads" portrayed as abandoning their children to live a lazy, carefree life.

24 Baker, *supra* note 10, at 2050–56; *see also* Mary Patricia Byrn & Lisa Giddings, *An Empirical Analysis of the Use of the Intent Test to Determine Parentage in Assisted Reproductive Technology Cases*, 50 Hous. L. Rev. 1295 (2012). Baker argues that differential treatment of sexual and nonsexual reproduction demonstrates that child support remains a penalty for sex, but I think it reflects exaggerated concern about the evidentiary difficulties of proving (or disproving) agreements when adults conceive a child through sexual intercourse or a genetic father donates sperm to a friend for private insemination. Bruce v. Boardwine, 770 S.E.2d 774, 778 (Va. App. 2015); E.E. v. O.M.G.R., 420 N.J. Super. 283, 285 (N.J. Super. Ch. Div. 2011).

25 *In re* Marriage of Hopper, 991 P.2d 960, 969 (Mont. 1999); *ex parte* Univ. of S. Alabama, 541 So. 2d 535, 537 (Ala. 1989).

26 Foster v. Foster, 655 S.E.2d 172, 178 (W. Va. 2007); State v. Deaton, 93 Tex. 243, 247 (1900) ("Parents cannot devest themselves of the obligation imposed upon them by their Creator"). The citations in *Foster* trace to Buchanan v. Buchanan, 170 Va. 458, 471 (1938), which rests only on a quote from Minor's *Institutes*, vol. I, that recites the conclusions of Pufendorf and Montesquieu without their reasoning. Pufendorf argued children belong to mothers in the state of nature but fathers obtain authority by virtue of the marital pact giving them authority over mothers – hardly a sound basis for modern paternity. Simone Zurbuchen, *Family and Marriage*, *in* The Cambridge Companion to Pufendorf 164 (Ian Hunter & Knud Haakonssen eds., 2022). On a more egalitarian note, Pufendorf also denied that procreation creates authority, which must rest instead on presumed consent. *See* Katharine T. Bartlett, *Rethinking Parenthood as an Exclusive Status: The Need for Legal Alternatives When the Premise of the Nuclear Family Has Failed*, 70 Va. L. Rev. 879, 887–90 (1984) (collecting natural law references in genetic paternity cases).

27 Kansas v. Bohrer, 189 P.3d 1157, 1163 (Kan. 2008) ("[p]arents have a common-law duty to support their minor children, regardless of any statute imposing such an obligation").

28 Baker, *supra* note 10, at 2045.

29 Lawrence v. Texas, 539 U.S. 558 (2003).

30 State v. Wood, 569 P.2d 1148, 1150 (Wash. 1977); *In re* Adoption of Marlene, 822 N.E.2d 714, 719 (Mass. 2005); L.W.K. v. E.R.C., 735 N.E.2d 359, 365 (Mass. 2000).

31 Harris, *supra* note 7.

The last argument that courts make for imposing duties on genetic parents appeals to causation rather than genetics. They cite Blackstone's argument that a parent must not allow their child to "perish," because their act brought the child into the world.[32] Genetic parentage is evidence of causal parentage, and sophisticated courts make this connection.[33] Chapter 3 explores this causal justification for parental duties in depth. This chapter focuses on genetic ties per se.

C *Legal Rights of Genetic Parents*

Most genetic parents who want parental rights can now obtain them. They are not automatically legal parents but can establish parentage by a petition or acknowledgment, although these paths may be limited if the child has a competing presumed parent.

1 Genetic Fathers with No Competing Marital Parent

The Supreme Court has protected constitutional parental rights since the 1920s, but the early cases accepted state law definitions of who counted as a parent.[34] To challenge state laws that excluded nonmarital fathers, the Court had to articulate an independent constitutional test for parentage. What emerged was the biology-plus-relationship test for constitutional paternity. This doctrine consists of three rules that set two clear endpoints but leave several vague boundaries.[35] State statutory and common law further refine these vague thresholds.

A CONDITIONAL CONSTITUTIONAL RIGHTS OF GENETIC FATHERS. The Court's first nonmarital father case, *Stanley v. Illinois*, established that genetic fathers with a "developed parent–child relationship" have a liberty interest in their children's care, custody, and control.[36] Stanley lived with his children and their mother for eighteen years. When the mother died, Illinois removed the children without a hearing because state law presumed unmarried fathers were unfit. The Court held that Illinois violated due process by removing Stanley's children without even giving him a hearing to challenge the conclusion that he was an unfit parent.[37]

32 1 William Blackstone, Commentaries *435. *See, e.g.*, State of Kansas/Iowa ex rel. Sec'y of Soc. & Rehab. Servs. v. Bohrer, 286 Kan. 898, 906 (2008); Bornemann v. Bornemann, 175 Md. App. 716, 727 (2007).

33 Cty. of Los Angeles v. Christopher W., 41 Cal. App. 5th 827, 835 (2019).

34 Pierce v. Society of Sisters, 268 U.S. 510, 534–35 (1925); Meyer v. Nebraska, 262 U.S. 390, 399 (1923); Prince v. Massachusetts., 321 U.S. 158, 166 (1944). Anthony Miller, *The Case for the Genetic Parent: Stanley, Quilloin, Caban, Lehr, and Michael H. Revisited*, 53 Loy. L. Rev. 395, 396 (2007) (noting that the Court allowed an aunt with custody to raise the child's claim in Meyer).

35 Meyer, *supra* note 18, at 762–63.

36 Stanley v. Illinois, 405 U.S. 645, 652 (1972).

37 *Id.* at 657.

In *Quilloin v. Walcott*, the Court ruled that if a genetic father fails to fulfill substantial responsibilities promptly, his interest in parenting receives no procedural or substantive protection.[38] *Quilloin* had visited his eleven-year-old son "on many occasions" but never lived with the child, sought physical or legal custody, or provided regular financial support.[39] The Court held that Georgia could terminate *Quilloin*'s rights and allow a stepparent adoption without any steps to notify *Quilloin* and based only on a judge's conclusion that the adoption served the child's best interests.

Together, these two cases establish that genetic parents have *conditional* parental rights. A genetic father has full constitutional parental rights if and only if he "demonstrates a full commitment to the responsibilities of parenthood by coming forward to participate in the rearing of his child."[40] The hard cases created by this rule are easy to imagine. First, what extent of child-rearing shows full commitment and how quickly must the genetic father perform it?[41] Second, what happens if the genetic parent has had no adequate opportunity to fulfill these child-rearing functions?

Lehr v. Robertson raised both issues. Lehr visited his genetic child after the birth, but the mother and her boyfriend (later husband) refused his help and secretly moved to another county. Lehr hired an investigator to find them. When he did find them, they threatened to sue Lehr for harassment. They also filed a petition for stepparent adoption in their county without notifying Lehr. In the meantime, Lehr filed a paternity action in his county, where the child had been born. At this point, the child was two. The judge in the adoption case knew about Lehr's paternity petition but finalized the adoption before Lehr had time to appear.

The Supreme Court reasoned that a genetic father like Lehr has a liberty interest in his "potential" or "inchoate" relationship with the child.[42] His genetic connection gives him an "opportunity that no other male possesses to develop a relationship."[43] If he "grasps that opportunity and accepts some measure of responsibility for the child's future," then he becomes a full constitutional parent. The state has a limited duty to protect this "opportunity" with minimal procedural safeguards. The state must at least offer some way for genetic fathers to ensure they will receive notice of any hearing that would terminate their parental rights.[44] New York satisfied due

38 Quilloin v. Walcott, 434 U.S. 246 (1978). Emily Buss, *"Parental" Rights*, 88 VA. L. REV. 635, 658–60 (2002).

39 *Quilloin*, 434 U.S. at 255.

40 Lehr v. Robertson, 463 U.S. 248, 260 (1983) (internal quotes omitted). This principle assumes there are no competing presumed parents. *See* I.C.3.

41 Meyer, *supra* note 18, at 763.

42 *Lehr*, 463 U.S. at 261 and n.17.

43 *Id.* at 262 (1983). Caban v. Mohammed, 441 U.S. 380, 393 (1979). Michael H. v. Gerald D., 491 U.S. 110, 128–29 (1989).

44 Mark Strasser, *The Often Illusory Protections of Biology Plus: On the Supreme Court's Parental Rights Jurisprudence*, 13 TEX. J. ON C.L. & C.R. 31, 67–78 (2007) (surveying meager state court protections for this opportunity).

process by offering a putative father registry. Had Lehr filed with the registry, the state would have automatically notified him of any adoption petitions. Because he waited over two years to file with the registry, the Court held that Lehr waived his constitutional right to notice.

What exactly is an opportunity right? Some courts describe genetic fathers' rights as "merely inchoate."[45] Others divide adoption challenges into two parts. Whether the genetic parent "has assumed his or her parental duties" is a "threshold determination as to whether the Constitution is substantively involved at all."[46] Both formulations suggest incorrectly that genetic parents have no constitutional rights until they fulfill parental roles, which is contrary to *Lehr*. Our analysis needs to be more accurate.

Genetic parents have a liberty to perform the caregiving tasks that satisfy the condition on their parental rights. *Lehr* established that this liberty receives weak *procedural* due process protections. It must also receive some *substantive* protection, although the scope of these substantive protections is not well established. The Supreme Court denied several certiorari petitions that would have raised precisely this issue.[47] Nevertheless, *Lehr* presupposes that states cannot give birth mothers the legal power to decide whether genetic fathers may become legal parents. It would be almost pointless to insist that states create a way for genetic fathers to ensure they receive notice of the adoption, if the birth father who manages to appear in court can only watch helplessly as the mother consents to adoption.[48]

For similar reasons, states must create some procedure for genetic fathers to establish parentage unilaterally. If genetic fathers could become legal parents only by a voluntary acknowledgment of paternity (VAP) or the marital presumption, their

45 Adoption of Michael H., 898 P.2d 891, 896 (Cal. 1995); Thurnwald v. A.E., 163 P.3d 623 (Utah 2007).

46 *In re* Adoption of G.L.V., 190 P.3d 245, 264 (Kan. 2008).

47 Serena Mayeri, *Foundling Fathers: (Non-)Marriage and Parental Rights in the Age of Equality*, 125 YALE L.J. 2292, 2354–63 (2015).

48 I say "almost" because one can coherently maintain that genetic parents have (1) parental rights conditioned on caregiving, (2) a privilege to perform caregiving, and (3) no claim to perform caregiving. This bundle of rights is isomorphic with property acquisition by capture. As Jennifer Hendricks explained in conversation, due process requires a hearing only to determine if the genetic father acquired rights by caregiving, so the hearing can be conclusory in any infant case. *See* Meyer, *supra* note 18 (Court did not settle father's substantive rights). However, *Lehr* assumes the genetic father's privilege to perform caregiving receives minimal substantive protections against interference by the gestational parent, a conclusion accepted by at least five justices in *Michael H.* and many state court decisions applying federal law. Meyer, *supra* note 18, at 766–69. I am skeptical of claims that the nonmarital father cases reflect ideological commitments to the "mother as primary parent" or to marital supremacy. Dolgin is correct that nonmarital fathers won only when they had fulfilled a role that the justices could see as equivalent to that of a husband in a nuclear family. Janet Dolgin, *Just a Gene: Judicial Assumptions about Parenthood*, 40 UCLA L. REV. 637, 649 (1992); *See also* Alice Ristroph & Melissa Murray, *Disestablishing the Family*, 119 YALE L.J. 1236, 1252–55 (2009); Douglas NeJaime, *The Constitution of Parenthood*, 72 STAN. L. REV. 261, 293–96 (2020). However, the fact central to that analogy is the parental care and guidance, not the relationship with the mother or the marital norms.

liberty to raise a child would be subject to the birth mother's consent.[49] Furthermore, genetic parents must have a claim to parenting time with newborns. Every child will be in the legal custody of some caregiver who has default authority to decide who else may spend time with the child. Without a claim to visitation, genetic fathers would be – like any other adult – under a duty *not* to pursue a parental role. States cannot give birth mothers de jure or de facto authority to prevent a genetic parent from establishing the relationship that will ground their parental rights.[50]

B STATE SPECIFICATIONS OF GENETIC FATHERS' RIGHTS. The above discussion exhausts the established content of the constitutional right, but it leaves many unanswered questions. Many of these gaps are filled in by state law that specifies genetic parents' right to perform caregiving and become parents.

Genetic parents are not automatically legal parents, but all states empower alleged genetic fathers to file a petition to establish paternity. In a timely petition, genetic evidence will be sufficient to establish paternity for purposes of child support and parental rights, unless the child has a competing parent or the genetic parent was a gamete donor.[51] If the birth parents are on good terms, they can instead sign a VAP at the hospital. After sixty days, the signed VAP receives the same preclusive effect as a judicial order of parentage.[52]

Once genetic parents establish legal parentage, they have a right to visitation, sometimes called "parenting time." They can seek legal custody (decisional authority) and physical custody (residential time), but if the parties cannot agree, a court will determine what custody arrangement serves the child's interests. Mere genetic fathers typically do not receive substantial rights unless they make a substantial effort to develop a relationship and provide financial support. Despite scholarly advocacy to increase involvement by nonmarital fathers, most unmarried genetic fathers still have secondary parental roles.[53] On the other hand, even if a genetic parent fails to exercise visitation or pay child support, courts will not terminate their rights unless someone else wants to adopt the child. Courts presume children benefit from having two parents, even if one is derelict.[54]

To prevent adoption, the genetic parent must act quickly to satisfy the condition on their parental rights. The demands and timing vary depending on the legal

49 Several state supreme courts have invalidated statutes that allowed an unmarried father to veto adoption only if he had shared a residence with the child. Adoption of Kelsey S., 1 Cal. 4th 816, 847 (1992); Raquel Marie X., 559 N.E.2d at 426. *See* Meyer, *supra* note 18, at 788.

50 Meyer, *supra* note 18, at 769 (describing consensus that "thwarted" genetic father has constitutional rights but also expanded notions of abandonment and waiver that courts use to narrow the threat to adoption by a late-acting father).

51 Some states also maintain a quick process for a putative father to acknowledge paternity in court. Int. of Armani S., 188 N.E.3d 327, 338 (IL App. (1st) 2020).

52 *See* 42 U.S.C. § 666(a)(5)(D)(ii).

53 Baker, *supra* note 10, at 2069–81.

54 Ayelet Blecher-Prigat, *Conceiving Parents*, 41 HARV. WOMEN'S L.J. 119, 163–64 (2018).

context.[55] Genetic parents can veto a *second-parent adoption* only if their conduct demonstrates a substantial and consistent commitment to parental responsibilities. They must support the pregnant mother, seek legal paternity, fulfill visitation, and pay child support. Courts are more demanding when the birth mother wants to place the child for adoption. A genetic parent can veto adoption only by accepting full custody. To facilitate infant adoption, many courts have developed aggressive theories of "prenatal abandonment," concluding that genetic fathers have "abandoned" their children by not expressing their unambiguous commitment to parenthood before birth, sometimes soon after conception.[56]

Courts offer clear reasons for demanding prompt action and unambiguous commitment: the pregnant parent can postpone her decision only for so long. They must decide whether to seek an abortion, arrange an adoption, or prepare to keep the child.[57] The physical reality of pregnancy lends an urgency to the gestational parent's decision that a mere genetic parent may not feel. Concern for child welfare also supports the early and conclusive resolution of infant adoptions. Genetic parents who knowingly fail to assert their rights should not be allowed to disrupt bonds that they allow to form between the child and adoptive or functional parents. Courts apply similar arguments even if the fathers did not know about the child, believing these fathers simply did not care enough to learn about the pregnancy.[58] Courts are more lenient toward absent genetic parents in other situations. When an older child's custodial parent dies, courts often favor genetic parents over stepparents or relatives, even when the genetic parent previously exhibited little concern for the child.

C UNCERTAIN JUSTIFICATION FOR GENETIC RIGHTS. What justifies the conditional rights of genetic parents, whether as a matter of constitutional or state law? Although the Supreme Court declared the Constitution protects the "private interest ... of [a] man in the children he has sired and raised," the justices never explained why genetic ties generate familial interests.[59] The Court's description of parental rights as the "counterpart" of parental responsibilities does indicate, at least, that the justices did not understand it as a simple egoistic interest in the psychological benefit of having a genetic family.[60] Lower courts offer no more assistance.

55 Laura Oren, *Unmarried Fathers and Adoption: Perfecting or Abandoning and Opportunity Interest*, 36 CAP. U. L. REV. 253, 267 (2007).

56 Mary M. Beck, *Prenatal Abandonment: Horton Hatches the Egg in the Supreme Court and Thirty-Four States*, 24 MICH. J. GENDER & L. 53 (2017). *See, e.g.*, Adoptive Couple v. Baby Girl, 570 U.S. 637 (2013) (Native American genetic father was not a legal father under Indian Child Welfare Act because he sent ambiguous texts to his pregnant girlfriend suggesting he did not want to raise a child unless she married him).

57 Lehr v. Robertson, 463 U.S. 248, 263–64 and n.20. *See also In re* Baby Girl T., 298 P.3d 1251, 1258 (Utah 2012); *In re* Adoption of A.A.T., 287 Kan. 590, 609–12 (2008).

58 Beck, *supra* note 56.

59 *See* Miller, *supra* note 34.

60 *Lehr*, 463 U.S. at 257.

Despite hundreds of opinions interpreting the unmarried father cases, I have found none that describe the interest of the genetic parent in any detail. Most assert bluntly that genetic fathers have a natural right to raise their children, regardless of whether the judge believes the child will have a better life with adoptive parents.[61]

Often, the courts switch perspectives to explain the value of genetic parenthood *for the child*. For example, quoting *Lehr*, the California Supreme Court wrote:

> [E]qually important is the loss to the child. The child has a genetic bond with its natural parents that is unique among all relationships the child will have throughout its life. "The intangible fibers that connect parent and child have infinite variety. They are woven throughout the fabric of our society, providing it with strength, beauty, and flexibility." ... [A] child is ill-served by allowing its mother effectively to preclude the child from ever having a meaningful relationship with its only other biological parent.[62]

As it stands, this passage is a non sequitur. Each child has exactly two genetic parents, but that does not explain why this semiunique empirical relation justifies rights.[63] Most of the passage is empty rhetoric, particularly the Supreme Court quote. It is unclear why it matters that genetic ties have infinite variety or how genetic ties contribute to society's beauty or flexibility. It is also unclear how benefits to children could justify liberty rights for adults, given that fundamental rights are typically justified by the interests of the rights-holder. Regardless of these shortcomings, perhaps the underlying idea is clear enough. Perhaps these courts believe that genetic connections are intrinsically valuable for parents and children, and parentage law should help realize this intrinsic value. I consider philosophical arguments to this effect in II.C.

Other courts argue that genetic parents have rights because natural instincts make them the best parents for the child.[64] The Supreme Court of Texas, for example, concluded that genetic fathers have "natural rights" of "constitutional magnitude" because "the ties of the natural relationship of parent and child ordinarily furnish strong assurance of genuine efforts on the part of the custodians

61 In Int. of B.G.C., 496 N.W.2d 239, 245 (Iowa 1992). Some state courts appeal to sex equality, arguing that adoption statutes violate equal protection if birth fathers do not receive the same protections as birth mothers. Adoption of Kelsey S., 823 P.2d 1216, 1235 (Cal. 1992). Such arguments assume and cannot justify genetic parenthood: the state needs a special justification for treating birth mothers and fathers differently only if the legal right to be a parent already rests on genetics rather than gestation. Jennifer Hendricks, Essentially a Mother: A Feminist Approach to the Law of Pregnancy and Motherhood 99–103 (2023).

62 Kelsey S., 823 P.2d at 1236 (quoting *Lehr*, 463 U.S. at 256).

63 *See, e.g.*, Melissa Moschella, *Rethinking the Moral Permissibility of Gamete Donation*, 35 Theoretical Med. & Bioethics 421, 432 (2014) (similar attempt to infer value from uniqueness).

64 *In re* Adoption of G.L.V., 190 P.3d 245, 263 (Kan. 2008); Hawk v. Hawk, 855 S.W.2d 573, 577 (Tenn. 1993) ("The parents are trusted with the custody of the child upon the idea that under the instincts of parental devotion it is best for the child."). Kim Everett & Lucy Yeatman, *Are Some Parents More Natural than Others?*, 22 Child & Fam. L.Q. 290, 302–03 (2010) (describing similar arguments for biological parenting in the UK House of Lords and Supreme Court).

to provide the child with the best care and opportunities possible."[65] This is known as the "natural affections" argument.[66] As proffered by courts, the argument is wildly incomplete. Courts offer no psychological, sociological, or anthropological evidence for their empirical claim about the efficacy of genetic incentives.[67] They do not compare the incentives of nonmarital genetic parents to those of stepparents, adoptive parents, or extended families. Finally, they fail to explain how the child's interests ground a right held by the parent. Nevertheless, II.B considers whether this stump of an argument can be worked into a plausible consequentialist theory.

2 Mere Genetic Mothers

Although no Supreme Court precedent directly addresses constitutional maternity, mere genetic mothers should have the same constitutional rights as genetic fathers. When an intended mother transfers ova to a clinic to be carried by her partner or a surrogate, the genetic mother is in the same situation as all genetic fathers. She has supplied half the child's genetic material. There is no legitimate reason to distinguish a person who supplies the egg carrying twenty-two autosomes and an X sex chromosome from a person who supplies the sperm that might carry either an X or Y sex chromosome. Some state supreme courts have held that the Equal Protection Clause (interpreted through the unmarried father cases) requires states to recognize the parentage of intended genetic parents who share sperm or eggs for assisted conception with their partner.[68] Once a genetic mother "demonstrates her commitment to accepting these responsibilities" and "in fact parent[s] and support[s] the child," her "inchoate interest has developed into a protected fundamental right to be a parent."[69]

65 In Int. of J.W.T., 872 S.W.2d 189, 194 (Tex. 1994) (quoting Wiley v. Spratlan, 543 S.W.2d 349, 352 (Tex. 1976)).

66 *See* Pamela Laufer-Ukeles, *The Relational Rights of Children*, 48 Conn. L. Rev. 741, 755 (2015) (discussing similar arguments in Parham v. J.R., 442 U.S. 584, 602 (1979), Bellotti v. Baird, 443 U.S. 622, 648 (1979), and scholarship of Elizabeth Scott and Emily Buss).

67 Texas case law traces parental incentives to the natural law argument that "God, in his wisdom, has placed upon the father and mother the obligation to nurture, educate, protect, and guide their offspring, and has qualified them to discharge those important duties by writing in their hearts sentiments of affection, and establishing between them and their children ties which cannot exist between the children and any other persons." State v. Deaton, 54 S.W. 901, 903 (Tex. 1900).

68 L.F. v. Breit, 736 S.E.2d 711, 722 (Va. 2013); D.M.T. v. T.M.H, 129 So. 3d 320, 339 (Fla. 2013); *In re* Adoption of Sebastian, 879 N.Y.S.2d 677, 689 (2009). *See also In re* Roberto d.B., 923 A.2d 115, 124 (Md. 2007) (same result under state equal rights amendment). For advocacy of this result, see Lynda Wray Black, *The Birth of a Parent: Defining Parentage for Lenders of Genetic Material*, 92 Neb. L. Rev. 799 (2013). For discussion of recent cases, see Jeffrey A. Parness, *The Constitutional Limits on Custodial and Support Parentage by Consent*, 56 Idaho L. Rev. 421 (2020); Michael J. Higdon, *Constitutional Parenthood*, 103 Iowa L. Rev. 1483, 1535–36 (2018).

69 D.M.T. v. T.M.H., 129 So. 3d 320, 339 (Fla. 2013).

While the doctrinal avenues vary, all states now regard a female who transfers ova to her partner as a legal parent in the same manner as a genetic father.[70] The states diverge regarding surrogacy because these agreements raise distinct concerns, which I discuss in Chapter 5. Accordingly, unless the case or context requires, I will use "genetic parent" whenever possible.

3 Genetic Fathers with Competing Marital Parents

It remains unsettled whether genetic fathers have constitutional rights when their children have presumed marital parents. The Supreme Court's only case about conflicting genetic and marital fathers resulted in a split decision.[71] Carole conceived a child with Michael while married to Gerald. For several years, she and the child lived intermittently with each man, and each man held himself out as the child's father. When Carole chose to stay permanently with Gerald, Michael sued for visitation. The California courts dismissed Michael's petition because only spouses could rebut the state's marital presumption.[72] The US Supreme Court affirmed in a split decision.

The Court did not decide whether Michael had a constitutional parental liberty interest. A four-justice plurality concluded that Michael had no liberty interest because the Constitution protects only interests deeply embedded in American law, and few states had ever recognized adulterous fathers as parents.[73] The four dissenting justices concluded that Michael demonstrated sufficient commitment to his parental roles to ground a liberty interest.[74] Justice Stevens cast the decisive vote against Michael without resolving this issue. Whether or not Michael had a liberty interest, Stevens concluded the family court had adequately weighed it against the child's interest in her intact marital family.[75] As a practical matter, the divided decision in *Michael H.* leaves states with the discretion to decide how to resolve competing paternity claims.

The states have split procedurally and substantively, reflecting the full range of options. At least nine states still do not permit nonmarital fathers to challenge an intact marital presumption.[76] For example, the Alabama Supreme Court ruled that "marital presumption outweighs genetics, so that as long as the husband persists in his parental roles, the marital presumption is conclusive."[77]

70 Douglas NeJaime, *The Nature of Parenthood*, 126 Yale L.J. 2260, 2300–02, 2373–75 (app. D) (2016).

71 Michael H. v. Gerald D., 491 U.S. 110 (1989); Higdon, *supra* note 68, at 1499; Meyer, *supra* note 18, at 785–86.

72 Michael H. v. Gerald D., 236 Cal. Rptr. 810, 817 (Ct. App. 1987).

73 *Michael H.*, 491 U.S. at 122–27 (Scalia, J. plurality).

74 *Id.* at 136 (Brennan, J., dissenting) (counting votes).

75 *Id.* at 136 (Stevens, J., concurring).

76 Susan Frelich Appleton, *Presuming Women: Revisiting the Presumption of Legitimacy in the Same-Sex Couples Era*, 86 B.U. L. Rev. 227, 234 (2006).

77 R.D. v. S.S., 309 So. 3d 146, 155 (Ala. Civ. App. 2020). *See also ex parte* C.A.P., 683 So.2d 1010, 1012 (Ala. 1996) (a male's "interest in judicially establishing his alleged biological relationship to the child is outweighed by the obvious objectives of the [parentage act], which are to provide for the

A handful of states swung entirely the other way, concluding that genetic paternity trumps the marital and residential presumptions.[78] The Tennessee Supreme Court held that the marital presumption cannot abrogate genetic fathers' constitutional rights.[79] Other states adopted similar statutory preferences for genetic parents.[80] Under the 1974 and 2002 Uniform Parentage Acts, evidence of biological paternity rebuts the marital presumption because these Acts treat the parentage presumptions as evidence of presumptive genetic paternity.[81]

The more recent trends favor judicial discretion. Genetic fathers can challenge the marital presumption, but genetic evidence cannot rebut it. Instead, genetic parentage creates a presumption on a par with others, which requires a court to apply rules for conflicting presumptions. In some states, the court must decide whether the marital or genetic presumption rests on the "weightier policy and logic," while in other states and under the UPA 2017, the court must decide which parent will serve the child's best interest.[82]

Unfortunately, the large volume of conflict cases has not improved opinion reasoning. Whether they favor marital or genetic fathers, courts rarely engage in well-reasoned analysis of the empirical or normative premises behind their legal rules.[83]

psychological stability and general welfare of the child and to afford legitimacy to children whenever possible.").

78 June Carbone & Naomi Cahn, *Marriage, Parentage, and Child Support*, 45 FAM. L.Q. 219, 223–24 (2011).

79 *In re* T.K.Y., 205 S.W.3d 343, 352 (Tenn. 2006).

80 Nev. Rev. Stat. Ann. § 126.051(2) (West); Mo. Ann. Stat. § 210.834.4 (West) ("Whenever the court finds that the results of the blood tests show that a person is presumed or alleged to be the father of the child is not the father of such child, such evidence shall be conclusive of nonpaternity."); Courtney v. Roggy, 302 S.W.3d 141 (Mo. App. W.D. 2009).

81 Matter of Paternity of AAAE, 471 P.3d 990, 996 (Wyo. 2020); UPA 1973 § 12 (describing relevant evidence to determine paternity as including evidence of intercourse at the time of conception, blood tests, and other "medical or anthropological evidence"); UNIF. PARENTAGE ACT § 631(1) (UNIF. LAW COMM'N 2002) [hereinafter UPA 2002] (a presumption or acknowledgment of paternity "may be disproved only by admissible results of genetic testing" and "a man excluded as the father of a child by genetic testing must be adjudicated not to be the father of the child"). The UPA 2002 recognized the "controlling supremacy of admissible genetic test results." UPA 2002 § 631, cmt. See also Jessica Feinberg, *Restructuring Rebuttal of the Marital Presumption for the Modern Era*, 104 MINN. L. REV. 243, 254 n.48 (2019).

82 *In re* Jesusa V., 85 P.3d 2, 14 (Cal. 2004); Greer *ex rel.* Farbo v. Greer, 324 P.3d 310, 319 (Kan. App. 2014); Doherty v. Leon, 472 P.3d 531, 535 (Ariz. Ct. App. 2020) ("there is no hierarchy among the statutory presumptions").

83 For example, the Maine Supreme Court tried to infer the strength of the policies from the burden of proof. Atkinson v. Hall, 556 A.2d 651, 653 (Me. 1989). In a non sequitur, it reasoned that the marital presumption must be at least as weighty as the genetic presumption because common law required proof beyond a reasonable doubt to rebut the marital presumption, while the newer statute required only clear and convincing evidence to rebut the genetic presumption.

Courts that sustain a strong marital presumption tend to rely formalistically on statutory language.[84] When they mention the underlying policies, they emphasize children's need to maintain stability in intact relationships.[85] This might sound like a promising child welfare argument, but courts rarely cite psychological or sociological evidence. They rarely grapple with the trade-off between the best result for the child in the immediate case and the systemic effects of their rule on families and child welfare.[86] Often, they appeal to normative dogma about the need to "protect the sanctity of family relationships."[87] Even that normative analysis is strikingly one-sided. When assessing the value of genetic ties, they mostly note that *Michael H.* upheld a strong marital presumption and cite heavily to Justice Scalia's plurality opinion.[88] This reliance is ironic. *Michael H.*'s historical approach to fundamental rights is designed to prevent federal courts from second-guessing state law based on their value judgments – not to lock states into historical policies without regard for their estimate of the underlying values.

The state courts that have struck down conclusive marital presumptions do only marginally better. They often assert the "significance of the biological link" without further explanation.[89] Many rely on dogmatic precedents like *Lehr*, which is especially problematic in this context because *Lehr* never purported to grapple with *competing* paternity claims.[90] Courts that favor genetic over marital fathers do marshal two more arguments. The first appeals again to natural affections, only this time against marital rather than adoptive parents.[91] Once again, courts rarely cite any empirical evidence. They rarely even recognize that they need to *compare* the incentives of genetic fathers with the incentives of birth mothers and marital fathers.[92] Nevertheless, I consider sophisticated versions of the natural affections argument in II.C below.

84 *See, e.g.*, Dawn D. v. Superior Ct., 952 P.2d 1139, 1146 (Cal. 1998); Sinicropi v. Mazurek, 729 N.W.2d 256 (Mich. App. 2006).

85 Carbone and Cahn, *supra* note 78, at 225.

86 The Alabama Supreme Court boldly asserted that preserving marital parenthood will "be in the child's interest in practically all cases" in a case where the custodial mother had remarried the biological father and they were living together with the child as a family. *Ex parte* Presse, 554 So. 2d 406, 412 (Ala. 1989).

87 For example, R.D. v. S.S., 309 So. 3d 146, 154 (Ala. Civ. App. 2020), asserts that preserving psychological stability is more important to child welfare than genetic ties, but its only authority boils down to a citation to *ex parte* Presse, 554 So. 2d at 412, a case which relied on legislative intent.

88 *Ex parte Presse*, 554 So. 2d at 414–18.

89 Callender v. Skiles, 591 N.W.2d 182, 190 (Iowa 1999) (citing *In re* B.G.C., 496 N.W.2d 239, 245 (Iowa 1992) (also simply asserting a biological interest without explanation)).

90 E.g., *In re* T.K.Y., 205 S.W.3d 343, 352 (Tenn. 2006) (citing four cases where a biological father tried to oppose an infant adoption).

91 Hawk v. Hawk, 855 S.W.2d 573, 577 (Tenn. 1993) ("The parents are trusted with the custody of the child upon the idea that under the instincts of parental devotion it is best for the child.") (quoting State *ex rel.* Bethell v. Kilvington, 45 S.W. 433, 435 (Tenn. 1898)).

92 In Int. of J.W.T., 872 S.W.2d 189, 194 (Tex. 1994).

Another common argument is that protecting genetic fathers will respect familial liberty in our pluralist society. Justice Brennan made this argument in his dissent from *Michael H*, but his argument is unsound. States must choose who gets to raise the child: the genetic, gestational, marital, or functional parent. A genetic parentage rule does not advance liberty or pluralism as such; it simply prioritizes one family form. Furthermore, the way many states "protect" genetic parents only shuffles authority among institutions without increasing familial liberty. If genetic parenthood merely creates another presumption, then a family court must choose among putative parents using an ad hoc judgment about the value of marriage, genetics, or function. By contrast, if the legislature adopts a strict hierarchy among the tests, the legislature declares a family policy categorically. A familial liberty argument can have merit, but it needs a more nuanced conception of the relationship between genetics and liberty, which I develop in III.A.

4 Genetic Parents and Assisted Reproductive Technologies

Despite the revolutionary potential of reproductive science, genetic parentage still plays a crucial role in parentage rules when adults use assisted reproductive technology (ART). As I mentioned earlier, genetic parents who donate their sperm or egg through a clinic can waive their right to be parents and will avoid parental duties. Donors can agree to share gametes with anyone who wants them or limit their donation to a specific person. Now in all states, a couple or a single parent can use a known donor without the risk of creating unwanted parentage.

Other genetic parents agree to share parenthood when using ART. Some states have preconception agreement statutes, which state that the birth mother's spouse (or maybe a partner) becomes a parent if they consent to ART. Where does the genetic-gestational parent get this authority? If the embryos were created from her eggs, then her genetic parentage gives her a right to be a parent to this child and the legal power to share parentage via statutory mechanisms. If the embryos were created using eggs from another woman, then a gestational parent can acquire parental authority only if the egg donor waives her right to be a parent or agrees to share parenthood with her (in the case of a lesbian couple). If a fertility clinic in the United States mistakenly implants the wrong embryos, as in *A.P. v. Manukyan*, the gestational parent loses the children to the genetic parents.

Although technology makes it possible to sever gestation from genetics, the driving force behind ART has always been a desire to procreate genetically. Couples who cannot conceive via sexual intercourse could adopt, but instead they expend significant resources to have a genetic child using technology. (Some women may pursue ART primarily to experience pregnancy and childbirth.) Many theorists have argued that this desire is so strong and the interest in procreation so important that individuals have a right to ART. Some argue that individuals have a negative right not to have the government interfere with their access to fertility treatments, while others argue that individuals have an affirmative entitlement to public funds for ART because it is a medical treatment for infertility.[93] Debates about the value of fertility treatments can be heated in nations with public health services, where resources spent on ART diminish public funds needed for other medical treatments.[94]

5 Open Adoptions and Open Gamete Donation

The last salient aspect of parentage law that recognizes the value of genetic ties is the "right to know" movement in adoption and assisted reproduction. Adoption law has long been ambivalent about genetic notions of family. When the number of adoptions peaked in the United States in the 1960s, adoption served as a substitute for sexual procreation. Infertile heterosexual couples – mostly married, white, and middle-class – sought to adopt infants who looked like them. States helped these adoptive families "pass" as genetic families by issuing a new birth certificate for the child and closing the adoption file so that neither the birth parents, the adoptive parents, nor the adopted child could later learn the truth. For similar reasons, adults involved in assisted reproduction often also insist on a right to secrecy. Dorothy Roberts revealed ways that the movement for adoptive and ART secrecy is wrapped up in racialized notions of family and the desire to avoid challenges to a "pure" white family.

As infant adoption reached its zenith, adoptive parents and children pushed back to "open" adoption files and to enable open adoptions with ongoing contact. The movement had several goals. One was to reduce the stigma of adoption by undercutting the normative ideal of a genetically related family. Another was to enable adoptive children to learn about their biological heritage. One reason is to learn about heritable diseases, but the central argument is that children want to know about their heritage. The two messages – contesting the genetic ideal and seeking genetic knowledge – exist in some tension. Nevertheless, they can be consistent. One can value information about one's genetic heritage and still believe that care relationships with adoptive parents establish genuine families that are not secondary to genetic families.

A movement with similar tensions exists in the world of donor conception. Naomi Cahn argues that the law should end anonymous gamete donations and force parents to disclose their child's status, insisting that children have a right to know their genetic heritage.[95] Others argue that denying parents the authority to choose when to disclose violates their privacy, forcing them to reveal their infertility in a way

93 John B. Appleby & Anja J. Karnein, *On the Moral Importance of Genetic Ties in Families*, *in* Relatedness in Assisted Reproduction: Families, Origins and Identities 79 (Fatemeh Ebtehaj et al. eds., 2014).

94 *See* 6.III.A.

95 Naomi Cahn, *The New Art of Family: Connecting Assisted Reproductive Technologies & Identity Rights*, 2018 U. Ill. L. Rev. 1443; Margaret Somerville, *Children's Human Rights and Unlinking Child–Parent Biological Bonds with Adoption, Same-Sex Marriage and New Reproductive Technologies*, 13 J. Fam. Stud. 179 (2007).

that can implicate their identity and social relations.[96] Professor Kimberly Leighton argues that both sides of this debate presume a normative tie between genetics and "real" families.[97] The parents' desire to "pass" as a genetic family "reinforces the hetero-bionormative assumption . . . that real and good families must be genetically related."[98] Conversely, advocates for the right to know assume that genetic identity has positive value and hiding it harms the child psychologically, which they give the pseudoscientific name of "genealogical bewilderment."[99] Leighton has correctly identified an (often implicit) normative assumption, but that is not a criticism if genetically related families do have some distinctive value.

II GENETICS AND MORAL PARENTHOOD

Although many legal academics oppose genetics as a basis for parentage, we cannot ignore the widespread folk intuition – shared by the law – that genetic parents have special rights and duties concerning their genetic children. One might suppose that genetic parents have moral duties and rights to raise their children that justify legal parenthood. Section A considers and rejects the idea that genetic parentage is necessary or sufficient for moral parenthood. Sections B and C consider arguments offered by courts and scholars for more limited claims about the rights or duties of genetic parents.

A *Counterexamples to Strong Genetic Theories*

Obvious counterexamples belie any claim that genetic ties are necessary or sufficient for parental rights or duties. Nevertheless, these counterexamples cannot bury the genetic theory.

1 Genetic Ties Are Not *Necessary* for Parental Rights or Duties

Genetic parentage is not necessary for parental rights or duties.[100] Adoption is the obvious counterexample. Marital and residential presumptions can also create

96 An Ravelingien & Guido Pennings, *The Right to Know Your Genetic Parents: From Open-Identity Gamete Donation to Routine Paternity Testing*, 13 AM. J. BIOETHICS 33, 36–37 (2013). In a clever twist, Ravelingien and Pennings argue that whatever arguments justify mandatory disclosure in adoption and donor conception equally justify mandatory routine paternity testing at birth to prevent misattributed paternity.

97 Kimberly Leighton, *To Criticize the Right to Know We Must Question the Value of Genetic Relatedness*, 13 AM. J. BIOETHICS 54 (2013).

98 *Id.* at 54.

99 Janet Farrell Smith, *A Child of One's Own: A Moral Assessment of Property Conceptions in Adoption*, *in* ADOPTION MATTERS: PHILOSOPHICAL AND FEMINIST ESSAYS 112 (Sally Haslanger & Charlotte Witt eds., 2005).

100 Nancy D. Polikoff, *A Mother Should Not Have to Adopt Her Own Child: Parentage Laws for Children of Lesbian Couples in the Twenty-First Century*, 5 STAN. J. C.R. & C.L. 201, 202 (2009).

nonbiological parenthood by barring challenges from genetic parents. Even states that allow genetic evidence for rebuttal often have statutes of limitations that exclude delayed challenges. Most states also apply the presumptions to spouses and cohabitants who could not *possibly* have genetic ties to the child, such as when lesbian couples conceive using artificial insemination. Many states allow a pregnant person and their partner to agree to parentage before using assisted reproduction. A handful also allow a birth mother to sign a voluntary acknowledgment of parentage with a nonbiological parent at birth. Even acknowledgments of *paternity* sometimes bind signatories who knew the alleged father had no genetic tie to the child.

Although they show genetic ties are not necessary for parenthood, these doctrines do still give genetic ties a central role. Adoption can proceed only if the genetic mother and father either consented or had their parental rights terminated. The presumptions, acknowledgments, and preconception agreements all require the participation of a birth parent, who is likely the genetic mother. If she is not, these doctrines apply only if the genetic mother and father either waive their parental rights or agree to share parentage with her. All the legal doctrines that enable nonbiological parentage presume genetic parents have the initial right to pursue parenthood and, thus, some authority to veto other potential parents.[101]

Sections B and C and Part III consider the scope of this initial right and its potential justifications. Before evaluating it, we must ask if genetics could be sufficient for moral parentage. For this task, it is helpful to distinguish between parental rights and duties.

2 Genetic Ties Are Not *Sufficient* for Parental Duties

Genetic parentage is often thought sufficient for parental duties – or at least child support. Under the influence of federal welfare reform, many states moved in this direction. Unfortunately, this proposition is demonstrably false.

A handful of fanciful counterexamples can make the point cleanly. Imagine a woman sloughs off skin cells on the street. A scientist collects them and reprograms them into stem cells, which are triggered to form ova and then fertilized to create embryos. The woman from the street is the genetic parent of any resulting children, yet she has no duty to support the children financially, much less to raise the children herself. Perhaps the example is missing some voluntary act by the genetic parent? Suppose a woman chooses to undergo surgery to remove her ovary and the

101 Black asserts that biological parents receive "primary parentage," while adoptive or presumptive parents have "derivative parentage" that must arise through the biological parent. Black, *supra* note 68, at 832. I reject this language because it suggests that genetics generates moral parentage, when in fact genetics only generates a liberty to pursue parenthood that becomes parentage only with caregiving.

surgeon secretly uses her ova to create children. Once again, the genetic mother seems to have no parental duties to her genetic children.[102]

Maybe the problem with gamete theft cases is that the children are unforeseeable. Compare two cases of unexpected children. First, a couple uses a fertility clinic to have a child. Afterward, the clinic carelessly implants their extra embryos in another woman. If these genetic parents do not want to be parents again, it seems like they have no duty to raise or support their unforeseen genetic children. Compare their situation to a woman who undergoes IVF with her gametes and unexpectedly ends up with triplets. Even if she did not want to raise multiples, she has some duty toward the reasonably foreseeable children.

While this pair of conclusions may suggest *foreseeable genetic parents* incur duties, I think the intuition has collapsed a genetic theory into a causal theory. The woman who had unintended triplets incurs duties because she performed a voluntary act that she could reasonably foresee might cause a child to exist. As I will explain in Chapter 3, causal parentage can justify limited personal duties. It is also the clearest rationale for child support. However, adults can cause a child to exist with no genetic ties. If the woman had used donor eggs, she would have had the same duties to the triplets. Genetic ties no longer make any independent contribution.

Admittedly, counterexamples using fanciful technology or gamete theft might generate unreliable intuitions, but more ordinary and unfortunate scenarios offer analogous counterexamples. The most salient cases involve conception by rape. Consider, first, the case of a female perpetrator who rapes a male victim under the influence of a drug like GHB. In all relevant respects, the male rape victim is analogous to a patient whose sperm was stolen from a fertility clinic. His genetic paternity does not obligate him to raise the child.

If a person becomes pregnant as a result of rape, the pregnancy adds complexity without altering the moral conclusion. The rapist forces his victim into a choice: carry the fetus to term or obtain an abortion. Someone might argue that the victim's choice to continue the pregnancy grounds a prima facie duty to raise the child, although the psychological trauma excuses her from those parental duties.[103] The excuse reveals the prima facie duty, or so the argument might go. On the contrary, I maintain that the rape victim's choice cannot generate *parental* duties. So long as a pregnant person exercises reasonable care to ensure the child has a valuable life, such as obtaining obstetric care and helping find adoptive parents, the gestational parent has benefitted the child without placing the child at any added risk. Why would this benevolent choice justify a further duty to raise the child? There is no need for an excuse. In any case, notice that,

[102] As Chapter 4 explains, some courts will – out of fear of evidentiary disputes and need to maintain privatized welfare – impose child support on men when the birth mother allegedly impregnated herself with sperm saved after oral sex or taken from discarded condoms.

[103] Even if a free choice to continue a pregnancy can generate duties, the choice might not be free in the right sense if the law interferes with abortion, trauma interferes with their ability to choose, or their belief that abortion is immoral leaves them no permissible alternative.

once again, the locus of the duty shifted away from genetics toward causation. The rape victim allegedly incurs a duty because their voluntary choice to continue the pregnancy created a child who needs a parent.[104] The same principles would apply if a woman became pregnant after being coercively implanted with an unrelated embryo. Genetic ties again do no moral work.

3 Genetic Ties Are Not *Sufficient* for Parental Rights

Genetic parentage is also insufficient for parental rights. As a matter of common-sense morality, a long-absent genetic parent has no right to waltz back into a child's life and assume parental responsibilities. The law on this point is a little more ambiguous. On the one hand, genetic parents are not legal parents until they establish parentage through a paternity petition or a VAP. On the other hand, if the child has only one legal parent, the parentage petition can be filed at any time during the child's minority, and the genetic parent will owe support and have a right to petition for visitation. But if the child does have a second presumed marital or residential parent, the genetic parent may find themselves excluded from parentage (at least after the statute of limitations). A child can also be adopted without giving the genetic father notice or a hearing if the genetic father did not reliably pursue a relationship or provide support. The court need give no regard to the genetic parent's wishes or interests.

The obvious response to these alleged counterexamples is to narrow the asserted right. Genetic parents have a right to be a parent *if* they promptly commit to parental responsibilities, and they have a liberty right to perform the caregiving necessary to demonstrate this commitment. Part III defends a version of this conditional liberty right.

Yet even this narrower conclusion faces apparent counterexamples. Anonymous sperm and egg donors have no right to seek parental status. An IVF technician who fraudulently uses their own gametes has no parental rights.[105] Similarly, a rapist should acquire no rights over a child conceived through rape.[106] Some states treat rapists as legal parents until a court finds them unfit, but with some encouragement

104 If one is still inclined to think genetic parentage alone creates parental duties, consider the following horrible but real case. A woman was raped while in a vegetative state at a long-term care facility. Steve Orr and Gary Craig, *In a First, a Comatose Rochester Woman Gave Birth. Today, Her Rapist Remains Behind Bars*, DEMOCRAT & CHRON., www.democratandchronicle.com/story/news/2019/01/11/comatose-woman-gave-birth-rochester-23-years-before-phoenix-case/2540086002/ (last visited Oct. 9, 2023). Suppose – now contrary to fact – the woman awoke after the child's birth. Does she have a duty to raise the child merely because of her genetic or gestational connection? She may choose to parent that child, but surely that is supererogatory. The need for an excuse does not even arise.

105 Rousseau v. Coates, No. 2:18-CV-205, 2022 WL 3910990, at *1 (D. Vt. Aug. 30, 2022) (two-million-dollar punitive award for physician who fraudulently used his own sperm).

106 Matter of R.V., 511 P.3d 148, 158 (Wash. App. 2022) (statute precluding sexual assault perpetrator from establishing paternity does not violate constitutional parental rights); Peña v. Mattox, 84 F.3d 894, 899–900 (7th Cir. 1996) (same).

by federal law at least thirty states now mandate termination of parental rights.[107] Are these viable counterexamples to a conditional right for genetic parents?

Gamete donation is easily explained by waiver. In contemporary American law, egg and sperm donors waive any parental rights at the time of donation. By contrast, anyone who transfers gametes to a clinic for their use or for use by their partner retains parental rights and duties. This rule might help explain why genetic parents like the Manyukans have parental rights – if there is a moral principle that can justify both a genetic liberty to parent and the power to waive that liberty.

Wrongful conception cases are more complex. I see two options to defuse the counterexample, each of which might be the principle behind modern statutes. Some statutes provide that rapists "forfeit" parental rights or courts "shall terminate" their parental rights.[108] Someone who believed genetic parentage is sufficient for conditional parental rights might say that a rapist or fraudulent IVF technician acquired a right to pursue parenthood but *forfeited* it because their conduct was wrongful or because they proved they would likely be bad parents. I prefer statutes that provide a court shall issue no order recognizing parental rights for rapists.[109] A mere genetic parent is not a legal parent (even a presumed parent) until they establish parentage by petition or a VAP. As I explain in III.C, the state may protect genetic parents' liberty to parent only if it limits this liberty as necessary to render it consistent with equal respect for the child and other adults. The law should not allow a rapist to use the victim's body to obtain custodial rights that perpetuate their control over the victim's life. Egregious wrongdoing should never generate rights, even temporarily.[110] Instead of a forfeiture rule, the law should deny that anyone can acquire rights through rape or fraudulent IVF.

* * *

[107] Parental Rights and Sexual Assault, (2020), www.ncsl.org/human-services/parental-rights-and-sexual-assault (last visited Jul. 7, 2023). Alabama terminates the parental rights of a defendant convicted of rape, but absent a criminal conviction the rape victim must prove by clear and convincing evidence that the rapist is "unwilling or unable to discharge parental responsibilities." Ala. Code § 12-15-319. Virginia maintains a similar regime. Jordan S. Miceli, *Note: The Haunting of Her House: How Virginia Law Punishes Women Who Become Mothers Through Rape*, 78 Wash. & Lee L. Rev. Online 129 (2021). Jay Mitzer, Annotation, *Visitation or Custody of Child Allegedly Conceived by Sexual Assault*, 54 A.L.R.7th Art. 7 (originally published in 2020).

[108] Mont. Code Ann. § 45-5-503.

[109] E.g., Ohio Rev. Code § 3109.50. Michigan's statute authorizes a court either to conclude the rapist is not the legal father or to make a paternity determination that they immediately revoke. Mich. Comp. Laws § 722.1445 Sec. 15(2).

[110] A forfeiture theory may receive undo support by mistaking the timing of legal procedures with a conceptual presupposition. Forfeiture and termination presuppose existing rights. A person must have parental rights before they can forfeit them by wrongdoing. Legal reasoning requires an ordered decision process. The rapist is not even an alleged parent if they are not the genetic parent, so a court must first determine that the rapist is the genetic parent before it concludes the rapist has no parental rights. That the legal procedures must follow this temporal order does not entail the rapist had parental rights for a brief moment until the court "terminated" them.

The above counterexamples demonstrate that genetic parentage is neither necessary nor sufficient for parental rights or duties. However, they leave several important possibilities open. Genetic parentage might be necessary or sufficient for the *initial* assignment of parental rights. Moreover, even if genetic parentage is not necessary or sufficient for initial parenthood, states may have good reasons to offer genetic parents the initial parenting opportunity. The remainder of this part considers these possibilities. Do genetic parents who conceive a child rightfully have a personal moral right to the liberty to fulfill parental responsibilities and rights?

B *Initial Parental Rights or Duties from Genetic Incentives*

Among American legal scholars, questions about the initial assignment of duties and rights immediately invite questions of efficiency. Informal consequentialism is the order of the day in law, so courts and scholars unsurprisingly use the "natural bonds of affection" argument to this effect.[111] The premise is that evolution favors incentives to aid one's progeny, and social norms exploit and enhance this connection, so genetic parents are more likely than anyone else to provide quality childcare and derive pleasure from caregiving work.[112] Biological parenting instincts are enhanced as child-rearing builds attachments and as cultural norms reinforce those incentives and attachments.[113] The "natural affection" argument appears frequently in judicial opinions and legal scholarship and occasionally in philosophical literature.[114] It comes in two normative flavors. The first is a child-centered theory, arguing that familial rights and duties should be designed to promote child well-being. The second is more broadly consequentialist, arguing familial rights and duties should be designed to benefit children, parents, and society overall. Does assigning parenthood to genetic parents improve welfare for children or for society generally?[115]

111 Nancy E. Dowd, *Parentage at Birth: Birthfathers and Social Fatherhood*, 14 Wm. & Mary Bill Rts. J. 909, 922–26 (2006).

112 David J. Herring, *Evolutionary Perspectives on Child Welfare Law*, *in* The Evolution of Violence 53 (Todd K. Shackelford & Ranald D. Hansen eds., 2014). Liao argues that everyone has a duty to ensure children receive love, but everyone cannot practically fulfill this duty at the same time, so a "primary duty bearer" can "be assigned based on criteria such as responsibility, [physical] proximity, ability, and motivation." S. Matthew Liao, The Right to Be Loved (2015). Biological parents are the natural candidates because they are typically causally responsible, often immediately present, and often have the strongest motivation.

113 Stephen G. Gilles, *On Educating Children: A Parentalist Manifesto*, 63 U. Chi. L. Rev. 937, 954 (1996).

114 *See* Brenda Almond, *Family Relationships and Reproductive Technologies*, *in* Having and Raising Children: Unconventional Families, Hard Choices, and the Social Good 103 (Uma Narayan ed., 2010); E. Gary Spitko, *The Constitutional Function of Biological Paternity*, 48 Ariz. L. Rev. 97, 118–21 (2006) (criticizing the argument); John Locke, Second Treatise of Government § 63 (The Project Gutenberg eBook ed.), www.gutenberg.org/files/7370/7370-h/7370-h.htm (last visited Sept. 25, 2023).

115 Philosophers have theoretical reasons to be skeptical that consequentialism can justify special duties for genetic parents. An act-consequentialist must decide how to act by weighing each person's welfare equally. A parent should devote resources to their child only insofar as doing so

Evolved incentives cannot justify our pervasive favoritism for genetic parents, at least not to the extent of current law and social norms. The natural affection argument falters as a matter of evolutionary and consequentialist theory. The argument is on especially thin ice if it is meant to show that genetic parents are the adults most likely to care for their children well.

Although kin selection is the central explanatory principle of evolutionary biology, it favors more discerning reproductive strategies than uniform affection for each genetic child.[116] A parent can dedicate resources to one child, increasing that child's likelihood of success, or spread resources among multiple children, hedging their bets. Which strategy is more effective likely varies according to the parent's species, sex, social status, and environmental context.[117]

Female primates expend substantial resources on gestation and nursing, which encourages investment in each child. Nevertheless, uniformly high investment in every child is an ineffective strategy. When resources are scarce, the environment is dangerous, or caregiving assistance is unavailable, females may delay reproduction or abandon children with low prospects. Male incentives likely vary with social status. High-status males with sexual access to multiple females have an incentive for promiscuity with little attention to each child. Low-status males, in contrast, can make themselves more attractive mates by devoting themselves to one female and her child, increasing the likelihood of paternity and maximizing each opportunity. Males may also invest in unrelated "stepchildren" because developing a reputation for partnership can lead to future reproductive opportunities.

Indeed, when imagining our evolutionary incentives for caregiving, a myopic focus on genetic parents is likely misleading. Human infants have an unusually long and demanding period of material dependency, so parents likely relied on social assistance while raising children. Wider circles of cooperative caregiving from grandparents, aunts, siblings, and groups were likely crucial to reproductive success.[118] Such alloparental care might also have allowed our human ancestors to be more flexible and opportunistic in their parental commitments, perhaps leading to less reliable male parenting.

increases overall welfare – precisely the opposite of parental partiality. Most parents lavish resources on their children that could generate far greater marginal benefits for less advantaged people. A central project of act-utilitarianism – from Bentham through Singer – has been to expand sympathy beyond families so that individual incentives better align with the general welfare. Any plausible consequentialist theory of parenthood must appeal to some form of rule-consequentialism.

116 For a devastating review of the sociobiological premises, see June Carbone & Naomi Cahn, *Which Ties Bind? Redefining the Parent–Child Relationship in an Age of Genetic Certainty*, 11 Wm. & Mary Bill Rts. J. 1011, 1023–39 (2002).

117 Sarah Blaffer Hrdy, Mother Nature: Maternal Instincts and How They Shape the Human Species ch. 3 (2000).

118 Sarah Blaffer Hrdy, Mothers and Others: The Evolutionary Origins of Mutual Understanding 100–09 (2009).

Outside evolutionary theory, history and anthropology offer ample reason to doubt genetic parents are uniformly invested in their children's best interests. All societies value parent–child relationships, but few conceive of parents as stewards obligated to care for each child for its own sake. Most societies have viewed children as resources for their parents and community.[119] Children provide free labor, offer parents security in old age, and carry on family legacies. Individuals and societies had incentives to care for children for self-regarding and instrumental reasons.

More precisely, they valued *some* children. For example, Western parentage law evolved to ensure the efficient transfer of land and title through male heirs. One heir was essential. Subsequent male children offered a backup but also threatened orderly succession and familial resources. Female children were a means to forge alliances with other families. Illegitimate children had no status. Social and economic conditions also generate differential investment in children. Parents invest in children differently based on anticipated returns to the parent and family – such as gendered expectations regarding labor tasks, future wages, or elder care.[120] Furthermore, infant exposure was common cross-culturally, occurring in Rome, medieval China and Japan, and Europe through the nineteenth century.[121] Our intuitions about the strength of genetic incentives – rather than reflecting "natural" affections – reflect a contingent confluence of Victorian ideals of childhood, the mid-twentieth-century ideals of nuclear family, the late-century push to privatize welfare, and twenty-first-century markets for ancestry tests and fertility treatment.[122]

Anyone still tempted to believe that wealth or moral progress has freed our contemporaries to indulge their natural familial affections need only look at modern child welfare statistics. Abandonment remains a problem. In the 1990s, American parents abandoned or excluded around 100,000 minors yearly, not including the half a million "runaways" who often leave to avoid parental abuse.[123] In 2020, 618,000 children were subject to *verified* abuse or neglect, which was 8.4 out of every 1,000 children.[124] Of these, 90 percent were victims of their biological parents.[125] The rates of abuse by genetic parents are lower than by stepparents but higher than by adoptive

119 Julia Grant, *Parent–Child Relations in Western Europe and North America, 1500–Present*, *in* The Routledge History of Childhood in the Western World 103 (Paula S. Fass ed., 2013).

120 Silvia Helena Barcellos, Leandro S. Carvalho & Adriana Lleras-Muney, *Child Gender and Parental Investments in India: Are Boys and Girls Treated Differently?*, 6 Am. Econ. J.: Applied Econ. 157 (2014).

121 Gregory A. Loken, *Thrownaway Children and Thrownaway Parenthood*, 68 Temple L. Rev. 1715, 1717 (1995); Gregory Hanlon, *Routine Infanticide in the West 1500–1800*, 14 Hist.Compass 535 (2016).

122 Janet L. Dolgin, *Biological Evaluations: Blood, Genes, and Family*, 41 Akron L. Rev. 347, 369 (2008).

123 Loken, *supra* note 121, at 1720.

124 Child. Bureau, Dep't Health & Hum. Servs., Child Maltreatment 2020, xi (2020), www.acf.hhs.gov/sites/default/files/documents/cb/cm2020.pdf. Some caution about this statistic is warranted because neglect cases often reflect a parent's financial difficulties and disparities in policing Black parents.

125 *Id.* at 27. Some 14 percent were maltreated by a nonparent (some by both).

parents.[126] Genetic incentives are consistent with exploitation, discrimination, and indifference – hardly a reliable mechanism to ensure quality, individualized caregiving.

In addition to its empirical weaknesses, the "natural affections" argument is curiously conservative for a consequentialist theory. Legal and moral rules should exploit evolutionary and cultural incentives, but why rest content with them? A community could craft its legal rules to incorporate other indicators of parenting quality, such as eagerness to parent, investment to create the child, voluntary acceptance of parenting duties, past parenting performance, or parenting knowledge and education.[127] Hugh Lafollette has famously argued that states should use parenting licenses to require parenting education and screen adults with a history of abuse.[128] Consequentialist social engineers should also consider whether the law can improve caregiving by redirecting evolutionary or cultural incentives. Perhaps it should leverage evolved incentives for kinship care to facilitate communal child-rearing.[129] The law can also create incentives, such as through financial support for all caregivers and for childcare. If the goal is to use empirical evidence to design child-rearing arrangements that promote child welfare, simplistic reliance on the genetic default is a poor choice.

On the other hand, social engineering requires vast amounts of information. Epistemically modest consequentialists might retreat to Burkean conservatism. If social norms tend to persist and spread because they generally promote social welfare, the near universality of child-rearing by biological parents could attest to its social utility. Perhaps lawmakers should assume society is better off maintaining its genetic default and limiting reform to the margins rather than attempting a revolutionary redesign of family norms. Unfortunately for this argument, we have plenty of evidence to reject the premise of this Burkean argument. Ideas about genetic parentage have not spread for salutary reasons, and genetic ties are a weak proxy for parenting quality.

Genetic ties are not a central feature of law because child-rearing by genetic parents is the arrangement most likely to facilitate child or social welfare. Genetic incentives are relevant but cannot be the whole story. When assessing familial arrangements, no community can ignore caregivers' incentives, whether genetic, gestational, cultural, financial, legal, or otherwise.

126 Marinus H. van IJzendoorn et al., *Elevated Risk of Child Maltreatment in Families with Stepparents but Not with Adoptive Parents*, 14 CHILD MALTREATMENT 369 (2009); John Archer, *Can Evolutionary Principles Explain Patterns of Family Violence?*, 139 PSYCHOL. BULL. 403 (2013).

127 YEHEZKEL MARGALIT, DETERMINING LEGAL PARENTAGE: BETWEEN FAMILY LAW AND CONTRACT LAW 103 n.22 (2019); Spitko, *supra* note 114, at 118–19 (arguing past caregiving is a better predicter of future caregiving).

128 Hugh LaFollette, *Licensing Parents Revisited*, 27 J. APPLIED PHIL. 327 (2010); Hugh Lafollette, *Licensing Parents*, 9 PHIL. & PUB. AFF. 182 (1980).

129 HRDY, *supra* note 118.

C Parental Rights (or Duties) from the Intrinsic Value of Genetic Parentage?

One might still believe that genetic ties are *intrinsically* valuable to parents and children. Our revealed preferences suggest we believe it.[130] Prospective parents pay exorbitant fees for fertility treatments, IVF, and gestational surrogacy.[131] Heterosexual couples who conceive rather than adopt reveal a similar preference. Many adopted or donor children desire to know about their genetic parents, which advocates argue should trump adults' desire for secrecy. Do these preferences track an objective value that could justify parental rights or duties for genetic parents?

I see two kinds of arguments to this effect in the existing literature. The first is a form of instrumental perfectionism. Genetic heritage is a valuable part of our identity, so the law should allow or require adults to raise their genetic children to promote this good for themselves and their children.[132] The second appeals to natural law or rights. Procreative parenting is a basic human good, so children and adults have a natural right to procreative families, and the state should help them realize this common good. Sections 1 and 2 argue that neither theory – even on its own terms – justifies parental rights or duties for genetic parents. This analysis also reveals that each theory relies on increasingly controversial premises about the state's authority to promote familial ideals. Accordingly, this part concludes with an external criticism that neither form of reasoning can legitimately justify legal rights for genetic parents.

1 Instrumental Perfectionism

Many people value procreative parenting because genetic heritage is part of their personal, familial, or community identity. Although "genetic essentialism" is subject to valid criticisms,[133] our genetic code is a necessary *part* of our identity. Do individuals have a right or a duty to raise their genetic children because this procreative parenting will contribute to valuable forms of personal or communal identity?

Before delving into the weeds, it is crucial to identify the straw men. The interesting assertion is not the genetic essentialist position that a person's DNA is their immutable essence. That proposition is implausible.[134] Our beliefs, experiences, and actions shape our identity. Even gene expression depends on environmental influences in

130 Margalit, *supra* note 127, at 89.

131 Saskia Hendriks et al., *The Relative Importance of Genetic Parenthood*, 39 Reprod. Biomed. Online 103 (2019) (finding patients would switch from genetic to nongenetic fertility treatments at a cost of 3,500 euros).

132 Christine Overall surveys other alleged values in biological procreation but none as plausible as genetic heritage. Christine Overall, *What Is the Value of Procreation?*, *in* Family-Making: Contemporary Ethical Challenges 89 (Françoise Baylis & Carolyn McLeod eds., 2014).

133 Leslie Bender, *Genes, Parents, and Assisted Reproductive Technologies: Mistakes, Race, Sex, and Law*, 12 Colum. J. Gender & L. 1 (2003).

134 Natural law theorists sometimes say that the information in our genetic code is part of our form, so growing up is the realization of our essence. Melissa Moschella, *The Wrongness of Third-Party Assisted Reproduction: A Natural Law Account*, 22 Christian Bioethics 104, 107 (2016).

the womb, childhood, and even adulthood. We could change portions of our genetic code without altering our identity, including large sections that have no apparent function and even some operative sections, like genes for hair color or lactose tolerance. Nevertheless, many abilities and characteristics central to our identity have genetic substrates. Some genes are necessary features of our identity, and we receive those genes from our genetic parents.

Jamie Nelson and David Velleman argue that this genetic heritage is essential to a valuable conception of human identity. According to Nelson, it contributes to our conception of narrative identity.[135] Each person's DNA is unique but not merely their own. We inherit it and pass it on. Shared genetic ties help us conceive of ourselves as part of a project extending beyond our lifetime, backward to our ancestors and forward to our progeny.[136] Many people feel deeply connected to their ancestral origins and culture, even if they only discover it as adults. Advocates for open adoption and donor conception (and critics of donor conception) argue that some children feel that they do not know themselves fully until they know their genetic heritage.[137] Barbara Woodhouse concludes that children have a right to know their identity as members of their genetic family.[138]

Velleman adds an embodied element to this narrative of intergenerational identity. Genetic inheritance is part of our identity as animal creatures.[139] It is written into our bodies. According to Velleman's surmise, being raised by genetic parents helps children come to terms with their bodies and characters. They benefit from seeing how their parents, siblings, relatives, and ancestors navigate the world with features and abilities like their own.[140] Some adopted or donor-conceived children report feeling less connected to their families because they lack distinctive physical commonalities.[141] They also describe potent emotions when they see photographs of ancestors with similar bodily features or hear stories recounting their shared abilities or interests.[142] Admittedly, culture and ideology influence which features and

135 Jamie Lindemann Nelson, *Genetic Narratives: Biology, Stories, and the Definition of the Family Essay*, 2 HEALTH MATRIX 71 (1992). Nelson also invokes notions of causal responsibility, which I discuss in Chapter 4.

136 While Nelson views genetic narratives as a bridge from an honored past to an anticipated future, others might build an identity out of discontinuity by opposing relatives they view with contempt and seeking a new start for their progeny. *See also* Velleman, *supra* note 5, at 375–77.

137 For empirical studies of the expressed desires of donor-conceived individuals and their psychological well-being, see A. Ravelingien, V. Provoost & G. Pennings, *Donor-Conceived Children Looking for Their Sperm Donor: What Do They Want to Know?*, 5 FACTS VIEWS VISION OBGYN 257, 259 (2013); Tabitha Freeman, *Gamete Donation, Information Sharing and the Best Interests of the Child: An Overview of the Psychosocial Evidence*, 33 MONASH BIOETHICS REV. 45 (2015).

138 Barbara Bennett Woodhouse, *"Are You My Mother?": Conceptualizing Children's Identity Rights in Transracial Adoptions*, 2 DUKE J. GENDER L. & POL'Y 107, 128 (1995).

139 J. DAVID VELLEMAN, BEYOND PRICE: ESSAYS ON BIRTH AND DEATH 61 (2015).

140 Velleman, *supra* note 5, at 259–60, 366–69.

141 Ravelingien, Provoost & Pennings, *supra* note 137 at 260–61.

142 Anderson believes involuntary genetic duties and associated social sanctions "help secure children's interests in having an assured place in the world, which is more firm than the will of their parents," as

abilities people believe are salient and heritable. Nevertheless, it is undeniable many people subjectively value these perceived connections.

Claims about the value of genetic heritage overlap with more controversial claims about the value of racial or ethnic community. Many communities build their identity around beliefs about biological descendance or relatedness. Some claims to sustain ancestral community seem morally pressing. Minorities who faced genocide, such as Jewish or Indigenous communities, claim a special interest in raising related children.[143] Other claims rest on empirically false, racist beliefs constructed to rationalize oppression. Americans crafted pseudobiological ideas about racial purity to sustain white supremacy.[144] Laws tied to genetic parenthood, such as strict child support or public financing of fertility treatments, may perpetuate racism by eclipsing forms of child-rearing and support crucial to communities of color, like kinship caregiving. Accordingly, many lawyers and philosophers argue we should challenge the social construction of genetic identity rather than treat the common preferences as valuable when deciding what goods children need to thrive.[145] Many are also simply unmoved by the alleged value of genetic heritage.[146]

I doubt philosophy can settle such controversies about intrinsic values. Fortunately, we do not need to settle this debate definitively. Even if genetic heritage has intrinsic value that can be disentangled from its genealogy, Nelson and Velleman do not have a sound argument for building moral or legal rights and duties from this value.

They are instrumental perfectionists about morality and law. Our moral duty is to promote whatever is intrinsically good. Adults have a moral duty and right to raise genetic children because it helps provide the adult and child with genetic heritage, which is intrinsically valuable.[147] They should not have donor-conceived children because "their children will be disadvantaged by the lack of a basic good on which most people rely in their pursuit of self-knowledge and identity formation."[148] The law, in turn, should help us realize intrinsic goods. The law can promote genetic heritage by giving legal rights to genetic parents, incentivizing genetic parenting, restricting donor conception, and maybe even requiring genetic procreation.[149]

well as tying children to networks of kinship caregiving. Elizabeth S. Anderson, *Is Women's Labor a Commodity?*, 19 PHIL. & PUB. AFF. 71, 80 (1990).

143 MARGALIT, *supra* note 127, at 125 n.88.

144 Roberts, *supra* note 12, at 258–60.

145 Carbone and Cahn, *supra* note 116 at 1025; SALLY HASLANGER, Family, Ancestry and Self: What Is the Moral Significance of Biological Ties?, *in* RESISTING REALITY: SOCIAL CONSTRUCTION AND SOCIAL CRITIQUE 158, 179–81 (2012); Heather Draper, *Why There Is No Right to Know One's Genetic Origins*, *in* PHILOSOPHICAL REFLECTIONS ON MEDICAL ETHICS 70, 72–73 (Nafsika Athanassoulis ed., 2005).

146 Overall, *supra* note 132, at 103–05; Robert Leckey, *Identity, Law, and the Right to a Dream*, 38 DALHOUSIE L.J. 525, 538–46 (2015).

147 Velleman, *supra* note 5, at 364.

148 *Id.* at 365.

149 Adeline A. Allen, *Surrogacy and Limitations to Freedom of Contract: Toward Being More Fully Human*, 41 HARV. J.L. & PUB. POL'Y 753, 794–95 (2018).

Many of the crucial moral and legal premises in these arguments are woefully underdeveloped.

Even if it is intrinsically valuable, is genetic heritage valuable enough that individuals have a prima facie moral right or duty to raise genetic children? Velleman labels it a "basic good," but his arguments can only establish that it is valuable, not that it is essential or even central. Many citizens have flourishing lives without deep ties to their genetic parents or ancestors. Genetic heritage is, at most, one prima facie good among many. It would be unwise to pursue it at a substantial cost to other goods undoubtedly central to childhood flourishing, such as being raised by loving caregivers in a supportive community.[150] Nelson and Velleman offer little evidence to assess the relative importance of genetic heritage, much less to show that it is so valuable that the balance of reasons tips toward procreative parenting in most cases.[151]

Moreover, not all children raised by their genetic parents develop a deep sense of heritage. The discourse about adoptees' "missing history" often presupposes, unrealistically, that other children develop a complete identity grounded in their true ancestry.[152] Many children know little about their ancestors, and much of what we learn from our family is fabricated. Even children raised by their parents may eventually develop different ethnic or cultural ties. Conversely, adoptive or donor parents can help their children learn about their genetic ancestry. Adoptive families also share many familial commonalities not caused by genetics. "Common upbringing, habits, [and] values" generate "identity-forming family resemblances" in language, mannerisms, and abilities, which may be as important to our identity as "biological resemblances."[153] Most societies have conceptions of "fictive kinship" to integrate nonbiological children into ancestral families and communities.

Even if genetic heritage is a significant value and best facilitated by procreative parenting, that still does not entail that genetic parentage should be sufficient for *legal* duties or rights. The inference to legal rules creates two more problems.

First, it adds another loose step in the means–ends reasoning. Simply imposing legal duties on genetic parents is unlikely to foster children's genetic heritage. And

150 Haslanger, *supra* note 145, at 168–70.

151 Appleby and Karnein, *supra* note 93, at 89–90. They also insist empirical data (not normative reasoning) must settle whether children fare better in genetic than in nongenetic families. *Id.* at 87. I worry their dedication to empiricism masks a problem akin to the one plaguing Velleman. Any empirical study using general measures of child welfare will submerge trade-offs among different values, including genetic heritage. Studies that break out dimensions of child welfare, like identity formation, find donor-conceived children in open families fare equally well on the salient measures. Susan Golombok, *Love and Truth: What Really Matters for Children Born Through Third-Party Assisted Reproduction*, 15 Child Dev. Persp. 103 (2021). However, one can draw general conclusions from disaggregated findings only by balancing effects on identity against other dimensions of welfare. Empiricism cannot end-run value pluralism.

152 Leckey, *supra* note 146.

153 Ezio Di Nucci, *IVF, Same-Sex Couples and the Value of Biological Ties*, 42 J. Med. Ethics 784 (2016).

no liberal state forces genetic parents to raise their children. It would violate adults' rights and be disastrous for children's well-being. Instead, states impose financial duties and give genetic parents the right to raise the child. Few nonmarital genetic fathers sustain deep connections with their children over time, especially if they never have physical custody and do not remain in a romantic relationship with the mother.[154] America's regime of genetic parenthood is poorly designed to foster genetic heritage. Of course, states could do more. A community dedicated to promoting genetic heritage could actively support procreative parenting with public financing.

Any such policy highlights the second problem with instrumental perfectionist arguments: their epistemic immodesty about values. A state's family policy must balance multiple values in a domain of intense and persistent disagreement. As objectivists about value, Nelson and Velleman must acknowledge that their judgment about the value of genetic heritage may be wrong. And as pluralists who recognize multiple values, they must also realize that they may have balanced or aligned the values incorrectly. It is one thing for the law to allow parents to pursue genetic families if they value them,[155] but it is quite another to design a legal system to promote genetic heritage that will sacrifice other intrinsic values for families and children. Instrumental perfectionists sensitive to the plurality of intrinsic values should be more hesitant to reach definitive moral conclusions in this uncertain domain, much less to impose their conclusions with legal coercion.

2 Natural Rights or Natural Law

Natural rights and law theorists offer a subtly different take on genetic parenthood. Instead of arguing that genetic parenthood produces valuable goods for children or parents, they insist that procreative parenting is an intrinsically valuable activity. If successful, this move would circumvent the problem of loose means–ends reasoning. To be persuasive, a natural law theory of genetic parenthood must articulate a convincing account of the unique good of procreative parenting, explain how this

[154] Marcia J. Carlson, Sara S. McLanahan & Jeanne Brooks-Gunn, *Coparenting and Nonresident Fathers' Involvement with Young Children after a Nonmarital Birth*, 45 DEMOGRAPHY 461 (2008); Joyce Y. Lee et al., *Longitudinal Relations Between Coparenting and Father Engagement in Low-Income Residential and Nonresidential Father Families*, 34 J. FAM. PSYCHOL. 226 (2020).

[155] Di Nucci argues it "would be morally reproachable for a parent to love a child less should they find out . . . that the child was not biologically tied to them" by genetics or gestation, which he claims shows that "biological ties ought not to be meaningful to the prospective parents." Di Nucci, *supra* note 153. This is a non sequitur. Once an individual accepts responsibility for a child, they have a duty to love the child as an individual independent of their characteristics – including genetic ties. This does not entail that a person choosing how to procreate ex ante might not prefer a child who shares their genetic heritage. Nor does it entail that a father may not seek genetic tests before committing to parental responsibilities. Heather Draper & Jonathan Ives, *Paternity Testing: A Poor Test of Fatherhood*, 31 J. SOC. WELFARE & FAM. L. 407, 411 (2009).

good generates a moral obligation for adults to raise their genetic children, and explain why this good and moral duty require legal rights and duties.

Some new natural law theorists link the good of procreative parenting closely to the good of heterosexual marriage, which they use to justify traditional restrictions on sexuality.[156] These arguments have been subject to thorough and well-deserved criticism.[157] Rather than rehash those criticisms, I want to consider a more limited possibility. Might parental rights and duties be grounded in the good realized when adults raise genetic children?[158]

A NATURAL RIGHTS FOR GENETIC PARENTS. Mathew Liao, a secular natural rights theorist, argues that raising our genetic children is a human right because parenthood is one aspect of "a characteristically good human life."[159] Everyone has a fundamental right to engage in the "basic activities" essential to a valuable human life, and the state must ensure everyone has adequate opportunities for these activities.[160] Procreative parenting is one such basic activity. Humans can create a new being who shares a core aspect of their identity and shape this being into their own person entitled to moral respect.[161] This project of procreative parenting has four aspects. The parent (1) creates a new being and (2) shapes that new being into (3) a distinct person who nevertheless (4) shares a core aspect of their genetic identity with the parent.

Liao's theory faces two problems that will trouble any attempt to justify genetic parenthood through an interest theory of rights. First, as Christian Barry and R.J. Leland argue, "procreative parenting" conjoins distinct activities.[162] Nearly all conceptions of a good human life recognize the value of raising a child, but many people believe this good can be realized by same-sex couples, adoptive parents, stepparents, or kin caregivers. Procreating (1 and 4) and parenting (2 and 3) are distinct activities, each of which might generate human rights on an interest theory. Why are genetic ties necessary to turn parenting into a basic activity that can ground rights? Liao offers two arguments that parenting per se is not a basic activity. Many

156 Velleman, *supra* note 5, at 370–71. John Finnis, *Marriage: A Basic and Exigent Good*, 91 MONIST 388 (2008).

157 *See, e.g.*, STEPHEN MACEDO, JUST MARRIED: SAME-SEX COUPLES, MONOGAMY, AND THE FUTURE OF MARRIAGE 38–59 (2017).

158 For a less natural law account of the same value, see CARSON STRONG, ETHICS IN REPRODUCTIVE AND PERINATAL MEDICINE: A NEW FRAMEWORK (1997).

159 LIAO, *supra* note 112, at 41.

160 *Id.* at 44, 170. *See also* Catherine Mills, *Reproductive Autonomy as Self-Making: Procreative Liberty and the Practice of Ethical Subjectivity*, 38 J. MED. PHIL. 639 (2013) (arguing positive freedom requires states to support "the capacities of individuals to adopt ways of life that accord with the reproductive choices and significant values that give meaning to their lives").

161 LIAO, *supra* note 112, at 156–57.

162 Christian Barry & R.J. Leland, *Do Parental Licensing Schemes Violate the Rights of Biological Parents?*, 94 PHIL. & PHENOMENOLOGICAL RES. 755 (2017); *see also* David Archard, S. *Matthew Liao, The Right to Be Loved*, 127 ETHICS 294 (2016).

people care deeply about procreation, going to great expense to conceive genetic children, and adoption seems like a secondary mechanism for nonideal situations when a child loses their biological parents.

Subjective preferences, even if widespread, offer weak evidence of objective value without some connection to more profound principles. Our preferences likely rest on intuitions about genetic heritage, which, as we just saw, cannot ground fundamental rights. Moreover, adoptive parents have long disputed this picture of their families as nonideal backups. Liao emphasizes his support for the valuable function of adoptive parenthood, but it cannot remove the slight implied by the position that only procreative parenting is a basic activity that justifies human rights. The theory also demotes other nonbiological routes to parentage that many people value, such as the marital presumption or donor conception. Admittedly, it is difficult to argue for intrinsic values. However, Liao wants to establish a basic right to procreative parenting that does not extend to parenting per se. Hence, he needs to identify stronger reasons for conjoining his four aspects.

In any case, Liao's theory faces a more fundamental problem. Any interest-based theory of rights appears to require a focus on the parents' interests as the rights-holder. Although Liao's overall project is to vindicate the child's right to love, his account of procreative parenting focuses on a parent's interest in shaping the life of their child.[163] This value accrues only to parents. Being shaped by one's genetic parent is not a basic good for the child. When adult and child interests are not symmetrical in this way, the adult's interests cannot justify parental authority without disrespecting the child. A devoted pianist might judge that his life is valuable only if he can shape a musical prodigy, but his interest cannot justify a claim to authority to shape a child's life. The child does not exist to serve his musical values. The child's life is their own. Similarly, adults cannot have a human right to parental authority simply because genetic parents have an interest in shaping the lives of their progeny.[164]

B NATURAL DUTIES FOR GENETIC PARENTS. Natural law theory suggests another way to infer parental *duties* from the good of procreative parenting. According to Finnis's principle of "practical reasonableness," individuals should act with the intention to realize all and only objective human goods.[165] We fall short of this ideal in three primary ways: (1) intentionally impeding the realization of objective human goods, (2) pursuing human goods in a manner inconsistent with their value, or (3) acting in ways indifferent to the realization of a human good.[166] For example,

163 LIAO, *supra* note 112, at 157.
164 James G. Dwyer, *Regulating Child Rearing in a Culturally Diverse Society*, *in* PHILOSOPHICAL FOUNDATIONS OF CHILDREN'S AND FAMILY LAW 273 (Elizabeth Brake & Lucinda Ferguson eds., 2018).
165 JOHN FINNIS, NATURAL LAW AND NATURAL RIGHTS 451 (2d ed. 2011).
166 *Id.* at 118–25, V.7.

knowledge is an objective good, so a person acts unreasonably by lying, engaging in bullshit,[167] or remaining ignorant.

Some natural law theorists use similar reasoning to oppose donor conception. Gamete donors and commissioning parents purposefully create a child with the intention to deprive the child of "the important benefits . . . of being loved and raised by their biological parents."[168] Donor conception is "incompatible with a will toward integral human well-being" because the adults are either purposefully rejecting an objective good or pursuing the good of parenthood in a manner that cannot realize its full value. Does similar reasoning entail that genetic parents must raise their children rather than pursue adoption?

Some natural law opponents of ART resist similar categorical conclusions about adoption.[169] The adoption decision is complicated. Thomists recognize a plurality of basic human goods and acknowledge that pursuing one good sometimes limits our opportunities to realize others.[170] Our duty is to adopt a harmonious life plan without arbitrary choices among goods or persons. A choice is said to be arbitrary if it is not guided by another basic good.[171] Birth parents must navigate multiple goods. They must judge (1) their ability to realize the good of procreative parenting by raising the child well, (2) other basic goods that they must forgo to raise the child, and (3) the familial good that the child could realize in an adoptive family. This adoption judgment is not a matter of calculation, whether egoist or utilitarian. It is an exercise in practical wisdom.

Sometimes, birth parents should reorient their lives to raise the child. Birth parents have an imminent opportunity to realize the good of procreative childrearing, which only they can realize for themselves and for the child.[172] While raising a child will interfere with their carefree lifestyle, it is arbitrary to forgo an objective good for a subjective preference. Parenting might also interfere with objective goods, like a meaningful career, but a person must not (so the argument would go) forgo an imminent familial good to pursue speculative goods realizable in other ways or on other occasions.[173] Sometimes, however, adoption is a reasonable choice. When birth parents are young, impoverished, or face mental health difficulties, taking on parental roles may permanently undermine the flourishing of the

167 Harry Frankfurt, On *Bullshit* (2005).

168 Melissa Moschella, *The Wrongness of Third-Party Assisted Reproduction: A Natural Law Account*, 22 Christian bioethics: Non-Ecumenical Stud. Med. Morality 104 (2016); David S. Oderberg, *Towards a Natural Law Critique of Genetic Engineering*, *in* Philosophical Reflections on Medical Ethics 109 (Nafsika Athanassoulis ed., 2005); Velleman, *supra* note 5, at 363.

169 Melissa Moschella, *Natural Law, Parental Rights and Education Policy*, 59 Am. J. Juris. 197, 208–09 (2014).

170 Finnis, *supra* note 165 at 120.

171 *Id.* at 103–10, V.2–V.5.

172 Moschella, *supra* note 63, at 426–29; Moschella, *supra* note 169 at 207–08.

173 Finnis, *supra* note 165, at 105.

parent or the child.[174] The child could have a flourishing life with an adoptive family, and the genetic parent may raise children when their life stabilizes.

The need for practical wisdom regarding adoption should cast donor conception in a different light. The adults plan to provide the child with a flourishing life, simply with a different balance of basic goods. No child's life can fully realize all the basic human goods. A parent must often judge how their child should balance different basic goods. They must decide, for instance, whether to send the child to a better school even if it interferes with their friendships. Prospective parents make similar judgments before conception. A person may choose to have kids with a musically challenged partner, even if their children will likely never realize certain aesthetic goods. Similarly, donors and intended parents forgo the good of procreative parenting to have a child who will realize other basic goods.

At most, natural law reasoning suggests that prospective parents (of all types) must consider the value of procreative parenting when choosing whether to conceive, adopt, or engage gamete donors and surrogates. Adults who choose nonbiological parenthood must also judge whether to help their children develop a relationship with their genetic relatives. Practical reasonableness does not require genetic parents to raise their progeny.

Suppose one is persuaded of the contrary position and believes that genetic parents ought to raise their children absent a strong countervailing basic good. Does that mean genetic parents must have *legal* duties or rights?[175] Must the state also restrict nonbiological parenting?

According to Finnis, law's function is to facilitate the "common good," which is the harmonious realization of both individual and collective goods.[176] Legal authority is needed to realize the common good in two ways.[177] Some basic goods could be realized in several ways, yet they can only be realized at all if most community members pursue them in the same way. Positive law offers a coordination point that serves as a *specification* of natural law. Procreative parenting has no need for legal specification. Other basic goods can in principle be realized without positive law, but they are difficult to realize without communal support through legal procedures. In such cases, positive law can *implement* natural law by (1) resolving epistemic uncertainty about who holds rights or duties, (2) clarifying how multiple rights or rights held by multiple individuals form a coherent system, or (3) providing positive and negative reinforcements to encourage individuals to pursue the good for themselves and the community. Is legal implementation pragmatically important to realize the good of procreative parenting?

174 Moschella insists genetic parents can forgo parenthood consistent with appropriate concern for the child only if they are "genuinely incompetent." Moschella, *supra* note 169, at 208–10; Moschella, *supra* note 63, at 436. I see no rationale for limiting the reasons in this fashion.

175 It is tempting to move, as does Moschella, *supra* note 168, from an individual's pursuit of the good to legal conclusions, but Finnis recognizes that legal rules require additional justifications.

176 Finnis, *supra* note 165, at 154–56, VI.8.

177 *Id.* at 281–90, X.7.

The outlines of the argument are easy to imagine. Paternity suits resolve uncertainty about who is a genetic parent. Custody petitions allocate parenting time and authority when both genetic parents want to raise their child but not together. If a genetic parent shirks parental responsibilities, child support law penalizes their failure and, in the process, buttresses social norms of parental responsibility.[178] The state should also directly support procreative parenting as part of its duty to serve the common good for parents and children. Not only should genetic parenthood be a ground for legal duties and rights, but states might actively encourage procreative parenting by offering subsidies for children or financing for fertility treatments or birth-related leave.[179]

Many of these "natural law" arguments shift toward instrumental reasoning, in which case they face challenges like those described in previous sections. In any case, even if they offer a sound rationale for genetic parenthood, none of them require a legal prohibition on nonbiological parenting. A state can promote the basic good of procreative parenting without coercively limiting the familial lives of other citizens who disagree about the value of genetic ties. Moreover, natural law theorists have good reason to refrain from such coercion because they recognize that many kinds of families can realize basic human goods for children and their caregivers.

* * *

Insofar as genetic heritage or procreative parenting are intrinsically valuable aspects of human life, individuals should consider this value when deciding whether to conceive genetic children and, having done so, whether to parent the child. However, this does not entail that genetic parents must adopt parental roles or that the state must restrict parenthood to genetic parents. Deriving the right from the good is a tricky business, even within a teleological moral theory. Even on their own terms, the perfectionist, natural rights, and natural law arguments cannot justify a conclusion that genetic ties are sufficient or necessary for parental rights or duties.

From an external perspective, this survey of genetic theories reveals a progressively worsening flaw. Perfectionist theories assume the state may encourage family forms that public officials (or theorists) judge valuable, and natural law theories purport to authorize coercion of citizens into these family forms. Yet, many citizens reject their ideals of genetic heritage or procreative parenting. Many reasonable citizens form their families through adoption, assisted reproduction, or kinship networks. A parentage regime steeped in perfectionist or natural law reasoning is likely to deny these families equal freedom to live by their judgments about valuable family

178 Scott Altman, *A Theory of Child Support*, 17 INT'L J. L. POL'Y & FAM. 173 (2003). I doubt child support encourages derelict parents to fulfill their role in ways that realize the procreative good, as opposed to encouraging a social vision of fatherhood as primarily financial.

179 Some natural law theorists might believe that procreative parenting is sufficiently valuable to restrict contraception or abortion (independent of arguments about fetal life). However, these laws damage obvious countervailing basic human goods like bodily integrity, and it is unlikely that coerced procreation will lead parents or children to realize familial goods.

ties. Even if the regime permits nonbiological parenthood, designing the legal regime to promote genetic heritage or procreative parenting denies equal respect to citizens who value nonbiological families.[180]

Teleological theories of genetic parenthood disrespect children too, even if their arguments are often framed in child-centric language. Adults' interests in genetic heritage or procreative parenting cannot justify a basic liberty right to be parents without treating children as subordinate to their genetic parents. If a child develops a different conception of the familial good, they can rightly accuse the state of using their childhood to facilitate a set of comprehensive genetic values that they – along with many reasonable citizens – reject. Adults cannot have a fundamental right to raise their progeny grounded directly in the basic interests of the adults. That does not mean, however, that a liberal-egalitarian state cannot protect genetic parents' liberty to raise their children.

III GENETICS IN A POLITICAL CONCEPTION OF PARENTAGE

The constitutional rights of genetic parents can be justified as a derived liberty right. Citizens enjoys a "derived liberty" if their freedom to act or not arises from the limits of legitimate reasons for law (as opposed to a list of interests of the person sufficiently fundamental to impose duties on others). Using a Kantian principle of equal liberty, I will argue that citizens should be free to pursue their procreative parenting projects insofar as those projects are consistent with equal liberty for the child and for other adults. If the state supports caregiving and maintains redistributive mechanisms, and if genetic parents maintain a commitment to fulfill parental roles, genetic parents should be free to raise their children.

One preliminary note. For most of this part of the present chapter, I assume the interests of the genetic mother and father align. Until Chapter 4 explains how gestation affects parental rights and duties, we cannot assess conflicts between genetic, genetic-gestational, and gestational parents.

A *Genetic Parentage as a Derived Liberty Right*

Norvin Richards has argued that genetic parental rights can be justified as derived liberty rights using Mill's harm principle.[181] Genetic parents do not harm anyone by bringing a child into the world. As long as their child-rearing does not harm the child, no consequentialist reasons exist to interfere with

180 Baker, *supra* note 10, at 2063 (arguing the DNA default "marginalizes" nongenetic families).

181 Norvin Richards, The Ethics of Parenthood 22–24 (2010); Giulia Cavaliere & César Palacios-González, *Lesbian Motherhood and Mitochondrial Replacement Techniques: Reproductive Freedom and Genetic Kinship*, 44 J. Med. Ethics 835, 838–39 (2018) (arguing a Millean harm principle justifies allowing mitochondrial replacement techniques for women at risk of mtDNA diseases and for lesbian couples who want a genetic tie to both parents).

their project to conceive and raise children. Genetic parenting may have some "negative effects," but whatever "negative effects parenting has in the normal cases are all of kinds that cannot be taken seriously, if the right to be at liberty is to have any significant content." Our "children suffer some range of [minor] mishaps, we provoke disapproval in those who would act differently, we contribute to the sometimes very deep disappointment of those who would want to adopt . . . , and there are others who might do a better job as parents than we would," but these are not "harms" that could justify interfering with the liberty of genetic parents.

Whatever its merits in general, Mill's harm principle has no place in parentage law. Applying it here misunderstands the nature of parenthood and, as a result, sets the wrong moral baseline. The harm principle justifies a space of derived liberty for self-regarding conduct. If an individual's conduct does not set back anyone else's interests, and if an individual is likely to judge their own interests better than others, then there are no sound consequentialist reasons for interfering with their liberty. The liberty to parent (for genetic parents or others) cannot be justified in this manner. Parents purport to create duties for their children and compel them to fulfill those duties. Parents insist third parties may not interfere as they use coercion to shape the child's life. Parenthood is anything but self-regarding, which makes *harm* entirely the wrong baseline.

Nevertheless, we can construct a sound argument for a derived liberty to engage in procreative parenting if we turn to the more complex liberty principle sketched in Chapter 1. Individuals should be free to pursue their ends, so long as those ends can be part of a system of law that enables everyone to enjoy equal liberty and respect. A community treats its members with equal respect only if it ensures everyone has a fair opportunity to make and act on their own judgments. This equal liberty principle can justify fundamental liberties like free expression, private rights like contracts, and the demands of distributive justice. Applying this principle to procreative child-rearing, individuals should be permitted to raise their genetic children unless restrictions on this liberty are necessary to ensure equal liberty or respect for children (Section B) or other adults (Section C).

B *Genetic Parentage and Equal Respect for Children*

The primary limits on genetic parents' liberty derive from the demands of respect for children as equal citizens. A legal system committed to equal respect cannot allow genetic parents to wield custodial authority over a child in a way that might deny the child a fair share of primary goods. Children's political entitlements, not some personal conception of harm or welfare, must set the moral baseline for evaluating any claim to parental liberty.

1 Genetic Parentage Conditional on Prompt Fulfillment of Parental Roles

A child can have no abstract objection to the default rule that allows genetic parents to choose to be the child's initial legal parent. Every infant is entitled to an adequate parent, not to any specific parent.[182] However, the genetic parent's custodial liberty must be subject to the same substantive conditions that restrict all parental rights. As I argued in Chapter 1, parental rights – genetic or otherwise – must be contingent on the adequate performance of parental functions. As an equal member of the community, each child is entitled to an intimate caregiver who will meet their material and relational needs and will guide them toward a flourishing childhood. Any community that allows a genetic parent to have custody when they cannot or will not fulfill this parental function denies the child's status as an equal citizen. All just legal systems must include some monitoring to ensure biological parents care for their children adequately.

The community must also demand that genetic parents demonstrate their commitment to parenthood promptly. An infant has a right to care immediately. The first months and years of caregiving are formative. The child will develop attachments with whoever provides their care, and continuity in this intimate relationship is essential to development. Children develop a right to a stable relationship with anyone who rightly occupies parental roles.[183] A legal system that afforded genetic parents an indefinite opportunity to pursue parenthood would violate its duty to ensure children have relational primary goods. To retain their liberty to raise the child, a genetic parent must prepare to raise the child during the pregnancy and assume a caregiving role before the child forms parental attachments with other rightful caregivers. Otherwise, the genetic parent must forfeit their liberty to be a parent.

To implement this abstract conditional liberty in law, officials must specify the substantive norms, design a procedure, and apply it in each case. If the legal rules rest content with an abstract standard – as has American constitutional law – some adjudicator will be required to assess the genetic parent's reasons for the delay and the depth of the child's bonds with their caregiver. Both assessments involve scalar facts and values, likely with vague thresholds. Courts may err in either direction. Some courts have removed four-year-old children from adoptive parents when the genetic father is faultless.[184] Others have approved infant adoptions even though the birth mother hid the pregnancy from the genetic father.[185]

States have methods to cabin this judicial discretion. To limit the time, they can enact paternity registries and a statute of limitations on paternity challenges. They could try to specify what counts as sufficient notice of the pregnancy and birth. Of course, these statutes would not eliminate the necessity of judgment. Instead, they

[182] *See* 1.II.B. Full proof of this claim awaits demonstration that a child has no claim right to be raised by causal procreators (Chapter 3) or gestational parents (Chapter 4).

[183] Children's right to a stable caregiver is defined and justified in 4.II.A.

[184] Meyer, *supra* note 18.

[185] Beck, *supra* note 56.

shift who exercises discretion and how they do so. To design the rules, legislators must imagine a prototypical parentage contest and judge how much time genetic parents need to learn about the child and commit to parenthood, considering typical reasons for delay and timelines for child development. Legislators must also judge what quality and quantity of infant caregiving is sufficient to maintain the liberty. So long as public officials make these judgments with public reasons, I have no moral reason to quarrel with which officials define the lines or precisely where each state draws its lines.

However, there is one pervasive mistake in this area of law. The promptness condition on genetic liberty should apply even if the child has only one other legal parent. Most statutes of limitation apply only if (1) the birth mother seeks second-parent adoption or (2) the child has another competing presumed or acknowledged parent. Unless the child has a potential "substitute" parent, a genetic parent can file a petition for paternity and visitation anytime during the child's minority. This rule is an unjustified remnant of the gendered "rule of two."[186] The ideological notion that each child is entitled to a mother and father morphed into an assumption that each child needs two parents. Nothing in the political conception of parenthood supports this conclusion.[187] Everyone has two genetic parents, but that does not entail that every child needs two legal parents. Giving dilatory genetic parents an indefinite right to return can disrupt a child's life with their single parent. Instead, the community should offer material support to single parents and protect their right to sole legal custody.[188]

2 Genetic Parentage Must Be Offset by Redistributive Mechanisms

The child cannot claim they were entitled to any specific parent, but might they object to the genetic parentage rule because another adult could have provided them with a better life? As I argued in 1.II.B.2.a, a child is not entitled to the best available parent. They are entitled to an adequate parent as defined by the community's judgment about what children need for a flourishing childhood and to develop into adults capable of living by their own judgment. Among the class of adequate parents, a liberal state cannot legitimately rank the value of the life that each parent may offer the child.

Even if a child cannot claim they were entitled to a "better" parent, they may still object to the *systemic effects* of the genetic parentage lottery. Following Dworkin,

186 Susan Frelich Appleton, *Parents by the Numbers*, 37 Hofstra L. Rev. 11 (2008).

187 *See* 1.II.B.2.b (justifications for limiting the number of parents). States also resist cutting ties with dilatory genetic parents because they mistakenly conflate parentage with causal duties of child support. Federal laws that effectively force states to allow mothers to seek child support indefinitely, Clark v. Jeter, 486 U.S. 456, 465 (1988), seem to imply that fathers should have an indefinite opportunity to decide whether to pursue parental rights.

188 Nancy E. Dowd, In Defense of Single-Parent Families 130–42 (1999). As I will argue in 3.II.A.4, causal parents can have a horizontal duty to support a custodial caregiver.

many liberal political philosophers worried about reconciling distributive justice with the inequality that results from their talents (and their market value) for which individuals are not responsible. Even if some portion of talent is genetic, the development of our abilities also depends on our parents' caregiving, economic assets, and social status. A community may allow genetic parents to raise their progeny while treating citizens as equals only if it also maintains redistributive mechanisms to offset this parentage lottery.

It is important not to oversell this point as a deep objection to genetic parenthood. The parentage lottery is one among many kinds of brute luck built into the basic structure. Everyone is born into social and legal structures that enhance or inhibit their life prospects. The legal rules for assigning parents are like rules for assigning elementary schools or fixing school funding. Furthermore, any parentage rule – genetic, gestational, adoptive, or otherwise – will have distributional effects. Caregivers will always have different strengths and economic resources. One might surmise that genetic parentage magnifies intergenerational inequality, but if people could become legal parents only through adoption, adoptive parents would still pass inequality to their adopted children. The United States does not adequately redress the distributive injustices arising from parenthood, but the fault does not lie with the genetic default per se.

3 Genetic Parentage Does Not Require Ex Ante Licensing

While every just state must ensure parents provide adequate care, the United States generally trusts biological parents with only sporadic oversight. Some philosophers have argued that states should do more *before* trusting a genetic parent to raise their child. Hugh LaFollette famously argued that our deference to genetic parents exposes children to an excessive risk of harm.[189] States investigate prospective adoptive parents to protect children, so they should adopt a similar parenting license to screen and train genetic parents to improve parenting quality. Does respect for children's status as equals *require* such parental licensing?

While LaFollette's parenting "licenses" created a splash, the licensure requirement was not truly radical. Parenthood has always been a state license. Birth parents need not apply for a parenting card, but the law determines who may parent a child, defines parents' exclusive privileges and authority, and conditions custody on adequate parenting subject to state oversight. Lafollette's real objection is that the current licensing regime in the United States – biological criteria for assigning parentage and only sporadic oversight through schools and doctors – is insufficient to ensure quality parenting. The radical aspect of his proposal is that the law should empower officials to screen and withhold parenting licenses *before birth*.

[189] Lafollette, *supra* note 128.

Ex ante parental licensing is not required for equal respect for children. Proponents of parenting licensure often compare parenting to other "dangerous activities" that require a license, such as driving. However, a state that allowed anyone to drive without a license would not be unjust, so long as the law still policed risky driving and compensated injured drivers. It would only be unjust if the law allowed people to continue driving with a history of recklessness (e.g., drunk driving) or with conditions that create excessive risks (e.g., blindness). A law that allows these drivers to impose these asymmetric risks on others demonstrates inadequate regard for their victims. By analogy, a state would fail to treat a child with equal regard if it allowed a genetic parent to retain custody despite a track record of unfitness and without adequate monitoring. Whether the law should screen parents before or after they take custody is a pragmatic question about the extent of the risks and the benefits and drawbacks of each form of monitoring. [190]

LaFollette's instrumental argument for ex ante licensure rests on three components. The first is an empirical assertion that biological parenthood (genetic or gestational) is a poor proxy for parenting quality, worse than other identifiable facts. The second is skepticism about formal rules. Since biology is an imperfect proxy, we could improve the assignment of parenthood by adding an ad hoc process to consider specific evidence about each parent. The last component is a preference for ex ante over inter se regulation. LaFollette seems to prefer ex ante interventions that seek to prevent injuries before they occur rather than either inter se monitoring to handle risks as they arise or ex post efforts to intervene only once harm arises.

The objections to ad hoc, ex ante screening are well rehearsed.[191] The procedure would be effective only if sociologists could identify reliable predictors of parenting quality and administrators would evaluate those indicators accurately. Neither is likely. It is difficult to imagine criteria of likely parenting quality that are not classist or sexist, such as an adult's level of education, availability for personal childcare, or caregiving motivation. Historically, technocratic efforts to identify "good" parents simply masked racist, classist, and ableist judgments.[192] Even if scientists could identify legitimate predictive factors, it is difficult to imagine officials administering

[190] Liao attempts to reject this argument categorically. He argues that states may not demand parents pass an ex ante competence test to obtain a parenting license, because if one has a freedom to parent only if one proves one will parent well, then one is not free at all. Matthew Liao, *Rightholding, Demandingness of Love, and Parental Licensing*, 94 PHIL. & PHENOMENOLOGICAL RES. 762, 768 (2017). By analogy, we would not have freedom of movement if we had to prove we would not trespass before we could move about. Even if Liao is right that parents have a fundamental right to parent, his argument against licensing gives inadequate weight to the need to harmonize that right with equal rights for the child. Ex post compensation for wrongdoing is sufficient to respect rights like property, but respect for the child's rights might require ex ante screening and inter se monitoring if there is a high likelihood that inadequate parenting will cause irreparable harm. That possibility cannot be ruled out a priori.

[191] Liam Shields, *Parental Licensing as Harm Reduction*, 28 HEALTH CARE ANALYSIS 424 (2020); PEG TITTLE, SHOULD PARENTS BE LICENSED?: DEBATING THE ISSUES (2004).

[192] Shields, *supra* note 191.

these standards accurately and fairly. Our child welfare system is systemically racist and classist, even when social workers and judges respond only to reported abuse and neglect.[193]

For similar reasons, LaFollette's more recent article opts for a mixed system: formal parentage rules and limited screening only for documented neglect or abuse. In the end, LaFollette lands not far from our current system. The primary difference is that officials would screen all birth parents for past abuse systemically rather than react haphazardly to reporting by healthcare or social workers about risky parents or potential abuse or neglect. Limited but universal screening might prevent some cases of neglect and avoid some arbitrary enforcement in our current system. Our current system of ad hoc reporting tends to target poor and minority birth mothers, scapegoating victims of distributive injustice rather than supporting their efforts to raise their children.[194] On the other hand, systematic screening might expand the dragnet, extending counterproductive penalties to all prospective and current parents. Even if screening were limited to adults previously charged with abuse, it would magnify the effects of past racial injustice in the child welfare system.

The community must ensure all children have able and willing parents, but its regulatory tools must also respect the equal status of the parents. It is difficult to imagine a legal system that protects children's rights without some ex ante and inter se monitoring of parents, but reform efforts would be better spent reimagining ways to support parents while protecting children, without threatening or punishing the adult victims of distributive injustice.[195]

4 Genetic Parentage Does Not Violate Liberal Neutrality

I argued above that the state fails to treat children and nonbiological families as equals if it designs parentage law to promote genetic heritage or procreative parenting. Yet, in this liberal system that I am reconstructing, the law respects adults' liberty to raise their genetic children *because* some reasonable citizens value genetic heritage or procreative parenting. The result is similar: parentage law facilitates the interests of adults at some cost to the interests of children. Furthermore, the community is not merely trading off independent interests. The genetic parent's project is to shape their child. They will use their coercive authority to encourage the child to adopt values, like genetic heritage or artistic excellence, not shared by all reasonable people. If it is illegitimate

193 Dorothy Roberts, Torn Apart: How the Child Welfare System Destroys Black Families – and How Abolition Can Build a Safer World (2022).

194 *Id.* Dorothy E. Roberts, Shattered Bonds: The Color of Child Welfare (2002).

195 Austin argues the state should screen parents for narrow factors that increase the likelihood of abuse or neglect, but rather than using the factors to prohibit parenting, the state would only monitor at-risk parents and offer additional support. Michael W. Austin, Conceptions of Parenthood: Ethics and the Family 94 (2016). Given our current system, it doubtful that this system would be effective or avoid the existing discrimination.

for the state to design parentage law to facilitate values like genetic heritage, why can the law empower a private person to pursue their own values through parenting without violating equal respect for the child?

This objection replicates two mistakes discussed in 1.II.C: the overstated liberal objection to shaping and the overstated priority of children's interests. First, shaping children is inescapable. No one can raise a child as a blank slate. If public officials raised children, they would still have to judge which comprehensive values would guide the child's life. The choice to raise the child to value strong genetic ties is not qualitatively different from a choice to raise the child to value aesthetics or philosophy. Second, this objection unjustly privileges children's interests. Parentage law should enable adults to pursue their own parenting projects, so long as this is consistent with children's status as *equal* members of the community. Equal respect does not require that we design children's law in ignorance of adult interests. No members of the community – including children – are entitled to a system of law that privileges their interests above all others. A genetic parent may have a liberty right to raise their child so long as they fulfill the child's right to a parent. From within the political conception of justice, an adult who wants to raise a child as part of their artistic household is no different from an adult who wants to raise a child as part of a biological family.

* * *

So long as the state conditions genetic parentage on prompt and adequate performance of parental roles and limits the distributive consequences of the parentage lottery, the law may afford genetic parents a liberty to raise their child consistent with equal respect for children.

C *Genetic Parentage and Equal Respect for Other Adults*

This brings us to the other half of the equal liberty question. Chapter 5 argues that all adults should have legal avenues to raise children even without being biological parents. However, this general liberty to parent cannot connect any particular adult with any particular child. Genetic ties allocate the initial liberty to raise a child. Is it consistent with equal liberty to give this initial liberty to genetic parents rather than others who might want to raise the child?

1 Liberty to Conceive and Raise Children

First, would any other adult have sufficient reason to demand that a couple refrain from raising their genetic child? Before the couple conceives the child, no one else has a claim to prevent them from using their own DNA to pursue this procreative project. An environmentalist might believe the couple should adopt rather than procreate, but they have no basis to demand the couple comply with their ethical judgments about procreation, nature, and future generations.[196] Once the child is born, no one else has a claim to take the child to raise themselves. A philanthropist might want to offer the child a "better" life, but they have no basis to demand that the genetic parents step aside so they can raise the child as they would prefer. No one has a right to insist that others refrain from pursuing their project to conceive and raise a genetic child.

This liberty to conceive and raise a child brings us closer to the contemporary genetic parenthood regime, but not all the way. A person has a "liberty" (a Hohfeldian "privilege") if they have no duty to refrain from the action. A liberty is not nothing, but it is not much. When I am at liberty to grab a coin off the ground, you can still snatch the coin first without wronging me.[197] The conclusion that each adult has a liberty to pursue their procreative parenting projects is essential, but it is still incomplete. Contemporary law affords genetic parents more than a mere liberty.

2 Claim Not to Procreate and Claim to Raise One's Genetic Progeny

The next step is to establish that the claim to *exclusive* use of one's DNA to create and raise a child is consistent with equal liberty. Both moral claims – a claim right not to procreate and a liberty right to raise one's genetic children – should also be part of a system of equal familial liberty.[198] It is helpful to begin with the jural opposites. Might others have a liberty to use our DNA to produce a child to raise themselves?

Most nonconsensual procreation will involve some other rights violation. I argued in II.A.3 that a community dedicated to equal respect could not allow a rapist's wrongdoing to generate parental rights, especially not over their victim. But what if someone collects skin cells that another person sheds on the street and uses them to create a child? This nonconsensual procreative project would not violate the genetic

196 Individual procreative liberty might have systemic consequences that threaten others' liberty, in which case the community may structure procreative liberty to ensure a system of equal liberty for all. For instance, if limits on population growth are necessary to prevent catastrophic climate change, then states might have legitimate authority to reduce procreation through incentives or perhaps coercion.

197 Glanville Williams, *The Concept of Legal Liberty*, 56 Colum. L. Rev. 1129, 1143 (1956).

198 The following argument is a deontological version of Professor Glenn Cohen's consequentialist argument for a right not to procreate. I. Glenn Cohen, *The Right Not to Be a Genetic Parent*, 81 S. Cal. L. Rev. 1115, 1153–58 (2007). Standard law and economics analysis suggests a right should be allocated initially to whoever values it most or, if that is costly to determine, whoever faces lower transaction costs to transfer the right should others value it more. Cohen argues both principles favor giving each person an initial right to control the use of their DNA for procreation. The welfare loss to a genetic parent who desires to avoid unwanted parenthood likely outweighs the welfare benefit to intended parents who desire to use their DNA but could easily find another donor. If that assumption is not true, then the intended parents should be able to buy the donor's DNA with low transaction costs. By contrast, if everyone started with an entitlement to use anyone else's DNA to procreate, the people who prefer not to procreate would not be able to negotiate with everyone else to buy back their entitlement. The only way to avoid unwanted procreation would be to engage in costly self-protective measures to avoid shedding DNA. Thus, a right not to procreate will likely increase overall social welfare. I have no quarrel with this as welfarist analysis, except its welfarism.

parent's right to bodily integrity. Yet, I suspect that most people feel they should have a claim to prevent others from using their genetic code in this way to create a child.[199] I also suspect that many would also feel, as did the Manyukans, that they have a right to raise the resulting child.

Imagine a society in which everyone has a liberty to use anyone else's DNA without their consent and a liberty to raise the resulting child.[200] When Mark discards a cup, Jim may grab it and use Mark's DNA to create a child to raise himself. Jim's choices determine the future of Mark's genetic family. If Mark believes that genetic parents have no duty to their children and genetic ties have little value, he will be untroubled by the possibility that Jim (or anyone else) is raising his genetic child.[201] However, we saw in II.C that many reasonable citizens conceive of themselves as members of families whose identity and duties extend across generations. If Mark does value genetic heritage, he will regard Jim's actions as a deep intrusion into his ability to shape his own familial life. This legal regime makes it extremely difficult for Mark to pursue his conception of the good life – difficult, but not impossible. No one can take DNA from Mark's body without violating his bodily integrity. He could try to control his genetic family heritage by guarding his body to avoid shedding DNA.

The world without a right not to procreate is structurally akin to the world without property rights described in 1.I.B.3 through the potter example. No one could pry an object from our hands without violating our bodily integrity, but they could permissibly take objects we need the moment we set them down. We might be able to survive in this world, but each person's ability to pursue permissible projects is subject to others' whims. Similarly, Mark's ability to pursue his valued genetic family is subject to other people's choices. Must his choices be subject to theirs? Is there any legitimate reason for a community *not* to give each person authority to decide how their DNA is used to create children, so that citizens who value genetic heritage can

199 Davis v. Davis, 842 S.W.2d 588, 603 (Tenn. 1992).

200 Americans do not need a hypothetical example. White Americans denied enslaved persons the right to decide whether to procreate by raping women and separating families. The difficulty with this real-life example is that the violation of slave's moral personhood was so pervasive that isolating its effect on familial liberty is difficult. Nevertheless, some abolitionists believed that violations of family integrity were one of slavery's core evils and that empowering formerly enslaved people to marry and form families was central to recognizing their personhood. FREDERICK DOUGLAS, MY BONDAGE AND MY FREEDOM, chs. II, III (1855), www.gutenberg.org/ebooks/202; JACQUELINE JONES, LABOR OF LOVE, LABOR OF SORROW (2010).

201 Cohen concludes the right not to have a genetic child is not terribly important. Glenn Cohen, *The Constitution and the Rights Not to Procreate*, 60 STAN. L. REV. 1135, 1164–65 (2007). He believes we want to control our genes to avoid "attributional parenthood," which is the emotional distress that an adult experiences if they, the child, or society believes they are not fulfilling parental duties. Cohen, *supra* note 198, at 1136–37. Cohen is being led astray by his subjective welfarism. *Id.* at 1139, 1154. Feelings of loss or guilt indicate the underlying intrinsic value or moral failing – their significance is not reducible to the subjective feeling. If I defame someone who is extremely self-assured, I still wrong them even if they do not feel psychological distress at the injury to their reputation.

pursue their familial projects without taking the drastic measure of constantly guarding their genetic material?

Someone might argue that giving genetic parents the right not to procreate limits procreative liberty for others. Denying Jim access to Mark's DNA does limit Jim's ability to procreate. However, this limitation of Jim's liberty violates a commitment to equal liberty only if it is necessary for Jim to use Mark's genetic code to have a family.[202] That is unlikely to ever be the case. The law can empower citizens to donate gametes and waive their parental liberty because genetic parents are not obligated to raise their genetic children.[203] If too few people donate voluntarily, intended parents or states can pay for gametes. States should also offer preconception agreements and parentage agreements at birth.[204] Parentage law can enable all citizens to enjoy familial liberty *without* a privilege to use others' DNA without their consent. The state can protect the ability of some citizens to pursue genetic heritage or procreative parenting while offering equal procreative and familial liberty to other citizens who want nonbiological families. The right not to procreate and a conditional liberty right to raise one's genetic children are consistent with equal liberty.

One final objection in this vein is worth considering. Some scholars argue that genetic parentage rules marginalize other family forms. Kathy Baker concludes that "the DNA default inevitably edifies a two-parent heterosexual family and diminishes any family structure not mimicking that ideal" because it is "[r]ooted . . . in genetic essentialism, exclusion, and heteronormativity."[205] I agree that existing legal rhetoric valorizes heterosexuality and marriage. In *Lehr*, the Supreme Court waxes on about how the "intangible fibers" of genetic parenthood "are woven through the fabric of society, providing it with strength, beauty, and flexibility."[206]

However, if officials avoided such blatant violations of public reason and appealed instead only to a derived liberty right, the genetic default itself would not be disrespectful. Admittedly, nongenetic families must jump through an additional hoop. They must obtain legal consent from the genetic parents before using their gametes or adopting a child. However, this consent rule does not rest on a public valorization of heterosexual families or belittlement of other family forms. It is necessary to enable citizens who value genetic heritage to pursue their conception of a valuable family. It "edifies" heterosexual family ideals only in the sense that citizens who value this form of family (or who value genetic ties in other family

202 It may be tempting to argue that Jim is using Mark as a mere means to his ends, in violation of Kant's Formula of Humanity. This objection begs the question, as Cohen has argued. Jim's choice to use Mark's genetic code treats Mark as a mere means only if Mark's personhood is tied to his genetic code, which is precisely what needs establishing. Cohen, *supra* note 198, at 1150. Instead of relying on Kant's doctrine of virtue, this chapter offers a juridical argument that the right not to procreate is a corollary of equal liberty to pursue family.

203 Why this waiver is consistent with the procreators' *causal* duty is explained in 3.II.B.2.

204 *See* 5.III.C and 5.III.D.

205 Baker, *supra* note 10, at 2063–64.

206 Lehr v. Robertson, 463 U.S. 248, 256.

forms) may pursue it. As a derived right, the genetic default protects citizens' liberty to build families they value. Laws that enable citizens to pursue reasonable conceptions of valuable families cannot be regarded as unjustly stigmatizing or marginalizing.[207] A liberal state has no legitimate reasons to deny genetic parents an exclusive right to control who uses their genetic code to procreate or a liberty right to raise their progeny.

3 Genetic Paternity Can Be Consistent with the Rights of Gestational Parents

The foregoing argument for genetic parentage as a derived right is crucially incomplete because it assumes away conflicts between birth mothers and fathers. Suppose a genetic-gestational parent does not want to share parenthood with a mere genetic parent. What additional conditions must be placed on the liberty rights of genetic parents to ensure they remain consistent with equal respect and liberty for the gestational mother? The full answer to this question must await the analysis in Chapter 4 about how gestation and childbirth might ground parental liberties. In the meantime, I want to allay one concern about genetic rights: a person's right to decide how their genetic code is used for procreation does not entail a right to control women's bodies.

To get some distance from ideological fights, consider first the ART cases involving fertility clinic negligence or gamete theft. Suppose that a person donates ova to a clinic for personal use in IVF. This person retains a right to decide how the clinic uses the ova to create zygotes. Once the clinic creates zygotes, the donor retains a right to prevent anyone else from using them. If the clinic ships the zygotes to another lab, the genetic parent should be entitled to an injunction prohibiting the second lab from allowing other people to use the embryos. Similarly, if a male donates sperm to a sperm bank for use by his partner, and a third party steals the sperm, the male should have a right to stop this person from using the sperm for artificial insemination.[208]

The moral situation changes once the gametes are inside another person. After insemination with sperm or implantation of an embryo, the mere genetic parents can have no further right to control procreation without compromising the bodily integrity of the pregnant person.[209] They have no right to demand that she use her body to create a child for them or end the pregnancy so they can avoid genetic

207 Critics may also argue that allowing adults to pursue genetic families perpetuates racism because the genetic ideals of parenthood evolved to serve racist conceptions of white supremacy. However, the genetic ideals discussed in III.C are not inherently racist, and genetic parentage cuts across socially constructed racial identifications. I suspect the better legal targets are the legal and social norms that hinder recognition of multiracial families and identities. Onwuachi-Willig, *supra* note 15, at 264, 271–76.

208 Sally Sheldon, *"Sperm Bandits," Birth Control Fraud and the Battle of the Sexes*, 21 Legal Stud. 460 (2001).

209 Planned Parenthood v. Danforth, 428 U.S. 52, 71 (1976).

parentage. The gestational parent's innate right to bodily integrity trumps the genetic parents' derived liberty right not to procreate.[210] Similarly, a male who engages in heterosexual intercourse loses any further right to control reproduction. He had a claim right to control whether his genetic code was used to create a child (i.e., everyone else had a duty not to use his sperm), but he exercised that control when he chose to engage in heterosexual vaginal intercourse. Only the pregnant person now has authority to decide whether to use emergency contraception, obtain an abortion, or carry the child to term.

These reproductive rights do not entail that genetic parents also lose their conditional parental liberty. After the birth, the gestational parent's bodily integrity is no longer at stake. A law that recognizes the genetic parent's liberty to raise an infant does not interfere with the birth parent's bodily integrity. It will, of course, limit the gestational parent's liberty to raise the child.[211] Does that deny equal respect to the gestational parent? We have returned to the second question raised by the Manukyan case. We need to know whether the work of gestation and childbirth generates claim rights that must extinguish genetic parents' derived and conditional parental liberty.

That question is investigated in 4.III.C, so I will only preview the conclusion here. The work of pregnancy and childbirth justifies a conditional liberty right. A gestational parent should have an opportunity to commit to parenthood so long as they obtain the gametes with a liberty to use them for their own procreative project. If they want to raise the child, the gestational parent should be a presumed parent. Perhaps they should also have a custody preference. However, gestational work does not justify full parental rights at birth that require extinguishing the genetic parent's conditional liberty, denying them any opportunity to parent the child.[212] All biological parents should have an opportunity to commit to parenthood.[213] If they do, they have a right to custody, but the extent of the custody will depend on their ability to coparent cooperatively.

* * *

The law can allow genetic parents to have the initial liberty to raise their children consistent with equal liberty and respect for the child and other adults. A genetic

[210] Cohen considers the possibility that "bodily integrity is a more 'important' kind of interest … than that of compelled genetic parenthood," which might justify a "meta-rule" among fundamental liberty rights in which the right not to be a gestational parent has lexical priority over the right not to be a genetic parent. Cohen, *supra* note 201, at 1163. While I reject the weighing of interests, an equal liberty approach provides the missing argument for this priority. Bodily integrity is a basic liberty (what Kant called an innate right), while the liberty to parent is a derived liberty that the law must specify to render it consistent with bodily integrity.

[211] Kathy Baker notes that current law forces the gestational parents to retain their parental status. Baker, *supra* note 10, at 2061. However, a causal parent (gestational or genetic) should have only a limited duty to support another's and the community's efforts to raise the child (2.II.B and 2.III.A–2.III.B); child support does not force gestational parents to raise the child, any more it forces men to be fathers.

[212] Blecher-Prigat, *supra* note 54, at 173 n.283.

[213] *Id.* at 159.

default can respect children if the state ensures genetic parents promptly provide adequate parenting and limits the distributional effects of the genetic parentage lottery (III.B). This initial assignment of parenthood respects equal liberty for other adults, who cannot have a claim to insist genetic parents refrain from procreation or a claim to create a child using another's genetic code to raise themselves (III.C). Finally, I will argue in Chapter 4 that the law can recognize genetic parents' liberty to fulfill parental roles consistent with equal liberty and respect for the gestational parent.

CONCLUSION

Genetic ties remain central to American parentage law. The strongest genetic laws are simply unjustified. Under the influence of federal welfare law, many states treat genetic paternity as sufficient for parentage, unless there is a competing presumption or the father is a sperm donor. No plausible moral principles justify treating genetic parentage as sufficient for full parenthood. The natural affections argument is contingent and speculative, and a state cannot legitimately design parentage to prioritize genetic heritage or procreative parenting.

Nevertheless, a liberal conception of parentage can justify a set of limited rights for genetic parents that are consistent with existing constitutional law. The Constitution protects the liberty of genetic parents to fulfill parental roles and thereby acquire full parental rights. This conditional right to be a parent is justifiable as a derived liberty right. Each citizen has equal freedom to pursue their vision of the valuable family only if each has a claim to decide whether a child is created from their DNA and a liberty right to raise their genetic children. Within the proper legal context, this initial liberty of genetic parents is consistent with equal respect for the child and other adults. The court appropriately allowed the Manukyans to parent their genetic child, although we have yet to consider whether A.P. should also have had a right to parent the child.

3

Parents by Procreation

At the age of thirty-four, Ricci Jones gave birth to a daughter whom she conceived during a two-week affair with Nathaniel J., who was then fifteen.[1] After convicting Ricci of "unlawful sexual intercourse with a minor," the district attorney turned around to sue Nathaniel for child support and welfare reimbursement. The court of appeals held that Nathaniel owed child support despite Ricci's conviction for statutory rape. Although Ricci was not permitted to argue that Nathaniel consented to sex because he was a minor, Nathaniel was "not an innocent victim of Ricci's criminal acts." Nathaniel "decided" to have sexual intercourse "[a]fter discussing the matter" with Ricci, so he bore responsibility for the child.

Although every American court to hear a similar case has reached the same result, many legal scholars find this result deeply troubling.[2] The law seems to say that Ricci committed a crime because Nathaniel was incapable of voluntarily consenting to sexual acts, yet Nathaniel owes child support because he voluntarily engaged in sexual acts that created a child. While I have little to say about the former claim, this chapter investigates the latter claim that individuals who are causally responsible for children have parental duties.

A causal theory of parenthood was central in the history of child support law, appearing in the common law under Blackstone and in the first child support statutes.[3] In the last few decades, courts leveraged causal arguments to extend support obligations and rights to lesbian coparents. Causal theories of parenthood were also central in the history of philosophy, espoused by philosophers as distinct as

[1] Cty. of San Luis Obispo v. Nathaniel J., 57 Cal. Rptr. 2d 843 (Ct. App. 1996).

[2] Ruth Jones, *Inequality from Gender-Neutral Laws: Why Must Male Victims of Statutory Rape Pay Child Support for Children Resulting from Their Victimization*, 36 GA. L. REV. 411, 418 (2001); Ellen London, *A Critique of the Strict Liability Standard for Determining Child Support in Cases of Male Victims of Sexual Assault and Statutory Rape*, 152 U. PA. L. REV. 1957 (2004); Michael J. Higdon, *Fatherhood by Conscription: Nonconsensual Insemination and the Duty of Child Support*, 46 GA. L. REV. 407 (2011).

[3] 1 WILLIAM BLACKSTONE, COMMENTARIES *435.

Kant and Sedgwick.[4] Few contemporary family law theorists take causal parentage seriously,[5] but it remains prominent in ethics. Several ethicists argue that causal parents have a duty to fulfill parental roles and, perhaps, a right to be parents.[6] Others argue that causal parents have a weaker duty to ensure the child has a valuable life, which they can satisfy by raising the child themselves or ensuring someone else raises the child.[7]

Causal theories of parenthood rest on a principle familiar to law: if an individual's voluntary act places another person at risk of harm, the individual incurs a special duty to the victim to prevent the harm. An adult whose voluntary acts cause a child to exist incurs a duty to the child to ensure that they receive the care they need.[8] Not only does the causal theory appeal to a persuasive principle, but it offers a neat corrective for genetic theories of parenthood. Many of the counterexamples to a genetic theory, such as conception by rape or gamete theft, are cases where parental duties seem unfair because the genetic parent did nothing to create the child. A causal theory also seems able to explain procreative parentage without sexual intercourse or genetic ties. An intended parent who encourages their partner to conceive with donor gametes incurs parental duties because their voluntary acts helped cause the child to exist. Some courts have surmised that genetic ties are a proxy for causation.[9]

Despite its apparent potential, causal parentage can offer only a tiny piece of the parentage puzzle. As Part II explains, causal parents incur genuine duties to the child because they are morally responsible for placing the child in a situation where the child will suffer without consistent emotional and physical caregiving. However, causal parents are not moral parents in the full sense for three reasons: causal duties cannot justify parental rights, are too weak to justify parental duties, and are held by

4 Immanuel Kant, *The Metaphysics of Morals, in* PRACTICAL PHILOSOPHY, AK 6:280, at 429 (Mary J. Gregor ed., 1999); HENRY SIDGWICK, THE METHODS OF ETHICS 249 (7th ed. 1981).

5 *But see* Donald C. Hubin, *Daddy Dilemmas: Untangling the Puzzles of Paternity*, 13 CORNELL J.L. & PUB. POL'Y 29, 65 (2003); Katharine K. Baker, *Bionormativity and the Construction of Parenthood*, 42 GA. L. REV. 649, 664 (2007).

6 BERNARD G. PRUSAK, PARENTAL OBLIGATIONS AND BIOETHICS: THE DUTIES OF A CREATOR 15–23 (2013) (procreators have a "prima facia, all-things-considered" obligation to "provide in person, support, warmth and affection during the child's minority and beyond – that is, to develop a loving parent–child relationship"); Lindsey Porter, *Why and How to Prefer a Causal Account of Parenthood*, 45 J. SOC. PHIL. 182 (2014) (causal parents, which she calls "makers," have a "pro tanto obligation to take on parental roles"); Michael Chobli, *Procreation Generates Parental Rights, in* Procreation, Parenthood, and Educational Rights: Ethical and Philosophical Issues 15, 28–29 (Jaime Ahlberg & Michael Chobli eds., 2017).

7 Jeffrey Blustein, *Procreation and Parental Responsibility*, 28 J. SOC. PHIL. 79 (1997); David Archard, *The Obligations and Responsibilities of Parenthood, in* PROCREATION AND PARENTHOOD: THE ETHICS OF BEARING AND REARING CHILDREN 103, 117 (David Archard & David Benatar eds., 2010); Giuliana Fuscaldo, *Genetic Ties: Are They Morally Binding?*, 20 BIOETHICS 64, 74–75 (2006).

8 Jamie Lindemann Nelson, *Parental Obligations and the Ethics of Surrogacy: A Causal Perspective*, 5 PUB. AFF. Q. 49 (1991); Archard, *supra* note 7, at 115–16; Daniel Callahan, *Bioethics and Fatherhood*, 1992 UTAH L. REV. 735.

9 Cty. of Los Angeles v. Christopher W., 41 Cal. App. 5th 827, 833 (2019).

too many actors who are not moral parents. Nevertheless, as I explain in Part III, causal parentage offers limited help with one core question for political parentage. As a matter of distributive justice, a community may fairly place part of the cost of child-rearing on individuals responsible for creating the child.

I CAUSATION IN PARENTAGE LAW

Causal theories of parenthood played a prominent role in rationalizing child support obligations, both in historical and modern law. While causation appears less frequently in legal justifications for parental rights, courts have leveraged causal arguments to expand parental duties and rights to nonbiological intended parents, including lesbian couples.

A *Causal Theory and Child Support Duties for Natural Parents*

The causal theory of parental duties has deep historical roots. Blackstone, citing Pufendorf, offers a causal justification for the parent's moral duty of support:

> The duty of parents to provide for the *maintenance* of their children is … an obligation … laid on them not only by nature herself, but by their own proper act, in bringing them into the world: for they would be in the highest manner injurious to their issue, if they only gave the children life, that they might afterwards see them perish. By begetting them therefore they have entered into a voluntary obligation, to endeavour, as far as in them lies, that the life which they have bestowed shall be supported and preserved. And thus the children will have a perfect *right* of receiving maintenance from their parents.[10]

The early English and American child support obligations were quite limited. Parents were required to pay only for minimal necessities, and the suit could be brought only by public officials, not the child or custodian. In the nineteenth century, American judges began creating common law causes of action that allowed any custodial parent to sue for support. By the twentieth century, every state had passed a private child support statute.[11]

Courts interpreting and defending these statutes invoked the traditional causal justifications. As one court explained, the statute "adding legal sanction to the parent's natural and moral obligation is an … exercise of the state's police power to compel those who are responsible for the child's existence to bear the burden of

[10] BLACKSTONE, *supra* note 3, at *435.

[11] Donna Schuele, *Origins and Developments of the Law of Parental Child Support*, 27 J. FAM. L. 807, 809–15 (1988); Daniel L. Hatcher, *Child Support Harming Children: Subordinating the Best Interests of Children to the Fiscal Interests of the State*, 42 WAKE FOREST L. REV. 1029, 283–84 (2007); Leslie Joan Harris, *The Basis for Legal Parentage and the Clash Between Custody and Child Support*, 42 IND. L. REV.611, 617 (2009).

the expense that its existence necessitates."[12] The state compels unmarried fathers to "contribute to the child's support and maintenance, thus relieving others upon whom otherwise the burden might chance to fall."[13] While contemporary courts are less likely to invoke natural duties, the causal justification persists. In 2019, a California appellate court wrote:

> A parent's duty to support his or her child is based in part on the state's interest in seeing that the child does not become a public charge, and the policy that those who are directly responsible for the child's existence should ordinarily bear the burden of support. Thus, a man who freely engages in an act which results in the conception and birth of a child is held responsible for the consequences of that act.[14]

While most judges recognize that child support duties should arise only from "free" or "voluntary" acts, few are sufficiently careful about the underlying notion of voluntariness. The sexual acts must be voluntary, but the law does not care about the actor's intentions or precautions regarding procreation. Sexual procreators owe child support even if they used multiple methods of contraception and intended to avoid conception.[15] A person can even owe child support if their sexual partner lied about taking contraception or about having had a vasectomy or tubal ligation.[16] To justify this rule, courts sometimes invoke tort law notions of presumed intent. For instance, one court reasoned that anyone who purposefully engages in sex is "deemed to have intended the natural consequences of his action."[17] Of course, pregnancy is hardly the "natural consequence" of sexual activity after a tubal ligation. Despite this rhetoric about presumed consent, parentage law does not care about sexual procreators' intentions or precautions. Accordingly, scholars often discuss child support law as "strict liability" for heterosexual intercourse.[18]

The scope of the causal parent's enforceable duties is limited. Courts describe parental obligations broadly, including the duty to love, guide, and raise the child.[19] Yet, no states enforce those parental duties. Coerced love might be a contradiction. Coerced child-rearing would likely be detrimental for the child. Moreover, coerced parenting raises concerns about involuntary servitude. Contract law invokes similar reasons to deny specific performance in service contracts, but family law further constricts the remedy for breach of parental duties. Family law will not award damages for a breach of parental obligations. A child cannot sue an absent parent for harm caused by their absence. Americans take this result for granted, but it was

12 McLain v. Meadows, 186 P. 411, 411–12 (Cal. Ct. App. 1919).
13 Schuele, *supra* note 11, at 836.
14 *Cty. of Los Angeles*, 41 Cal. App. 5th at 833 (internal citations and quotes omitted).
15 Jill E. Evans, *In Search of Paternal Equity: A Father's Right to Pursue a Claim of Misrepresentation of Fertility*, 36 Loy. U. Chi. L.J. 1045, 1074 (2004).
16 L. Pamela P. v. Frank S., 449 N.E.2d 713 (N.Y. 1983).
17 Kristine M. v. David P., 135 Cal. App. 4th 783, 790 (2006).
18 London, *supra* note 2, at 1958; Blustein, *supra* note 7.
19 *In re* Adoption of Lybbert, 453 P.2d 650, 652–53 (Wash. 1969).

not inevitable. Israel allows a child to sue their absent genetic parent in tort for emotional damages.[20] In the United States, a causal parent's only enforceable duty is economic support.

How does the state determine how much financial support a parent owes? Historical nonsupport actions allowed officials to sue relatives for reimbursement of pauper support. Statutory reforms gave family courts discretion to award custodial parents whatever support was "'suitable,' 'just,' 'reasonable,' 'proper,' 'fit,' 'sufficient,' or 'necessary.'"[21] Despite this aspirational language, support awards were sporadic and minimal. Courts remained "quick to note that [the father] was liable only for absolute necessities."[22] Judges showed little interest in the actual costs of raising a child and even less interest in sustaining a child's expected standard of living or in protecting maternal welfare.

Dissatisfied with the miserly and inconsistent awards, Congress required states to establish child support formulas in the 1980s. Rather than try to define a set of necessities, all states require noncustodial parents to share a percentage of their income with the child. States fix the percentage, ranging from 17 to 30 percent, based on what intact families with similar income typically spend. These percentages far exceed the modest share set in most European countries, where awards remain around 10 percent to "ensure a basic level of support from the absent parent."[23] Most American states exempt a small amount of income for the basic needs of impoverished obligors, and they tailor off the percentage for high-income obligors. They will also typically reduce the award if the obligor has shared custody, on the assumption that the obligor pays for the child's expenses while in their custody. Support awards terminate when a child turns eighteen, but courts may extend them if the child has disabilities and cannot support themselves.[24]

What does the parent's obligation to share their income mean in practice? When the obligor has income, a child support award can contribute significantly to a child's well-being. Among low-income custodial parents, child support awards represent 45 percent of their household income.[25] Wealthy obligors pay substantially more than their child needs in any objective sense.[26] At the other end of the income spectrum, impoverished obligors pay only a nominal amount that offers little

[20] *See* Benjamin Shmueli, *Love and the Law, Children Against Mothers and Fathers: Or, What's Love Got to Do with It?*, 17 Duke J. Gender L.& Gender 131, 157–60 (2010) (discussing CA 2034/98 Amin v. Amin [1999] [Isr.]).

[21] *L. Pamela P.*, 449 N.E.2d at 715; Schuele, *supra* note 11, at 835.

[22] Schuele, *supra* note 11, at 836.

[23] John Eekelaar, *Child Support as Distributive and Commutative Justice*, *in* Child Support: The Next Frontier 151, 153 (Marygold Shire Melli & J. Thomas Oldham eds., 2000).

[24] Yost v. Yost, 2003-Ohio-3754, at ¶ 10 (Ohio Ct. App.).

[25] Off. Child Support Enforcement, Annual Report to Congress FY 2013 (2016), www.acf.hhs.gov/sites/default/files/documents/ocse/fy2013_part_1_narrative_and_national_performance.pdf (last visited Mar 8, 2024).

[26] Dep't of Revenue v. Mason M., 790 N.E.2d 671, 675 (Mass. 2003) (goal to allow children to enjoy their parents' higher standard of living, above mere subsistence).

benefit to the child. Some states even take these payments as reimbursement for welfare given to the custodial parent. Even if the award is small, it can lock the noncustodial parent in a cycle of poverty because the arrears will accumulate and cannot be discharged in bankruptcy. Courts try to coerce payment by revoking the parent's driving license or sending them to prison for civil contempt, exacerbating the cycle.

B *Causal Theory as a Basis for Duties and Rights for Nonbiological Parents*

In a series of pivotal California cases, causal duties played a crucial role in expanding parentage to nonbiological intended parents. In the 1968 case *People v. Sorenson*, the California Supreme Court held that a husband owed child support for a child conceived with donor sperm. "[U]nable to accomplish his objective of creating a child by using his own semen, [the husband] purchase[d] semen from a donor and use[d] it to inseminate his wife to achieve his purpose."[27] He incurred "an obligation of supporting those for whose existence he is directly responsible" because "without [his] active participation and consent the child would not have been procreated."[28]

Courts still find this deliberate causation theory persuasive in artificial insemination cases. In 2003, the Supreme Court of Illinois reasoned:

> The allegations demonstrate a deliberate course of conduct with the precise goal of causing the birth of these children .... [I]f an unmarried man who biologically causes conception through sexual relations without the premeditated intent of birth is legally obligated to support a child, then the equivalent resulting birth of a child caused by the deliberate conduct of artificial insemination should receive the same treatment in the eyes of the law. Regardless of the method of conception, a child is born in need of support.[29]

Many states have statutes with similar language making a spouse a parent if they "consent" to artificial insemination using donor sperm.[30] Although these statutes use the term "consent," the concept of consent captures the relevant idea poorly.[31] These spouses help cause the child to exist by supporting and planning artificial insemination with their wives. While *Sorensen* emphasized the act of insemination to draw a parallel with conception by intercourse, the underlying point in all these cases is that the nonbiological parent helped cause the existence of a child.

Twenty-five years after *Sorensen*, its causal theory formed the backbone of a groundbreaking surrogacy opinion, *Johnson v. Calvert*. Unlike the prior cases that used causation to establish duties, *Johnson* tries to use causation to assign

27 People v. Sorensen, 437 P.2d 495, 500 (Cal. 1968).

28 *Id.* at 499.

29 *In re* Parentage of M.J., 787 N.E.2d 144, 152 (Ill. 2003) (citations omitted).

30 *See* Chapters 1 (political conception) and 5 (agreements).

31 Causal and contractual arguments are not exclusive, and some courts invoke both. *See* Levin v. Levin, 645 N.E.2d 601, 604–05 (Ind. 1994).

relative priority for parental rights. Anna Johnson entered a gestational surrogacy contract to carry a zygote created with Crispina Calvert's egg and Mark Calvert's sperm. When their relationship deteriorated, each woman sought a declaration of legal maternity. The California Supreme Court determined that the parentage statute recognized gestation and genetics as independent grounds of maternity but offered "no clear legislative preference."[32] The court chose Crispina but foreswore the two obvious rationales: the surrogacy contract was enforceable or genetics trumped gestation.

Instead, *Johnson* invoked a causal theory. Crispina and Mark were the child's legal parents because, "but for their acted-on intention, the child would not exist." Although Anna's "gestational function was also necessary to bring about the child's birth," the Calverts would not have allowed Anna to implant their zygote if she had "manifested her own intent to be the child's mother." For support, the court turned to academic scholarship, quoting Professor Lawrence Hill at length. Hill argued that "while all of the players in the procreative arrangement are necessary in bringing a child into the world, the child would not have been born but for the efforts of the intended parents .... [T]he intended parents are the first cause, or the prime movers, of the procreative relationship."[33] The court drew upon "similar" quotes from Professor Marjorie Shultz and Andrea Stumpf that blended intent with causation.[34]

The court's argument is obviously missing a premise. A counterfactual theory of causation cannot distinguish between intended, genetic, and gestational parents, all of whom are necessary. The Johnsons acted first, but as tort and criminal law have long recognized, being the first actor in a chain of events does not make one the sole cause or the most important cause. As I discuss in II.B.3, the law can distinguish among these many causal parents only with a more discerning conception of actual causation or some additional principles of proximate causation.

Regardless, *Johnson*'s causal theory remained a useful tool. Although Crispina was both an intended and genetic mother, similar reasoning allowed courts to expand maternity to intended mothers *without biological ties* to the child. Courts found this novel step easier because the first such cases harkened back to the roots of the causal theory: imposing child support on adults trying to shirk responsibility.[35] In the

32 Johnson v. Calvert, 5 Cal. 4th 84, 92 (1993).

33 *Id.* at 94. (citing John Lawrence Hill, *What Does It Mean to Be a "Parent"? The Claims of Biology as the Basis for Parental Rights*, 66 N.Y.U. L. Rev. 353, 415 (1991)).

34 *Id.* at 92 (quoting Marjorie Maguire Shultz, *Reproductive Technology and Intent-Based Parenthood: An Opportunity for Gender Neutrality*, 1990 Wis. L. Rev. 297, 309 (bargained-for intentions should fix parentage because "reproductive technology 'dramatically extend affirmative intentionality. ... Steps can be taken to bring into being a child who would not otherwise have existed.'"); Andrea E. Stumpf, *Redefining Mother: A Legal Matrix for New Reproductive Technologies*, 96 Yale L.J. 187, 196 (1986) ("[t]he mental concept of the child is a controlling factor of its creation, and the originators of that concept merit full credit as conceivers")).

35 *See In re* Marriage of Buzzanca, 61 Cal. App. 4th 1410, 1423, 1425–26 (Cal. Ct. App. 1998) (using causal theory to impose duties on intended nonbiological mother who tried to avoid gestational surrogacy agreement).

seminal case *Elisa B. v. Superior Court*, the California Supreme Court used causal reasoning to impose child support duties on a lesbian coparent.[36] Elisa encouraged her partner Emily to conceive a child through artificial insemination. They coparented the child for years. Although this apparently satisfied the statutory residential presumption, Elisa tried to avoid child support by arguing she was neither a genetic nor gestational mother. The court refused to allow Elisa to rebut the presumption because she had "actively participated in causing the children to be conceived with the understanding that she would raise the children as her own."

Family scholars often interpret the residential presumption as a functional parentage rule, but the court regarded its causal reasoning as necessary. A caregiver could rebut the residential presumption if he "voluntarily provides support for a child who was conceived before he met the mother" because "the Legislature surely did not intend to punish [him] … by transforming that act of kindness into a legal obligation." In contrast, Elisa "acted together with the birth mother to cause the child to be conceived." Elisa could not rebut the presumption because the "Legislature would have intended to impose upon the presumed father or mother the legal obligation to support the child whom she caused to be born."

C *Problematic Legal Applications of Causal Theory to Biological Parents*

A handful of courts have held that genetic fathers owe child support even if the birth mother conceived the child by raping him while he was unconscious.[37] These cases are inconsistent with a causal theory (not to mention sexist). The unconscious genetic father performed *no act* that could give rise to duties, much less a voluntary one. Such cases generally do not refer to the father's responsibility. Instead, they assert that the innocent child should not be denied support because of the mother's alleged wrongdoing.

Closer to the fold, but still troubling, are sperm theft cases. A few courts have held that a man owes child support even if the birth mother inseminated herself with sperm that she retained after oral sex or retrieved from his discarded condom.[38] In these cases, the genetic father is a cause of the child's existence. His voluntary sexual act led to ejaculation, a necessary condition for the child's birth. However, imposing parental duties in these cases violates principles of proximate causation that delimit moral responsibility, as I discuss in II.B.

The last class of problematic child support cases involves statutory rape. Courts uniformly impose child support obligations on male victims of statutory rape as

36 Elisa B. v. Superior Ct., 37 Cal. 4th 108, 124 (2005).

37 S.F. v. State *ex rel.* T.M., 695 So. 2d 1186, 1189 (Ala. Civ. App. 1996); *In re* Paternity of Derek S.H., 642 N.W.2d 645 (Wis. Ct. App. Feb. 26, 2002).

38 State v. Frisard, 694 So. 2d 1032, 1035 (La. Ct. App. 1997); Phillips v. Irons, No. 1-03-2992, 2005 WL 4694579, at *1 (Ill. App. Ct. Feb. 22, 2005) (a tort claim seeking damages, rather than a challenge to paternity); Peter v. Gibson, 477 S.W.3d 402 (Tex. Ct. App. 2015) (discussed in Dov Fox, *Reproductive Negligence*, 117 Colum. L. Rev. 149 (2017)).

young as fourteen.[39] Some argue that these teenage boys voluntarily engaged in sexual intercourse to create this child who needs support. These assertions appear to conflict with the criminal law's premise that minors are incapable of consenting to sex. Faced with this incongruity, courts insist that the needs of the innocent newborn take precedence over the financial interests of the not-quite-innocent teenager. This argument is particularly galling in cases like *Nathaniel J.*, where the state is suing for reimbursement of welfare payments, so the payments offer no benefit to the infant.[40]

These three cases reveal a mistaken understanding of the relationship between causal duties and distributive justice. These courts perceive, but misunderstand, the distributive justification for child support. America has chosen to place the cost of meeting children's needs on the adults who create children. The courts correctly conclude that children cannot be denied these basic goods simply because one procreator acted wrongfully. That does not mean, however, that the community can justly shift the cost of meeting the child's need onto the *involuntary* procreator.[41] I discuss these distributive implications in III.C.

II CAUSATION AND MORAL PARENTHOOD

Causal parenthood is a viable ground for personal duties to children, but those duties are too limited to ground parenthood. Moreover, causal parenthood cannot generate personal parental rights of any kind. Section A describes the limited causal duties of procreators, while Section B explains why causal parenthood cannot directly ground the full set of parental duties or rights.

A *The Personal Duties of Causal Parents*

Causal theories of parental duties rest on a "causation of peril" principle that is familiar to tort law.[42] If an agent's voluntary act places another at imminent risk of serious harm, then the agent has an affirmative duty to take reasonable measures to prevent this risk from resulting in injury. Tort and criminal law focus on holding actors liable when their failure to rescue causes harm, but the creation of risk is the trigger for this affirmative duty – as it might be for parentage. Anyone whose voluntary act contributes to bringing a child into existence incurs a duty to the child to ensure they receive the care and support they need for a valuable life.

39 Higdon, *supra* note 2, at 423–26.
40 *Id.* at 425; Hatcher, *supra* note 11, at 1037.
41 L. Pamela P. v. Frank S., 449 N.E.2d 713, 715 (N.Y. 1983) (arguing wrongdoing among parents does not affect duties to the child).
42 Restatement (Third) of Torts: Liability for Physical and Emotional Harm § 39 (Am. Law Inst. 2010).

1 Causation of Peril as a Ground for Affirmative Duties

Despite its settled legal status, the causation of peril principle is rarely subject to thorough philosophical analysis.[43] The following hypothetical will help illustrate and clarify causal duties. I refer back to it throughout the chapter.

> **Drowning Rescue**: Barry was walking down a pier when he stumbled on a loose board and knocked Carrie into the ocean. Dylan takes advantage of the commotion to deliberately push Evelyn off the pier. Felicia was fishing when she saw Carrie and Evelyn fall into the water.

All three people on the pier ought to help the drowning victims. Felicia's duty of beneficence includes a duty to help the drowning victims. I will assume, somewhat controversially, that everyone has an imperfect duty to help others in need merely by virtue of the victim's value as a fellow person. Beneficence may be a weak moral duty, but it is a duty, nonetheless.

Dylan and Barry have an additional, special duty to their respective victims. By his wrongful push, Dylan incurs a duty to Evelyn to rescue her from the peril he caused. He wronged Evelyn by pushing her in, and if he culpably omits to save her from drowning, he wrongs her again.[44]

Dylan's duty to rescue is qualitatively distinct from a duty of beneficence, as shown by two distinctive features. First, it is a "special" duty. Only Dylan (not the others) owes this duty to Evelyn, and Dylan owes this duty only to Evelyn (not to Carrie). By contrast, a principle of benevolence gives everyone an equal duty to rescue Evelyn and Carrie. Second, Dylan's duty correlates with Evelyn's claim to his assistance. Evelyn may demand Dylan save her at substantial risk to his well-being. Moreover, he is not at liberty to choose to save Carrie instead. Evelyn has no similar claim against a bystander like Felicia. Bystanders may balance their imperfect duty to rescue against other duties, the risk to themselves, and other comparably valuable ends. Felicia may choose to save Carrie because they are fishing buddies or may forgo saving anyone because she is a weak swimmer.

Some ethicists might deny that Barry has a special duty to Carrie, thinking his situation is akin to Felicia's. He was innocently walking on the pier, just like she was innocently fishing. One might insist that an agent incurs a duty to rescue only if their act that created the risk was wrongful. According to this view, the duty to rescue is an instance of the duty to mitigate harm caused by prior wrongful acts. Dylan committed culpable wrongdoing by shoving Evelyn. He must pay damages if she develops hypothermia, but he ought to pull her out to prevent the injury in the first place. Barry, in contrast, did nothing culpable. His stumble was an innocent accident. If

43 For an exception, see Larry Alexander, *Duties to Act Triggered by Creation of the Peril: Easy Cases, Puzzling Cases, and Complex Culpability*, *in* The Ethics and Law of Omissions 180 (Dana Kay Nelkin & Samuel C. Rickless eds., 2017).

44 Larry Alexander & Kimberly Kessler Ferzan, Reflections on Crime and Culpability: Problems and Puzzles 69 (2018).

Carrie hit her head on the way over the rails, Barry should not have to compensate her for the stitches. Given that Barry has no duty to repair this harm caused by his innocent act, it may seem strange that he has a duty to mitigate harm caused by his innocent act.

In contrast, I and the authors of the Third Restatement of Torts think Barry has a special duty to aid Carrie. Compare Barry's relationship to the two victims. He played no role in creating Evelyn's peril. Barry and Felicia are equally bystanders of Evelyn's predicament. In contrast, Barry's conduct caused Carrie's peril. Admittedly, walking on the pier is reasonable, but it does carry some risks, as parents of young children know. Before Barry stumbled, he had no reason to believe his stroll posed any special risk to Carrie. Things change when he bumps her into the water. Once he knows his conduct has created a risk of grave harm, he must manage this risk. Barry's duty to rescue is an instance of the duty to act with reasonable care, considering all the circumstances that an actor knows or should know about.

The following variant may help illustrate why Barry incurs this duty to Carrie:

> As Barry* is walking up the pier, he notices a loose board behind Carrie*. On his way back down the pier, Barry* forgets about the board, trips, and knocks Carrie* into the water.

Once aware of the loose board, Barry* should increase his estimate of the risk that he will stumble on the pier. The general duty of care requires Barry* to remember and avoid the broken board. Similarly, once Barry is aware that he has bumped Carrie, he knows his walk creates more danger than usual. Barry's duty of ordinary care requires him to manage the heightened risk of this walk. Morality and law do not hold Barry responsible for the stumble but for his response afterward. He had no reasonable opportunity to prevent Carrie from hitting her head, but he has an opportunity to save her from drowning. Innocent causers of peril have an affirmative duty to take reasonable steps to mitigate the danger they create.[45]

2 Causation of Peril Justifies Duties for Causal Parents

Causation of peril principles generate special duties for procreators. Anyone who knows a child needs care should help because of the general duty of beneficence, but

[45] As Kim Ferzan pointed out, a fact-relativist about wrongs would insist that whether Barry wronged Carrie depends on the objective facts, while his evidence affects only his culpability, but I agree with Alexander that our permission to act in ways that create risks is belief-relative because risk is an epistemic concept. Larry Alexander, *Recklessness, Agent-Relative Prerogatives, and Latent Obligations: Does Belief-Relativity Trump Fact-Relativity with Respect to Our Rights?*, 51 PHILOSOPHIA 2639 (2023). Culpability for creating the risk might matter in other ways. Actors who create peril purposefully or recklessly may incur more stringent rescue obligations, which might require greater efforts during the rescue or raise the standards of justification or excuse. *See* ALEXANDER & FERZAN, *supra* note 44 at 75–79 (developing a sophisticated analysis of conditions for culpable omission).

the people whose voluntary acts foreseeably caused this child to exist have a special duty to the child.[46] Had they not created a child, the child would not be at risk of deprivation. It is as if they intentionally or accidentally bumped the child off a pier.[47] The causal parent incurs a special duty regardless of their intentions or culpability regarding the risk of procreation.[48] Even adults who have sex using all reasonable contraceptive methods still incur an affirmative duty to the resulting child.[49]

What precisely is the procreator obligated to do? Anyone who creates a risk of harm has a duty to take reasonable steps to remove the peril they created. The peril they create fixes the content of their duty. Dylan must take reasonable steps to save Evelyn from drowning. He need not fix all her life problems. Sometimes it is challenging to specify the relevant baseline to distinguish harms from benefits, but some baseline is necessary to distinguish the special duty to rescue from the general duty of beneficence.

Archard offers a sensible first pass at specifying the baseline for the peril that procreators create for a child. Because they created a "vulnerable human being who will suffer harm, and most probably die, without the care that only adults can provide," the causal parent incurs a "duty to rescue the child from its helpless condition by the provision of care and protection."[50] They must try to ensure the child has a "life worth living" until the child is old enough to assume responsibility for their own care.[51]

46 Michael W. Austin, Conceptions of Parenthood: Ethics and The Family 40 (2016).

47 Archard, *supra* note 7, at 117; J. David Velleman, Beyond Price: Essays on Birth and Death 104–05 (2015). In an attempt to distinguish these cases, Archard argues that a driver who hits a pedestrian incurs a duty from the "direct production of the risked harm," but the causal parent acquires a duty from "performance of the risky action and a failure to take further steps to avoid" harm. No viable moral or metaphysical distinction could mark this direct/indirect boundary. Both parent and driver create a risk and incur a duty to manage it. Perhaps it would clarify the intuitions to imagine that the pedestrian, like the child, is not yet physically injured. Suppose to avoid the car, the pedestrian jumped off a bridge into the ocean. Now the driver, like the parent, breaches their causal duty only if they omit to act to prevent harm.

48 Blustein, *supra* note 7, at 85.

49 In her "Hazmat Theory" of parenthood, Weinberg argues we incur parental responsibilities because we "control" our gametes, and if "we do things that put our gametes at risk of joining with others and growing into persons, we assume the costs (and rewards) of that risky activity." Rivka Weinberg, The Risk of a Lifetime: How, When, and Why Procreation May Be Permissible 60–61 (2016). Focusing on the risk of procreation rather than the peril to infants has counterintuitive implications. Like a tort theory focused on risks rather than harms, Weinberg's theory has an air of duties floating in the ether. Tort or criminal law could be modified to treat risk creation as sufficient for wrongdoing. A speeding driver disrespects everyone in the vicinity exposed to risk, even if no one is hurt. However, this assumes specific people are risked. It makes less sense to say parental responsibilities attach whenever an adult *risks* procreation. The creation of a child seems necessary for parental duties.

50 Archard, *supra* note 7, at 111.

51 *Id.* at 115–18. This counterfactual formulation threatens a deadly difficulty. Conception is a necessary condition of everything that happens to a child. Procreators expose their children to all of life's risks. Benatar argues that all procreators wrong their children because they expose the child to a substantial risk that their life will not be worth living overall. David Benatar, Better Never to Have Been: The Harm of Coming into Existence (2008). It is tempting to respond that procreators benefit the child by bringing them into existence, but this would set too low a baseline. If a painful and short life is better than not existing at all, then procreators owe children next to nothing. On the other hand, it is not

Causal parents can fulfill this duty to the child by raising the child personally or taking reasonable steps to ensure the child has an adequate caregiver.

In most circumstances, procreators are not required to raise the child personally. This limit on the duty naturally follows from causation of peril principles. Causal duties are outcome-oriented. The agent is obligated to try to reduce the risk of injury they created, but if the peril to the victim subsides for other reasons, so does their duty.[52] Return to the pier example. Circumstances dictate what Barry must do to save Carrie from drowning. If Barry is the only person around, maybe he should jump in the water. If Carrie falls into the water next to a kayaker who pulls her out, Barry is off the hook. The phrase "duty to rescue" is misleading. Barry's duty is not to rescue Carrie. He must take steps reasonably likely to prevent her from drowning.

Analogously, causal parents must take reasonable steps to ensure their child receives care. The law can justly punish birth parents who abandon infants where no one can find them. What further actions the causal parents must take will depend on contingent factual circumstances. The most important contextual facts include the availability of substitute caregivers and the level of social support for children.[53] Once a reliable caregiver is meeting the child's relational and generic needs, the peril to the child created by the causal parent diminishes.

On the other hand, if the child is unlikely to receive adequate care or material support, the only course of action reasonably likely to give the child an adequate life might be for the causal parent to raise the child themselves.[54] Onora O'Neill recounts the story of Jean-Jacques Rousseau and Thérèse Le Vasseur, who left five

clear that antinatalists can articulate a baseline that renders their conclusion coherent. *See* Sarah Hannan, Samantha Brennan & Richard Vernon, Permissible Progeny?: The Morality of Procreation and Parenting (2015). To decide that *being brought into existence* harms the child, one must compare the net value of life for this existent person with the net value of nonexistence – but in the counterfactual world where they are never born, there is no thing for which nonexistence has positive or negative value for purposes of comparison. Fortunately, our exploration of causal parenthood can bypass this metaphysical problem. Suppose Benatar is correct that procreation creates an unreasonable risk that a child will have a negative life. This shows procreators act culpably. Yet not all procreation will end with a completed wrong. The child might end up with a wonderful life. We must still ask what morality demands that procreators do to manage the risk to the child. I do not see why the only reasonable course of action is for procreators to shoulder personal responsibility for everything that subsequently happens to the child – any more than the only reasonable way for procreators to manage the risk that a child will not be raised adequately is to personally raise them. Regardless of where one sets the baseline (at an adequate or worthwhile life), the causal duty requires managing the risk, not personally preventing it.

52 Alexander, *supra* note 43, at 188.

53 Greater culpability *regarding conception* may generate more stringent duties to ensure a child receives care, but as Amanda Porter has argued, even purposeful procreation cannot transform the causal duty into a duty to parent personally. Porter, *supra* note 6. Culpable risk creation would increase the *stringency* of a duty to rescue without altering its content. Dylan's deliberate shove does not turn his duty to rescue into a duty to improve Evelyn's life. A woman who purposefully conceives a child but places the child for adoption has not wronged the child, so long as she ensures the child receives a loving parent. For a contrary contractarian argument, see Weinberg, *supra* note 49 at 176–77, 222–23.

54 Archard, *supra* note 7, at 118.

infants on the doorsteps of overburdened foundling hospitals.[55] Rousseau rationalized their actions, arguing that the orphanage would raise the children to be satisfied peasants, which he thought was more than he could offer. In fact, infants in foundling hospitals suffered neglect and high death rates. Rousseau's choice demonstrated negligent disregard, if not reckless indifference, for the welfare of the children he brought into the world. A causal parent commits culpable wrongdoing if they fail to take reasonable steps to ensure the child will receive the care necessary for a valuable life. In a society like sixteenth-century France, the causal duty of a procreator might be quite burdensome.

Fortunately, this situation is uncommon in contemporary developed societies. In a society with "an organized social scheme of child adoption with an assured historic record of general success," causal parents who arrange for infant adoption have taken reasonable steps to ensure the child has the emotional and material caregiving needed for a valuable life.[56] This conclusion tracks the law of adoption and gamete donation. Birth parents and gamete donors have no ongoing legal duty to ensure the child's welfare. Our society tells biological parents it is reasonable to trust adoptive or intended parents to meet the child's needs.[57]

3 Objections to Causal Parents "Transferring" Their Duties Through Adoption

Some causal theorists object that causal parents cannot "discharge" their duty to the child by "transferring" their duty to adoptive or intended parents. These arguments that causal parents must care for their child personally are unpersuasive.

The first set of arguments insists that the obligor can fulfill their special duty to the child only by personally raising the child. Nelson, for instance, argues that I, as a procreator, cannot transfer my duties to intended parents because "the best I can do is predict that they will fulfill their duties, but my relations to my own agency is categorically different; I can bring myself – at least sometimes – to perform my duties."[58] If Nelson truly intends to draw a categorical distinction, his moral premise is vastly overbroad. It would entail that we may never rely on third parties to help us meet our duties. If the objection is not categorical, and instead Nelson's worry is about predicting success, then a similar worry extends to one's own parenting. I can control my willingness to fulfill my duty, but I cannot guarantee its outcome.[59] Sometimes I can even predict that others will do a better job. Most new parents feel this anxiety. Fortunately, morality does not fault us for not

55 Onora O'Neill, *Begetting, Bearing, and Rearing*, *in* HAVING CHILDREN: PHILOSOPHICAL AND LEGAL REFLECTIONS ON PARENTHOOD 25 (William Ruddick & Onora O'Neill eds., 1979); Archard, *supra* note 7, at 122–24.

56 Archard, *supra* note 7, at 121; AUSTIN, *supra* note 46, at 53 (arguing causal duty is satisfied if one has a "strongly justified belief that the future caretakers . . . will be good parents").

57 Tim Bayne, *Gamete Donation and Parental Responsibility*, 20 J. APPLIED PHIL. 77 (2003).

58 Nelson, *supra* note 8, at 60.

59 Bayne, *supra* note 57, at 83; Fuscaldo, *supra* note 7, at 73.

achieving outcomes, only for not taking reasonable steps in pursuit of mandatory ends. Causal parents must personally take reasonable steps to ensure the child receives care.[60]

In any case, it is a mistake to suppose adoption ever really "transfers" or "discharges" the causal parent's duty. An obligor can *discharge* a perfect duty by performing its required act. A seller who delivers the promised goods to the buyer discharges their contractual obligation. An obligor cannot discharge their duty by delegating performance to a third party, even if delegation is reasonable.[61] If a seller hires a delivery service that absconds with the buyer's goods, the seller has not discharged their duty. The duty to rescue is similar. Barry can discharge his duty by pulling Carrie out of the water. If he calls a lifeguard to save her instead, Barry takes a reasonable step to secure her rescue but has not discharged or transferred his duty. If the lifeguard hits a rock while diving off the pier, Barry must pursue other reasonable means of rescue.

Similarly, a causal parent who relies on a substitute caregiver has not discharged or transferred their causal duty to the child. The risk that a child will suffer inadequate care does not disappear because someone is currently parenting the child. The adoption might fail. The child may be orphaned. If the child loses her caregiver, and the causal parent knows or should know, then the causal parent should find another way to secure the child's needs. Maybe causal parents should even check in on adoptive families periodically, though I argue below that the community has good reasons *not* to recognize this duty. Through all these changing circumstances, the content of the causal parent's duty remains the same: take reasonable steps to ensure the child receives the care necessary for a valuable life.

A second set of objections focuses on the child.[62] Bernard Prusak argues that causal parents have a duty to raise the child personally because children have needs that only a causal parent can meet.[63] He begins his account by endorsing Seana

60 A few Kantian ethicists argue that a procreator may impose life on the child consistent with respect for the child as a person (or consistent with equal liberty) only if the procreator commits to ensuring this choice goes well from the child's perspective, which they argue justifies a duty to raise the child personally. Porter, *supra* note 6; WEINBERG, *supra* note 49, at 176–77; Chobli, *supra* note 6. While intriguing, their arguments tend to conflate ethical duties regarding maxims of respect with juridical duties necessary to ensure equal liberty.

61 It conflates delegation with novation to argue that adoption is an extension of the parent's authority to delegate care to nannies or teachers. *See, e.g.*, Fuscaldo, *supra* note 7, at 73–75.

62 Porter argues every child has a claim to caregiving, and this claim must correlate with a duty held by someone, and causal parents are the only viable candidate. Porter, *supra* note 6, at 194. In Chapter 1, I argued that children are entitled to caregiving and parents in the same sense that they are entitled to any primary goods, which are claims held against the community.

63 *See also* AUSTIN, *supra* note 46, at 45 (relying on intuition that children have a unique need for relationship with their causal parents); WEINBERG, *supra* note 49, at 74–79. Similar perfectionist arguments for genetic parents were rejected in 2.II.C. VELLEMAN, *supra* note 47, at 111–15. Another possibility is that children suffer psychological harm from parental abandonment because our social norms encourage children to expect to be loved by their biological parents. Scott Altman, *A Theory of Child Support*, 17 INT'L J. L. POL'Y & FAM. 173, 191–92 (2003).

Shiffrin's view that procreation is a "morally hazardous activity because in all cases it imposes significant risks and burdens upon the children."[64] Even if the child's life does turn out to be worthwhile, the causal parent compels the child to bear the inevitable pains, disappointments, and losses of a typical life. Prusak argues that procreators who compel a child to face life must offer the relationship of "unconditional love, abiding interest, and deep-rooted concern" that the child needs "to be fortified against, prepared for, and reconciled to life's burdens and travails."[65] Having a "deep parent–child relationship" with one's procreators "may reconcile a child to the fact and conditions of his or her existence . . . in part because they 'permit children to confront, hold responsible, show gratitude toward, and receive comfort and instruction from those who have given them this burden-riddled mixed benefit' – which of course only the procreators did."[66]

What, exactly, is the child holding the procreators responsible for? Not for ensuring they receive the relational goods of parental caregiving or for helping them form attachments with their family or community. As Prusak reiterates, adoptive parents can fulfill those functions. What distinguishes causal parents is that they are responsible for the child's existence. Because "no one other than one's procreators – with the possible exception of the Creator – can be called on to answer for the fact of one's being,"[67] procreators have a duty to help "reconcile the child with existence."

I find this position puzzling. Parents are not morally responsible for answering the riddle of life's meaning for their children. No one can answer existential questions for you. Parents must provide the material, relational, and psychological goods that fortify children against the vagaries of life. That might include inculcating whatever virtues stave off existential angst, whether that is fortitude, optimism, or wise naivety. However, such virtues can be taught equally well by biological, intended, or adoptive parents. These adults should avoid making these existential issues more difficult for children – as they might by hiding the circumstances of a child's birth. Accordingly, Prusak's worry may counsel against anonymous gamete donations and closed adoptions. It does not entail that causal parents have a pro tanto duty to parent the child personally.

4 Causal Parents' Adjacent Moral Duties

Two counterintuitive implications of the causal theory need to be addressed. First, many people will disapprove of a birth parent who walks away from an infant for no reason, even if the child receives loving adoptive parents. Society expects birth parents to find the adoption decision difficult and feel regret if they must choose

64 Seana Valentine Shiffrin, *Wrongful Life, Procreative Responsibility, and the Significance of Harm*, 5 Legal Theory 117, 137 (1999). Unlike Prusak, Shiffrin does not conclude procreators must raise the child personally, only that they must pay child support, participate in "justificatory dialogue about the child's origins," and (perhaps) act as backup parents. *Id.* at 140, 145, 147.

65 Prusak, *supra* note 6, at 36–37.

66 *Id.*

67 *Id.* at 37.

adoption. The child will expect their birth parent to have some good reason. Such regret and demands have no place in causal duties. When the lifeguard saves Carrie, Barry has no reason to regret not saving her personally. Second, the causal theory disagrees with law and common-sense morality about what should happen if birth parents disagree about adoption. In a causal theory, the custodial parent's caregiving fulfills the causal parent's duty to the child. In our society, the birth parent who would prefer adoption is stuck with parental duties.[68] The law will not force them to exercise visitation, but "[t]he fact the minor child does not suffer deprivation of necessary food, clothing, lodging, medical or surgical attention because such needs are being supplied by another does not abrogate the parent's obligation."[69]

Causal duties cannot justify these two moral intuitions. So long as the child has a dedicated caregiver who meets their relational and material needs, the causal parent does not have a perfect duty *to the child* to do anything more. The child's only claim against a causal parent is to ensure someone provides care and support. Whether this care comes from a third party or another causal parent is irrelevant.[70] However, other wider moral concerns may help mitigate the sense that these conclusions are counterintuitive.

In addition to the causal duty to the child, causal parents have two other related moral duties: (i) a duty of beneficence and (ii) a duty to the caregiver to assist with caregiving's burdens. These moral duties can reduce, but not eliminate, the gap between parenthood and the responsibilities of causal parents.

A CAUSAL PARENT'S IMPERFECT DUTY OF CARE TO THE CHILD. Everyone has an imperfect duty of beneficence to help some people sometimes. In Kantian terms, we must adopt the well-being of others as one of our ends. We must be willing to help when circumstances require it. Often, conventional social structures like associations, neighborhoods, or families provide concrete opportunities for acts of beneficence. If social norms allow a birth parent to raise their child, this opportunity provides a salient moment to dedicate themselves to another's well-being – perhaps the most critical moment they will ever experience.

This perspective helps capture another common attitude toward parenthood. If causal parents had a perfect duty to raise the child, then birth parents deserve little praise. They do only what morality strictly requires. By comparison, Barry deserves little praise for throwing Carrie a life preserver, but risking his life to save her would be praiseworthy. Similarly, if causal parents have only an imperfect duty to fulfill parental roles personally, then a causal parent's commitment to raising the child can be morally praiseworthy.

68 Ayelet Blecher-Prigat, *Conceiving Parents*, 41 HARV. WOMEN'S L.J. 119, 142 (2018).

69 *In re* Amos, 614 B.R. 866, 873 (Bankr. E.D. Mo. 2020); Cty. of Los Angeles v. Christopher W., 41 Cal. App. 5th 827, 833 (2019); People v. Sorensen, 437 P.2d 495, 500 (Cal. 1968).

70 This is a virtue of causal duties because, as I explain in II.B.3, the class of causal parents includes individuals like IVF technicians, who have no claim to care for the child personally.

Conversely, if a causal parent walks away for trivial reasons, this choice *might* reveal that they lack adequate regard for the child as a person whose well-being matters for its own sake. Suppose they choose not to parent simply because they are squeamish about diapers. This choice would be analogous to a situation where Felicia chooses to reel in her fish rather than throw a lifebuoy. Felicia's omission did not violate Carrie's rights, but it did violate Felicia's imperfect duty to make others' well-being her end. Although the moral analysis of the rescuer and the causal parent are *structurally* similar, the moral *conclusion* will rarely be. Felicia knew Carrie's dire need could be alleviated by a nearly costless action. No one who values others' lives could allow someone to drown so she can reel in a fish. Causal parents have a much wider range of permissible judgments.

First, a causal parent may care about the child's welfare and still choose not to raise them personally. One way to support a child's well-being is to raise the child oneself; another is to ensure the child receives a loving home with others. Which option is better for the child is underdetermined as a conceptual matter. The child could live many different valuable lives. Assuming all the potential parents will care for the child, it is impossible to say whether the child will have a better life raised by one birth parent, both birth parents, or adoptive parents. The child will simply have different lives. The empirical uncertainty is also daunting. A causal parent may reasonably predict the child will be raised well by adoptive parents or the other birth parent, yet the child's life might be improved further if the causal parent sticks around. Their presence could offer another emotional bond, additional financial resources, and another caregiver to divide the burden. Causal parents should not make this judgment lightly. Nevertheless, allowing someone else to raise the child does not *necessarily* demonstrate a lack of proper regard for the child's well-being.

Second, a causal parent often has adequate reasons not to raise the child. Because they have an imperfect duty to raise the child, causal parents may – indeed should – weigh this opportunity to benefit the child against their other moral duties and valuable ends. They should consider alternative avenues to contribute to the welfare of others, including their existing children, future children, and the general good. Causal parents may even consider their own well-being. As I argued in 1.I.B.1, we may balance the fulfillment of imperfect duties to others against pursuing our ends. Morality does not demand agents abandon all their ends to pursue others' welfare. A young parent may conclude that raising a child would require abandoning all their life projects. Such parental self-sacrifice is supererogatory, not morally required.

The causal parents' duty of beneficence can help explain some common intuitions about the moral weight of adoption decisions. A causal parent can fulfill their duty to the child by raising the child or by ensuring the child has a loving parent, but this decision is not morally neutral like choosing a flavor of ice cream. The child's birth offers an imminent opportunity for some causal parents to fulfill their duty of beneficence. A child may expect their birth parent to have good reasons for forgoing parenthood. Causal parents who walk away for trivial reasons fall morally short by revealing inadequate regard for the child's well-being, although not in a manner that violates the child's rights.

B CAUSAL PARENT'S PERFECT DUTY TO SUBSTITUTE CAREGIVERS. In addition to their causal and imperfect duties, causal parents might incur a personal duty to assist whoever raises the child, whether the other birth parent or an adoptive parent. I have said nothing yet about these horizontal duties between adults. To establish whether the causal theory can ground horizontal duties that justify the assignment of parental duties, we must determine what an agent who causes peril owes to the victim's rescuer. Like the duty to rescue, this question has received little philosophical attention. Consider two additions to the drowning case:

> **Drowning Rescuers**: A lifeguard employed by the pier dives into the water and pulls Evelyn to safety. A bystander physician performs a medical procedure on Evelyn necessary to save her life.

Dylan should help the lifeguard pull the victims ashore and help the physician resuscitate her. Afterward, Dylan owes the rescuers a debt of gratitude. He might also have a legal duty to compensate the physician for the medical treatment she gratuitously rendered, although he has no such duty to the professional lifeguard.[71]

A causal parent might incur similar duties to assist or compensate whoever cares for the child, whether this caregiver is a volunteer adoptive parent or another causal parent (intended or biological). Merle Weiner argues that when an absent biological parent uses the custodial parent to satisfy their duties to the child, they are "freeloading" off the custodial parent's efforts.[72] Similarly, David Archard suggests procreators sometimes exploit the moral virtue of adoptive parents who take on parental roles for needy children.[73]

Notice that these are special duties owed to the caregiver, not the child.[74] The direction of the duties makes them a poor fit for child support law. Courts insist that the child holds the claim to support, which custodial parents only hold in trust for

71 Limited duties to professional risk-takers: the firefighters' rule. DAN B. DOBBS, PAUL T. HAYDEN & ELLEN M. BUBLICK, THE LAW OF TORTS § 363 (2d ed. 2011).

72 MERLE H. WEINER, A PARENT-PARTNER STATUS FOR AMERICAN FAMILY LAW 162, 416–17 (2015). *See also* Ayelet Blecher-Prigat, *The Costs of Raising Children: Toward a Theory of Financial Obligations*, 13 THEORETICAL INQUIRIES LAW 179, 199, 207 (2012) (arguing for horizontal duties among coparents but not based only on causal grounds). *But see In re* Peterson's Est., 225 N.W.2d 644, 647 (Wis. 1975) (denying any such duty absent promise).

73 Archard, *supra* note 7, at 126; *See also* Don Hubin, *Procreators' Duties: Sexual Assymetries*, *in* THE OXFORD HANDBOOK OF REPRODUCTIVE ETHICS 301 (Leslie Francis ed., 2016) (asserting it is "pro tanto wrong" to create a being who will suffer without care and "to impose unchosen costs on others to avoid that suffering").

74 Causation grounds what Merle Weiner calls a "derivative obligation" between coparents, because this first parent is obligated to ensure the child's needs are met and thus obligated to the second parent who meets those needs. WEINER, *supra* note 72, at 83; Blecher-Prigat, *supra* note 72, at 199–200.

the child.[75] This principle underlies the rule that a custodial parent cannot waive the child's right to support, even if both parents want to exchange reduced financial support for reduced visitation.[76] Child support is a vertical, not horizontal, duty.

Nevertheless, courts have difficulty denying the connection between the two. For example, in *Sickels v. State* a non-custodial father fled the country to avoid paying $84,000 in child support. After the children were adults and no longer needed support, the father moved back to Indiana, where he was convicted of felony nonsupport. The Indiana Supreme Court held that the custodial mother may receive the arrearage as "restitution" because it "presumed" she exceeded her own duty to support the children to make up for the shortfall from the noncustodial parent.[77]

The judgment is fair, but its reasoning is unpersuasive. If the father had died instead, the mother would have done all the same things without exceeding her duty to the child. The parent's duty is fixed by the child's needs. By analogy, suppose that both Dylan and the lifeguard have a duty to take reasonable steps to effectuate the rescue. If the lifeguard saves her, he has not done more than was required. That is why Dylan does not need to compensate the lifeguard. By contrast, Dylan might have to compensate the physician, who has no independent duty to rescue Evelyn. It is puzzling that a birth parent should have to pay the custodial parent, given that the latter has an independent obligation to the child.[78]

On the other hand, apportionment law recognizes one comparable situation. Suppose both Dylan and the lifeguard omit to save Evelyn. Evelyn's estate can recover a wrongful death award from either of them.[79] If the lifeguard pays the entire judgment, he can seek a contribution from Dylan. So long as Dylan has assets, the law will divide their damages. It would seem unjust to the lifeguard if Dylan could avoid his remedial duty simply because the lifeguard fulfilled his remedial duty. There might be similar relations among cocausal parents. Their joint action created a child who needed care. As Weiner argues, the custodial parent's actions enriched the noncustodial parent by fulfilling the latter's independent duty to the child. Accordingly, the noncustodial causal parent must pay child support as restitution.

A restitutionary approach can align the moral and legal duties more neatly than first appears possible, but this rationale emphasizes another profound discrepancy in child support law. Noncustodial parents must pay child support to custodial parents but not to adoptive parents.[80] The adoptive parent has no preexisting duty to the child. They seem like a complete volunteer, more akin to the physician than the

75 Sickels v. State, 982 N.E.2d 1010, 1013 (Ind. 2013).

76 Perkinson v. Perkinson, 989 N.E.2d 758, 762 (Ind. 2013).

77 *Sickels*, 982 N.E.2d at 1013–14.

78 *See* Dep't of Health & Rehab. Servs., Child Support Enf't v. Holland, 602 So. 2d 652, 655 (Fla. Dist. Ct. App. 1992); Martin v. Martin, 480 So.2d 683 (Fla. Dist. Ct. App. 1985).

79 *Defendants who are under a duty to protect plaintiff from another's negligence*, Dan B. Dobbs, Paul T. Hayden & Ellen M. Bublick, The Law of Torts § 499 (2d ed. 2011).

80 Kansas v. Bohrer, 189 P.3d 1157, 1168 (Kan. 2008).

lifeguard. If support from the coparent enriches the noncustodial parent, then adoptive parenting enriches all the causal parents.

Some people might argue that when adoptive parents choose to become substitute parents, they waive any claim for financial assistance from former parents. This answer simply pushes the question backward. Why is it fair to demand adoptive parents waive their claim to financial support from the causal parent as a condition of adoption?

One answer might be that adoptive parents desire to be parents and benefit from the experience. Imagine Felicia was delighted to have a chance to rescue someone, so she eagerly jumped in to save Carrie. It is hard to see why Barry owes Felicia more than gratitude. Wealthy couples desperate to adopt infants look like eager rescuers, so perhaps causal parents have no duty to assist them.

On the other hand, this scenario cannot justify a categorical rule. Infants are a small fraction of all adoptions. Most adoptions are motivated by benevolent concern for children who need parents. Suppose Dylan sees that Felicia is considering whether to jump in to save Evelyn, so he delays his rescue until Felicia concludes reluctantly that no one else will help. Dylan used Felicia to fulfill his duty. In a similar fashion, Rousseau exploited the foundling hospital's benevolent intentions to save needy infants. Many adoptive parents are similarly reluctant rescuers. Relatives often step up when birth parents cannot or will not care for a child. These adoptive parents will hopefully find joy in their parent–child relationships, but this hardly justifies the causal parent's decision. Whether a causal parent should assist or compensate the adoptive parents seems to depend on the circumstances of the adoption.

I suspect the best reason to treat adoption as categorically different from single parenthood has nothing to do with causal parents' vertical duties to the child or horizontal duties to the caregiver. Instead, it appeals to the child's distributive right to a parent. The community has a collective duty to ensure each child has an adequate parent. It must not allow anyone to retain parental rights who is unable or unwilling to provide the child with a flourishing life.[81] For similar reasons, the community should also avoid giving causal parents an incentive to hold onto parenthood simply to avoid financial duties. Law redistributes some portion of the costs of parental care to adoptive parents to facilitate children's right to a parent.

* * *

Causal parenthood generates several personal obligations to the child and other adults. Causal parents have a duty to the child to take reasonable steps to ensure the child has a valuable life. This includes a duty to ensure the child has an adequate caregiver, whether by raising the child personally or finding adoptive parents. In

[81] Many states make parents pay child support for children in foster care, partly to make parents demonstrate their continued commitment and partly to reimburse the state. This demand is likely counterproductive. Most of these parents lack resources to pay, and establishing a child support order at the time of removal is correlated with a six-month longer stay in foster care. Maria Cancian et al., *Making Parents Pay: The Unintended Consequences of Charging Parents for Foster Care*, 72 CHILD. & YOUTH SERVS. REV. (2016).

a modern society with adoption networks, causal parents will rarely be required to parent the child personally. Nevertheless, the decision to raise a child personally remains morally freighted. The birth of a child presents (some) causal parents with a unique chance to fulfill their imperfect duty of beneficence. They may decline, but if they do, they may still incur a duty to assist the person who cares for the child.

B *Limitations of the Causal Theory of Moral Parentage*

Unfortunately for the causal theory of parenthood, causal duties have three substantial limits that prevent them from grounding parental rights or duties.

1 Causal Duties Cannot Justify Parental Rights

Like many ethicists, causal theorists assume a fiduciary theory of parental rights, according to which adults acquire parental authority to fulfill their parental duties.[82] As Blackstone wrote, "[t]he *power* of parents over their children is derived from the former consideration, their duty; this authority being given them, partly to enable the parent more effectually to perform his duty, and partly as a recompence for his care and trouble in the faithful discharge of it."[83] Unfortunately for the causal theory, causal duties simply cannot justify parental rights in this manner.

It is common to suppose that "a duty must carry with it the entitlement to perform it,"[84] but this principle is not uniformly true. Crucially, a duty to rescue does not entail a liberty to rescue. The appearance of contradiction dissolves once we specify the moral relations at play.

Someone who creates peril has *no claim to rescue their victim personally*. Barry cannot complain if Felicia swims faster and preempts his rescue attempt. It would be natural to suppose that Barry must at least have a liberty to rescue Carrie. On the contrary, a causer often has *no privilege to rescue personally*. If Felicia is more likely to rescue Carrie, Barry ought to stay out of her way. It would be perverse if Barry's duty to rescue, which he incurred by placing Carrie in danger, entailed a privilege to increase her peril by interfering with Felicia's rescue.[85] Other people may even have *a privilege to compel a causer not to rescue personally*. If one lifeguard swims out to rescue Carrie, another lifeguard may stop Barry from diving into the water. The label "duty to rescue" is a misnomer. The duty is to take reasonable steps to remove the

82 Jeffrey Blustein, Parents and Children: The Ethics of the Family 104–14 (1982); Jeffrey Shulman, The Constitutional Parent: Rights, Responsibilities, and the Enfranchisement of the Child (2014).

83 Blackstone, *supra* note 3, at *440.

84 John Eekelaar, Family Law and Personal Life 67 (2006); Chobli, *supra* note 6, at 29 (arguing redistributing children from procreators to better nonbiological parents would be "unjust, as it permits the procreators who incurred these obligations in the first place to circumvent them").

85 Anca Gheaus, *The Best Available Parent*, 131 Ethics 431, 440 (2021).

victim's peril, and sometimes that means deferring to more effective rescuers or social schemes for rescue.

Because of these inherent limits, causal duties simply cannot ground parenthood. The causal parent's duty to ensure the child receives adequate parental care does not entail a claim or privilege to care for the child personally. Causation of peril principles do not even justify giving causal parents the right to decide who will adopt the child; Barry has no right to decide who saves Carrie. The law allows birth parents or gamete donors to pick adoptive or intended parents, but this power cannot be justified by their causal duties. These limits may be surprising, but we will see they are appropriate given other features of causal duties, most importantly that many people are causal parents who should have no right or duty to raise the child (Section 3).

2 Weakness of the Causal Duty

Even if causal duties cannot justify parental rights, one might still hope they can ground parental duties. The law can enforce the causal parents' personal duty to the child, but those causal duties fall short of ordinary notions of parental moral and legal duties.

As Elizabeth Brake has argued, a procreator's causal duties are weaker than parental moral duties in two ways. First, a causal parent must ensure the child has a valuable life until the child becomes self-sufficient, but a parent must ensure their child has a loving environment to flourish until at least late adolescence, well past natural self-sufficiency.[86] Second, the disjunctive causal duty can be satisfied by substitute caregivers, but core parental duties cannot be "outsourced" in this manner.[87] A parent may hire sitters and order takeout, but they must personally provide the material and attitudinal care necessary to develop the bonded parental relationship essential to child development.[88] In Chapter 1, I argued that a parent must also exercise substitute judgment to guide the child's life – another function that parents must fulfill personally.

One might expect that causal duties could at least justify child support, which is where causal ideas have most influenced law. On the contrary, our child support law aligns poorly with the duties of causal parents. No states set guidelines relative to what a child needs for a valuable life. Instead, they require parents to share their income with the child. As a result, awards often exceed or fall short of children's

[86] Elizabeth Brake, *Willing Parents: A Voluntarist Account of Parental Role Obligations*, *in* PROCREATION AND PARENTHOOD: THE ETHICS OF BEARING AND REARING CHILDREN 151, 160–61 (David Archard & David Benatar eds., 2010). In fairness to Archard, he argues causal parents have "parental duties" but denies that they have full "parental responsibilities" in Brake's sense.

[87] *Id.* at 160.

[88] *Id.* at 168.

needs.[89] Moreover, child support lasts until the age of majority. One might imagine that this mirrors the end of causal duties upon attainment of self-sufficiency, but children could be self-sufficient at a much younger age if not for legal restrictions on child labor. The community, not nature, determines the length of childhood dependency.

3 Worries Akin to Proximate Cause

The last and well-known difficulty is that causal parentage is overinclusive. A person is a causal parent if their voluntary act was necessary to bring a child into existence. This counterfactual definition encompasses many people not ordinarily regarded as parents or procreators, including the technician who performs in vitro fertilization, the gamete donors who supply the eggs and sperm, the child's biological grandparent, and even an aunt who pesters her niece into getting pregnant. All these individuals have a special causal duty to ensure the child has a valuable life. Some ethicists accept this implication, using it to object to cavalier sperm donation.[90] Others resist this apparent absurdity, which Giuliana Fuscaldo labels the "too many parents" problem.[91]

Why is it a problem that some children have too many causal parents? It is not a metaphysical objection, as if a child simply cannot have this many parents. Every event is part of an infinite chain of causes. Anyone whose acts were necessary to bring a child into existence is a cause. We might not typically call all these people "parents" as a matter of ordinary language, but this type of semantic objection is unpersuasive. We could revise usage or adopt a new term to accommodate our moral insights. I chose "causal parent." Some scholars worry that having too many causal parents creates moral conflict, but pragmatic concerns need not threaten the conclusion that each causal parent has a moral duty to the child.[92] Their duty, like any duty to rescue, entails a duty to coordinate to ensure the child has a valuable life.

There is a problem in this vicinity, but it is not about having *too many* parents. The above list of marginal causal parents is a simple list of putative counterexamples. Any theory that entails these individuals have parental duties must be unsound, or so the argument goes. As a matter of common-sense morality, most of these individuals have no special duty to the child, much less parental duties. We could revise those common intuitions, but one might also think that extending causal duties to these individuals is unfairly demanding.[93] Special duties seem especially disproportionate for the marginal causal parents who make little contribution, like the pestering aunt,

89 Blecher-Prigat, *supra* note 68, at 165 (arguing but-for causers would be obligated only to meet basic needs).

90 Nelson, *supra* note 8, at 59.

91 Fuscaldo, *supra* note 7, at 72.

92 *But see* WEINBERG, *supra* note 49, at 58; Teresa Baron, *A Lost Cause? Fundamental Problems for Causal Theories of Parenthood*, 34 BIOETHICS 664, 668 (2020).

93 Baron, *supra* note 92, at 668.

but they may even seem unfair for core causal parents who act without culpability, such as the person whose sexual partner lied about using contraception.

These worries should sound familiar to lawyers. They mirror problems that tort law handles under the rubric "proximate causation." The law maintains two distinct causal doctrines: factual and proximate. The former refers to metaphysical causation, which law usually equates with counterfactual dependence. The latter is a set of doctrines to handle problems that arise because counterfactual dependence is less discriminate than intuitions about responsibility. In some cases, a defendant's wrongful acts were necessary to bring about the injury, but we intuitively assign responsibility to some other person or event. In other cases, the defendant was part of an unusual or lengthy chain of counterfactual causes that threatened to saddle the defendant with unfairly excessive liability. Both are part of the too-many-parents problem. Accordingly, advocates of causal parentage suggest that some theory of "the primary and proximate cause" of the child's existence might resolve these problems, but they typically offer no developed theory that could do so.[94] We must consider proximate causation in more detail.

Subsection a begins by defusing part of the objection. It argues that, contrary to many people's first instinct, even marginal causal parents have special duties to the child, maybe even to raise the child. The next sections ask whether principles of proximate causation can alleviate anxiety about causal duties either by narrowing the class of causal parents with duties (Subsection b) or explaining why it is fair to impose duties on them (Subsection c). While causal duties conflict less with common sense than first appears, proximate causation only appears to solve the problem because it switches topics from the parents' causal duties to concerns of distributive justice. Demonstrating this conclusion requires a relatively deep dive, but the analysis proves useful for another reason. It reveals why judicial opinions like *Nathaniel J.* take their mistakenly absolutist approach to child support duties. Causal theorists and judges alike conflate causal duties with distributive principles.

A UNUSUAL CAUSAL PARENTS HAVE A DUTY TO THE CHILD. Many of the putative counterexamples – fertility technician and pestering aunts included – do bear some moral responsibility to ensure the child receives adequate care. They might even be obligated to raise the child in extraordinary circumstances. I suspect the contrary intuitions have little to do with personal causal duties and instead rest on principles of familial liberty and excusing conditions in contemporary societies.

94 Fuscaldo, *supra* note 7, at 70; Archard, *supra* note 7, at 118; Nelson, *supra* note 8, at 54; AUSTIN, *supra* note 46, at 39, 44. Technically, causal parentage uses causation of risk to *assign affirmative duties*, not to determine when a person's breach of their duty caused the kind of harm that justifies moral or legal responsibility. Only the latter is truly a question of proximate causation. However, using causation of peril as a ground for affirmative duties creates similar problems because the peril often has too many counterfactual causes. Alexander, *supra* note 43, at 184.

The following hypothetical will help isolate the personal and political intuitions about the duties of causal parents. I will return to it again in Part III.

> **Deserted Island IVF**: Ann, Ben, Cam, and Dana are stranded on a deserted island. Ann and Ben want a child but cannot conceive through sexual intercourse. Cam, a physician, agrees to help Ann and Ben. She extracts Ann's eggs, fertilizes them with Ben's sperm, and implants the embryo in Ann. Dana plays no part in the plan or its execution. Ann gives birth to Eve, but just hours later Ann and Ben die tragically in an accident on the island.

Should Cam or Dana have primary responsibility for Eve?

If Cam's only relevant duty were beneficence, then Cam and Dana would have the same moral duty to raise Eve. That would be the natural conclusion if Eve had washed ashore in a basket. However, Cam chose to bring a child into the world. Admittedly, Cam believed the child would have two eager parents who would provide excellent care, but there was always a risk something might happen to Ann and Ben. Cam and Dana do not have the same obligation to Eve because Cam helped create Eve. Accordingly, Cam has a special duty to ensure Eve has a valuable life.

I suspect that the intuition that fertility professionals have no duty to the children they create rests on political concerns not applicable on a deserted island.[95] Western societies facilitate adults' right to procreate. Public policy encourages reproduction, even subsidizing ART. If fertility clinics, physicians, or donors had a legal duty to ensure the child has a valuable life, fewer clinics would offer fertility services, and fewer donors would offer sperm or eggs. Fertility clinics might screen intended parents in ways that intrude on their privacy and discriminate based on class or genetics. Clinics, donors, or birth parents would be incentivized to check on the growing child, further intruding on the privacy and liberty of intended or adoptive families and possibly interfering with their effort to build parent–child attachments.[96] A duty to screen and supervise would also signal that the community distrusts nonbiological parents.

95 Jason Hanna, *Causal Parenthood and the Ethics of Gamete Donation*, 33 Bioethics 267, 269 (2019). Hanna identifies some of these problems but treats them as a reason to conclude that fertility technicians and donors have no causal duties. He likens technicians to employees in risky industries. Coal miners help create the risk of environmental damage, but if they reasonably believe their employer will remedy the site, they are not personally liable if the company defaults. *Id.* at 270. I believe this analogy cuts the other way. The causal contributions of a miner, foreman, and executive differ only in degree. Miners are morally obligated to exercise reasonable care to protect neighboring communities – that is why they may mine only if they reasonably believe the company will mitigate. However, law exempts employees from tort liability for reasons of distributive justice and practicality. Individual employees have little power to switch industries or influence corporate decisions, and it is pointless to impose vast liability on employees with no assets to pay. These political concerns ought not distort judgments about personal moral duties. A miner has an ethical duty to help prevent and remedy pollution, such as by whistleblowing or cooperating with plaintiffs.

96 *Id.* at 271.

Accordingly, the law allows medical professionals, gamete donors, and birth parents (but not adoption agencies) to assume that intended and adoptive parents will provide the child with a valuable life, with ongoing support and monitoring from the state as necessary. Like the pier lifeguards who restrain private rescuers, the community can even prohibit causal parents like birth parents, donors, or clinics from trying to personally intervene to oversee the child's family. For reasons of political morality, the law displaces the duty of these causal parents. This does not show that they never had a personal duty in the first place.

On the deserted island Cam faces a different political situation. The group has no policy encouraging procreation, no willing substitute parents, and no impersonal redistributive mechanisms. The technician's personal causal duty comes to the fore when their choice to create a child imposes a substantial and direct burden on another discrete individual. Ann, Ben, and Cam's plan risks placing significant burdens on Dana, who might even have objected to sharing the island's limited resources with a child. Cam, therefore, has a duty to reduce the burden that her actions inflict on Dana, which is a duty that might have analogs even in contemporary society. In a nation struggling to prevent child trafficking, a fertility technician who notices the same client using multiple surrogate mothers ought to investigate the supposed "parent." Some legal systems already impose limited duties on fertility clinics to protect children. The United Kingdom demands fertility clinics deny a client's request for embryonic treatments that might be detrimental to the future child.[97]

The island hypothetical has three lessons. Many people whose voluntary acts cause a child to exist incur a special duty to ensure the child has a valuable life, even if they are not parents as a matter of ordinary language. Consequently, a bare causal theory needs supplemental principles to allocate caregiving duties among multiple causers, as well as between the causers and bystanders. Finally, our all-things-considered judgment about what a causal parent must do for the child likely reflects a host of political reasons about how to fairly allocate social burdens. All three issues are perennial concerns of proximate causation.

B CAN PROXIMATE CAUSE NARROW THE CLASS OF CAUSAL PARENTS? Could principles of proximate causation tailor the duties of causal parents so they align more closely with distinctively parental duties? One might first hope that they can narrow the class of causal parents with duties to the child. Three principles grouped under the rubric of proximate cause might serve this purpose.

97 EEKELAAR, *supra* note 84; Richard F. Storrow, *The Bioethics of Prospective Parenthood: In Pursuit of the Proper Standard for Gatekeeping in Infertility Clinics*, 28 CARDOZO L. REV. 2283 (2006) (arguing fertility clinics' duty to avoid harm to a future child requires screening prospective parents to ensure they can provide "minimally acceptable care").

i **Foreseeability** The first – and least helpful – is the foreseeability principle commonly invoked by theorists of causal parentage. Fuscaldo, for instance, argues that adults who conceive a child cannot "reasonably foresee" that their voluntary act will result in a grandchild years later.[98] Foreseeability is an intuitive limit on legal duties. Tort law insists it is fair to hold a person responsible for injuries they cause only if the risk of this type of injury is foreseeable.[99]

Unfortunately, foreseeability is too vague to avoid the salient counterexamples for causal parentage.[100] The fertility technician and pestering aunt know that their conduct increases the likelihood that a child will be born. Indeed, that was their purpose. A foreseeability principle would not let grandparents off the hook either, considering that 85 percent of American women give birth to a biological child.[101] Even gamete theft and mistakes are foreseeable. It is unlikely that technicians will use the wrong gametes or thieves will steal from the clinic, but the clinic's managers can foresee these risks and have a duty to take precautions against them, such as by creating labeling protocols and locking the embryo storage.

One might be tempted to argue that a person is responsible for managing the risk of procreation only if it is *reasonably* foreseeable, hoping that the modifier raises the degree of probability needed to trigger causal duties.[102] However, sexual procreators will incur causal duties even if they use multiple contraceptive methods to reduce the risk of conception. Rather than simply raising the probability threshold, the reasonableness modifier supplements foreseeability with unrelated and implicit moral ideas. Our temptation to say that fertility patients cannot reasonably foresee embryo theft or that grandparents cannot reasonably foresee grandchildren has less to do with the likelihood of these events than with our sense that it is unfair to hold patients or grandparents responsible for managing these contingencies. We should confront those fairness concerns explicitly rather than cloak them in the language of foreseeability.

ii **Intervening Agents** Foreseeability's classic competitor is sometimes called the directness test. Historically, common law judges hoped to find natural breaks in the infinite chain of necessary conditions. If certain types of events intervened between

98 Fuscaldo, *supra* note 7, at 70.

99 Benjamin C. Zipursky, *Foreseeability in Breach, Duty, and Proximate Cause*, 44 Wake Forest L. Rev. 1247 (2009).

100 Many tort scholars lament the "slipperiness" of foreseeability. *See* David G. Owen, *Figuring Foreseeability*, 44 Wake Forest L. Rev. 1277 (2009). Some hope to give foreseeability more precision using the "harm within the risk" test: an individual's unreasonable act is a proximate cause of the victim's harm only if the risk of causing this type of harm was among the risks that made the act unreasonable. Restatement (Third) of Torts: Liability for Physical and Emotional Harm § 29 (Am. Law Inst. 2010). Whatever its own merits, this test offers no help with the counterexamples to causal parentage. Anyone who increases the risk of a child being born – that is all causal parents – increases the risk that the child will suffer without adequate care.

101 Gretchen Livingston, *Childlessness*, Pew Research Center (May 7, 2015), www.pewresearch.org/social-trends/2015/05/07/childlessness/ (last visited Mar. 8, 2024).

102 Hubin, *supra* note 73, at 314–15.

the defendant's wrongful act and the plaintiff's injury, then the law would not deem the defendant a cause of the injury. The law recognized two salient types of superseding causes: natural catastrophes and deliberate human agents.[103]

These superseding cause ideas are no help for fertility technicians or surrogates. No intervening causes let them off the hook, because they are part of a concerted effort to produce the child. Contrary to the intuitions of the California Supreme Court and Lawrence Hill, proximate cause doctrines would not privilege the duties of the intended parents because they initiated the plan to have a child. All joint and concurrent causers share moral responsibility.[104]

Other potential counterexamples do raise issues relating to the directness doctrines. One might argue that a biological parent's deliberate decision to have sex or undergo IVF cuts off the chain of causation from pestering aunts and gamete donors.[105] Several justifications exist for treating intervening human agents as breaking causal chains. One idea might be that humans have free will, so prior events never cause their actions. I find libertarian theories of free will indefensible, so I focus on a more plausible reason.

Prusak argues that pushy relatives should not be regarded as causers, because they merely "provide considerations in view of which responsible agents may act." He is correct that the niece remains responsible for her decision. Sometimes, an agent is not morally responsible because a third party caused her conduct by bypassing her processes of deliberation or will formation. They might, for example, create a loud noise that startled her, causing her to bump into someone. The aunt's conduct is not comparable. Even if she incessantly reminds her niece of the reasons for having kids, the niece remains responsible for her choice to undergo IVF.

I am sympathetic to this picture of agency, but it only demonstrates that the niece is morally responsible. It does not show the aunt was not a cause of the niece's decision or relieve the aunt of moral responsibility. Unless one assumes

103 Although doctrinally housed in proximate cause, directness principles are sometimes interpreted as reflecting kernels of wisdom about metaphysical causation necessary to correct for overinclusive counterfactual tests. Michael S. Moore, Causation and Responsibility: An Essay in Law, Morals, and Metaphysics 103–04 (2010) (discussing Hart and Honore).

104 Fuscaldo, *supra* note 7, at 74.

105 Other scholars make less persuasive arguments to similar effect. Cohen argues sexual procreators are causes because their act is sufficient to cause a child, but gamete donors are not because additional subsequent acts must be completed to create the child. Glenn Cohen, *The Constitution and the Rights Not to Procreate*, 60 Stan. L. Rev. 1135 (2007). No theory of causation requires sufficiency or cuts off liability for any intervening human event. Bayne argues donors have no causal duty because they transfer property rights in their gametes to the recipient, which transfers moral authority over whether to use the gametes and, thus, cuts off the donor's causal duty. Bayne, *supra* note 57, at 79. Fuscaldo accuses Bayne of assuming a false "last causer" theory of intervening causation, Fuscaldo, *supra* note 7, at 74, but Bayne's mistake is moral not metaphysical. Bayne's moral premise is that the new owner's right to exclusive control relieves the prior owner of moral responsibility, even if the prior owner transferred the property knowing of its intended use. This over-inclusive moral principle would exonerate all arms dealers.

that deliberate human decisions are contracausal (just a roundabout appeal to a libertarian account of free will), it must be possible for one person to be *a* cause of another's conduct by influencing their deliberation. This causal premise fits common intuitions in other situations. For example, a teacher's advice can affect a student's career choices. Moreover, moral responsibility for human decisions does not need to be all or nothing. The student may bear relatively more responsibility for deciding whether to act on the teacher's advice, but the teacher remains responsible for how they influence their student's deliberation. A similar perspective manifests in child support cases for nonbiological parents. Someone who convinces their partner to undergo insemination with donor sperm is a cause of the child's birth, even if their partner must decide to go through with the procedure. The causal role of the partner and the pestering aunt are different in degree, not kind.

Even if we sometimes cause others' deliberate actions, that does not mean we are always *morally* responsible for those decisions. Moral reasons (as opposed to metaphysical ones) limit the scope of our moral responsibility. When we are responsible for others' downstream choices, we must factor their choices into our decisions. Their choices fix the scope of our moral liberty.[106] Sometimes it is morally unacceptable to demand that we restrain ourselves to avoid influencing others' actions. The most salient cases involve downstream *wrongful* actors. Tort law retains its strictest superseding cause rule for subsequent intentional torts or criminal acts.[107] I am not liable if someone hotwires my car to take it on a joyride, even if they can steal my car only because I parked it on a high-crime street. Criminal activity should not determine the extent of our liberty to travel around a city. In contrast, I do bear some responsibility if I leave my keys in the ignition. Tort law will hold a defendant liable for a third party's wrongful acts if we regard the defendant's conduct as improper precisely because it creates too great an opportunity for wrongful acts.

How do such *moral* intervening agent principles apply to parentage cases? They do not relieve gamete donors of their causal duty. The donor sold their gametes precisely so that someone else could use them to conceive a child.[108] They might, however, defuse other problem cases. When embryos are stolen from a clinic, the genetic parents should have no special duty to the child. Similarly, a genetic father should have no duty of support if a woman impregnates herself with sperm taken from a discarded condom. By engaging in voluntary sexual intercourse, he increased the probability of procreation, and he bears responsibility for that risk; however, that risk dissipates once he discards the condom. He should not be held morally

106 Kimberly Kessler Ferzan, *Omissions, Acts, and the Duty to Rescue*, *in* The Ethics and Law of Omissions 217 (Dana Kay Nelkin & Samuel C. Rickless eds., 2017).

107 Restatement (Third) of Torts: Liability for Physical and Emotional Harm § 34, notes to cmt. e (Am. Law Inst. 2010).

108 Fuscaldo, *supra* note 7, at 68.

responsible for managing the risk that his sexual partner might steal his sperm from the trash, any more than donors should be responsible for managing the risk of a break-in at the clinic. His sexual partner inappropriately used him to achieve her end of having a child, and the law inappropriately used him to satisfy the community's duty to meet the child's needs.

Intervening agent principles must be applied carefully to parentage to avoid illicit inferences. Men's rights advocates often insist that unwilling fathers should not owe child support, because they cannot choose whether to end the pregnancy through emergency contraception or abortion. The first mistake in this line of argument is its implicit assertion regarding factual causation. It suggests the mother is the "real" cause of the child's birth because she chose to continue the pregnancy. This is false. Their joint sexual act set a chain of events in motion. The pregnant woman later omits to intervene in ways that could prevent the zygote from growing into a child. Her omissions are necessary conditions for the child's birth, but omissions do not break causal chains.

Fixing the metaphysical mistake helps clarify the moral one. The unwilling father's other suggestion is that it is unfair to hold him morally responsible because if he had the right to decide whether to continue the pregnancy (which he did not), then he would have chosen to prevent the zygote from developing into a child who needed care. Even if this counterfactual is true, the moral premise is not. His voluntary choice created a risk of procreation. He had an opportunity to prevent this risk by abstaining from sex or using adequate contraception. The law justly denies him any further right to manage this risk because the woman has a liberty right over her body.

That is bad luck for him, but it is an ordinary kind of luck. Someone who creates a risk often loses control over the subsequent chain of events. If I injure you, I have no right to dictate your medical care. If I spill chemicals on your land, I have no right to control your cleanup. Even if these downstream agents make unreasonable choices, the initial actor is not relieved of *all* moral responsibility. If a physician's negligence or your unreasonable cleanup efforts increase the extent of damage, then I can argue at most that we should share responsibility. With an unintended pregnancy, the woman's choice to carry the fetus to term is neither unforeseeable nor unreasonable. Her choice is not the type of intervening act that could justify cutting off the genetic father's duty to the child to meet the needs that he helped to create.

iii **Scalar Causal Contributions** Some counterexamples to causal parentage, especially grandparents, invite an analogy to proximate cause cases with long or unusual chains of causation. Tort scholars often view these rules as instrumental policy limits, but one might also interpret them as raising issues of factual causation. For example, Michael Moore contends that the causal force of one event peters out as it passes through intervening events in a causal chain.[109] A scalar theory of causation might remove some sting from the too-many-parents problem.[110]

Perhaps the grandparents and aunt are necessary but small causes.[111] Many highly contingent events must occur between the conception of the parent and the conception of the grandchild. On a process theory of causation, the physical force exerted by the grandparent's decision has been exhausted. Similarly, the aunt's nagging was only a tiny part of the mother's decision to get pregnant. Reminding someone of a reason influences their choice, but perhaps that small influence is overwhelmed by the agent's own mental processes.

Although Archard warns against "reading off" degrees of moral duties from the magnitude of causal contributions, it is plausible to suppose there is some relationship.[112] Common-sense morality would recognize a direct relation: other things being equal, the greater one's role in bringing a child into existence, the more stringent one's duty. Alternatively, causal duties might arise only after the agent's contribution exceeds a certain threshold. Perhaps the grandparents and aunt have no duty because they made negligible contributions compared to the birth mother. Alternatively, one might allocate responsibility based on relative causal contributions. Lesser causes, like grandparents or pestering aunts, would be backups for primary causes, like the gestational mother.

A scalar theory of causation is unlikely to remove all responsibility from marginal causers, but weakening the duties might blunt the objection that they are unfairly demanding. On the other hand, scalar theories may reinforce the other difficulties. First, they may strengthen the duty of the IVF technicians. When infertile heterosexual couples can only conceive using IVF, the technician arguably exerts as much causal influence as gamete contributors. Under a probability theory, the probability of conception without the technician's intervention is near zero. Second, gestational mothers might always be the most significant cause. Under a process theory of causation, for example, the gestational mother's physical effort to sustain the fetus constitutes the bulk of physical processes that create the child – much greater than the mere contribution of an egg or sperm.

I raise these issues as difficulties, not counterexamples. These enhanced duties might be acceptable if other moral or legal principles remedy the collateral implications.[113]

109 MOORE, *supra* note 103, at 121–23. *But see* Larry Alexander & Kimberly Kessler Ferzan, *"Moore or Less" Causation and Responsibility*, 6 CRIM. L. & PHIL. 81, 84–85 (2012) (criticizing the notion of scalar causation).

110 MOORE, *supra* note 103, at 500. According to a probabilistic theory, event 1 causes event 2 if it increases the probability of event 2 relative to background probability. On a process theory, event 1 causes event 2 if it transfers some physical force to event 2.

111 *Id.* at 275–77.

112 Archard, *supra* note 7, at 113.

113 In 5.III.D it will be argued that intended parents can agree with the lab, donors, and surrogate about how to allocate parental duties.

C CAN PROXIMATE CAUSE REDUCE THE DEMANDINGNESS PROBLEM? Even if marginal causal parents have weaker or secondary duties, their causal duties might generate burdensome demands in unusual circumstances, as in the deserted island hypothetical. Is it fair that lab technicians, pestering aunts, and grandparents incur a duty to ensure the child has a valuable life? as above, if it does not have cascading effects, I would prefer a paragraph break here. Marginal parents foreground the fairness problem, but similar unfairness can arise even among prototypical parents. Consider unintentional pregnancies. One in 1,600 women who engage in regular heterosexual intercourse for a year will become pregnant *despite always* using both oral contraceptives *and* condoms (1 in 82 for average rates of missed pills or misused condoms). Only this couple will incur causal duties to a child, even though 1,600 couples engaged in identical conduct. Causal parentage looks even less fair if it ignores culpability regarding procreative risks. This couple took all reasonable precautions, yet they have the same duty as couples who recklessly took no precautions or even deliberately got pregnant.

These examples raise many potential fairness problems that must be disentangled. Two potential objections should be set aside. First, some scholars suggest these examples show that causal parentage is an objectionable form of strict liability.[114] Taken literally, this is a category mistake. It conflates conditions for the existence of a duty with conditions for its breach. Everyone who causes a child to exist is obligated to ensure the child has a valuable life, but no one violates this duty unless they fail to take reasonable steps to ensure the child receives care. A man who never knows he fathered a child has not wronged the child by his absence.

Second, the one out of 1,600 careful couples who happen to conceive a child experience "resultant luck."[115] A set of low-probability contingencies aligned for this couple to create a child and incur a duty. Resultant luck raises moral puzzles, but the puzzles are no more problematic for causal parentage than any other duty that requires causation. Many people drive while intoxicated. Only the unlucky drunk drivers who cause an accident will incur a duty of repair. If resultant luck is morally problematic, we must revise a vast swath of our moral and political judgments, as true skeptics about the moral relevance of causation advocate.[116]

The parental demandingness objection that creates a genuine problem concerns what Nagel calls "circumstantial luck." Cam's duty to Eve became more onerous than Cam anticipated because of Adam and Betty's deaths. This unfortunate event is

114 Joseph Millum, *How Do We Acquire Parental Rights?*, 36 Soc. Theory & Prac. 112, 80–81 n.3 (2010); Higdon, *supra* note 2, at 421. The plausible version of the "strict liability" objection denies that an actor can incur a duty to rescue unless the act that created the peril was wrongful. Some parentage authors assume this general principle is true, Hubin, *supra* note 73, at 313. However, I argued in II.A.1 that innocent causation grounds a duty to rescue.

115 Carolina Sartorio, *Resultant Luck*, 84 Phil. & Phenomenological Res. 63 (2012).

116 Kimberly Kessler Ferzan & Larry Alexander, *Confused Culpability, Contrived Causation, and the Collapse of Tort Theory*, *in* Philosophical Foundations of the Law of Torts 406 (John Oberdiek ed., 2014).

one of many contingent circumstances that affect the onerousness of Cam's duty. The island might suffer a drought that reduces its natural food supply, or Cam might suffer a physical injury that makes it more difficult to forage. In these unfortunate circumstances, it seems unfair for Cam to continue bearing the brunt of caregiving or support obligations for Eve.

Again, these fairness arguments have instructive analogs in tort law. Suppose a camper negligently builds a campfire that starts a forest fire. The nearby river would typically contain this fire, but freak winds push sparks over the river to burn down a city. Holding the camper responsible for this fortuitous destruction strikes many as unfair.[117] Although it is tempting to think the objection that causal duties are excessive (in tort or in parentage) is a problem of proximate causation, this objection is more perspicuously framed as a problem of distributive justice.

Consider tort law first. The law empowers accident victims to seek a remedy when an agent wrongfully causes them injury. This theory of relational justice can lead to disproportionate burdens on either side. A wrongful actor must remedy all the injuries they cause, even if greater than reasonably anticipated. Conversely, the injured victim receives no compensation if the actor's conduct was reasonable. This result is just *as between the actor and the victim*, but it may still seem unfair for society to impose all the injury costs of socially permissible activity on victims. The community must decide which valuable but risky activities are permissible and how to distribute the cost of likely injuries. Similarly, it seems unfair to impose extensive injury costs on defendants, even culpable ones, when the injuries are vastly more than anticipated or the cost is more than one person can reasonably bear. Even if this result is just as between the two parties to the suit, that does not mean the results are just, all things considered.

Proximate cause doctrine reasonably punts on these problems. Courts hearing tort cases have jurisdiction only over two parties and only for one incident. This is a poor context for resolving distributive justice problems. Similarly, even if it is just for Cam to bear the cost of parenting rather than Dana, that does not settle the distributive question when a drought arises. The distributive problem created by causal duties is not limited to marginal causal parents. If Ben had survived to raise Eve himself, it would have been unfair to insist that he meet all of Eve's needs on his own through the drought. The duties of a causal parent can become unfairly burdensome under challenging circumstances, primarily when there are no other willing caregivers and the material costs of caregiving are high. In fact, this distributive problem is not even limited to causal parents. If Dana had eagerly volunteered to raise Eve, the drought would still have made her voluntary duty of support unfairly demanding.

Sometimes, the circumstances that render our duties unfairly burdensome depend on genuine luck, like a drought. Often, the circumstances result from collective political decisions, like agriculture policy. The United States makes infant adoption easy for birth parents but offers little financial assistance to birth parents

[117] Ryan v. N.Y. Central, 35 N.Y. 210 (1896).

who choose to raise their children. The argument that parental duties are too demanding for marginal causal parents is not really an argument against duties for causal parents per se. It is a typical problem of distributive justice. The distributive unfairness simply becomes glaring when caregiving or support duties rest on a weak initial trigger, such as for the pestering aunt who played a small causal role with little culpability. Instead of imagining that notions of proximate cause will realign extensive causal duties with our intuitions about fairness, we should address intuitions about distributive fairness directly.

C *Causal Creation Cannot Justify Parental Rights*

This chapter has focused primarily on procreators' duties and alleged fiduciary rights, but causation might be relevant for a different reason. One might think that an adult obtains a claim to parent a child simply *because they created the child*. Such possessory arguments dominated the history of parent–child relations until the rise of children's rights, which put any analogy between children and property on the defensive.[118] Contemporary defenders of this variant of the causal theory do not typically assert that creation justifies parental rights, for good reason. A child is an independent person. The fact that I brought a child into being (or commissioned someone to do so) cannot directly give me the authority to shape the child's life without treating the child as a subordinate being who exists to serve my ends.

Nevertheless, similar arguments persist; they simply use different moral premises to infer parental rights from causation. Some scholars argue that birth mothers have parental rights because they perform the work of gestation to create the child. These scholars often invoke Lockean labor principles, but they equate gestation with child-rearing work rather than the creation of physical objects of property. Accordingly, I consider this argument in Chapter 4 in a section on gestational caregiving (4.II.B). A second argument might resonate more closely with the reasoning of the California Supreme Court in *Johnson*. Perhaps anyone who decides to create a child to raise themselves has a right to parent the child. This position assumes that some causal parents (genetic, gestational, or intended parents) have the authority to settle among themselves who will parent the child because they initiated the procreative project, so I consider this possibility in Chapter 5 on agreements (5.III.D).

* * *

118 Barbara Bennett Woodhouse, *"Who Owns the Child?": Meyer and Pierce and the Child as Property*, 33 Wm. & Mary L. Rev. 995 (1991). The patriarchal argument, traceable through Aristotle to even earlier ideas, is that a biological father owns his children because he created the child from his "seed." *Id.* at 1043. Barbara Hall recently developed a nongendered version of this argument that priority for genetic parents can be inferred from bodily self-ownership, but it has been subject to trenchant criticism by Kolers and Bayne. Barbara Hall, *The Origin of Parental Rights*, 13 Pub. Aff. Q. 73 (1999); Avery Kolers & Tim Bayne, *"Are You My Mommy?": On the Genetic Basis of Parenthood*, 18 J. Applied Phil. 273 (2001).

Causal parents incur genuine causal duties to the child. Anyone whose voluntary acts cause a child to exist incurs an affirmative duty to take reasonable steps to ensure the child has a valuable life, which they can fulfill either by finding substitute caregivers or fulfilling caregiving roles personally. Adults incur this causal duty whether they cause the child to exist through voluntary sexual intercourse, regardless of their intentions about procreation, or through "artificial" means, such as by encouraging a gestational mother to undergo artificial insemination.

Nevertheless, causal duties cannot generate a personal theory of moral parenthood. Someone who creates a risk does not have a liberty right to fulfill their causal duty, so causal parenthood cannot ground a right to raise the child. Causal duties are also too weak to explain parental duties, most importantly because causal parents have no duty to raise the child personally. These limitations on causal duties are fitting because the class of causal "parents" is quite broad, including fertility technicians, pestering aunts, and grandparents. Even these secondary causal parents might end up with caregiving duties in extraordinary circumstances. Our resistance to these causal duties rests primarily on political concerns about familial liberty and distributive justice rather than interpersonal morality.

Despite all these limitations, causation may remain relevant to a political vision of parentage. To see why, we must confront directly those distributive principles which proximate cause doctrines try to sneak in through the back door.

III CAUSATION IN A POLITICAL CONCEPTION OF PARENTAGE

In Chapter 1, I noted two central questions that the political conception of parentage must answer: Why may a community fairly impose the collective duty to raise a child on an individual? And do any individuals have a claim to occupy the parental office? Causal parentage offers a *limited* response to the first fairness question. To see how, we must reorient the causal theory. Causal theorists focus on the duty causal parents owe the child. They neglect the second type of causal argument offered in the legal justification for child support.

Like Blackstone, California courts insist that the state forces biological fathers to pay child support to "reliev[e] others upon whom otherwise the burden might chance to fall."[119] Other courts expressly recognize that child support is a "tax" on voluntary sexual procreators because they, not the state, retain primary responsibility for the child's welfare.[120] This argument is not about what the causal parent owes the child but what they *owe other adults*. It is an argument about distributive justice. Fairness suggests that the individuals who create a child should bear a larger share of

[119] McLain v. Meadows, 44 Cal. App. 402, 403 (Cal. Ct. App. 1919).

[120] N.E. v. Hedges, 391 F.3d 832, 836 (6th Cir. 2004). Trying to undercut constitutional objections, some courts absurdly assert that child support involves no state action because the duty is imposed by "operation of nature, not statute." Child Support Enf't Agency v. Doe, 125 P.3d 461, 469 (Haw. 2005).

the child-rearing costs than their relatives, neighbors, fellow citizens, or the state.[121] This argument, sounding in political morality, is fit for a political theory of parentage. The community must collectively decide what role causal responsibility should play in a just allocation of the cost of meeting children's basic needs.

A *Causal Parentage as a Distributive Principle*

Causal responsibility has some appeal as a principle of distributive justice. The underlying moral intuition is simple: You did it, you pay for it. Why is it fair to make everyone else pay for your voluntary choices? Luck egalitarians worked this intuition into a theory of distributive justice. Inequalities are fair (or more so) if they result from voluntary choices that the individual made within an otherwise fair framework of interaction.[122]

Fairness offers one reason to allocate some child-rearing costs *to causal parents rather than bystanders*. Child support rests on a luck-egalitarian intuition that individuals who choose to engage in sex should bear a larger share of child-rearing costs.[123] This intuition is particularly persuasive in small groups, as we saw in the island hypothetical above. It is unfair to Dana if Ann, Ben, and Cam can deliberately create Eve and then demand that Dana pay an equal share of the costs to raise Eve. Similar intuitions were central to the California Supreme Court's opinion in *Elisa B.* The court had previously held the state could not impose child support on an unrelated man who helped the birth mother raise her newborn, but it could demand support from Elisa because she voluntarily helped create the child.[124]

Causal responsibility might also help fairly allocate costs *among multiple causal parents*, as discussed above in 2.II.B.3. A community may decide that it is fair for a larger share of child-rearing costs to fall on the causal parents who make a larger contribution or act with greater culpability, such as sexual procreators and intended parents, rather than marginal or less culpable causal parents, like grandparents or unintentional procreators.[125] If a community insists that causal parents must pay for

[121] Foster v. Foster, 221 W. Va. 426, 432 (2007).

[122] Richard J. Arneson, *Luck Egalitarianism Interpreted and Defended*, 32 PHIL. TOPICS 1 (2004).

[123] Laura Oren, *The Paradox of Unmarried Fathers and the Constitution: Biology Plus Defines Relationships; Biology Alone Safeguards the Public Fisc*, 11 WM. & MARY J. WOMEN & L. 47 (2004).

[124] Altman argues that such distributive intuitions assume parents should pay because (a) parents seek or gain some benefit from procreation, which treats child support as a "user fee," or (b) they caused this need through *wrongful* behavior. Altman, *supra* note 63, at 187–88. Neither assumption is attractive. Fortunately, neither is necessary. Luck egalitarianism treats personal responsibility as relevant to the fair allocation of social costs, irrespective of whether the individual benefits personally or their act was wrongful.

[125] The California Supreme Court hoped causal principles could also justify priority for intended parents over surrogates, but their argument to this conclusion is unsound. Surrogates may enter the chain of events later than intended parents, but surrogates and lab technicians arguably make larger causal contributions. Ben recruited Cam, but Cam extracted the eggs, created the embryos, and implanted them. They also act with equal culpability – all act with the purpose to create a child. Intuitions about the fair allocation of parenthood between intended and causal parents must rest on preconception agreements.

some of the child's financial support, it might also allow them to volunteer to raise the child. Offering this option is a sensible approach, but it is by no means morally required.

B The Limits of Causation as a Distributive Principle

Even if a community can reasonably assign some child-rearing costs on the basis of causal responsibility, this is not the only distributive concern. Distributive justice is not this simple. Contemporary mass societies distribute many social costs caused by voluntary choices rather than insisting these costs must fall on the individual citizens who cause them.

This would be true even on the hypothetical deserted island. Suppose Dana walked among the tide pools and stepped on a jellyfish that causes temporary paralysis. During her recovery, Dana needs help to feed herself. She voluntarily chose to take this risk and imposed a new cost on the group, yet it is fair to ask the group to help with the costs of her recuperation.

The objection to imposing costs on others cannot be absolute. I suspect the objection gets illicit support from its superficial similarity to the equal liberty principle that I discussed in Chapter 1, which does have an absolute flavor. No one can have the moral power to impose duties on others unilaterally. It is tempting to think that Dana's choice about where to stroll imposed a duty on the others to assist her, but this misunderstands the moral relations. A community has a collective duty of justice to meet members' basic needs. Dana's choice and injury altered the facts that determined what justice required. She did not impose a new duty on the group. Justice always depends on circumstances and choices in this way.

Some of the relevant circumstances will be brute facts, like the year's annual rainfall. Others will be created by individual choices responding to brute facts, like a farmer's decision to plant specific crops. Still others are created by communal choices, like sustaining a market economy in which farmers' ability to meet their own needs depends primarily on their ability to sell crops.

As a result, it is often misleading to focus on the consequences of one choice in isolation when evaluating matters of distributive justice. The circumstances of justice are the collective result of everyone's actions, and the community must distribute those benefits and burdens fairly. Causal responsibility is relevant to fair distribution, but it is rarely a sufficient basis to determine the just allocation of social costs.[126] While some philosophers treat the luck principle as constitutive of justice, even many luck egalitarians recognize that causal responsibility is one principle that must be aligned with others, whether prioritarian, sufficientarian, or otherwise.[127]

[126] Arneson, *supra* note 122, at 5; Larry S. Temkin, *Egalitarianism Defended*, 113 Ethics 764, 177–78 (2003).

[127] Carl Knight, *Luck Egalitarianism*, 8 Phil. Compass 924 (2013).

Not even tort law is a pure system of corrective justice. By default, it is insensitive to distributive justice. A tortfeasor whose wrongful act causes injuries must compensate the victim even if it will increase inequality because the tortfeasor is unjustly poor or the victim is unjustly rich. Nevertheless, tort law also respects relational justice, allowing adults to allocate responsibility for accidents between themselves through express contracts, consent, and assumption of the risk.[128] Distributive concerns also enter tort law directly through the proximate cause doctrines discussed in Part II that protect defendants from excessive liability. Tort liability is also cabined by distributive systems external to tort law. Certain welfare payments are exempt from tort judgments, and tort debts are dischargeable in bankruptcy.

C *Causal Parentage as One among Many Distributive Concerns*

For similar reasons, it is a mistake to focus exclusively on causal responsibility when selecting a fair principle for distributing child-rearing costs. Causal parenthood must be integrated with other principles of fairness grounded in distributive or relational justice. Chapter 5 will consider relational justice among procreators. This section offers a few speculative remarks about distributive justice. My goal is not to defend a particular distribution of child-rearing costs. However, child support would need (at least) four major reforms to approximate a plausible system of responsibility-sensitive distributive justice.

First, American child support formulas would need to be fundamentally revised to approximate the models of Continental Europe. Under European formulas, each parent is responsible for a share of the child's basic needs. This system comports with distributive principles that assign a portion of the social cost of raising a child to those causally responsible for the costs. In contrast, American states demand that parents share their income with their children. Parents must pay the same share as typically spent by two-parent families with similar incomes. Wealthy obligors owe more than any reasonable measure of the child's need, and indigent obligors owe less.[129] The underlying thought is that a child is entitled to the level of affluence that they would have received had their biological parents raised them together. This hybrid of causal duties and distributive justice misconstrues both the causal parent's duty and the child's distributive entitlements.

Impoverished parents raise the second problem. The community must respect the distributive entitlements of children *and parents*. Modern child support law exacerbates injustice by taking resources from already unjustly impoverished parents.[130]

[128] Eekelaar treats concerns about how to allocate costs between causal and custodial parents as issues of "commutative justice." Eekelaar, *supra* note 23.

[129] Truly wealthy obligors have financial planning tools to shield their income. Allison Tait, *Debt Governance, Wealth Management, and the Uneven Burdens of Child Support*, 117 Nw. U. L. Rev. 305 (2022).

[130] *Id.* at 309–16.

Child support awards can cement a noncustodial parent in poverty. Unpaid arrearages accumulate and cannot be discharged in bankruptcy. States resort to extraordinarily coercive remedies to enforce these debts, from suspending driving licenses to civil imprisonment. These burdens fall disproportionately on minorities, especially African Americans. Actors in the child support enforcement system also reinforce gender and racial stereotypes, particularly that mothers are default custodians, fathers' primary duties are financial, and poor persons of color engage in irresponsible procreation.[131] Furthermore, custodial parents who receive state welfare must sign over their child support rights to the state. When the obligor makes payments, some states continue to take this money as reimbursement for welfare.[132]

This system is absurd if child support is meant to reflect principles of causal responsibility that fairly allocate costs between causal parents, custodial parents, and society. The community has no legitimate interest in shifting all public welfare expenses onto private individuals, especially when doing so exacerbates distributive injustice for the parents and offers little (or no) benefit to the child or custodial parent.

Feminist scholars have long criticized the "privatization of dependency" that drove welfare reform in the late twentieth century.[133] Congressional conservatives opposed most financial support for low-income families, even minimal requirements of justice like food and housing assistance. To skirt this collective obligation, Congress sought to extract more support from noncustodial fathers to "reimburse" taxpayers for the minimal welfare poor children received.[134] Congress showed little concern for how this would compound the distributive injustices already facing impoverished parents. Similar reforms occurred in the United Kingdom. Parliament explicitly pegged support payments to the child's welfare entitlement.[135] The welfare entitlement reflected the state's judgment about children's basic rights, yet the government used this amount to define the private child support obligations. No reasonable conception of distributive justice would insist that causal parents reimburse the state for all or most of a child's basic needs.

Although child support often begins with this absolutist lens, even the guidelines bend to distributive problems at the extremes. Some American statutes have a "self-support reserve."[136] A small amount of income is set aside for the parent's basic

131 Tonya L. Brito, *Nonmarital Fathers in Family Court: Judges' and Lawyers' Perspectives*, 99 Wash. U. L. Rev. 1869 (2021).

132 Tait, *supra* note 129, at 311.

133 Susan Frelich Appleton, *Illegitimacy and Sex, Old and New*, 20 Am. U. J. Gender Soc. Pol'y & L. 347, 360–62 (2011).

134 Linda D. Elrod, *Child Support Reassessed: Federalization of Enforcement Nears Completion*, 1997 U. Ill. L. Rev. 695, 697.

135 Eekelaar, *supra* note 23, at 154–55.

136 Stacy Brustin, *Child Support: Shifting the Financial Birden in Low-Income Families*, 20 Geo J. on Poverty L. Pol'y 1, 11–15 (2012).

needs, not subject to the child support percentage. Others specify a lower income threshold, below which the noncustodial parents should pay nothing or a nominal amount, around $50. Unfortunately, many courts quickly conclude that obligors are not trying hard enough to meet their obligations. They impute income to unemployed obligors, setting the award as if the obligor worked full-time at minimum wage. This judicial tendency reflects the absolutist starting premise of child support.

The third necessary revision would be to child support rules when a child is conceived through rape, sperm theft, or statutory rape. Courts often insist that these biological parents cannot be excused from their duty of support because the child's needs always outweigh the adult's needs. No responsibility-sensitive theory of distributive justice would support these outcomes or their reasoning. The child's needs do not have categorical priority over adults' needs, and causal responsibility does not have categorical priority over other principles of justice. No plausible system of distributive justice would hamper the life of the statutory rape victim for no added benefit to the infant. Courts make an added mistake when they impose support on victims of rape or sperm theft. These genetic parents did not make a voluntary choice to conceive. They are not even a causal parent. Demanding child support from them is like demanding it from a random stranger, except worse because it compounds the victim's injury.

Why do courts ignore these distributive concerns? Judges appear to think it disrespects the infant to consider how financial duties affect the biological parents. I suspect these courts are conflating child support with a causal duty, a mistake encouraged by the litigation posture. A child exists who needs support. The only parties before the court are the child, the biological parents, and (sometimes) the state. If this were a tort case, concerns about distributive fairness could only be offered as an excuse for not enforcing the parent's relational duty to the child – that is why distributive justice gets pushed to the margins of tort law. Our child support regime, in contrast, is distributive at its core. We seek a fair allocation of the social costs of child-rearing between causal parents, caregivers, and the community. Causation does create a relation *between the child and the adult*, and I suspect courts mistakenly assume this empirical relation settles the distributive relation *between the adult and society*. Many of these adults, however, have no causal duty to the child. Even if they do, the salience of their causal duty is easily overblown because the courts focus only on the parties before them. Judges are unlikely to address distributive questions coherently when the litigation context constricts their vision to a narrow set of private individuals.

The final revision is more systematic. A liberal-egalitarian theory must think more subtly about the foundational premise that causal parents impose costs on fellow citizens. Focusing on causal responsibility may lead theorists, as it has judges, to conflate ethical judgments about personal duties with systemic political judgments about justice.[137] Unfortunately, my deserted island hypothetical plays into this tendency. Eve's birth creates potential burdens for Dana without clear offsetting benefits. Any child-rearing burdens not met by Eve's three causal parents will fall entirely on Dana, a bystander who bears no personal responsibility. The extent of those costs also depends primarily on natural facts about child development and the island's natural resources, for which Dana also bears no responsibility.

None of these three crucial facts hold when we evaluate the justice of child-rearing arrangements in political communities. First, if causal parents do not raise the child, the costs of child-rearing need not fall directly on a single, unwilling bystander. Political communities can collectively manage the social cost of child-rearing. They can build adoption networks to find volunteer parents and use taxation to spread the financial and opportunity costs. Second, the cost of raising a child in a community is a function of the basic structure that it has overlain on natural facts. For example, a state's decision to mandate education and prohibit child labor determines how long youth remain financially dependent. Third, the law regulates childhood in these ways because children are essential to sustain the community. Many legal scholars and philosophers argue that children produce a net social benefit to society over their lifetime, which raises the question of how to justly distribute the costs of producing this collective good.[138] The more children are viewed as a communal investment, and the more social arrangements affect the cost of child-rearing, the more the community should pay rather than causal parents (or caregivers).

This book will not seek to resolve these difficult questions about the just distribution of child-rearing between causal parents, caregivers, and the community. The point is simply that causal responsibility is one – but only one – among many *distributive* principles. Within a responsibility-sensitive conception of distributive justice, the people whose voluntary acts create a child justly bear some of the child-rearing costs. Nevertheless, American child support law exaggerates causal responsibility in its effort to dodge our collective responsibility for children.

CONCLUSION

Child support cases frequently invoke two causal arguments: a biological parent wrongs their child by not providing financial support, and a biological parent must support their child to avoid imposing child-rearing costs on the community. While both strands begin with intuitive premises, the arguments support only limited

[137] Heather Draper & Jonathan Ives, *Paternity Testing: A Poor Test of Fatherhood*, 31 J. Soc. Welfare & Fam. L. 407, 411–12 (2009) (carefully distinguishing moral and financial fatherhood yet still grounding both in personal relations rather than distributive justice).

[138] Martha Fineman, The Autonomy Myth: A Theory of Dependency (2004); Serena Olsaretti, *Children as Public Goods?*, 41 Phil. & Pub. Aff. 226 (2013); Liam Shields, *Children as Public Goods: At What Cost?*, http://liamshields.com/wp-content/uploads/2018/12/Children-as-Public-Goods-at-what-cost.pdf (last visited June 19, 2024).

personal or political obligations. Causal parents have a personal duty to the child to ensure the child has a valuable life, but this causal duty does not typically require personal caregiving or even financial support. According to luck egalitarian theories of distributive justice, a community may insist that causal parents pay for some of the social costs of child-rearing. However, responsibility for one's voluntary choices is only one factor in a just allocation of child-rearing costs among causal parents, caregivers, and the community.

This picture of causal parentage allows us to identify the mistakes made in *Nathaniel J.* Nathaniel was too young to give the kind of genuine consent that would make Ricci's conduct permissible, but he did engage in voluntary conduct that created a child and, thus, had a personal duty to ensure the child received care. Nothing suggests Nathaniel violated his personal causal duty to the child. While he did not seek custody himself, there was no suggestion that the child faced any risk of neglect. Instead, the court insisted that Nathaniel owed the state compensation for the financial support that it paid to the child's foster parents. Even if the community believes that causal parents should bear some of the child-rearing costs from their voluntary acts, that does not entail a minor victim of sexual exploitation must pay this cost. The court mistakenly treated Nathaniel's causal duty to the child as if it settled the just distribution of social costs between Nathaniel and the state. No just system would hamper a teenager's life simply to reimburse the state, especially when it offers no benefit to the infant.

4

Parents by Caregiving

Jennifer Peck and Sarah Sinnott wanted to adopt a child from Guatemala.[1] Their daughter was from Guatemala, and they wanted the siblings to share the same national origin. Unfortunately, the agency would not facilitate same-sex adoptions. Jennifer adopted a child, M.P., in Guatemala, and they planned to perform a second-parent adoption for Sarah back in Vermont. Unfortunately, soon after their return, Jennifer's parents passed away, and Sarah became ill. They never completed the Vermont adoption. Nevertheless, they treated Sarah as an equal parent. Sarah took maternity leave and then returned part-time so she could be the primary caregiver. M.P. referred to Sarah as "Mom," and Jennifer introduced her as M.P.'s mother. Four years later, the couple broke up. They created a custody agreement, which worked for three more years. Then their relationship soured, and Jennifer cut off all ties between Sarah and the children. When Sarah sued for custody, the lower courts concluded that Sarah lacked statutory standing to seek custody of M.P. because she was neither her biological nor adoptive parent.

The Vermont Supreme Court reversed the lower courts by embracing a "de facto parent" doctrine. The court's central intuition was that Sarah was a parent because, with Jennifer's consent, she committed to raising the child and provided emotional and physical care for long enough to develop a parent–child relationship. This is the core of *Sinnott*, which I will call a "caregiver theory" of parentage. *Sinnott* also exemplifies ambiguities latent in this perspective. The opinion circles amorphously around ideas about intentions, plans, commitments, consent, agreements, caregiving, and labor. Sarah might have obtained parental rights because Jennifer agreed to shared caregiving or parenthood, because Sarah committed to parenthood, because Sarah fulfilled caregiving labor, or because Sarah and the child developed a relationship deserving protection.

Caregiver theories typically go under different labels, which I avoid because they hide similar ambiguities that obscure normative analysis. Many family law scholars would classify *Sinnott* as a "functional" parentage case. Although she had no formal

[1] Sinnott v. Peck, 180 A.3d 560, 562, 572 (Vt. 2017).

status, Sarah should have parental rights because she fulfilled caregiving functions that built parental attachments for the child. At the same time, functionalists often argue that caregiving reveals the adult's commitment to the child.[2] Functionalists lean heavily on this ambiguity between caregiving and commitment because most of them also want to justify a presumption for gestational parents.[3] Although gestation does not develop parental bonds for the child, it can demonstrate commitment to future caregiving.

Ethicists, on the other hand, are more likely to see *Sinnott* as an example of "voluntarism." Moral voluntarists will conclude that Sarah incurred parental *duties* because she accepted parental roles voluntarily.[4] Unfortunately, this "voluntarist" label masks a similar ambiguity. Voluntarists often insist that adults can accept parental roles either by caring for a child or by committing to raising a child. Adoptive parents like Jennifer commit to parenthood expressly, but most biological parents commit only implicitly by bringing their children home and caring for them.

Which grounds parental rights and duties: caregiving or commitment? A person may raise a child without committing to being a parent; conversely, a person may commit to raising the child before doing any caregiving. This chapter briefly departs from the book's typical structure to disentangle these two related grounds for parenthood. The opening interlude that follows offers a conceptual analysis to distinguish a caregiver theory from a moral power theory. The remaining sections return to the book's typical format to evaluate the caregiver theory.

2 Nancy E. Dowd, *Parentage at Birth: Birthfathers and Social Fatherhood*, 14 WM. & MARY BILL RTS. J. 909, 917–19 (2006) (social fatherhood defined by nurture also includes commitment to duties).

3 *See, e.g.*, Douglas NeJaime, *The Constitution of Parenthood*, 72 STAN. L. REV. 261, 371–73 (2020). Some scholars argue intent should be determinative because it is a reliable predictor of subsequent caregiving. Dara E. Purvis, *The Origin of Parental Rights: Labor, Intent, and Fathers*, 41 FLA. ST. U. L. REV. 645 (2013); Linda D. Elrod, *A Child's Perspective of Defining a Parent: The Case for Intended Parenthood*, 25 BYU J. PUB. L. 245, 249 (2011). Functionalism is ambiguous in other ways as well. Many family-law functionalists prefer standards to rules. *E.g.*, Nancy D. Polikoff, *This Child Does Have Two Mothers: Redefining Parenthood to Meet the Needs of Children in Lesbian-Mother and Other Nontraditional Families*, 78 GEO. L.J. 459, 463–64 (1989); Douglas NeJaime, *The Nature of Parenthood*, 126 YALE L.J. 2260, 2338–39 (2016). These ambiguities are regrettably cross-cutting. Rules (e.g., a marital presumption) might be more accurate proxies for caregiving than standards (e.g., de facto parent doctrine) given the limits of litigation, judicial competence or bias, and parties' incentives. Philosophers may see a third ambiguity: parenthood might be a functional kind. *See, e.g.*, DAVID ARCHARD, THE FAMILY: A LIBERAL DEFENCE 10 (2010). A "functional kind" is a category defined not by a natural property (genetic parent) but by a role it plays (raising a child). Different individuals can realize functional roles in multiple ways. Anyone who cares for a child is their parent. This helps explain why attempts to identify parents functionally seem circular, such as insisting adults "have parental rights and obligations … based on their conduct of having parented the child and, as a result, formed a parent–child bond." Courtney G. Joslin & Douglas NeJaime, *How Parenthood Functions*, 123 COLUM. L. REV. 319, 329–30 (2023).

4 Elizabeth Brake, *Willing Parents: A Voluntarist Account of Parental Role Obligations*, *in* PROCREATION AND PARENTHOOD: THE ETHICS OF BEARING AND REARING CHILDREN 151 (David Archard & David Benatar eds., 2010).

The intuition driving caregiver theories of parenthood is that an individual becomes a parent by performing the caregiving that establishes a psychological parent–child relationship. Part I traces strands of the caregiver theory throughout parentage law, especially in constitutional parental rights, the parentage presumptions, and recent reforms like de facto parenthood. Part II isolates three distinct moral principles that can generate personal duties and rights for caregivers: a voluntary undertaking duty, a labor-based right, and estoppel principles. None of these caregiver rights or duties can ground parentage because they cannot explain who may care for a child, why caregivers would obtain broad authority over the child's life, or why caregivers must accept conventional parental duties. Part III argues that a political theory of parenthood is necessary to fill these crucial gaps in the moral principles around caregiving. Nevertheless, caregiving must remain central to any theory of parentage that respects children's status as equals.

TWO KINDS OF VOLUNTARIST THEORIES

The first class of voluntarist theory insists parenthood is a social role that adults voluntarily accept, akin to a professional role. Medical students obtain professional obligations by swearing an oath to uphold the standards of the medical profession. Ethicists like Onora O'Neil and Elizabeth Brake believe adults obtain parental duties through a similar process by voluntarily accepting the social role of a parent.[5] Adults have various ways of accepting parenthood. Nonbiological parents can commit through adoption, signing a parentage acknowledgment, or entering a preconception agreement. Some biological parents also make express commitments, such as by signing a paternity acknowledgment or filing a parentage petition. More often, biological parents accept parental duties through conduct exhibiting subjective commitment, such as bringing the child home rather than placing them for adoption.

Some theorists would label this set of ideas "intentional" or "contractual" parenthood. I will call them "normative power" theories. What unites them is an assumption that individuals sometimes have a moral power to create parental rights or duties through an act of commitment or acceptance, expressed in the right manner in the right context. Normative power theories effectively assimilate all parentage rules to adoption. The different rules merely reflect differences in the timing or procedure for commitment.[6] From a voluntarist perspective, Sarah became a parent either when she orally agreed to the adoption plan with Jennifer in Guatemala or when she brought the child home to Vermont with a subjective commitment to raising the child.

[5] *Id.*; Onora O'Neill, *Begetting, Bearing, and Rearing, in* Having Children: Philosophical and Legal Reflections on Parenthood 25 (William Ruddick & Onora O'Neill eds., 1979).

[6] *See, e.g.*, Janet Farrell Smith, *A Child of One's Own, in* Adoption Matters: Philosophical and Feminist Essays 112, 126–27 (Sally Haslanger & Charlotte Witt eds., 2005).

The second class of voluntarist theories emphasizes caregiving relationships over moments of commitment. An adult becomes a parent by voluntarily performing the material and emotional caretaking that builds a deep relationship with a child. Parental duties and rights arise once caregiving forms this parental relationship rather than through commitment per se. From a caregiving perspective, Sarah became a parent when she had raised the child long enough to develop deep interpersonal bonds. For the first few days or weeks, her parental rights and duties were tenuous. After seven years, their parent–child relationship was established beyond question.

Such caregiver theories are voluntarist only in a weaker sense. Parental rights and duties arise through the adults' voluntary conduct rather than being ascribed based on a natural kind like genetic parentage or a social category like marital status. While the adult's caregiving conduct must be voluntary rather than forced, they need not deliberately commit to being a parent per se. Most caregivers are genuinely committed to parenthood, but child-rearing could generate parental duties even with no express or subjective commitment to parenthood. A stepparent or foster parent might, at some point, incur parental duties regardless of their intentions or preferences.

Both varieties of voluntarism offer many putative benefits. First, they are parsimonious. They purport to unify parenthood for biological, functional, and adoptive parents under a single principle. Second, they align parentage with other special duties that an individual owes to specific people, as opposed to general duties that everyone owes to everyone else. Most special duties arise in relationships that we form voluntarily, like contracts, clubs, or friendships. Third, voluntarism easily explains why parental duties vary across societies. Parental duties are defined by social conventions that parents accept by voluntarily entering the social role. Fourth, voluntarism seems to address worries about demandingness. If adults enter their parental roles voluntarily, then the complaint that parental duties are unfairly demanding loses much of its force.

With all these apparent virtues, can either form of voluntarism offer a complete theory to ground personal duties or rights between a parent and child? The short answer is no. Both caregiving and normative powers are essential to a pluralist theory of parentage, but individually they are woefully incomplete. Chapter 5 considers normative powers theories. The remainder of this chapter evaluates the caregiver theory.

I CAREGIVER THEORIES IN PARENTAGE LAW

Caregiving principles were implicit in the marital presumption and gained constitutional status in the US Supreme Court's nonmarital father cases. In intervening years, the caregiver theory spread throughout parentage law, driven by attachment theory in developmental psychology and feminist demands for recognition of caregiving labor.

A *Caregiving in Constitutional Parental Rights*

1 Caregiving is Necessary to Complete Genetic Parent's Constitutional Rights

As I explained in Chapter 2, genetic parents have a constitutional right to be a parent *conditioned on adequate caregiving*. Parents have constitutional rights to fulfill their concomitant responsibilities to raise the child.[7] This duty affects constitutional parentage. As *Lehr v. Robertson* explained, a genetic parent acquires parental rights only if he "demonstrates a full commitment to the responsibilities of parenthood by coming forward to participate in the rearing of his child."[8] This oft-quoted sentence replicates the ambiguity described in the preliminary part of this chapter: genetic parents demonstrate commitment through child-rearing. Other passages in *Lehr* emphasize the priority of the relationship built through child-rearing. The Court noted that "the importance of the familial relationship, to the individuals involved and to the society, stems from the emotional attachments that derive from the intimacy of daily association, and from the role it plays in promoting a way of life through the instruction of children."[9] Numerous lower-court opinions reaffirm the necessity of caregiving relationships to constitutional parenthood. Subjective commitment is insufficient. For example, the Utah Supreme Court concluded genetic parent retains their parental opportunity only if they are "shouldering significant responsibility with respect to the daily supervision, education, protection, or care of the child."[10]

While commitment is necessary, it is the primary focus only in newborn cases when the genetic parent has not had sufficient opportunity to perform caregiving. When a genetic parent makes ambiguous statements or acts in equivocal ways during pregnancy, a court may conclude that they waived their parental opportunity.[11] The gestational mother must make plans, so the genetic parent must participate or get out of the way. Even in these cases, subjective commitment is necessary but not sufficient. A genetic parent must offer to help with the pregnancy as soon as they know or should know about it. More

7 Jeffrey Shulman, The Constitutional Parent: Rights, Responsibilities, and the Enfranchisement of the Child (2014).

8 463 U.S. 248, 257 (1983) (internal quotations omitted).

9 *Id.* at 262 (quoting Smith v. Org. of Foster Fams. for Equal. & Reform, 431 U.S. 816, 844 (1977) and Wisconsin v. Yoder, 406 U.S. 205, 231–33 (1972)).

10 *In re* Adoption of T.B., 232 P.3d 1026, 1035 (Utah 2010) (internal quotation omitted). *See, e.g.*, T.R.F. v. Felan, 760 P.2d 906, 910 (Utah Ct. App. 1988) (Unwed father had properly acknowledged his child where he "received the child into his home for brief visits and on occasion his child would spend the night … [and] also visited the child at the child's mother's home. [He] took the child to Texas to meet his family. He held the child out to the public and to his family as his own.").

11 Mary Beck, *Prenatal Abandonment: Horton Hatches the Egg in the Supreme Court and Thirty-Four States*, 24 Mich. J. Gender & L. 53, 89–119 (2017).

importantly, they must take steps to prepare to care for the child and follow through once the child is born. If the gestational parent wants to place the child for adoption, a mere genetic parent can object only by accepting full legal and physical custody.[12]

2 Caregiving may be a Ground for Birth Mother's Constitutional Rights

The constitutional parental rights of gestational parents may rest on a relationship generated by pregnancy. The US Supreme Court has said little about the grounds of constitutional maternity, but scholars and lower courts have tried to infer its principles from the equal protection cases brought by genetic fathers. The Court has held it is not sex discrimination to give gestational mothers an automatic right to veto adoption while insisting genetic fathers must first prove commitment through caregiving.[13] Similarly, the federal government may allow gestational mothers to transmit citizenship automatically but require genetic fathers to legitimate their children before they turn eighteen.[14] In both cases, the Court appears to reason that the law may treat gestational parents and genetic fathers differently because gestation and childbirth are caregiving work that creates an incipient relationship with the child.[15] If this reasoning is correct, genetic-gestational parents have constitutional parental rights at birth.

It is unclear whether the same reasoning should apply to surrogacy. A "traditional surrogate" agrees to conceive a child using her own eggs and promises to waive her parental rights in favor of the intended parent or parents. As the genetic mother and gestational carrier, some courts have held the surrogate has constitutional parental rights, which a state can terminate only by following traditional adoption rules.[16] Even the UPA 2017, which takes a proenforcement approach, allows a genetic surrogate to void their agreement for seventy-two hours after the birth – the same time frame as for rescinding an adoption.[17] Since mere genetic parents receive no similar special protections, one might think the constitutional analysis of gestational surrogacy would be similar. Gestational and traditional surrogacy involve the same work, cause the same bodily changes, and may lead to the same attachments. Nevertheless, many statutes and the UPA 2017 treat gestational surrogacy agreements as

12 Adoption of Michael H., 898 P.2d 891, 896 (Cal. 1995); Robert O. v. Russell K., 604 N.E.2d 99, 103 (N. Y. 1992).

13 Caban v. Mohammed, 441 U.S. 380, 389 (1979).

14 Tuan Anh Nguyen v. I.N.S., 533 U.S. 53, 65 (2001).

15 Katharine K. Baker, *The DNA Default and Its Discontents: Establishing Modern Parenthood*, 96 B. U. L. Rev. 2037, 2060–61 (2016).

16 *In re* Baby, 447 S.W.3d 807, 832 (Tenn. 2014).

17 UPA 2017 § 814(a)(2).

binding under certain conditions.[18] Two prominent cases have expressly rejected parental rights claims by gestational surrogates.[19]

3 Caregiving may be Sufficient for Constitutional Rights

If a person must be a caregiver to have constitutional parental rights, can someone get those rights solely by caring for a child? The US Supreme Court has not addressed this question, but some lower courts have concluded that adults without genetic ties can acquire constitutional parental interests by fulfilling parental roles.

Some cases conclude that caregiving en route to satisfying a presumption is sufficient to establish constitutional parental rights. This happens most often when the birth mother's cohabitant holds out the child as their own but has not met other statutory requirements for the residential presumption. In *In re Jerry P.*, J.R. was living with his partner when she conceived and believed he was the father.[20] They separated during the pregnancy because he tried to get her to stop using drugs. After the birth, J.R. visited the child daily in the ICU. The child welfare agency took the child from the hospital directly into state custody. J.R. visited the foster home as often as permitted, even after DNA tests proved he was not the genetic father. The child eventually came to call him "Daddy." The foster parents and birth mother supported J.R.'s parentage claim, but the juvenile court concluded J.R. had no right to custody because he was not the genetic father and never lived with the child, as required by the residential presumption.

The California appellate court reversed because it would be unjust if "a man who has established a loving, nurturing parental relationship with a child can be denied presumed father status because, through no fault of his own, he cannot physically bring the child into his home ... because ... DCFS [Department of Children and Family Services] ... made it impossible."[21] The parent–child relationship stems not from genetics but "from the emotional attachments which derive from the intimacy of contact between the parent and child."[22] J.R. and the child developed these bonds during his visitation, so he had constitutional parental rights. The court's approach treats the presumptions like genetics. A presumptive parent has a conditional liberty to care for a child, and once they do so, they have full parental rights.

In a more common scenario, a cohabitant or relative helps raise a child alongside the legal parent. Several state supreme courts have held that an unrelated adult can

18 Michael J. Higdon, *Constitutional Parenthood*, 103 IOWA L. REV. 1483, 1535–36 (2018).

19 Johnson v. Calvert, 851 P.2d 776 (Cal. 1993); P.M. v. T.B., 907 N.W.2d 522, 542 (Iowa 2018). *See also* J. R. v. Utah, 261 F. Supp. 2d 1268 (D. Utah 2002) (statute granting legal maternity to gestational carrier surrogate violated substantive due process rights of genetic parents).

20 *In re* Jerry P., 95 Cal. App. 4th 793, 816 (2002). *See also* Adoption of Kelsey S., 823 P.2d 1216 (Cal. 1992).

21 *In re Jerry P.*, 95 Cal. App. 4th at 804.

22 *Id.* at 817. *But see In re* S.C., No. F073961, 2017 WL 728298, at *6 (Cal. Ct. App. Feb. 24, 2017) (unpublished opinion) (expressing skepticism about *In re Jerry P.*, but in a case where man did little during pregnancy or after birth).

acquire constitutional parental rights if they live with the child and, with the parent's consent, fulfill the parental responsibilities that build attachments for the child.[23] Because the caregiver becomes a coequal parent, these courts conclude that the de facto parent has a constitutional right to custody. I discuss de facto parent doctrines in detail in the state law section B.4 below.

4 Constitutional Parental Rights for Relative Primary Caregivers

Several courts have also extended some constitutional rights to relatives who have acted as surrogate parents.[24] The US Supreme Court recognized that kin caregivers have constitutional liberty interests akin to parental rights. In *Moore v. East Cleveland*, the Court held that East Cleveland violated a grandmother's right to familial association because its single-family zoning rule prohibited her from living with grandsons born from two different fathers. Moore did not bring the claim as a parent, but she did have legal custody of one of her grandsons.

Relying on *Moore*, the Second Circuit held that a relative who had served as the children's custodial caregiver acquired parent-like constitutional rights. Rivera raised her half-siblings "almost from birth" for over six years, including ten months as a legal foster parent after their mother entered a psychiatric institution. When the state denied her petition for guardianship, the Second Circuit concluded that the state violated Rivera's "liberty interest in the integrity and stability of her family."[25] Quoting extensively from *Moore*, the court reasoned that relatives who live in the same household often "take on major responsibility for the rearing of children," especially in times of adversity such as economic need or after a parent's death.[26] Rivera's interest in custody of her "surrogate children" was "rendered more compelling" because the children had a complementary interest in sustaining their long-standing familial relationship with Rivera, their "surrogate mother."[27]

The Constitution might also extend limited protection to relatives who perform significant caregiving without custody or guardianship. In *Johnson v. City of*

[23] *In re* Parentage of L.B., 155 Wash. 2d 679, 710, 712 (2005) ("The State is not interfering on behalf of a third party in an insular family unit but is enforcing the rights and obligations of parenthood that attach to de facto parents; a status that can be achieved only through the active encouragement of the biological or adoptive parent by affirmatively establishing a family unit with the de facto parent and child or children that accompany the family."); Smith v. Guest, 16 A.3d 920, 931 (Del. 2011) (because caregiver has a parental interest, "allowing [her] to pursue that interest through a legally-recognized channel cannot unconstitutionally infringe on" the birth parent's rights).

[24] Sacha M. Coupet, *Ain't I a Parent: The Exclusion of Kinship Caregivers from the Debate over Expansions of Parenthood*, 34 N.Y.U. Rev. L. & Soc. Change 595 (2010).

[25] Rivera v. Marcus, 696 F.2d 1016 (2d Cir. 1982).

[26] *Id.* at 1023 (quoting Moore v. City of East Cleveland, 431 U.S. 494, 504–05 (1977)).

[27] *Id.* at 1026, 1028. *See also* Ellis v. Hamilton, 669 F.2d 510, 514 (7th Cir. 1982) (concluding "a great-aunt, an adoptive grandmother, and a de facto mother and father all rolled up into one" had a "liberty interest in the society of her grandchildren," but ultimately holding state gave her adequate process). *But see* K.K. v. Berks Cty., No. 5:15-CV-00475, 2016 WL 1274052, at *6 (E.D. Pa. Mar. 31, 2016) (denying liberty interest in similar circumstances but with shorter custodial caregiving).

Cincinnati, the city violated a grandmother's right to familial association because the "drug exclusion zone" around a school prevented her from watching her grandchildren and taking them to school.[28] Johnson did not live with the children, but she had a liberty interest because she had "been an active participant in the lives and activities of her grandchildren, with the consent and support of the children's mother."[29] In contrast, when a relative has not performed substantial caregiving, courts routinely deny that genetic relatedness and emotional bonds can justify a constitutional interest in custody, visitation, or adoption.[30]

B *Caregiver Theory in Modern State Parentage*

The caregiver theory is embedded deeply and broadly in state parentage law. Formal rules like marital and residential parentage often serve as proxies for caregiving, and many states have been expanding protection for caregivers through estoppel and de facto parenthood.

1 Marital Presumption as a Caregiver Presumptions

The spouse of the birth mother is a presumed parent at birth, and they retain their parental status unless someone challenges their parentage within the statute of limitations. The marital presumption applies to most children because around 60 percent of children are born to married women. Historically, the marital presumption's primary purposes were to reinforce gender norms of the marital family, shield the husband's patrilineality, and ensure his right to child labor.[31] Currently, the presumption applies without regard to the spouse's sex or gender, even when a birth mother and their partner plan conception with donor gametes. This modern marital presumption reflects three distinct inferences: (1) the spouse is likely the child's genetic parent before the birth; (2) the spouse likely intended to be a parent and helped with the pregnancy; and (3) after the birth, the spouse likely helped raise the child.[32]

Recognizing the imperfect overlap of the three bases, some scholars try to tame the presumption. Susan Appleton, for example, argues that the marital

[28] Johnson v. City of Cincinnati, 310 F.3d 484 (6th Cir. 2002).

[29] *Id.* at 501.

[30] Mullins v. State of Oregon, 57 F.3d 789, 794 (9th Cir. 1995); Brown v. Ives, 129 F.3d 209 (1st Cir. 1997); Thompson v. Ashe, 250 F.3d 399 (6th Cir. 2001) (nonresident grandmother had no associational right that prevented public housing from adopting no-trespass rule that prohibited her from "visiting" her grandchildren).

[31] Susan Frelich Appleton, *Presuming Women: Revisiting the Presumption of Legitimacy in the Same-Sex Couples Era*, 86 B.U. L. Rev. 227, 246, 285–86 (2006).

[32] Courts also invoke two question-begging rationales: it "promotes the family unit" and it ensures the child has two sources of financial support. McLaughlin v. Cty. of Pima, 401 P.3d 492, 499–500 (Ariz. 2017). A general policy to promote families offers no reason to identify one person as part of the family. A child's need for two sources of support cannot explain why this support must come from the spouse.

"presumption today reflects the belief that someone legally connected to the woman bearing the child likely planned for the child, demonstrated a willingness to assume responsibility, or provided support (emotional and/or economic) during the pregnancy, in turn supporting the expected child."[33] Two doctrines add support to this idea that marriage primarily serves as a proxy for prebirth commitment: the spouse is a presumed parent at birth before they perform any caregiving, and the presumption sometimes applies to donor conception cases even though the spouse cannot be a genetic parent. States have long applied these doctrines to husbands and, once marriage was opened to same-sex couples, extended them to female spouses of gestational parents as well.[34]

Nevertheless, the rebuttal process demonstrates that the presumption also continues to serve as a proxy for genetics and postbirth caregiving. In paternity challenges regarding newborns, courts routinely allow genetic evidence to rebut the marital presumption.[35] If the husband is not a genetic parent, the law will not force him to pay child support for the infant or force his wife to share parenthood. When spouses plan donor conception, courts often need another statutory or equitable principle to justify refusing to rebut the presumption.[36]

Paternity challenges regarding older children are cast in a different light that reveals the role of caregiving. The statute of limitations and its exception confirm the centrality of caregiving. After two years, the marital presumption becomes conclusive – unless the spouse never resided with the child and never held themselves out as a parent. The UPA assumes that any spouse who meets these criteria has fulfilled parental roles sufficient to establish a parental relationship.

In a few states, even if the challenge is timely, the court must still determine whether a "rebuttal of the presumption would be appropriate in the circumstances of the case."[37] Although this is an all-things-considered test, most courts insist that

33 Appleton, *supra* note 31, at 285–86. *But see* Joanna L. Grossman, *The New Illegitimacy: Tying Parentage to Marital Status for Lesbian Co-Parents*, 20 AM. U. J. GENDER SOC. POL'Y & L. 671, 719–20 (2012) ("The partner's functional role in parent-like activities over a period of time . . . would seem a much better indicator of consent to share the role of parent than whether the couple said vows to each other at some point.").

34 *In re* Pima Cty. Juv. Severance Action No. S-114487, 876 P.2d 1121, 1129 (Ariz. 1994); Treto v. Treto, 622 S.W.3d 397, 401 (Tex. App. 2020) (collecting cases with lesbian spouses). The US Constitution should require this extension. The Supreme Court held that prohibiting same-sex marriage violated the fundamental right to marry because it denied same-sex couples an equal ability to form families. Obergefell v. Hodges, 576 U.S. 614, 667–68 (2015). *See also* Pueblo v. Haas, 999 N.W.2d 433, 445–46 (Mich. 2023) (holding *Obergefell* required extending an equitable marital presumption to same-sex spouses who would have enjoyed it if able to marry); Pavan v. Smith, 582 U.S. 563 (2017) (refusal to include lesbian spouse on a birth certificate violated right to marry). Unfortunately, the Court's recent adoption of historicist methods for defining fundamental rights challenges this reasoning for treating parentage presumptions as protected by the right to marry. Dobbs v. Jackson Women's Health Org., 597 U.S. 215, 231 (2022).

35 Ambrose v. Ambrose, 536 S.E.2d 855, 857 (N.C. App. 2000).

36 McLaughlin v. Jones *ex rel.* Cty. of Pima, 401 P.3d 492, 501 (Ariz. 2017).

37 *In re* Jesusa V., 85 P.3d 2, 13 (Cal. Ct. App. 4th 2004).

parental relationships take priority over genetics.[38] The "core consideration" is "in preserving and protecting the developed parent–child . . . relationships which give young children social and emotional strength and stability."[39] Other states place even greater emphasis on parental roles. The Alabama Supreme Court concluded that a husband's paternity may not be challenged so long as he "has been discharging his parental obligations of support, love, and companionship toward the child, and the husband displays a commitment to continuing in his parental role, with all that it entails."[40] Alabama's lower courts extended similar reasoning to the residential presumption, reasoning that the law should "protect the sanctity of such parental relationships over that of a party claiming only a biological connection."[41]

2 Parentage by Estoppel

Other states reach similar results through equitable estoppel. Even in states that treat the presumptions as evidence of genetic paternity, courts still feel the need to protect the children who develop relationships and the adults who invest in caregiving. Accordingly, they reach for equity. A court may estop a party from introducing genetic evidence to rebut a parentage presumption if the evidence contradicts their past deliberate representations about parentage.[42]

Traditional estoppel cases involve paternity deception. A birth mother cannot deny her husband's paternity if her knowing "deceit and inaction" caused him to believe he was the genetic father, encouraged him to reorganize his life to provide emotional and financial care for the child, and allowed the husband and child "to develop deep emotional ties with each other."[43] Some recent cases apply paternity by estoppel even when both spouses knew the genetic facts, because preserving the presumed parental relationship serves the child's interests.[44] As the Supreme Court of Pennsylvania explained:

38 Alisha C. v. Jeremy C., 808 N.W.2d 875, 890 (Neb. 2012); Turner v. Whisted, 607 A.2d 935, 940 (Md. 1992); Nicholas H. v. Kimberly H., 46 P.3d 932 (Cal. 2002). States may also require courts to consider the child's interests before admitting DNA evidence, N.A.H. v. S.L.S., 9 P.3d 354, 361–64 (Colo. 2000); Kamp v. Dep't of Hum. Servs., 980 A.2d 448, 464 (Md. 2009), or allow a court to deny testing for "good cause." D.W. v. R.W., 52 A.3d 1043, 1057 (N.J. 2012).

39 Neil S. v. Mary L., 131 Cal. Rptr. 3d 51, 57 (Cal. Ct. App. 4th 2011).

40 *Ex parte* Presse, 554 So. 2d 406 (Ala. 1989); R.D. v. S.S., 309 So. 3d 146, 154 (Ala. Civ. App. 2020).

41 C.E.G. v. A.L.A., 194 So. 3d 950, 958 (Ala. Civ. App. 2015); D.I. v. I.G., 262 So. 3d 651, 658 (Ala. Civ. App. 2018).

42 White v. White, 293 S.W.3d 1, 17 (Mo. Ct. App. 2009).

43 Randy A.J. v. Norma I.J., 677 N.W.2d 630, 641 (Wis. 2004).

44 Christopher Y.Y. v. Jessica Z.Z., 69 N.Y.S.3d 887, 895 (N.Y. App. Div. 2018); Shondel J. v. Mark D., 853 N.E.2d 610, 616 (N.Y. 2006). Other courts refuse to apply estoppel if both parents knew the genetic facts because neither party made or relied on any false representations and applying estoppel would allow adults to skirt adoption rules. *E.g.*, Barber v. Barber, 77 P.3d 576, 579–80 (Okla. 2003); *In re* Donovan L., 198 Cal. Rptr. 3d 550, 558 (Cal. Ct. App. 4th 2016).

> Absent any overriding equities in favor of the putative father, such as fraud, the law cannot permit a party to renounce even an assumed duty of parentage when by doing so, the innocent child would be victimized. Relying upon the representation of the parental relationship, a child naturally and normally extends his love and affection to the putative parent. The representation of parentage inevitably obscures the identity and whereabouts of the natural father, so that the child will be denied the love, affection and support of the natural father. … While the law cannot prohibit the putative father from informing the child of their true relationship, it can prohibit him from employing the sanctions of the law to avoid the obligations which their assumed relationship would otherwise impose.[45]

Unlike traditional estoppel, which focuses on equity between parents, this expanded estoppel focuses on representations made to the child.[46] When a birth mother and a presumed parent encourage their child to develop parental attachments, neither party may use genetic evidence to avoid shared custody or child support. Neither parent can complain of unfairness when the law prevents them from contradicting their own past statements to benefit themselves at the child's expense.[47]

Equitable estoppel will typically not apply in two salient cases. First, a deceived husband can typically end a parental relationship that he created without reason to doubt his genetic paternity. Many courts conclude that a husband who never knowingly made false statements to the child or mother cannot be estopped from ending the parental relationship.[48] However, a few states will apply estoppel to hold men to parenthood if they choose not to "insist on a scientific test of paternity before initiating a parental relationship."[49] Second, estoppel is somewhat narrower than the conclusive marital presumption. If a genetic father is entitled to file a paternity petition and does so in a timely fashion, the marital couple cannot use estoppel to deny the genetic father's parental rights. This would allow the couple to end-run the rules of adoption and abandonment.[50]

3 The Residential Presumption

A substantial minority of states have a residential presumption that achieves directly for nonmarital couples what a marital presumption with rebuttal and estoppel

45 K.E.M. v. P.C.S., 38 A.3d 798, 807–08 (Penn. 2012).

46 Shondel J. v. Mark D., 7 N.Y.3d 320, 331, 853 N.E.2d 610, 616 (2006) ("To the child, Mark represented himself as her father.").

47 Nicole M. Riel, *The Other Mother: Protecting Non-Biological Mothers in Same-Sex Marriages Notes*, 31 Quinnipiac Prob. L.J. 387, 403 (2017).

48 K.E.M., 38 A.3d at 820; Clevenger v. Clevenger, 11 Cal. Rptr. 707, 714 (Cal. Ct. App. 1961). Jana Singer, *Marriage, Biology, and Paternity: The Case for Revitalizing the Marital Presumption*, 65 Md. L. Rev. 246, 262 (2006).

49 Shondel, 853 N.E.2d at 616 (denying estoppel requires knowledge).

50 Corey D. v. Travis R., 858 S.E.2d 857, 865 (W. Va. 2021).

doctrines does indirectly.[51] Twelve states have statutory presumptions modeled on the UPA 1973, under which an individual is presumed a parent if they receive a child into their home and hold the child out as their "natural child."[52] Seven have statutes similar to the UPA 2017, under which an individual is a presumed parent of a child if they "resided in the same household with the child for the first two years of the life of the child, … and openly held out the child as the individual's child."[53] The older statutes have no time frame or age limit but require holding out as a "natural parent." The newer act eliminates the reference to natural parents but applies only if the adult lives with a newborn for two years. Both limitations invite the question, Who is the target of this presumption? Does it protect birth parents who believe they are genetic parents (or had a preconception agreement), or does it protect any caregiver?

Some states with the older statute interpret "natural child" as a reference to genetic parentage.[54] The biological interpretation has substantial support in the text and legislative history. The drafters of the UPA 1973 designed the residential presumption as a substitute for the marital presumption for unmarried fathers, both of which they imagined offered "external" proof of which man is the probable father.[55] This biological interpretation fits the ordinary language and the act's rebuttal provisions. The act lists the evidence relevant for rebuttal, and it is exclusively evidence of biological paternity.[56] Nevertheless, other state courts have interpreted the "natural parent" language to encompass nonbiological fathers who hold themselves out as parents, even if all the parties knew the biological facts.[57] Appealing to purposive statutory interpretation, these courts reason that the residential presumption serves the state's "interest in preserving and protecting the developed parent–child relationships which give young children social and emotional strength and stability."[58] For the same reasons, some courts have extended their statutory residential presumption to the nonbiological parent in a lesbian couple.[59]

51 Leslie Joan Harris, *Obergefell's Ambiguous Impact on Legal Parentage*, 92 CHI.-KENT L. REV. 55, 85 (2017).

52 *Id.* at 78 n.113. UPA 1973 § 4.

53 UPA 2017 § 204(a)(2).

54 L.P. v. L.F., 338 P.3d 908, 915 (Wyo. 2014); Pippin v. Pippin, No. M2018000376COAR3CV, 2020 WL 2499633, at *6 (Tenn. Ct. App. May 14, 2020). Minnesota amended the uniform act to remove the ambiguity, requiring the father to "hold out the child as his biological child." Minn. Stat. § 257.55, subd. 1(d) (discussed in *In re* Welfare of C.M.G., 516 N.W.2d 555, 558 (Minn. App. 1994)).

55 Harry D. Krause, *The Uniform Parentage Act*, 8 FAM. L. Q. 1, 9 (1974).

56 UPA 1973 § 12. This genetic assumption carried over into the structure and reporter commentary on the UPA 2002. The drafters eliminated all the rules for resolving conflicting presumptions because "[n]owadays the existence of modern genetic testing obviates this old approach" by "mak[ing] it possible in most cases to resolve competing claims to paternity." UNIF. PARENTAGE ACT § 204 cmt. (UNIF. LAW COMM'N 2002). *In re* Guardianship of Madelyn B., 98 A.3d 494, 500–01 (N.H. 2014).

57 Chatterjee v. King, 280 P.3d 283, 293–94 (N.M. 2012); Partanen v. Gallagher, 59 N.E.3d 1133, 1135 (Mass. 2016); *In re* Guardianship of Madelyn B., 98 A.3d 494, 501 (N.H. 2014).

58 *In re* Nicholas H., 46 P.3d 932, 938 (Cal. 2002).

59 Harris, *supra* note 51, at 80 (citing four states).

This functionalist conclusion is easier to reach in the few states that adopted the UPA 2017, which drops any reference to "natural" parents and applies without regard to the sex or gender of the presumed parent. On the other hand, this provision applies only to individuals who live with a newborn, which suggests that, rather than a purely functionalist test, it captures intended parents who have a preconception agreement and coparent after the birth.[60] This narrower interpretation fits some of the case law. When one biological mother argued that the state may not force a second mother onto her single-parent family, the Massachusetts Supreme Court responded that they were always a two-parent family because they had planned conception together and coparented as equals since birth.[61] Allowing genetic rebuttal would deprive the child of emotional and financial support of a person whom the child always regarded as their second parent.

4 De Facto Parenthood

A few courts expanded estoppel beyond its role as a defense to rebuttal, treating it as an independent source of legal parentage. For example, in *Strickland v. Day* the Mississippi Supreme Court held that a birth mother, Kimberly, could not challenge the parentage of her ex-wife, Christina.[62] Kimberly "made numerous representations that Christina was an equal coparent" in a preconception agreement, birth announcements, and daily life with the child. Because of "her belief of and reliance on Kimberly's representations, Christina clearly changed her position" by serving as the "primary caretaker for at least the first year of the child's life" and "taking on all the responsibilities and rewards that accompany parenthood." The court estopped Kimberly from taking this "position . . . wholly inconsistent with her earlier position" because allowing Kimberly to deny Christina's parental status would harm Christina and the child.

Eight states have adopted a functionalist standard for legal parenthood.[63] Under the de facto parenthood doctrine, an individual becomes a legal parent if they, with the existing legal parent's consent or encouragement, lived with the child and "assumed obligations of parenthood by taking significant responsibility for the child's care, education and development" for a "length of time sufficient to have established with the child a bonded, dependent relationship parental in nature."[64]

60 This element may exclude kin caregivers. Joslin and NeJaime, *supra* note 3, at 339 n.131.

61 Partanen, 59 N.E.3d at 1138. A handful of cases apply a residential presumption to adults who have custody without legal authority. *In re* Salvador M., 4 Cal. Rptr. 3d 705, 709 (2003) (adult half-sibling took custody of a child after their mother's death, telling him she was his mother).

62 239 So. 3d 486, 494 (Miss. 2018) (the opinion does not invoke the marital presumption).

63 Gregg Strauss, *What Role Remains for De Facto Parenthood?*, 46 Fla. St. U. L. Rev. 909, 919 n.58 (2018). The highest courts in New York, Kansas, Oklahoma, and Vermont initially rejected de facto parenthood but later recognized a narrow class of parents who helped plan a child's conception or adoption and then took on parental roles. *Id.* at 916 n.40.

64 Conover v. Conover, 146 A.3d 433, 447 (Md. 2016) (adopting test developed in *In re* Custody of H.S. H.-K., 533 N.W.2d 419, 436 (Wis. 1995)). The UPA 2017 codified a version of this test with a significant

The Vermont Supreme Court used de facto parenthood to resolve the case of Sarah, Jennifer, and M.P. that opened this chapter. These courts reason that children develop parental attachments with their residential caregivers regardless of the adult's legal status.

Another group of states do not treat caregivers as legal parents but nevertheless allow them to seek custody or visitation on equal terms with a legal parent.[65] Typically, when a third party seeks visitation or custody over a parent's objection, federal constitutional law requires the court to give "special weight" to the parent's judgment. States effectuate this deference either by raising the substantive standard, so a petitioner must prove denying visitation will cause harm, or raising the evidentiary standard, so a petitioner must prove by clear and convincing evidence that visitation serves the best interests of the child.[66] Many courts and scholars argue that added parental deference is no longer necessary if the "third party" proves de facto parenthood. Because the legal parent encouraged their partner and child to form familial bonds and because disrupting such bonds tends to be harmful, the court may intervene to decide whether preserving this nonparental relationship is in the best interests of the child.[67]

Many of these disputes arise when a parent and their partner end their relationship, while others arise when a legal parent has entrusted a child to a nonparental caregiver. According to Joslin and NeJaime's survey of appellate cases on functional parenthood (parentage and custody), in 47 percent of these cases, the legal parent was not currently or had never served as the child's primary caregiver.[68] As the New York Court of Appeals has explained, these entrustment cases may be handled under abandonment law if the parent maintains little contact or under nonparental custody statutes if the parent maintained a relationship. Under the latter doctrine, the legal parent retains their status, but their judgment is no longer entitled to judicial deference, because the caregiver "is, in essence, acting as a parent with primary physical custody" and "mak[ing] important decisions affecting the child's life."[69]

II CAREGIVING AND MORAL PARENTHOOD

This chapter began with an apparently simple intuition: parents are the people who care for children. This intuition turns out to be complicated, legally and morally. Lawyers and ethicists use the caregiver theory for very different purposes. Section A investigates the ethicists' argument that caregivers incur parental

addition at § 609: a de facto parent must have "held out the child as the individual's child," which would seem to exclude relative caregivers.

65 Strauss, *supra* note 63 at 919–20.

66 *Id. See, e.g., In re* K.H., 773 S.E.2d 20, 31 (W.Va. 2015).

67 *In re* Care & Prot. of Sharlene, 840 N.E.2d 918, 926 (Mass. 2006); A.H. v. M.P., 857 N.E.2d 1061, 1071–72 (Mass. 2006). Strauss, *supra* note 63, at 971–77 (discussing evidence of harm).

68 Joslin and NeJaime, *supra* note 3, at 363–66.

69 Suarez v. Williams, 44 N.E.3d 915, 921 (N.Y. 2015).

duties by voluntarily caring for a child, which in turn justifies their right to parental authority. Section B explores the lawyer's argument that caregivers acquire parental rights because caregivers and children develop an interest in their caregiving relationship.

A *Caregiving as a Ground for Duties*

In the 1970s, Onora O'Neill and Judith Jarvis Thomson argued that parenthood is a social role that adults accept through their voluntary actions.[70] Their view aligned with the contemporaneous US Supreme Court opinions holding that a nonmarital father becomes a full parent by fulfilling parental responsibilities, except these philosophers sought to explain parental duties rather than rights. They believed the burden of parental duties may fall on someone only when they voluntarily accepted parenthood, in some sense. Once they have voluntarily accepted parental duties, an adult may be entrusted with the parental rights needed to fulfill them. As it turns out, these theories are less voluntarist than the label suggests. Although they gain much intuitive appeal from an analogy with consensual duties, voluntarist theories are better understood as reflecting a causal duty generated by a voluntary undertaking.

1 Voluntary Acts that Count as Acceptance

The first step to clarify voluntarist theories of parental duties is to ask what a person must do to accept the parental role. In her famous abortion article, Thomson asserted, "If parents do not try to prevent pregnancy, do not obtain an abortion, and then at the time of birth of the child do not put it out for adoption, but rather take it home with them, then they have assumed responsibility for it . . . and . . . cannot now withdraw support."[71] This scattershot strategy is inadequate. It is unclear which, if any, of these acts or omissions are necessary to "assume responsibility." Indeed, as Chapters 3 and 4 demonstrated, most of these acts or omissions are irrelevant to parental duties. Even purposeful conception does not entail parental duties.

Why, then, do voluntarists like Thomson or O'Neill care about this chain of events? It brings the biological parents to the critical juncture where they must choose: care for the child themselves or find an adoptive family. I take the most plausible voluntarist position to be that a person acquires parental duties by taking a child into their custody. All parents must make this choice, whether they bring the child home from a hospital, orphanage, or foster home. But why assume that anyone

[70] Judith Jarvis Thomson, *A Defense of Abortion*, 1 PHIL. & PUB. AFF. 47 (1971); O'Neill, *supra* note 5; *see also* JAMES G. DWYER, THE RELATIONSHIP RIGHTS OF CHILDREN 146 (2006).

[71] Thomson, *supra* note 70.

who chooses to bring a child into their home also chooses to undertake parental duties?

Elizabeth Brake argues that someone who brings a child into their home tacitly accepts the parental role and its accompanying duties.[72] A person "tacitly accepts" a social role if they perform the action that social conventions treat as entering the role, with an "awareness of the role and its obligations and that what one is doing amounts to entering it, and further, that one wishes, or intends, or at least believes oneself to be thereby taking on the [social] role."[73] According to this view, a custodian need not *choose parental duties*. In fact, they do not even need to choose the parental role per se. When social conventions treat bringing a child home into one's home as generating parental duties, anyone who knows about this convention and still brings a child into their home knows that they have taken on the social role. They tacitly accepted moral duties of parenthood regardless of their intentions or beliefs about what they owe the child.

Brake expects tacit acceptance to have the same moral force as express consent or promises. An adult who tacitly accepts parental roles by bringing a child into their home incurs parental duties just like an adoptive parent who expressly consents to fulfill parental roles. Unfortunately, this analogy obscures the moral relations at stake. To understand the duties created by voluntary custodial caregiving, we need to excise analogies with acceptance or consent – tacit or otherwise.

2 Caregiver Duties Are Not Justified by Acceptance

Voluntary caregiving theories cannot appeal to consent in its two paradigmatic senses. First, consent sometimes transforms a duty into a privilege.[74] When Adam consents to allow Ben to enter his house, he waives Ben's duty not to trespass, turning it into a privilege to enter. Consent in its waiver sense can be express or tacit. Adam might consent expressly with an utterance, such as "Come on in, Ben," or an act with the same conventional meaning, such as waving Ben in. Adam can also consent tacitly if he is willing to allow Ben to enter and does not protest as Ben does so. Consent, in this sense, cannot explain why an adult's choice to bring a child home creates parental duties. The adult who supposedly consents to being a parent is not waiving anyone's duty. Furthermore, waivers do not create duties. One person's waiver creates another person's privilege. As we will see in Part III, consent in this waiver sense is crucial to parentage by estoppel, but it applies only when someone else already has parental rights.

In its second paradigmatic sense, consent can allow an agent to accept new duties. When I tell the principal that I will serve as the school crossing guard, my consent

[72] Brake, *supra* note 4.

[73] *Id.* at 156.

[74] Heidi Hurd, *The Normative Force of Consent*, *in* The Routledge Handbook of the Ethics of Consent 44, § 4.2.1 (Peter Schaber & Andreas Müller eds., 2018).

creates a promise-like duty. Consent in this promissory sense can also occur through an act with conventional meaning. If I find the crossing-guard vest on the sidewalk and put it on, my conduct might be conventionally understood as consenting to fulfill crossing-guard duties. Some adults do consent to parentage in this sense, such as by adopting a child or signing a parentage agreement. I find it implausible to suggest that consent as conventional promises explains all parental duties. Someone who brings a child home is not making an implied-in-fact promise to anyone (see also 5.II.B).

What Brake calls "tacit acceptance" is not a kind of consent. It is something fundamentally different: a conditional privilege. A person has a *conditional privilege* to perform an action if they have a privilege to do it (i.e., no duty not to), but if they do, one of their other moral relations changes. Some adults have a liberty to take custody of a child, but if they do, they incur a duty to care for the child. To understand the moral principles behind voluntary caregiver theories, we must clarify the difference between these conditional privileges and consent.

Imagine Frank is walking on Broadway in New York City when Evan brushes against him. Frank, who suffers from haphephobia, complains strenuously. Evan might respond that Frank consented to incidental contact when he chose to walk on the sidewalk, but Frank can honestly reply that he never expressly consented to be touched and was subjectively unwilling to be touched. Evan might retort that Frank chose to walk on a New York sidewalk knowing that social norms treat incidental contact as permissible, so he tacitly consented to such contact.[75] Tacit consent does no moral work here. Evan's position is that Frank may walk on Broadway only if he gives up his claim against incidental contact. In other words, Frank had a conditional privilege.

Maintaining this formal distinction between consent and conditional privileges is essential to prevent illicit appeals to the principle of *violenti non fit injuria* (to a willing person, it is not a wrong). Consider a classic consent situation. Ann's consent to spar with Betty entails that Betty does not wrong Ann by punching her. Suppose someone said, "I know Ann was willing for Betty to punch her, but why did Ann lose her claim against being punched by Betty?" She was willing to be punched! Ann's willingness waived Betty's duty. Conditional privileges do not have the same moral implication. Frank chose to walk down the street. He was not willing to be touched. There is no necessary connection between walking and waiver. It is perfectly sensible to ask, "I know Frank chose to walk on the sidewalk, but why did Frank lose his claim against being touched by Evan?" Insisting that Frank tacitly consented obscures the missing moral premise. One must explain why pedestrians lose their claim against incidental contact by exercising their privilege to walk on the sidewalk.[76]

75 As Ferzan argues, the actor here cannot opt out and probably never has an option to avoid opting in. Kim Ferzan, *Dissent-Sensitive Permissions*, 41 LAW & PHIL. 397 (2022).

76 M. Beth Valentine, *Constructive "Consent": A Problematic Fiction*, 37 L. & PHIL. 499, 512–13 (2018).

It is tempting – but inadequate – to say Frank chose to accept the risk of contact because he cared more about going to a Broadway show than risking contact. This argument begs the question. It assumes Frank may be forced to choose between seeing a show and risking contact. He made a rational choice among his options, but why can society force him into this choice? As Elizabeth Anderson reminds us, "Consent to an option within a set cannot justify the option set itself."[77] Unlike in the waiver situation, we need a justification for this condition on Frank's liberty of movement. Many are available. Maybe the state, as the owner of public ways, has plenary power to set conditions for the use of sidewalks. Maybe travel would be too costly if individual pedestrians could opt out of incidental contact. My preferred justification, returning to the theory of Chapter 1, is that this limitation is necessary for equal liberty. No one can have the freedom to travel in a city unless all pedestrians yield their claim against *de minimus* contact. Frank cannot assert a liberty to walk on the sidewalk and a special exemption from the general legal rules that make this liberty possible for everyone.[78]

We are now equipped to understand the relationship between custody and conditional privileges. Suppose Frank brings an orphan child into his home and knows that others will interpret this act as accepting parenthood. Nevertheless, one cannot validly infer that Frank accepted the conventional parental duties. Maybe Frank rejects modern norms about parenting, such as the norm that parents (mothers anyway) must sacrifice their lives for their children. Maybe he intends to let his live-in mother raise the child. Maybe he plans to raise the child through infancy and then place the child for adoption. Maybe he plans to treat the child as a servant. Contemporary Americans find that abhorrent, but childhood indentures persisted through the nineteenth century.[79] A person can take custody of a child without accepting the conventional parental role, even if the adult knows about the parenting social conventions.

Fortunately, acceptance is the wrong moral framework. Caregiving duties are a condition of the privilege to take custody. No one may take custody of a child without incurring the caregiving duties defined by social or legal norms. Regardless of Frank's express declarations or subjective intentions, regardless of what he accepts or consents to, Frank incurs a duty to care for the child by bringing the child into his home. Caregiving duties are voluntary only in a limited sense. They arise whenever an adult voluntarily brings a child into their home. Again, we must avoid the temptation to say that Frank chose caregiving duties because he valued the child's

77 Elizabeth Anderson, Private Government: How Employers Rule Our Lives (and Why We Don't Talk about It) 61 (2017).

78 One should also ask what mental states are necessary for the triggering act to have its moral effect. If the moral consequence is trivial or obvious, then anyone who exercises the antecedent liberty may be subject to "strict liability." Clueless tourists cannot complain about being bumped as they walk down Broadway. Morality becomes more solicitous if the exercise of a privilege triggers significant moral consequences and if agents are unlikely to be aware of them.

79 Naomi Cahn, *Perfect Substitutes or the Real Thing?*, 52 Duke L.J. 1077, 1110–13 (2002).

presence in his home more than he valued his carefree life without child-rearing obligations. Frank's choice to take custody cannot justify socially imposed caregiving duties any more than his choice to walk justified his waiver of bodily integrity. Caregiving duties are a limit imposed on Frank's privilege to take custody of a child. Moral, social, and legal norms force Frank to choose between the liberty to care for the child and a life free of child-rearing duties.

3 Children Acquire a Right to Continued Care from Their Caregiver

Because caregiving duties arise from a conditional privilege rather than consent, we need additional moral premises to justify conditioning custody on a moral or legal duty to care for a child. Ordinarily, the fact that I voluntarily start some activity is not enough to ground a duty to do it well or continue doing it. In narrow circumstances, however, the law does impose such duties. One helpful analog to caregiving duties is the tort doctrine of voluntary undertakings.

Individuals have no general affirmative duty to rescue strangers from a risk they have not created, but once a bystander voluntarily undertakes a rescue, they incur a duty to pursue the rescue in a reasonable manner.[80] The best justification for this duty appeals to risk creation. A bystander's rescue attempt may deter others from starting their own rescue. If the bystander then abandons their attempt or acts incompetently, then their rescue efforts will worsen the victim's situation.[81] In a classic torts case, Zelenko had a heart attack in Gimbel's department store.[82] Employees helped Zelenko to their infirmary but did not provide treatment or call an ambulance. Because Zelenko was hidden away, no one else could see he needed help. Zelenko had no legal claim to anyone's help, but he had a right to demand the employees not to increase his risk by preventing a competent rescue. Although described as an affirmative duty, the voluntary undertaking principle is just a corollary of the general duty not to act in ways that create unreasonable risk to others.

Voluntary undertaking principles can justify indefinite caregiving duties for custodial caregivers. These parent-like duties arise in two steps. First, when anyone takes physical custody of a child, they prevent others from meeting the child's basic needs – just like the Gimbel employees did. In addition, taking custody in our society expands a child's dependence beyond the privacy of the home. Our social norms treat caregiving roles as exclusive. Once an adult has taken custody of a child, others believe they should not intervene. In this respect, custodians are more like

80 Restatement (Third) of Torts: Liability for Physical & Emotional Harm § 42 (Am. Law Inst. 2010).

81 If omissions are not causes, then double prevention cases must rest on counterfactual responsibility as an independent basis of desert. Michael S. Moore, Causation and Responsibility: An Essay in Law, Morals, and Metaphysics 62–65 (2010).

82 Zelenko v. Gimbel Bros., 287 N.Y.S. 134, 135 (Sup. Ct. 1935).

paramedics than bystanders. Just as everyone is expected to stay out of the paramedics' way, third parties have no right to monitor a custodian to ensure they feed the child nutritious food and read them bedtime stories. Anyone who voluntarily takes custody of a child incurs a duty to meet the child's basic needs because taking custody prevents anyone else from fulfilling the child's needs.[83]

Second, once an adult performs custodial caregiving for a substantial time, the child's reliance interests deepen and change in character. Even basic caregiving generates emotional bonds. Disrupting the child's attachments may cause psychological harm. Accordingly, anyone who takes custody of a child has a duty to manage the risk created by the child's attachments. If the adult only has custody for a short time or the child does not develop strong relational bonds, then the adult can manage the transition to another caregiver. At some point, however, the risk of psychological harm from a caregiving transition may become too great, in which case the voluntary custodial caregiver incurs a duty to remain in the role.

No one may engage in voluntary custodial caregiving without incurring these caregiving duties. Biological parents, adoptive parents, stepparents, kin caregivers, and foster parents incur the same duty in the same way. The same duties arise if three adults take an infant into their home or neighbors take in a runaway teenager. Voluntarists may be tempted to say that adults accept caregiving duties by choosing to take custody, but this is misleading in the same way that it was misleading to say Frank accepts the risk of contact by choosing to walk down Broadway. Frank cannot take custody of a child and reject caregiving obligations. Custodial caregivers incur duties regardless of whether they expressly or tacitly accept duties.

Caregiver duties also generate something akin to parents' relational rights. This might be surprising given Chapter 3. The caregiver theory appeals to principles of reliance causation, and I previously explained that causal duties ordinarily do not generate duty-rights. An agent who creates a risk of harm has a duty to prevent it, but they generally have no duty or right to prevent the harm personally. However, causal duties can require personal performance if an agent creates a risk that only they can prevent. Procreation creates a generic need for *some* caregiver. In contrast, long-term custodial caregiving creates a relational need for *this specific* caregiver. Others could perform generic caregiving tasks like housing, feeding, or changing diapers, but substituting caregivers may damage the child's emotional well-being and interfere with their development. The child needs a relationship with this caregiver. Because

83 This argument coincides with what Kolers and Bayne describe as a "causation of neglect" theory, with two crucial clarifications. Avery Kolers & Tim Bayne, *"Are You My Mommy?": On the Genetic Basis of Parenthood*, 18 J. Applied Phil. 273 (2001). First, unlike tort remedies for completed wrongs that presuppose causation of harm, family law need not wait to intervene until *after* a parent causes neglect. Risk of harm creates an affirmative caregiving duty that can be enforced prospectively. Second, Kolers and Bayne reject a causation of neglect theory because they think it necessarily sets too low a baseline because adults need only avoid making a child's situation worse. As I explain in II. A.4.b and III.B, the baseline should not be set as if parenthood were a relationship between private persons but rather recognizing it as a political office to ensure children's primary goods.

they caused the child to develop this need, the custodial caregiver has a duty to care for the child personally.

Furthermore, caregiving relationships may be important enough to children to entail that third parties, including the state, owe a duty to a child not to interfere with their established relationships. The child's relational needs may also justify a limited amount of discretionary authority for their caregivers. Someone must decide what the child eats, when they play, and what they read. In theory, third parties could have the authority to make these decisions. In practice, such direct external management might disrupt the child's developing attachments because they see the caregiver as a cook or housekeeper rather than someone who has taken personal responsibility for their well-being.[84]

4 Limitations of the Caregiver Theory of Parental Duties

Voluntary custodial caregiving can generate personal duties to a child, and these duties can even justify some child-rearing discretion. Nevertheless, voluntary undertaking principles have shortcomings that prevent caregiving duties from grounding full parental rights or duties.

A CAREGIVING DUTIES CANNOT JUSTIFY PARENTAL RIGHTS. Caregiving duties cannot justify parental rights. The child's needs justify the caregiver's duty to raise the child and the third parties' duties to not disrupt the relationship. Duties to the child cannot justify personal rights for the caregiver. An individual has a personal moral right only if the right is grounded in respect for their interests or autonomy.[85] Caregiving duties are more akin to a duty to act in defense of others. If a third party tries to disrupt the child's caregiving relationship, the caregiver is obligated to prevent this interference to defend the child's interests. The right belongs to the child, not the caregiver.

These caregiver obligations also justify narrower authority than parenthood. The child needs to sustain the caregiving relationship, but the caregiver can fulfill their function without exclusive authority to decide who else builds a relationship with the child. Similarly, caregivers need some discretion to decide how to meet the child's daily needs, but they do not need wide-ranging authority to shape the child's experiences by their vision of a valuable life. Parenthood's fiduciary authority vastly exceeds basic caregiving obligations.

84 Ferdinand Schoeman, *Rights of Children, Rights of Parents, and the Moral Basis of the Family*, 91 ETHICS 6, 14–16 (1980).

85 Harry Brighouse & Adam Swift, *Parents' Rights and the Value of the Family*, 117 ETHICS 80, 90–91 (2006). Legal scholars often try to ground parents' constitutional rights in children's welfare, but perhaps legal rights (unlike personal moral rights) can be justified by others' interests. *See, e.g.*, E. Gary Spitko, *Constitutional Function of Biological Paternity: Evidence of the Biological Mother's Consent to the Biological Father's Co-Parenting of Her Child*, 48 ARIZ. L. REV. 97, 106 (2006).

Indeed, some caregivers have no duty – or corresponding right – to maintain permanent custody. Live-in nannies, relatives, and stepparents fulfill caregiving responsibilities that create emotional attachments for the child. All the adults involved in these arrangements have a duty to manage the relationships to protect the child from psychological harm.[86] Nevertheless, nannies can leave their jobs, and parents can fire nannies. Grandparents can help without incurring a duty to raise the child, and parents can seek help from relatives without transferring their rights. Parents can cohabit without consenting to adoption by the cohabitant. The line between caregivers who become parents and those who remain third parties is often fixed, not by a difference in their caregiving or in the child's psychological relationships, but in the relationship *between the adults* with respect to the child.

B CAREGIVING DUTIES CANNOT JUSTIFY THE CONTENT OF PARENTAL DUTIES. A caregiving theory cannot justify parental duties, because it suffers from baseline difficulties akin to the causal theory. A custodian incurs a duty to the child because they deny others access to the child, so the content of caregiving duties depends on what they prevent the child from receiving. No one can prevent a child from receiving their basic material needs (food and shelter) or relational needs (conversation necessary for language development). That causes the child harm, just like the employees caused harm to Zelenko by hiding him during his heart attack. A duty not to cause harmful neglect is uncontroversial, yet far from parental duties.

One intuitive approach might insist that an adult may not take custody of a child if it makes the child worse off. This suggests a counterfactual baseline: a custodian must provide at least as valuable a life as the child could expect to receive from other potential caregivers. An inattentive caregiver is likely better than an orphanage, but they also keep the child away from loving adoptive parents. According to this approach, the content of caregiving duties rests on two contingent social facts: who else would likely raise the child, and what care would they likely provide.

Unfortunately, using empirical facts to fix the counterfactual baseline generates three new problems. First, one can only assess the counterfactual by specifying the relevant community. A caregiver in rural Pennsylvania might owe a child the kind of care that would otherwise be offered by families in their Amish community, the rural county, Pennsylvania, America, or the world. There is no natural reference class. Second, a community may set its conventional bar too high or low from a normative perspective. A wealthy community may have many childless adults eager to devote their entire lives to a child. Impoverished birth parents seem to wrong their newborns by not placing them for adoption. An impoverished society may have low caregiving standards. Medieval peasants left infants swaddled and hanging on the

[86] For example, perhaps a short-term cohabitant should maintain emotional distance by behaving like a friend rather than a parent for the child and, if cohabitation ends, manage the transition rather than disappearing abruptly from the child's life.

door while they tended fields. Peasants seem to owe little to their children because the only alternative caregivers are unable or unwilling to provide more. Last, a counterfactual baseline sits uneasily with the ethical intuition underlying voluntarism. It seemed fair to insist adults fulfill arduous caregiving duties because they took custody of the child voluntarily. However, if the content of caregiving duties is fixed by contingent social norms, like helicopter parenting or sacrificial motherhood, it seems less fair to insist that no one can take custody of a child without incurring a duty to meet these arbitrary norms.

Together, these problems suggest the caregiver theory needs a moral baseline. If children have a basic right to certain material or relational goods, no adult may take custody of a child in a way that will deny the child these rights. Of course, that renders the caregiver theory dependent on a freestanding theory of children's rights. In III.A, I explain how the political theory of parentage provides a normative baseline to show why no one may take indefinite custody of a child without incurring full parental duties as defined by the community.

C THE PRIVILEGE TO CARE FOR A CHILD. The final problem is that caregiving theories are necessarily incomplete. Anyone who takes custody of a child incurs a duty to meet their need for emotional and physical care. Under this principle, even kidnappers incur caregiving duties! In a sense, that is surely correct. A kidnapper incurs a duty to care for the child. If they do not, they commit another crime. Yet surely the kidnapper's caregiving cannot generate parental duties, much less rights.[87] A voluntary caregiving theory must use some external principle to explain who has a privilege to take custody of a child and to meet their material and relational needs. Caregiving theories cannot explain the liberty to parent.

This incompleteness raises a related question-begging worry, one which ties back to the baseline problem. There is a crucial difference between cases of rescue and custody. Every bystander has a privilege to rescue a drowning victim. If the first rescuer deters subsequent rescuers, it is incidental to their purpose and dependent on contingent facts. Parents do not deter other caregivers incidentally or contingently. Most parents claim a right to raise their children without interference from relatives, neighbors, or other busybodies. A parent is more like a rescuer who yells at bystanders that they must stay away. Voluntary rescuers have no such authority. Lifeguards have this authority, but it rests on an institutional justification for socializing rescues. We cannot support a caregiver theory by arguing custodians incur parental duties because they deter others by asserting a moral claim to exclusive authority. All the moral work would be done by some prior, unspecified justification for allowing them to assert parental authority.

* * *

87 Relationships founded on wrongdoing often generate abstruse obligations.

Despite the label, "voluntarist" theories of parental duties do not rest on express or tacit acceptance of parental roles. Caregiving duties are a condition on the privilege to take custody of a child. No one may take custody without incurring a personal, affirmative duty to meet the child's material and relational needs. Once this caregiving generates relational attachments for the child, the custodian incurs an additional duty to remain in the caregiver role.

Caregivers' personal duties look more like parental duties than anything surveyed so far, but they still cannot ground parenthood. The child's need for caregiving cannot justify the wide-ranging authority of parenthood. Because of baseline problems, a voluntary undertaking principle cannot define the content of parental duties. Last, and perhaps most importantly, all caregiver theories are incomplete insofar as some external principles are necessary to explain which adults have a privilege to care for a child.

B *Caregiving as a Source of Parental Rights*

Caregiving plays a fundamentally different role in legal scholarship. Functionalist family law scholars typically seek to invest caregivers with parental rights. They rarely emphasize the caregiving duties of functional parents, likely because lawyers think about parental duties primarily through the lens of child support. The UPA 2017 allows de facto parents to establish parental rights but rejects unsolicited duties. According to a survey by Courtney Joslin and Doug NeJaime, only 5 percent of all functional parent claims involve a legal parent or government attempting to impose duties.[88]

Caregiving might generate parental rights in two ways. First, caregivers who invest labor in raising a child may develop relational interests sufficient to justify parental rights. This theory might be extended to the work of pregnancy and childbirth. Second, a court may allow nonparental caregivers to establish parental rights after a legal parent has allowed them to raise the child long enough to make ending the relationship detrimental to the child.

1 Caregiving Labor Alone Cannot Ground Parental Rights

The most promising attempts to ground parental rights in caregiving use a labor theory of rights, which has been advanced by Dara Purvis, Leslie Bender, Gary Spitko, and Jennifer Hendricks, among others. The core moral intuition is that adults acquire parental rights by performing caregiving labor that generates relational interests deserving of respect.[89]

88 Joslin and NeJaime, *supra* note 3.

89 Leslie Bender, *To Err Is Human – ART Mix-Ups: A Labor-Based, Relational Proposal*, 9 J. Gender Race & Just. 443 (2005); Purvis, *supra* note 3; Spitko, *supra* note 85; Jennifer Hendricks, Essentially

Joseph Millum offers the most analytically developed labor theory of parental rights.[90] He begins with a Lockean "principle of justice that reward should be proportional to work."[91] When a person invests their labor in a project, they develop an interest in continuing the project to realize the goods that it produces. So long as the agent's labor is "morally deserving work," others ought to respect the agent's investment-based interests by respecting their right to control the objects necessary to continue their project. One crucial limit of this "investment principle" is that it can only justify control rights consistent with the moral status of the object. For example, it cannot justify a right to slavery and probably not animal slaughter.

Under this principle, a caregiver acquires a right to control a child's life by performing substantial caregiving work to help the child flourish.[92] Having invested in "deserving" care work to fulfill the child's needs, the caregiver deserves an opportunity to realize the goods of parenting that their work made possible. The goods of parenting for the adult include (1) the relationship of intimacy with the child; (2) the love and respect that children usually feel for parents; (3) the ability to share valued pursuits with the child that gives meaning to their lives, such as participation in ballet or religion; and (4) even the child's labor toward the family business, such as on a farm in an agrarian society.[93] These interests of the caregiver justify claims on others and on the state, including a duty to allow the caregiver to retain authority over the child's life.[94]

Labor theories of parental rights are promising. Legally, they might help justify the trend toward functional parentage rules (although courts deny that their goal is to protect adult interests). Philosophically, they might plug significant holes in a caregiver theory of parental duties. With its focus on adult interests, a labor theory can justify claim rights for parents. They might even justify a right to authority over a child if this authority is necessary to realize the good of parenting. Finally, a labor theory might explain who has the liberty to raise a child. The work of pregnancy

A MOTHER: A FEMINIST APPROACH TO THE LAW OF PREGNANCY AND MOTHERHOOD (2023). *See also* Shoshana L. Gillers, Note, *A Labor Theory of Legal Parenthood*, 110 YALE L.J. 691 (2001).

90 JOSEPH MILLUM, THE MORAL FOUNDATIONS OF PARENTHOOD 25–27 (2018).

91 *See also* Purvis, *supra* note 3, at 656 (noting the Lockean labor principle rests on the idea that the person "deserves [rights] as a reward for the virtue of having created the major part of its value"). Millum offers a formal statement of his "investment principle": all other things equal, an agent has an interest that can ground rights with respect to any object or entity (over which people can acquire rights) in proportion to the effort that the agent spent to produce a good object or entity of its kind. My rephrasing here incorporates some of his technical refinements. The "all things equal" rider recognizes other principles may conflict with or outweigh the investment principle, most obviously that some things are already owned and some people work together as part of an agreement that specifies how they will allocate any goods produced.

92 MILLUM, *supra* note 90, at 28, 31.

93 *Id.* at 50–53.

94 *Id.* at 52–53.

generates relational interests that might justify parental rights at birth.[95] A labor-based theory promises a tidy theory of parenthood, with parental rights and duties grounded in the same source.

A CAREGIVING LABOR CAN GENERATE RELATIONAL RIGHTS BUT NOT PARENTAL RIGHTS. The first step to evaluating a caregiver theory of parentage is to investigate how this investment principle applies to child-rearing. One deep challenge arises immediately. Allowing adult labor to generate rights over children seems to violate the Kantian principle of equal liberty described in Chapter 1. No one may wield unilateral moral authority over others. That is precisely what makes parenthood puzzling.[96] Yet, under a caregiving labor theory, an adult can give themselves authority over a child's life by unilaterally deciding to raise a child. No one may have a moral power to set themselves as an authority over others in this manner. To add insult to injury, the adult claims authority over the child because it serves the adult's interests. It seems the adult is using the child as a means to facilitate their own ends.

A similar problem arises within a Lockean perspective. Locke recognized that a person may appropriate objects through their labor only if the new property rights do not diminish others' liberty (that is why the acquisition is permissible only if "there is enough, and as good left in common for others").[97] An adult cannot acquire parenthood without diminishing other's liberty. When a person acquires parental rights through caregiving, these rights directly limit the child's liberty and the liberty of other adults to raise the child. The same tension can be seen by comparing the labor theory of parental rights with other contexts involving adults, as Jim Dwyer has argued.[98] Suppose a beachgoer nurses a shipwrecked sailor back to life. The beachgoer performed morally valuable labor to meet the sailor's basic needs. The sailor should be grateful, but the beachgoer has no claim to authority over the sailor. Morality does not countenance debts of charity that would reduce any recipient, adult or child, to a subservient position of obedience.

B STRATEGIES TO RECONCILE A CLAIM TO AUTHORITY WITH THE CHILD'S EQUAL STATUS. I have encountered three strategies to reconcile a labor-based parental right with the child's status as an equal member of society. None succeed.

First, no genuine conflicts would arise if the relational interests of the caregiver and child were naturally coextensive. Recall the court's argument in *Rivera* that the

95 Spitko, *supra* note 85, at 109; Purvis, *supra* note 3, at 679. Spitko and Hendricks further claim that gestational parents have *full* parental rights, sometimes including a right to exclude the genetic parent and to place their child for adoption without the genetic parent's consent. Spitko, *supra* note 85, at 105; HENDRICKS, *supra* note 89. I consider this claim in Part III below.

96 ARCHARD, *supra* note 3, at 37, 55.

97 JOHN LOCKE, SECOND TREATISE OF GOVERNMENT § 33 (The Project Gutenberg eBook ed.), www.gutenberg.org/files/7370/7370-h/7370-h.htm (last visited Sept. 25, 2023).

98 James G. Dwyer, *Deflating Parental Rights*, 40 L. & PHIL. 387 (2021).

sister and her siblings had a complementary interest in their surrogate-mother relationship.[99] Children need to maintain their parental attachments, and parents benefit from their relationship with their children. If these interests are coextensive, then protecting caregivers' interests will always protect the child's rights.

This first strategy might suffice for narrow caregiving liberties. The only way to preserve the child's relational attachments is to allow the caregiver to continue daily caregiving tasks, including some limited authority over the child's life. Law can protect the child's relational interests only by protecting the caregiving's authority and, thus, the adult's relational interest.

Unfortunately, this strategy cannot expand caregiving rights into parental rights, as Harry Brighouse and Adam Swift have explained. The relational interests of children and parents are not coextensive.[100] Parents have an interest in shaping a child to share their values, which can limit the child's life opportunities in ways that do not align with the child's interests. An engineer might set out to make their child into a scientist, but the child has no ex ante interest in being a scientist. One develops interests of this specificity only when old enough to have one's own talents, preferences, and values. A parent may have an interest in directing a child's life, but the child has no obvious symmetrical interest in being shaped by this person for eighteen years.

According to Brighouse and Swift, the only way to ensure the interests of parents and children align sufficiently is to restrict which interests of adults count toward grounding parental rights. The next two strategies seek to create this laundered alignment.

One might insist that children's rights have categorical priority over any interests of the parent in their child-rearing project. The caregiver's interests in the goods of parenting cannot "override" the child's deep interests.[101] Accordingly, caregivers simply never obtain moral rights that conflict with their children's rights.

This strategy misses its primary target. The argument may be sound with respect to innate rights, which do have this kind of lexical priority. Because each child has an innate right to bodily integrity, parents may not withhold medical treatment even if they believe salvation depends on it. Unfortunately, innate rights were never the real problem. There is no a priori reason to suppose that children's distributive entitlements have similar categorical priority. For many parents, part of the value of child-rearing is shaping the child. A parent who values science may enroll their child in robotics summer camp to stimulate the child's interest in STEM, even if the child would have preferred playing in the woods. Parents may even make self-interested decisions that affect children's educational opportunities. A parent seeking career advancement may relocate to a town with worse schools. A child's distributive

99 Rivera v. Marcus, 696 F.2d 1016 (2d Cir. 1982).

100 Harry Brighouse & Adam Swift, Family Values: The Ethics of Parent–Child Relationships 94 (2014).

101 Millum, *supra* note 90, at 57.

entitlements do not always trump a parent's interest in shaping the child – or even the parent's own self-directed interests.

Even if one acknowledges that parents' interests generate prima facie moral rights, one might nevertheless insist that parents' duties constrain how they exercise their parental rights. Millum, for example, argues that children's rights are "an absolute constraint on the exercise of parental rights" because parents have a duty to use their rights only to facilitate the child's interests.[102] A fiduciary theory of parental authority alone cannot affect the needed reconciliation. A parent genuinely trying to decide in their child's best interests may still interpret the child's basic rights according to the adult's own comprehensive values. For instance, a parent genuinely trying to evaluate their child's right to education may conclude that education should be limited to avoid directly conflicting with the child's religious faith.

To undercut this possibility, Millum insists that the parent's duty is to satisfy the child's basic entitlements as understood by the community. To justify insisting that parents must subordinate their own judgment to that of the community, Millum returns to a voluntary acceptance theory of duties. An adult acquires parental rights when they labor to fulfill the caregiving duties that they incurred by voluntarily entering the social role of parent. Thus, adults can acquire parental rights only by providing whatever goods society believes children deserve. This move repeats the above mistake regarding "tacit acceptance." Caregivers do not expressly or implicitly consent to fulfill social norms solely by choosing to care for a child. An adult who believes contemporary parenting norms harm children may take custody precisely to protect the child from modernity. Some other reason – outside the caregiver theory – is necessary to explain why society can demand that adults either forgo raising children or raise children by conventional norms.

Adults' interests in parenting exceed children's interests in caregiving. Accordingly, any labor theory that tries to ground parental rights directly in adults' interests will appear to use children as a means to adult ends.

2 Gestation Cannot Ground Parental Rights

An extension of the caregiver theory argues that the work of gestation and childbirth generates relational interests sufficient to ground parental rights at birth. Anca Gheaus offers the most philosophically sophisticated version of this argument. She identifies two reasons for the gestational parent's initial claim. First, pregnancy and childbirth are physically, financially, and emotionally costly.[103] Nine months of bodily changes and physical work culminate with labor and delivery, all of which carry a significant health risk.[104] Gestation also restricts a person's ability to pursue other projects and transforms their

102 *Id.* at 56–58.

103 Anca Gheaus, *The Right to Parent One's Biological Baby*, 20 J. Pol. Phil. 432, 447–49 (2012).

104 Leslie Bender offers a descriptive account of the physical costs. Bender, *supra* note 89, at 486–87.

relationships with friends, coworkers, and lovers. While these costs represent "one good reason" for parental priority, Gheaus recognizes that this is only one reason that "may perhaps be overridden by other reasons such as considerations of . . . gender fairness" for men or nonbiological parents. Accordingly, she thinks the full justification for a birth presumption must appeal to the "incipient intimate relationship with the baby." Pregnancy is "often a conscious, intentional project ... [that] contains much anticipation and planning," and this intentional bodily experience typically (not always) creates emotional bonds between a mother and the newborn.[105] Rejecting rights at birth "would likely destroy [these] already existing intimate relationships between newborns and their bearing parents."[106]

Despite its intuitive appeal, a caregiver theory of gestational parenthood has difficulties. Even if parental rights could be justified by caregiving work, the caregiving theory cannot be easily extended to encompass gestational work.[107] These two different kinds of work do not generate the same relational interests. The relational interests created by gestation are deeply asymmetrical, falling primarily on the side of the bearing parent. Newborns display preferences for the voice or smell of their gestational mothers, but the newborn's incipient relational interests do not correspond to the gestational parent's interests in an anticipated future parental relationship. Whatever difficulty the caregiver theory faces in reconciling the interests of the caregiver and child, the problem is magnified for pregnancy.

Two responses might preserve parental rights for gestational parents. Someone who accepts that parentage principles must appeal only to children's interests might still argue that the newborn's incipient bonds break a presumptive tie among possible parents. For reasons that should now be familiar, I am dubious of attempts to compare an infant's interests in a future relationship with gestational, genetic, intended, or adoptive parents. The other option – which I will endorse in III.C – is to reject the moral premise of the objection. A community can allocate authority over a child to facilitate adult interests without disrespecting the child as an equal. I will argue that the interests of the gestational parent cannot justify parental rights directly, but the state can recognize and protect those interests with a parentage presumption.

[105] Gheaus, *supra* note 103, at 449–50.

[106] *Id.* at 450.

[107] Gheaus insists she is not offering a labor theory, but otherwise the moral principle underlying her theory is difficult to discern. As a matter of personal morality, the fact that I incurred a cost to confer an unrequested benefit on another person does not give them a duty to me, much less give me authority over them. Costs matter as a matter of distributive justice, but an unequal distribution of social costs justifies systemic redistribution – not piecemeal authority over the person who received the benefit.

3 Caregivers Can Acquire Limited Rights through Equitable Estoppel

Case law and legal scholarship on functional parenthood typically focus on whether caregivers may receive parental rights over the objection of an existing parent. The proponents' typical argument is that legal recognition of the functional parent does not violate the legal parent's rights because they waived their objection by consenting to shared caregiving. This argument reflects an important insight, but the proper analogy is estoppel or forfeiture rather than waiver.[108] The difference and its implications become clear once we isolate the Hohfeldian incidents at play.

When we touch gloves in the boxing ring, I waive my objection to you punching me. My consent changes your duty not to touch me into a privilege to punch me. Consent in this paradigmatic sense – as a moral power to transform a duty into a privilege – is essential to initiate caregiving relationships. Suppose that Gina, a legal parent, allows Haley, her partner, to care for her two-year-old child. Gina waives her objection to Haley intervening in the child's life, giving Halley a privilege to care for the child. Gina may also allow Haley to make decisions for the child, delegating some parental authority to her. American law has long recognized that stepparents sometimes act *in loco parentis*, in place of the parent.

Consent to share caregiving does not entail consent to share parenthood.[109] A parent may intend to share their privilege to care for their child or their decision-making powers without intending to waive their power to decide whether the caregiver becomes a permanent parent. Both are exercises of familial autonomy, but it is essential not to conflate them.[110] Various laws empower parents to consent to share parenthood. Gina could consent to a second-parent adoption or, in a few states, sign a parentage acknowledgment (see Chapter 5). Perhaps states should also recognize oral parentage agreements, which often appear in de facto parenthood cases. In one case, the legal mother and her husband held an "informal 'adoption' ceremony called 'sprouts and roots,' which celebrated their union as a family and held the child out to their family and friends as [his] 'adopted' daughter in spirit and intention."[111] Gina and Haley never tried to create permanent parental rights. When Gina invites Haley into her family, she exercises her power to give Haley caregiving privileges and powers without waiving her authority to alter those relations.[112]

Nevertheless, Gina might have waived her power in the forfeiture sense, which the law often protects through equitable estoppel. A court may prevent an individual

[108] Strauss, *supra* note 63, at 965–70.

[109] June Carbone, *From Partners to Parents Revisited: How Will Ideas of Partnership Influence the Emerging Definition of California Parenthood?*, 7 Whittier J. Child. & Fam. Advoc. 3 (2007) (arguing that legal parent must "hold out" the child as their own or similar course of action to establish consent to confer all of parental status).

[110] Joslin, for instance, argues that when a legal "parent exercises her autonomy interest by inviting someone else into the family, the law must recognize that exercise of choice in family form." Courtney G. Joslin, *Autonomy in the Family*, 66 UCLA L. Rev. 912, 953 (2019).

[111] Kilborn v. Carey, 140 A.3d 461, 462 (Me. 2016).

[112] Smith v. Jones, 868 N.E.2d 629, 630 (Mass. App. Ct. 2007).

from exercising her legal right if she failed to assert the right when she knew others would rely on her continued forbearance, and allowing her to assert the right now either unfairly harms them or advantages her.[113] Equitable servitudes are a well-known example.[114] Suppose a property owner decides to allow her neighbor to use a dirt road across her land. Typically, she can choose to withdraw his privilege at any time. But if he paves the road and she watched silently as he worked, a court may decide it would be inequitable to allow her to withdraw his privilege before he receives a reasonable benefit from his investment.[115] The owner does not lose her right to exclude generally, but only her claim to exclude her neighbor from the road insofar as necessary to protect his reasonable reliance. Similar estoppel principles can justify functional parenthood doctrines if we focus on the reliance interests developed by the child.

As a default, legal parents should be allowed to ask others to help care for their child without losing their power to modify those arrangements. Parents have a basic right to shape their familial lives for themselves and their children, which includes deciding whether to live with a cohabitant or relative. Parents should be able to rely on these partners or relatives to help with child-rearing. When a parent wants to alter these arrangements, they must consider how it will affect the child's well-being and development. However, children can manage transitions. Many children live temporarily with marital or nonmarital stepparents, and few children maintain deep ties with former stepparents.[116] Relationship decisions affect child welfare but are not categorically different from other major decisions, such as whether to relocate or convert. States should trust parents to judge which relationships are good for their child and their family. Accordingly, parents' constitutional rights protect their relational authority by requiring parental consent for second-parent adoption and deference to their visitation decisions.

Similarly, a parent facing a health crisis, military deployment, demanding work schedule, or short incarceration should also be able to turn to their partner, relatives, or friends for help without risk of losing their parental rights.[117] The parent–child

[113] Dennis Klimchuk, *State Estoppel*, 39 L. & PHIL. 297 (2020) (but following McFarlane, Klimchuk assumes estoppel requires a representation or a promise).

[114] RESTATEMENT (THIRD) OF PROP.: SERVITUDES § 2.10 (AM. LAW. INST. 2000).

[115] Commentary disagrees about whether estoppel requires reliance on the owner's express representations and whether the owner must know about the reliance. T. Leigh Anenson, *The Triumph of Equity: Equitable Estoppel in Modern Litigation*, 27 REV. LITIG. 377 (2007); Stewart E. Sterk, *Estoppel in Property Law Essay*, 77 NEB. L. REV. 756, 776–79 (1998).

[116] Strauss, *supra* note 63, at 975–76.

[117] Price v. Howard, 484 S.E.2d 528, 537 (N.C. 1997). Taylor v. Stafford, No. 2009-CA-001720-ME, 2010 WL 2540357, at *1 (Ky. Ct. App. June 25, 2010) (a mother sent to prison for eight months entrusted custody to the grandmother, who sought caregiving help during her grueling work schedule from friends, who then challenged both for custody). Many parents in the military must have a family care plan for training or deployment, e.g., Army Command Policy, Army Reg. 600-20 § 5–3 (Dep't of the Army July 24, 2020), and some state courts and statutes have made special provision for custody delegations during deployments. ANN M. HARALAMBIE, 1 HANDLING CHILD CUSTODY, ABUSE, AND ADOPTION CASES § 7:3 (3d ed. 2023) (Military deployments).

relationship can be sustained despite periodic absences, particularly with community support. In some cultures, long-term kinship care is common. Relative caregivers may do not want to permanently replace the child's parent. Accordingly, most states have a procedure that enables parents to arrange a temporary guardianship for their child.

At some point, however, a parent's absence approaches abandonment. The "modern child is considered a person, not a subperson over whom the parent has an absolute and irrevocable possessory right."[118] A parent who leaves their child in another's custody for years with only occasional contact has demonstrated their lack of commitment to fulfilling their duty of care and guidance. In such circumstances, courts rightly conclude that the parent "forfeited" their right to physical and decisional custody and any accompanying legal deference.[119] The community may not defer to a parent who is not fulfilling their fiduciary functions. If the child's custodian petitions for custody or the state files a neglect action, a court must reach an independent judgment about which caregiving arrangement will serve the child's relational needs.

A similar forfeiture argument may justify legal rights for coresidential partners or relatives. Ample evidence suggests that children typically develop deep attachments with any primary caregiver, such that abruptly ending these relationships creates a significant risk of psychological harm to the child.[120] Joslin and NeJaime estimate that alleged functional parents served as the child's primary caregiver in 94 percent of the cases in which the courts recognized afforded rights to the functional parents.[121] If the parent encouraged their child to develop a parent-like relationship with the caregiver and then seeks to abruptly end their caregiving relationship, the law may conclude that these scenarios carry sufficient risk of harm that the state may abandon its default deference to parental judgment. The parent's consent to a caregiving relationship evolved into a forfeiture of their right to deference. A court may review the parent's decision to ensure it complies with their fiduciary duty to give adequate weight to the child's interests.

Returning de facto parenthood to its estoppel origins helps clarify its consent element. The parents must consent to caregiving. Unless parents waived the caregiver's duty not to interfere, the caregiver had no privilege to raise the child at all. Suppose a teacher secretly cultivated parent-like bonds with a child. Laws that allowed such bonds to create a claim to visitation

[118] *In re* K.H., 773 S.E.2d 20, 29 (W. Va .2015).

[119] State *ex rel.* Combs v. O'Neal, N.W.2d 231, 236 (Neb. Ct. App. 2003). According to Joslin and NeJaime, in almost half of the "functional parenthood" cases, the caregiver was the child's only reliable caregiver because the legal parent was not serving as a primary caregiver. Joslin and NeJaime, *supra* note 3.

[120] Strauss, *supra* note 63, at 974–76 (finding no evidence of risk for secondary caregivers like stepparents).

[121] Joslin and NeJaime, *supra* note 3, at 25–28.

would undermine parents' relational authority.[122] However, legal parents do not have to consent to share parenthood. De facto parenthood is not informal adoption. It is legal enforcement of the parent's fiduciary duty to meet the child's relational needs. When the legal parent has left the child's relational needs to a custodian or encouraged the child to form bonds with a coresidential caregiver, the parent forfeits their authority to arbitrarily terminate these caregiving relationships.

States could enforce parents' fiduciary duties with regulation, but direct oversight would be ineffective and intrusive, and officials would just displace parents' reasonable judgments with other contestable values. Instead, most states crafted narrow legal tools that empower a small class of private individuals to challenge specific parental decisions in court. These functional doctrines are justifiable, but states should not pretend these doctrines simply enforce the legal parent's familial choices. This equivocation obscures the state's burden to justify its premise – in general and specific to a particular child – that preserving a caregiver relationship over parental objection serves children's well-being. The community has decided that parents who share caregiving forfeit their claim to deference becuase of the general risk to child welfare, so the law may demand an independent judicial assessment about whether ending the caregiver relationship in this specific case denies the child their primary relational goods.

* * *

When caregivers raise a child, the adult and the child develop an interest in sustaining their intimate relationship. Respect for these complementary interests justifies a limited claim against interference by other adults and the state. However, this caregiving theory cannot justify a broad parental authority to shape a child's life. Nor can it explain how anyone obtains the initial or subsequent privilege to raise a child. While estoppel principles cannot ground parenthood directly either, they do explain why parents forfeit their exclusive authority by encouraging their child to form attachments with a custodian or coresidential caregiver.

III CAREGIVING IN A POLITICAL CONCEPTION OF PARENTAGE

Caregiving will remain central to the political conception of parentage. Having untangled the principles behind caregiver theories, we can now reconstruct functional parentage rules using the political conception to fill gaps in the personal theory of caregiver duties or rights.

[122] I am thinking of Miss Honey, the teacher in *Matilda*, but what makes her moral claim to parenthood sympathetic is that Matilda's parents were so neglectful that they effectively abandoned her. Roald Dahl, Matilda (1988).

A *Political Parenthood Is a Condition on a Custodial Caregiving Privilege*

As concluded in II.A, the personal theory of caregiving cannot (a) identify a nonarbitrary baseline to specify the content of duties generated by voluntary caregiving or (b) justify coercing individuals to fulfill conventional parenting norms as a condition of caregiving. Political parenthood fills both gaps.

First, principles of justice supply the moral baseline needed for a caregiver theory. No one may take indefinite custody of a child without incurring a political duty to ensure the child receives their distributive rights, including their generic and relational primary goods specified by the legitimate political authority.

Consider first ordinary goods. The community must ensure that each child has adequate primary goods, including material goods such as food, services such as education, experiences such as play, and relational goods such as a caregiver. Anyone who takes custody of a child prevents others from supplying the child's primary goods. If the custodian does not supply them, then the custodian's conduct will deprive the child of their baseline entitlements. The community cannot, consistent with equal respect for the child, allow anyone to take custody of a child without a political duty to ensure the child receives their primary goods. The duty created by voluntary custodial caregiving is not fixed by what other adults would provide. Even if no one else is willing to raise the child, the child is entitled to a fair share of primary goods. Even if wait lists for adoption are full of wealthy parents, the child is only entitled to a fair share of primary goods. Less wealthy or less lavish parents do not deny their children anything to which the child is entitled.

For similar reasons, the state may not allow anyone to take indefinite custody of a child without full parental status. Every child has a political right to a parent. The community must ensure every child has a caregiver with the duty and authority to decide on the child's behalf how the child will live a flourishing life. Children's claim to a parent must trump adults' liberty to undertake custodial caregiving. Otherwise, adults would be permitted to take custody of a child to serve their own ends. They could take in a teenager for cheap labor. They could bring an infant home to experience the joy of caring for a baby with a plan to pass the child off in the terrible threes. An adult may take custody of a child consistent with equal respect for the child only if the adult incurs a legal duty to act on the child's behalf throughout their minority. The legal privilege to perform custodial caregiving must be conditioned on full parental duties, as specified by the public conception of justice.

Political parental duties must be voluntary, but only in the same limited sense as personal caregiver duties. Parental duties substantially limit an adult's liberty to pursue their own ends. A community that imposed parental duties on an arbitrary citizen would be using them as a mere means to meet the child's needs. The state must have reasons to impose parental duties on particular adults that respect them as equal citizens. As explained in II.A.2, it is not enough to say that a caregiver accepted the social role of a parent or that our conventions treat taking custody as acceptance of that role. Fortunately, the adult's consent to, acceptance of, or knowledge about the parental duties is irrelevant. The community can justify this limit on custodial liberty directly. A state that allowed anyone to undertake indefinite custodial caregiving without full parental duties would fail to ensure the child's primary goods.

The fact that an adult voluntarily accepts custody is necessary but not sufficient to reconcile parental duties with equal respect for adults. Parental obligations significantly restrict the liberty of adults to pursue familial lives. To reconcile this limitation with equal respect, the state has a duty to support parents financially and structurally and to affirmatively address gender inequality and distributive injustice.[123] Moreover, while caregiving alone cannot generate parental rights, states should consider offering secondary forms of legal recognition for nonparental caregivers who help meet children's needs, such as financial support, employment leave, and antidiscrimination protections in housing.[124]

B *Caregiver's Political Claim to Parental Authority*

Political parenthood can also explain why parents can acquire their own claim to parental authority. As concluded in II.B, the relational rights justified by caregiving labor cannot justify parental authority. Because the three methods of reconciling adult and child interests failed, any attempt to justify parental authority directly by a caregiver's interest in shaping a child seems to treat the child as a means to the adult's welfare. The child's political right to a parent provides the symmetry needed to explain why parents can hold a right to shape a child's life.

Young children have a political right to parental *authority*. Every child needs a parent to judge how the child will use their primary goods to pursue a coherent conception of a flourishing childhood. A parent can choose on a child's behalf only by exercising judgment based on the parent's values. The parental duty to ensure children receive primary goods leaves broad leeway – as wide as the range of valuable lives in a liberal pluralist society. This discretion opens space for adults to develop their own claim to parental authority. As they raise a child, a custodial caregiver develops an interest in this project of guiding the child's life by their values. The exercise of parental authority is itself good *for the parent*. As a child is raised by their custodial caregiver, the child develops an interest in continuing to have their life guided by this adult. A portion of the caregiver's interest in shaping the child is symmetrical with the child's interest in having this caregiver guide their life.

This portion of symmetrical interests can justify a claim to parental authority for the adult, but only insofar as their project is consistent with equal respect for the child.[125] A parental caregiver's only legitimate interest is in exercising authority on

[123] *See* 1.II.C.3; Maxine Eichner, The Supportive State: Families, Government, and America's Political Ideals (2010).

[124] Melissa Murray, *The Networked Family: Reframing the Legal Understanding of Caregiving and Caregivers*, 94 Va. L. Rev. 385, 409–15, 450–52 (2008).

[125] It must also be consistent with equal respect for other adults, discussed in Sections C and D below.

the child's behalf. Parents may not use their children to serve their own interests. For example, a parent may not exploit their child for labor. However, a parent can insist their child do chores that contribute to the child's welfare as part of the family and help the child develop a sense of responsibility.

Parental loyalty conflicts are not always problems of self-interest. A parent can violate their fiduciary duty by using their child for valuable ends. Consider parents who push their children into careers at a young age. The world is a better place because James Mill pushed his son John Stuart to become a philosopher, but he undoubtedly used his son. Other parents may draft their children into valuable crusades, such as combatting deforestation or climate change. Parents may argue that their decisions serve their child's well-being because the child shares their environmental or aesthetic values. This argument involves a contradiction. An adult may wield authority to set ends for a child only if the child cannot set ends for themselves. The parents might instead argue that they are not merely using the child because the child will come to share the parent's values. This begs the question. A parent cannot justify irrevocably shaping a young child's life toward one value by arguing that, after this shaping, the child will come to share that value.

What does this mean for religious education, the most discussed source of loyalty conflicts? Several faculties related to spirituality are arguably primary goods. All children have an interest in developing some appreciation for the nature of existence and humans' place in it. A liberal political community cannot legitimately supply these values. Because the parent's interest in shaping their children spiritually offers one realization of a primary good for the child, the community can recognize that parents have a liberty right to educate children in their religious or scientific beliefs and practices. As the US Supreme Court recognized, children need parents to prepare them for roles that the state cannot. However, the child's primary goods remain cabined by familiar liberal principles. As an equal citizen over a full life, the child's interest is in having an adult guide their life until the child can live by their own spiritual judgment. Young children need parents to provide spiritual values that will shape their lives, but children also need parents to act with an awareness that the child is their own person and not attempt to subvert their development. Caregivers who exercise discretion within these bounds acquire a legitimate parental right to use their conception of the good to guide their children's lives.

C *Caregiving, Gestation, and the Initial Assignment of Parentage*

So far, I have concluded that no one may engage in custodial caregiving without incurring full parental duties (II.A) and that custodial caregivers acquire a right to continued parental authority once the child develops a symmetrical interest in having the caregiver guide their life (II.B). Is that not the whole ballgame? Unfortunately, no. If parental rights arise through custodial caregiving, some other principles must determine who has a privilege to take custody of a child.

1 The Initial Allocation of Parental Liberty: Genetics and Gestation

Contrary to the hope of some philosophers and legal scholars, pregnancy and childbirth are not a form of parental caregiving that justifies full and exclusive parental rights at birth.[126] The strategy set out in II.B for reconciling caregivers' interests with equal respect for children cannot be applied to the interests formed by gestational parents during pregnancy and childbirth. Pregnant people sacrifice for the welfare of the future child, altering their bodies and lives to carry the fetus. However, this gestational work is not work to guide the child's life. Gestation is not the kind of caregiving function that grounds parental rights.[127] A gestational parent may develop an interest in their projected future relationship with the child, but the child does not have a symmetrical interest in a parental relationship with this adult. The interests of the gestational parent cannot justify parental rights directly without treating the child's life as a means.

That does not mean gestation is irrelevant to parentage law. A gestational parent takes on a profound procreative project, and if their project includes raising the child they are carrying, then they should have a conditional liberty to raise the child. In other words, gestational parents have a derivative liberty right to raise the child. A presumptive parental liberty for gestational parents is consistent with equal respect for the child and other adults.[128]

Suppose a gestational parent obtains donor sperm and eggs from a fertility clinic for their own use. No one else has a moral right to demand this person refrain from pursuing a gestational procreative project. Any such moral claim would deny the gestational parent's innate right to bodily integrity. Furthermore, no one else has a moral claim to raise the child after the birth. The gestational parent used their body and their labor to create this child. A third party could have a right to raise the child only if they had a right to use the gestational parent's body and labor to facilitate their child-rearing projects. Thus, an adult who undertakes a gestational project has a derived liberty to perform custodial caregiving.

The law must limit gestational parents' caregiving liberty to ensure it remains consistent with equal respect for the child and other adults. First, to respect the child, a gestational parent's custodial privilege (like any caregiving privilege) must

[126] *See, e.g.*, Spitko, *supra* note 85; Jessica Feinberg, *Parent Zero*, 55 U.C. DAVIS L. REV. 2271 (2021); HENDRICKS, *supra* note 89, at 39–41, 104–07.

[127] *Contra* Appleton, *supra* note 31, at 275.

[128] While I agree with *Lehr* that birth makes the "parental relationship clear," the relationship entails only a conditional parental liberty rather than full parenthood, so it need not rest on stereotypes about women as "draftees" and men as "volunteers," even if it may reinforce those social norms. Karen Czapanskiy, *Volunteers and Draftees: The Struggle for Parental Equality*, 38 UCLA L. REV. 1415, 1458–59 (1990); NeJaime, *supra* note 3, at 296–97. As Serena Mayeri describes the drafting of the *Lehr* opinion, Justice O'Connor insisted that Justice Stevens remove language (mirroring his dissent in *Caban*) that strongly implied physical and psychological bonds created by gestation justified maternal responsibility. Serena Mayeri, *Foundling Fathers: (Non-)Marriage and Parental Rights in the Age of Equality*, 125 YALE L.J. 2292, 2365–68 (2015).

be conditioned on commitment to parental duties. The law could demand birth parents commit to parental duties expressly. However, their willingness to incur pregnancy's burdens – its work, pain, risks, and costs – demonstrates their commitment unless they seek adoption. Furthermore, most (not all) pregnant people develop an emotional bond with the fetus, which is facilitated by biological processes, the work of pregnancy, and their imagined future. Cultural norms also exert pressure on pregnant people to identify with the fetus and plan for parenthood. The law has ample reasons to trust a gestational parent to care for the child. Accordingly, the states may presume the birth parent is a legal parent unless they opt out of the parental role.

This birth presumption does not entail exclusive parental rights. Gary Spitko and Jennifer Hendricks have argued (independently) that gestational parents meet the commitment prong of the genetics-plus-commitment test, so they have exclusive constitutional rights to choose to be a single parent or place the child for adoption.[129] Part of the appeal of this argument rests on a mistaken understanding of the moral function of commitment. Commitment satisfies the condition necessary for custodial caregiving. It does not justify parental authority directly.[130] Once a gestational parent takes on the role of raising the child and begins fulfilling the child's right to a parent, the adult and child develop symmetrical claims against interference with their relationship. A gestational parent who has not committed to raising the child has no fundamental right to shape the child's life, such as by deciding unilaterally whether to place the child for adoption.

Moreover, gestational parents' caregiving liberty must be reconciled with any similar caregiving liberty of other adults. As I argued in Chapter 2, genetic parents have a derived liberty to raise their progeny because many reasonable citizens believe procreative child-rearing is central to a valuable life. When a man engages in voluntary vaginal intercourse or a woman shares her eggs with her partner for IVF, these genetic parents waive any further right not to procreate. Any such right would violate the pregnant person's bodily integrity. However, genetic parents do not necessarily waive their privilege to raise the child. Gestation does not justify a right to exclusive parenthood. To preserve equal liberty, the law must maintain a legal process for genetic parents to commit to parenthood and seek shared custody. Without a unilateral tool like genetic parentage petitions, the birth presumption gives the gestational parent a right to limit the genetic parents' liberty to raise their genetic children.[131]

129 Spitko, *supra* note 85; HENDRICKS, *supra* note 89.

130 While many reasons support parental liberty for gestational parents, those reasons cannot be simply combined to justify an exclusive right to choose who else may be a parent for the child. *Contra* Feinberg, *supra* note 126, at 2320–21.

131 Jennifer Hendricks, in her Commentary on Chapter 4 at the University of Virginia School of Law Workshop on Reconstructing Parentage (Nov. 10, 2023), argued that this rule licenses genetic parents to use women's gestational capacity as a resource for genetic parents' familial ends. This objection is

Last, pregnancy may generate child-rearing liberty only if the gestational parent had a privilege to use the gametes for their procreative and child-rearing projects. This condition is met if a genetic mother conceives a child through voluntary heterosexual intercourse, regardless of the genetic father's procreative intentions. It is also met in most cases of assisted reproduction, as I argue in 6.III, except when the gestational surrogate agrees to carry an unrelated child on behalf of the intended parents. Furthermore, as I explained in 3.III.B, a gestational parent cannot acquire the privilege to raise a child if they acquired gametes wrongfully through rape or gamete theft. A legal rule that treated gestational parents as legal parents in these situations would empower gestational parents to use genetic parents for their own familial ends.[132]

2 Custodial Defaults among Gestational, Breastfeeding, and Genetic Parents

Although gestational and genetic parents have conditional parental liberties, that does not mean the law must treat them equally for purposes of custody. A state may adopt a custodial default for gestational parents. The work of pregnancy and childbirth is evidence that the gestational parent is earnestly committed and will provide quality care. By comparison, mere genetic parents have little evidence of similar commitment. At most, they can point to planning conception deliberately; preparing to raise the child, such as arranging a nursery or attending parenting classes; and assisting with the pregnancy, such as providing financial assistance or attending appointments and birth classes. These differences can justify a short-term presumption in favor of primary custody for a gestational parent, including a liberty to bring the child home from the hospital.

This custodial default does not justify a right to exclude genetic parents from postbirth caregiving. Separated birth parents can share custody of an infant. The unequal custody default should not persist once a genetic or intended parent demonstrates their commitment to the child and their ability to work cooperatively with the custodial gestational parent. The law can facilitate the adults' efforts to share coparenting responsibility.[133] Perhaps it will turn out to be the case, as some surmise, that few genetic parents will commit to equal parenting, even if the system

sound in cases of rape and when a genetic parent prevents a gestational parent from obtaining an abortion. In cases where a gestational parent plans to complete the pregnancy anyway, a right to share parenthood would use them as a mere means only if their labor entitled them to exclusive liberty to raise the child – the objection presupposes a gestational theory of parenthood.

132 Lies about contraception raise similar problems, but I am uncertain how fraudulent conception should affect biological parents' parental liberties. One might treat lies by genetic and gestational parents differently. A genetic father who lies about contraception imposes significantly on a gestational parent's bodily and reproductive liberty, while a gestational parent who lies about contraception limits the father's reproductive liberty while also investing in gestational labor.

133 Existing law can implement this only via shared custody or parenting time, but Mele Weiner argues the law should replace joint custody, which is often applied as a formalistic equality rule for conflictual relationships, with a coparenting status designed to facilitate cooperative coparenting.

supports it.[134] Nevertheless, only gender stereotypes could justify a general presumption against substantial shared parenting time. Many people assume gestational parents have stronger caregiving instincts than genetic parents (especially genetic fathers), but custody law must not reproduce traditional gender stereotypes that place an asymmetrical parenting burden on women, as feminists like Sylvia Law argued decades ago.[135]

If the infant is breastfed, then the child and breastfeeding parent have an additional interest in primary custody, especially early on while breastfeeding is being established.[136] The law may legitimately facilitate breastfeeding because the evidence suggests it is better than formula for an infant's physical health.[137] This rationale, however, does not justify exclusive residential or physical custody. Sometimes the genetic parent can induce lactation or obtain donor breastmilk. Even if they cannot, they may still receive blocks of parenting time, especially during the day. The birth parents can also share decisional authority, such as the decision on whether to use daycare. If a genetic or intended parent reliably works around breastfeeding to care for an infant, their parenting time can be gradually increased with pumped breastmilk or supplemental formula. As Meghan Boone argues, laws designed to facilitate lactation (whether in employment, public accommodations, or parentage) should avoid unnecessarily reinforcing gendered roles that marginalize nontraditional families.[138]

A custodial preference for breastfeeding parents will be controversial. On the one hand, it facilitates a massive investment in child-rearing work that builds relational attachments. It may also have expressive benefits. It offers public support for unpaid familial work traditionally assigned to women and hidden by privacy norms. On the other hand, allowing the breastfeeding parent to set the parenting schedule may prevent the noncustodial parent from getting enough caregiving time to build deep relational bonds. Although the rule is technically gender-neutral because some trans

Merle Weiner, *Thinking Outside the Custody Box*, 2016 U. ILL. L. REV. 1535, 1571. *See also* Clare Huntington, *Postmarital Family Law: A Legal Structure for Nonmarital Families*, 67 STAN. L. REV. 167, 227–28 (2015) (arguing law should presume equal access to facilitate parenting by nonmarital fathers).

134 *Compare* Katharine K. Baker, *Bargaining or Biology: The History and Future of Paternity Law and Parental Status*, 14 CORNELL J. L. & PUB. POL'Y 1, 51–52 (2004), *with* Huntington, *supra* note 133, at 186, 225.

135 United States v. Virginia, 518 U.S. 515 (1996). Sylvia A. Law, *Rethinking Sex and the Constitution*, 132 U. PA. L. REV. 955, 995–98, 1007–08 (1984); Mayeri, *supra* note 128, at 2343–46, 2360–61 (recounting similar arguments by feminist lawyers in nonmarital father cases, but they also favored unilateral adoption for birth mothers).

136 Kate Baxter-Kauf, *Breastfeeding in Custody Proceedings: A Modern-Day Manifestation of Liberal and Conservative Family Traditions*, 15 RICH. J. L. & PUB. INT. 627 (2011).

137 *See, e.g.*, Cesar G. Victora et al., *Breastfeeding in the 21st Century: Epidemiology, Mechanisms, and Lifelong Effect*, 387 LANCET 475 (2016); Kori Martin, *Parenting Plans and the Breastfed Child A Look at How Breastfeeding Is Used as a Factor in Parenting Time Allocations for Divorcing Parents in the U. S.*, 2 CLINICAL LACTATION 25 (2011).

138 Meghan Boone, *Lactation Law*, 106 CAL. L. REV. 1827, 1878–80 (2018).

men can nurse infants, the community will likely interpret it as a public endorsement of gendered parenting that essentializes women as mothers. Legislators openly trumpet lactation laws as facilitating traditional family values in ways that perpetuate sex stereotypes.[139]

D *Caregiving and Subsequent Allocations of Parentage*

When a caregiver enters the life of a child who already has a legal parent, the fact of caregiving alone cannot justify extending rights to this new caregiver. Once an adult performs caregiving with this privilege, their caregiving can begin to justify rights for the child and for the adult caregiver. An adult has a privilege to pursue the caregiving roles that can ground parental duties and rights only in three circumstances:

(a) no one else has a legal claim to the parental relationship, and the caregiver takes custody with the state's permission to pursue parental roles;
(b) a current or prospective legal parent has the legal power to consent to parentage by a third party, and this legal parent exercises that power; or
(c) the existing legal parents consented to share caregiving privileges with a third party, who provided sufficient care and guidance for the child to develop parental attachments, so ending the relationship would harm the child.

Obviously, the third opportunity reflects the reliance principles behind parenthood by estoppel, as I explained in II.B.3. This opportunity applies primarily to two narrow circumstances when the law may extend parenthood to a caregiver over the parent's objection.

The first is long-term guardianships. Arranging a temporary guardianship can be a reasonable exercise of parental authority when a parent faces a health crisis, military deployment, or short imprisonment (II.B.3). The parent–child relationship can be sustained despite periodic absences, especially with support from extended family or the community. Nevertheless, at some point, an absent parent has proven themselves no longer able or willing to fulfill the child's right to care and guidance. As some courts describe this situation, "the parent may no longer enjoy a paramount status . . . if he or she fails to shoulder the responsibilities that are attendant to rearing a child."[140] A state may specify this boundary through the law of abandonment or de facto parenthood. In either case, the community is exercising its authority to specify children's basic right to parental care and guidance. The child has a right to a parent, and if this role is fulfilled by someone who is not a legal parent, that custodial caregiver develops their own right to sustain their parental project. Long-term custodians should be able to petition a court for parentage or permanent custody (parentage in all but name), so a court can reach an independent judgment about

139 *Id.* at 1873.
140 Price v. Howard, 484 S.E.2d 528 (N.C. 1997).

which adult fulfilled parental roles sufficiently to maintain rightful authority over the child.

Similar forfeiture notions may justify doctrines like the residential presumption or de facto parenthood that elevate stepparents or relatives to parental status after they coparent a child in a shared household. These doctrines are not justified as an exercise of the legal parent's autonomy, but they can be rendered consistent with appropriate respect for the legal parent's familial liberty. The parent has a liberty to seek caregiving assistance and authority to judge the child's relationships, but if a parent shares too much authority for too long, they forfeit their ability to withdraw those powers. Legal parents need not expressly agree to share parenthood, but they must implicitly treat their cohabitant or relative as a coparent.[141] They must hold one another responsible for caregiving, expect to make major decisions together, and treat one another as coparents in interactions with the child and the community. The child who views both adults as dedicated to and responsible for care and guidance will develop a right to be parented by the caregiver, who in turn develops correlative parental obligations and a right to sustain the parenting project.[142] The legal parent forfeits not only their relational authority over visitation but also their authority to withdraw the parental powers they implicitly shared.

Several parentage law doctrines operationalize these ideas. The marital and residential presumptions reflect an evidentiary premise that someone who lives with a child likely performs the care and guidance that builds parental attachment with the legal parent's permission (as I explain more in 6.II.D). The statute of limitations for rebutting the presumptions reflects the community's estimate of the time children take to develop parental attachments. States may supplement the presumptions with a standard, such as de facto parenthood or parentage by estoppel. When these standards create legal parenthood, the law empowers courts to define, using common law processes, how much caregiving and decision-making legal parents may share without forfeiting their claim to exclusive authority.

CONCLUSION

No one may take indefinite custody of a child without full parental duties. Caregivers can incur parental duties by taking a child into their home voluntarily, but these duties are not justified by the caregiver's acceptance or by reliance causation. Parental duties are a condition on the liberty to perform indefinite

141 Unlike Jeffrey Parness, I would not call this a case of "apparent consent," because that term wrongly implies a moment of agreement; however, Parness is correct that these doctrines cannot be applied over the objection of a noncustodial parent who has not acted in a way that forfeits their authority. Jeffrey A. Parness, *The Constitutional Limits on Custodial and Support Parentage by Consent*, 56 IDAHO L. REV. 421, 443 (2020).

142 The caregiver's parental duties include support obligations, which requires revising existing laws and model acts that only allow a caregiver to bring a claim. Jeffrey A. Parness & Matthew Timko, *De Facto Parent and Nonparent Child Support Orders*, 67 AM. U. L. REV. 769 (2017).

custodial caregiving. The law must force adults to choose – no custody or full parenthood – because the community is obligated to ensure that every child receives a fair share of primary goods, including a parent who meets their need for caregiving and supplies value judgments to guide their childhood. Once an adult commits to this parental role, the adult can acquire full parental rights because the adult and child develop a symmetrical interest in this assignment of authority over the child's life.

Unlike child-rearing, the work of pregnancy and childbirth cannot justify full and exclusive parental rights. However, gestational labor can justify a conditional liberty to raise the child. Parentage law should respect the conditional caregiving liberty of gestational and genetic parents, while recognizing that these initial legal parents may want to agree to share parenthood with nonbiological intended parents.

5

Parents by Agreement

Over a spring brunch, David, his husband Raymond, and their friend Samantha "devised a plan" to conceive and raise a child together.[1] That summer, David and Raymond alternated delivering sperm to Samantha for insemination. In September, the three announced Samantha's pregnancy on social media wearing matching shirts that said, "This guy is going to be a daddy" and "This girl is going to be a mama." David attended the pregnancy appointments with Samantha, and all three attended a natural childbirth course. Raymond arranged sixteen weeks of paternity leave. They hired an attorney to draft an agreement but never signed it.

Samantha had a home birth in May at David and Raymond's house. After testing identified David as the genetic father, he and Samantha signed an acknowledgment of paternity. They named the baby Mathew Z. S.-G. to reflect his heritage: Mathew from Samantha's family, Z. from Raymond's father, and S. and G. from Samantha and David's surnames. After a week of recuperating at the men's house, Samantha brought Matthew to her residence. David and Raymond had "regular daytime parenting time," but overnight visitation was "slow to start because Mathew was nursing on demand." When talking to Matthew, the adults referred to Samantha as "Momma," David as "Daddy," and Raymond as "Papai," Portuguese for father.

That fall, the parties' relationship became "strained" because David and Raymond wanted more parenting time. They filed a petition seeking joint custody with Samantha. Everyone agreed that Samantha and David were legal parents. The only question was Raymond's status. Samantha was willing to allow Raymond visitation but resisted declaring him a legal parent. As the family court acknowledged, neither the parentage statute nor precedents authorized the court to recognize three legal parents. However, the state's highest court had recently held, under the custody statute, that a nonbiological intended parent who helped her partner plan conception and raise the child could seek custody "as a parent."[2] Extending this

1 Raymond T. v. Samantha G., 74 N.Y.S.3d 730, 731 (N.Y. Fam. Ct. 2018).

2 *Id.* at 964 (discussing *In re* Brooke S.B. v. Elizabeth A.C.C., 61 N.E.3d 488 (N.Y. 2016)).

precedent, the family court held that Raymond could also seek custody as a parent because he participated in the group's preconception plan.

This conclusion fits a trend in parentage law. Over the last three decades, states have slowly expanded the legal tools that allow adults to allocate parenthood among themselves. In fertility clinics, individuals provide sperm, eggs, or gestational services that enable others to be legal parents. In maternity wards, birth mothers and their partners sign forms agreeing to share parenthood. In adoption agencies, birth parents and adoptive parents agree to adoption with ongoing visitation. In courts, legal parents and their partners agree to second-parent adoption. Part I describes the evolving landscape of legal agreements to create parentage for unrelated adults. Why can private individuals decide who has the authority to shape a child's life?

Over the last three chapters, I concluded that our intentions affect our political rights and duties to children. Although biological parents are not automatically legal parents, they acquire parental rights when their conduct demonstrates their commitment to custodial caregiving. Might commitment be the core of all parentage?[3] Many family law scholars support intentional theories of parentage because allowing adults to arrange parental rights facilitates autonomy, diversity, and LGBTQ+ equality.[4] Some ethicists support voluntarist theories because a person who consents to parental duties cannot claim the burdens impose unfairly on their autonomy.[5] The intentional and voluntarist theorists reflect genuine insights, but their core concepts cannot justify parental rights or duties. Part II argues that any attempt to ground parenthood in intentions, consent, promises, or contracts is bound to fail because these normative powers are justified by the agents' authority over their own lives.[6] Extending those reasons to justify parenthood treats children as a subordinate means to adults' ends.

Nevertheless, liberal states should enable adults to become parents deliberately and prospectively without regard to biological relatedness. Many people want to pursue nonbiological parenthood, and parentage law has tools that can empower unrelated adults to become parents in ways that respect the child and the biological, presumed, and legal parents. Withholding these tools disrespects nonbiological

3 Jeffrey A. Parness, *The Constitutional Limits on Custodial and Support Parentage by Consent*, 56 Idaho L. Rev. 421 (2020) (attempting to unify these doctrines as cases of parenting by "consent," but a concept that includes explicit, implicit, apparent, and presumed consent, as well as various forms of waiver or forfeiture, is too multifarious to provide insight).

4 Martha M. Ertman, Love's Promises: How Formal and Informal Contracts Shape All Kinds of Families (2016); Melanie B. Jacobs, *Parental Parity: Intentional Parenthood's Promise*, 64 Buff. L. Rev. 465 (2016); Yehezkel Margalit, Determining Legal Parentage: Between Family Law and Contract Law (2019).

5 Elizabeth Brake, *Willing Parents: A Voluntarist Account of Parental Role Obligations*, *in* Procreation and Parenthood: The Ethics of Bearing and Rearing Children 151 (David Archard & David Benatar eds., 2010). *See also* Melanie B. Jacobs, *Intentional Parenthood's Influence: Rethinking Procreative Autonomy and Federal Paternity Establishment*, 20 Am. U. J. Gender Soc. Pol'y & L. 489 (2011).

6 Some material in Parts I and II of this chapter were previously published in Gregg Strauss, *Parentage Agreements Are Not Contracts*, 90 Fordham L. Rev. 2645 (2021).

parents and LGBTQ+ citizens, implying they are not able to or worthy of participating in the political office of parenthood.[7] As Part III concludes, a liberal-egalitarian state has sound reasons to recognize various normative powers regarding parentage, including second-parent adoption, parentage acknowledgments, preconception agreements, and perhaps surrogacy.

I NORMATIVE POWERS IN PARENTAGE LAW

To understand the new legal tools for privately arranging parenthood, it is essential to begin with the traditional means for deliberately adding new parents.

A *Adoption*

Adoption creates a legal parent–child relationship between a child and an adult who is not their presumed or biological parent. When a child has no legal parents, adoption creates a new legal family. A child is available for adoption only if their biological or legal parents have died, consented to termination of their parental rights, or had their rights terminated for neglect, abuse, or abandonment.[8] When a child has one legal parent, this parent can consent to adding a new parent through stepparent or second-parent adoption. A second parent can adopt only if any other claims to parenthood have been extinguished.

Adoption law has been shaped to protect parent–child relationships, including the constitutional rights of biological and legal parents.[9] A birth mother must give written consent to the adoption after the birth, sometimes after a waiting period.[10] She can also change her mind for a short period, ranging from a day to a few weeks.[11] If she revokes her consent, some states return the child automatically, while others direct courts to use a best-interests test.[12] The liberty of a mere genetic parent receives weaker legal protections, as discussed in Chapter 2. Some states treat a genetic father's consent to adoption during the pregnancy as binding. Some courts hold that genetic fathers waive their rights if they fail to demonstrate unambiguous

7 The US Supreme Court recognized that access to legal families implicates equality among citizens. It held that states cannot deny civil marriage to same-sex couples because denying their legal ability to form families on equal terms slanders their dignity as equal citizens. Obergefell v. Hodges, 576 U.S. 614, 675–76 (2015).

8 *See* 2 HANDLING CHILD CUSTODY, ABUSE AND ADOPTION CASES § 14:5 (2021).

9 UNIF. ADOPTION ACT § 2-401 cmt. (UNIF. LAW COMM'N 1994) (describing how consent provisions were crafted to accommodate the Supreme Court's unwed father cases); Michael J. Higdon, *Constitutional Parenthood*, 103 IOWA L. REV. 1483, 1499 (2018).

10 *See* 1 ADOPTION LAW AND PRACTICE § 2.11(1)(a) (2021).

11 Elizabeth J. Samuels, *Time to Decide? The Laws Governing Mothers' Consents to the Adoption of Their Newborn Infants*, 72 TENN. L. REV. 509, 541 (2004).

12 1 ADOPTION LAW AND PRACTICE § 8.02(1)(a)(i).

commitment during the pregnancy.[13] When birth parents have a right to veto adoption, they can also choose who adopts the child by consenting to waive their parental rights only for their preferred adoptive parent.[14]

Adoptive parents must also pass two layers of state screening: status limits and ad hoc review. An adoptive parent must be at least eighteen years old, sometimes twenty-one.[15] Other status rules rest on assumptions about which adults can raise children well, including controversial family ideals. Until recently, many states required or encouraged matching by race in foster care and adoption.[16] Despite purportedly barring consideration of race in custody cases, the US Supreme Court repeatedly turned away constitutional challenges to the use of race in adoption and foster care until Congress barred consideration of race by statute.[17] Most states banned joint same-sex adoption in the last quarter of the twentieth century, but the last such prohibitions have fallen to constitutional challenges.[18] Nevertheless, some private adoption agencies still refuse to serve same-sex couples, insisting that their religious liberty gives them a right to do so.[19]

Another set of controversial rules concerns marital status. Historically, only married couples could adopt, but most states now allow adoption by a single person.[20] Most also allow unmarried couples to adopt jointly or pursue second-parent adoption, although a minority still require marriage for joint adoption.[21]

13 *Id.* § 2.11. *See generally* Mary M. Beck, *Prenatal Abandonment: Horton Hatches the Egg in the Supreme Court and Thirty-Four States*, 24 MICH. J. GENDER & L. 53 (2017).

14 1 ADOPTION LAW AND PRACTICE § 2.11(4)(a) (2021); Teri Dobbins Baxter, *Respecting Parents' Fundamental Rights in the Adoption Process: Parents Choosing Parents for Their Children*, 67 RUTGERS U. L. REV. 905, 917–40 (2015) (describing birth parent's statutory, nonconstitutional right to choose in Tennessee and California).

15 CHILD WELFARE INFO. GATEWAY, WHO MAY ADOPT, BE ADOPTED, OR PLACE A CHILD FOR ADOPTION? (2020), www.childwelfare.gov/resources/who-may-adopt-be-adopted-or-place-child-adoption/ (last visited Jan 31, 2024).

16 1 ADOPTION LAW AND PRACTICE § 3.06(3)–(4) (2021).

17 Katie Eyer, *Constitutional Colorblindness and the Family*, 162 U. PA. L. REV. 537 (2013); Solangel Maldonado, *Bias in the Family: Race, Ethnicity, and Culture in Custody Disputes*, 55 FAM. CT. REV. 213 (2017) (demonstrating courts still use race expressly and implicitly in custody).

18 Kari E. Hong, *Parens Patri[Archy]: Adoption, Eugenics, and Same-Sex Couples*, 40 CAL. W. L. REV. 1, 38–42 (2003). Campaign for S. Equal. v. Miss. Dep't of Hum. Servs., 175 F. Supp. 3d 691, 710 (S.D. Miss. 2016) (federal right to marry); Fla. Dep't of Child. & Fams. v. Adoption of X.X.G., 45 So. 3d 79 (Fla. Dist. Ct. App. 2010) (violates state constitution).

19 Fulton v. City of Philadelphia, 141 S. Ct. 1868, 1875 (2021). Miracle Hill Ministries, the largest foster agency in South Carolina, requires prospective foster parents to accept a list of articles of evangelical Christian faith. *See Foster Care*, MIRACLE HILL MINISTRIES, https://miraclehill.org/how-we-help/childrens-ministries/foster-care/ (last visited Mar. 30, 2022).

20 2 HANDLING CHILD CUSTODY, ABUSE AND ADOPTION CASES § 14:4 (2021).

21 NATIONAL CENTER FOR LESBIAN RIGHTS, *LEGAL RECOGNITION OF LGBT FAMILIES* 2–3 (2019), www.nclrights.org/wp-content/uploads/2013/07/Legal_Recognition_of_LGBT_Families.pdf; COURTNEY G. JOSLIN, SHANNON MINTER & CATHERINE SAKIMURA, LESBIAN, GAY, BISEXUAL AND TRANSGENDER FAMILY LAW § 5:2 (2023–24 ed. 2023). Courts have rejected arguments that the Constitution demands states extend stepparent adoption to unmarried couples. Sheardown v. Guastella, 324 Mich. App. 251, 263 (2018); Hawkins v. Grese, 68 Va. App. 462, 475 (2018).

That minority position, shorn of express homophobia, rests on an empirical assumption that marriage is a proxy for commitment, resources, and stability.[22] On the other end of the spectrum, some states are loosening the connection between adoption and romantic relationships. A few courts have allowed a grandparent to adopt their grandchild to coparent alongside their own child.[23]

Prospective adoptive parents must also complete an ad hoc review. A court must judge whether adoption is in the child's best interests.[24] Most states require a social worker or counselor to investigate the parents' and ensure their home is "suitable."[25] These investigations can be wide-ranging. Florida, for example, "considers such factors as physical and mental health, income and financial status, duration of marriage, housing, and neighborhood, among others."[26] Courts insist the state has a duty to investigate to ensure the adoptive parents will care for the child adequately, and prospective adoptive parents, unlike biological parents, have no preexisting right to custody.[27]

Critics insist the investigations are slow, costly, intrusive, and discriminatory. A home study can take months and cost a few thousand dollars.[28] Vague standards allow social workers and judges to apply their own values and biases, often to the detriment of adults who are single, less wealthy, LGBTQ+, or disabled or have a different religion, ethnicity, or race than the child.[29] Scholars argue that investigating adoptive parents implies that nonbiological parents are second-class parents.[30] These objections often form the central motivation for new parentage agreements.

B *Agreements by Gestational Parents to Share Parentage of Newborns*

The first three types of agreements allow birth mothers to bypass adoption by consenting to share parentage with their partners at conception or soon after birth.

22 *In re* Jason C., 533 A.2d 32 (N.H. 1987); Vanessa A. Lavely, *The Path to Recognition of Same-Sex Marriage: Reconciling the Inconsistencies Between Marriage and Adoption*, 55 UCLA L. Rev. 247, 287 (2007). Scholars rightly question the sincerity and efficacy of this policy. Jessica R. Feinberg, *Friends as Co-Parents*, 43 U.S.F. L. Rev. 799, 824 (2008); Richard F. Storrow, *Rescuing Children from the Marriage Movement: The Case Against Marital Status Discrimination in Adoption and Assisted Reproduction*, 39 U.C. Davis L. Rev. 305, 336–48 (2005).

23 *In re* Adoption of A.M., 930 N.E.2d 613 (Ind. Ct. App. 2010); *In re* Abby D., 839 A.2d 1222 (R.I. 2004). *But see In re* Adoption of M.R.D and T.M.D., 145 A.3d 1117 (Pa. 2016).

24 *In re* Adoption of A.A.B., 877 N.W.2d 355, 362–63 (S.D. 2016).

25 *See* 1 Adoption Law and Practice § 4.12 (2021); *Adoption Home Study Requirements by State*, Adoption Network (2020), https://adoptionnetwork.com/adoption-laws-by-state/homestudy-requirements/ (last visited Jan. 31, 2024).

26 Lofton v. Sec'y of Dep't of Child. & Fam. Servs., 358 F.3d 804, 810 (11th Cir. 2004) (citing Fla. Admin. Code Ann. r. 65C-16.005(3) (2003)).

27 *E.g.*, *id.* at 809–11.

28 Jessica Feinberg, *A Logical Step Forward: Extending Voluntary Acknowledgments of Parentage to Female Same-Sex Couples*, 30 Yale J.L. & Feminism 99, 112–13 (2018).

29 Leah Whetten-Goldstein, *Building Up Families by Breaking Down Marital Status as a Barrier to Adoption*, 54 U.S.F. L. Rev. 373, 388–90 (2019); Rachel H. Farr & Abbie E. Goldberg, *Sexual Orientation, Gender Identity, and Adoption Law*, 56 Fam. Ct. Rev. 374, 378 (2018).

30 Douglas NeJaime, *The Nature of Parenthood*, 126 Yale L.J. 2260, 2318–19 (2016).

1 Preconception Agreements

Thirty-eight states have statutes that authorize a female who undergoes donor insemination or IVF to agree to share parenthood with a partner.[31] The statutes apply only when a female conceives using artificial means with the intention to parent the child. They cannot be used by surrogates or by anyone who conceives through sex.[32] Most also apply only to spouses; only ten statutes expressly apply to unmarried couples.[33]

According to these statutes, a birth mother's spouse is a parent if he or she "consents to assisted reproduction"[34] or "agreed … to the insemination."[35] Most say nothing more about the content of the agreement. Under the UPA 2017, "an individual who consents … to assisted reproduction by a woman with the intent to be a parent of a child … is a parent."[36] The grammar of this provision suggests that consent to the procedure and intent to be a parent are distinct requirements, but the proof provisions indicate that "consent" refers to a plan to coparent. Consent can be proven by a written record signed by the birth mother or by clear and convincing evidence of "an express agreement entered into before conception that the individual and the woman intended that they both would be parents of the child."[37]

Preconception agreement statutes have a few formal requirements. Unlike the UPA, most states require consent in writing before conception.[38] A few recognize agreements entered into after insemination during pregnancy, although none explain how a spouse can agree to insemination that already occurred.[39] It also remains unclear when the agreement becomes binding to make the partner a parent. Most contested litigation occurs either in a custody battle years later or when a woman wants to use zygotes for IVF after the parties separate. Not all statutes address embryo disputes, and courts vary in their response.[40] The UPA 2017 provides that a partner is not a parent if they withdraw consent before implantation.[41]

31 *Id.* at 2260, app. B at 2367–69; June Carbone & Naomi Cahn, *Jane the Virgin and Other Stories of Unintentional Parenthood*, 7 U.C. Irvine L. Rev. 511, 518 (2017).

32 *See, e.g.*, Mo. Ann. Stat. § 210.824 (West 2021).

33 NeJaime, *supra* note 30, at 2260 & app. B.

34 Tex. Fam. Code Ann. § 160.703 (West 2021).

35 Ariz. Rev. Stat. Ann. § 25-501(B) (West 2022); Mich. Comp. Laws Ann. § 333.2824(6) (West 2022); Mo. Ann. Stat. § 210.824.

36 UPA 2017 § 703.

37 *Id.* § 704(b)(1). A court can also find "consent to parentage" of a donor-conceived child by applying a test that mimics the residential presumption. *Id.* § 704(b)(2).

38 *See, e.g.*, Ariz. Rev. Stat. Ann. § 25–501; Mo. Ann. Stat. § 210.824.

39 Ariz. Rev. Stat. Ann. § 25–501(B) ("agreed … to the insemination … after the insemination occurred"). In the UPA 2017, *oral* express agreements must be "entered into before conception," but "consent in a *record* [may be entered] before, on, or after the birth of the child." § 705(b).

40 2 Handling Child Custody, Abuse and Adoption Cases § 9:8.50 (2021).

41 UPA 2017 §§ 102(22), 707; I. Glenn Cohen, *The Right Not to Be a Genetic Parent*, 81 S. Cal. L. Rev. 1115, 1124 (2007).

2 Voluntary Acknowledgment of Parentage

In ten states, a birth mother can sign a "voluntary acknowledgment of parentage" to share parenthood with her partner, regardless of the partner's sex, so long as the child has no other presumed parent.[42] Parentage acknowledgments evolved out of the acknowledgments of paternity discussed in Chapter 2. Although paternity acknowledgments were designed to establish genetic paternity, some couples used them "to memorialize their relationship as co-parents" even when they knew the man was not the genetic father.[43] Some courts have held that signatories are bound even if they knew their averments were false, effectively treating the form as an agreement to share parenthood.[44] However, no states allow gestational parents to sign a paternity acknowledgment with their female partner.[45] Parentage acknowledgment statutes follow through on the agreement logic, applying without regard to the sex of the nonbiological parent. When I refer to a parentage acknowledgment, I am referring to these broader statutes.

States rarely dictate the content of voluntary acknowledgments of parentage. Federal law states that parties must receive oral and written notice of "the legal consequences of, and the rights ... and responsibilities that arise from, signing the acknowledgment."[46] Nevertheless, state forms often focus on *procedural* consequences, some almost exclusively.[47] New York's model form requires the parties to affirm they "understand that signing this Acknowledgment of Parentage is voluntary and will establish parentage of our child."[48] The remainder of the form explains how to rescind or challenge such acknowledgment. Other state forms describe parental duties or rights. Maryland's model form explains that it "constitutes a legal finding of parentage" and that "legal parents ... are the joint natural guardians of their minor child," which "means that both parents are jointly responsible for the support of their child" and "have equal rights to custody of the child."[49]

42 *See, e.g.*, Conn. Gen. Stat. Ann. §§ 17b-27, 46b-476, 46b-477 (West 2022); *FAQ: Voluntary Acknowledgment of Parentage (VAP)*, GLAD, www.glad.org/voluntary-acknowledgment-of-parentage/ (last visited Jan. 31, 2024) (updated list of statutes and forms as of July 2022).

43 Leslie Joan Harris, *Voluntary Acknowledgments of Parentage for Same-Sex Couples*, 20 Am. U. J. Gender Soc. Pol'y & L. 467, 478 (2012).

44 State *ex rel.* Sec'y of Dep't for Child. & Fams. v. Smith, 392 P.3d 68, 79 (Kan. 2017); Leslie Joan Harris, *Reforming Paternity Law to Eliminate Gender, Status, and Class Inequality*, 2013 Mich. St. L. Rev. 1295, 1330 (2013). *But see* Bedell v. Price, 828 S.E.2d 263, 268 (Va. Ct. App. 2019).

45 Susan Hazeldean, *Illegitimate Parents*, 55 U.C. Davis L. Rev. 1583, 1711, table 6 (2021).

46 42 U.S.C. § 666(C)(1).

47 *See, e.g.*, Acknowledgment of Parentage, Wash. State Dep't of Health, DOH 422-159 (Mar. 2021), https://perma.cc/5JXN-F26E.

48 Acknowledgment of Parentage, N.Y. Off. of Temp. & Disability Assistance, LDSS-5171 (Apr. 2021), https://perma.cc/BEH3-PZHY.

49 Affidavit of Parentage, Md. Dep't of Health (2020), https://perma.cc/D3V3-CEXT. *See also* Voluntary Declaration of Parentage, Cal. Dep't of Child Support Servs., DCSS 0909 (Jan. 2020), https://perma.cc/6Q75-NUQT; Voluntary Acknowledgment of Parentage, Cmlth of Mass., R-130-02112011, https://web.archive.org/web/20210101023825/https://www.mass.gov/doc/voluntary-acknowledgement-of-paternity/download.

3 Marital Presumption

The marital presumption is the traditional, sometimes obfuscating, way for a birth mother to agree to share parentage. A birth mother's spouse is a presumed parent, whether the couple married before the conception, during the pregnancy, or soon after the birth.[50] The spouse remains a parent until someone successfully rebuts the presumption in court.[51]

The marital presumption has served many functions: protecting the child from the legal and social harms of illegitimacy, providing an inference to genetic paternity, promoting marriage, and reflecting spousal agreement.[52] Some scholars argue that in contemporary law it functions primarily as a presumed agreement.[53] Piggybacking on social norms around marriage, the law infers that the birth mother consents to share parentage and the spouse commits to coparent.

Agreement notions always played a role in the marital presumption. Until the late twentieth century, only spouses had standing to challenge the presumption. Even if everyone knew the husband was not the biological father, the spouses could preserve their family by agreeing to raise the child together to the exclusion of the genetic father.[54] A small minority of states still retain this "conclusive" marital presumption.[55] The agreement aspect took center stage when courts started applying the marital presumption even where a spouse could not be a biological parent – first when a husband encouraged his wife to use donor sperm and later when lesbian couples planned conception. As discussed in Chapter 2, many seminal ART cases focused on causation, while more recent cases emphasize the preconception agreement. At least one court allowed spouses to jointly disavow the marital presumption when they separated *after* conception but *before* birth.[56]

Of course, genetic ties remain relevant to the marital presumption. Most parents who rely on it are heterosexual husbands whose wives conceived in sexual intercourse. DNA tests are typically sufficient to rebut the presumed paternity during the child's infancy.[57] The determining factor seems to be state policies about the value of marriage and genetic heritage, not the private intent of the parties.[58] The possibility of genetic rebuttal conflicts with the theory that the marital presumption is a proxy for agreements, but

50 UPA 2017 § 204(a).

51 *Id.* § 204(b).

52 Jessica Feinberg, *Restructuring Rebuttal of the Marital Presumption for the Modern Era*, 104 MINN. L. REV. 243, 249–51 (2019).

53 Katharine K. Baker, *Bargaining or Biology: The History and Future of Paternity Law and Parental Status*, 14 CORNELL J. L. & PUB. POL'Y 1, 25 (2004); June Carbone & Naomi Cahn, *Nonmarriage*, 76 MD. L. REV. 55 (2016).

54 *See, e.g.*, Brinkley v. King, 701 A.2d 176 (Pa. 1997).

55 June Carbone & Naomi Cahn, *Marriage, Parentage, and Child Support*, 45 FAM. L.Q. 219, 224 n.26 (2011) (one-third); Feinberg, *supra* note 52, at 269 (six).

56 *See, e.g.*, Chimienti v. Perperis, 98 N.Y.S.3d 251, 254 (App. Div. 2019).

57 Feinberg, *supra* note 52, at 252; Carbone and Cahn, *supra* note 55, at 222–30.

58 Carbone and Cahn, *supra* note 31, at 536–37.

perhaps these ideas are reconcilable. When spouses' commitment to coparent is premised on the assumption that a husband is the genetic father, a timely genetic rebuttal looks like the recission of an agreement for unilateral or mutual mistake.

C *Agreements to Share or Transfer Parentage before or at Birth*

In the above doctrines, a gestational parent agrees to share parenthood with a nonbiological parent. A mere genetic parent cannot initiate these agreements. When a male conceives a child, whether in an affair or surrogacy, their spouse is not a presumed marital parent.[59] Similarly, birth mothers can enter into preconception agreements or acknowledgments only if they intend themselves to parent.[60] Those doctrines cannot be used by couples who can procreate only with the assistance of a surrogate, which excludes all gay male couples and lesbian or heterosexual couples in which the female partner(s) cannot carry a child. In these families, the nonbiological intended parent may become a legal parent only through second-parent adoption or surrogacy.

1 Surrogacy Agreements

Most states allow *some* surrogates to enter into agreements to waive parental rights before the birth.[61] Nearly all states treat a genetic surrogate, who carries a child conceived with her own eggs, differently from a gestational surrogate, who carries a child conceived from the egg of an intended parent or donor. Genetic surrogates cannot enter into a binding agreement before the birth. They are presumed parents who must follow adoption processes.[62] In contrast, twenty-four states passed statues allowing gestational surrogates to establish parenthood for commissioning parents before the birth.[63] In states without statutes, gestational surrogacy contracts are highly uncertain.[64]

Around half of surrogacy statutes treat intended parents automatically as legal parents based only on the agreement.[65] Others require a judicial hearing, but even some of these allow parties to obtain a judgment during pregnancy that is effective at birth.[66] Courts must enter a parentage order, usually having no discretion to

59 Jessica Feinberg, *After Marriage Equality: Dual Fatherhood for Married Male Same-Sex Couples*, 54 U.C. Davis L. Rev. 1507, 1523 (2020).

60 UPA 2017 § 302(a).

61 This summary is heavily indebted to Courtney G. Joslin, *(Not) Just Surrogacy*, 109 Calif. L. Rev. 401 (2021).

62 *Id.* at 463–73. UPA 2017 § 201(1).

63 *See* Joslin, Minter & Sakimura, *supra* note 21, at § 4:2.

64 *Id.* § 4:3.

65 Joslin, *supra* note 61, at 439.

66 Joseph Williams, *New Surrogacy Law Brings Opportunities but Practitioners Beware*, N.Y. State Bar Ass'n (2021), https://nysba.org/new-surrogacy-law-brings-opportunities-but-practitioners-beware/ (last visited Jan. 31, 2024); Steven H. Snyder & Mary Patricia Byrn, *The Use of Prebirth Parentage Orders in Surrogacy Proceedings*, 39 Fam. L.Q. 633, 634–35 (2005).

evaluate the parents or the interests of the future child.[67] Like a voluntary acknowledgment of parentage or preconception agreement, a surrogacy contract effectively circumvents adoption screening.

Unlike these other agreements, surrogacy statutes impose substantial regulations. Some rules are designed to ensure informed consent. Some or all parties may need to undergo medical or psychological evaluations. Often, the surrogate must have had a prior successful birth. The surrogate may also need an independent lawyer.[68] Other regulations seem designed to facilitate family law policies. Five states insist that intended parents must be married, have a medical need for surrogacy, and complete a home study. All statutes allow commissioning parents to reimburse medical expenses, and many authorize them to offer "reasonable compensation."[69]

Surrogacy contracts often contain lifestyle and medical provisions, the enforceability of which is less certain. Lifestyle provisions dictate the surrogate's behavior regarding matters like drinking, smoking, exercise, diet, and numerous other real or imagined health risks.[70] Some contracts even empower intended parents to monitor the surrogate.[71] Other provisions may allocate authority over medical decisions such as selective reductions, abortions, pregnancy treatments, and birth procedures. Most statutes protect surrogates' authority over medical decisions relating to their bodily integrity, but some authorize parties to transfer medical decision-making to intended parents. A few of the latter use sweeping language that would include deciding whether a surrogate has an abortion or a Cesarean section.[72]

2 Known Donors and Open Adoption

When donors sell gametes to a fertility clinic, they sign a contract waiving parental rights.[73] I do not regard this contract as a parentage agreement because it neither creates nor transfers parentage. The waiver poses no novel problems. The law has long allowed biological parents to waive parental rights, yielding their children to the state or adoption agencies. The gestational parent who carries donor gametes becomes a parent through biology, a presumption, or a statute – not through an agreement with the donor.

67 Joslin, *supra* note 61, at 439.

68 Joslin, Minter & Sakimura, *supra* note 21, at § 4:2.

69 Joslin, *supra* note 61, at 433–39, 452–53, app. B.

70 Hillary Berk, *The Legalization of Emotion: Managing Risk by Managing Feelings in Contracts for Surrogate Labor*, 49 L. & Soc'y Rev. 143, 157–58 (2015).

71 *Id.* at 156–57; Joslin, *supra* note 61, at 446–47; Rachel Rebouché, *Contracting Pregnancy*, 105 Iowa L. Rev. 1591, 1611–12 (2019).

72 Joslin, *supra* note 61, at 444–47; Rebouché, *supra* note 71, at 1614–23.

73 Rene Almeling, *Gender and the Value of Bodily Goods: Commodification in Egg and Sperm Donation*, 72 Law & Contemp. Probs. 37, 57 (2009); NeJaime, *supra* note 30, at 2300.

Agreements reenter the picture with "known donors." Some people who donate eggs or sperm want to retain a right to contact or visit their genetic child.[74] The duties and rights of known donors, and their ability to contract around them, vary by state.[75] Known-donor agreements are similar to open-adoption agreements. Adoptive parents may promise to give birth parents ongoing information, communication, or visitation.[76]

Traditionally, open-adoption contracts were unenforceable. Adoptions were surrounded by secrecy to recreate the appearance of a heterosexual biological family. Adoption severed all legal relationships between a child and the birth parents, so adoptive parents could not be forced to fulfill preadoption promises to allow visitation.[77] In the early 2000s, the tide turned. Almost all birth mothers now select and meet the adoptive parents, and around two-thirds of private adoptions include some postadoption contact.[78] Twenty-nine states now expressly authorize open-adoption contracts.[79] Yet, these "contracts" are enforceable only in a limited sense. The agreements are incorporated into the adoption decree, so if the parties later disagree, the court has the authority to decide if the child will benefit from ongoing visitation.[80]

D *Agreements to Tailored Parenthood*

In rare scenarios, adults may enter into an agreement to alter aspects of parenthood. One example might be an agreement to coparent by more than two adults. Such an agreement might be explicit, as in the case of David, Raymond, and Samantha. In other cases, families form complex de facto family units based on implicit agreements. Only a handful of states authorize three parents by statute, but functional parent tests open the door to these arrangements.[81]

Legal scholarship contains anecdotes about written parenthood contracts. Professor Martha Ertman describes her contract with Victor, a longtime friend, sperm donor, and cross-country coparent.[82] They signed a preconception agreement akin to a shared custody agreement. Her model contract specifies living

74 Lauren Gill, Note, *Who's Your Daddy: Defining Paternity Rights in the Context of Free, Private Sperm Donation*, 54 WM. & MARY L. REV. 1715, 1742–43 (2012).

75 NAOMI R. CAHN, THE NEW KINSHIP: CONSTRUCTING DONOR-CONCEIVED FAMILIES 95–96 (2013).

76 *See* 3 ADOPTION LAW AND PRACTICE § 13-B.01 (2021).

77 *See id.*; Lisa A. Tucker, *From Contract Rights to Contact Rights: Rethinking the Paradigm for Post-Adoption Contact Agreements*, 100 B.U. L. REV. 2317, 2349–50 (2020).

78 *Id.* at 2324.

79 *See* CHILD WELFARE INFO. GATEWAY, POSTADOPTION CONTACT AGREEMENTS BETWEEN BIRTH AND ADOPTIVE FAMILIES 2 (2019), https://perma.cc/AB65-Q46B.

80 Tucker, *supra* note 77, at 2352–53.

81 *See* Naomi Cahn & June Carbone, *Custody and Visitation in Families with Three (or More) Parents*, 56 FAM. CT. REV. 399, 402–03 (2018).

82 MARTHA M. ERTMAN, LOVE'S PROMISES: HOW FORMAL AND INFORMAL CONTRACTS SHAPE ALL KINDS OF FAMILIES 8, 18, 199–207 (2016).

arrangements, assigns decisional authority, allocates responsibility for day-to-day and significant expenses, and commits to therapy and mediation for disagreements. I am unaware of any cases deciding whether such a contract is enforceable, but I doubt it. Custody agreements among divorced parents are "enforceable" only in the limited sense that a court considers the agreement as evidence of the best arrangement for the child. Custody agreements are always subject to revision for a substantial change in circumstances.[83]

II NORMATIVE POWERS AND MORAL PARENTHOOD

The legal trend toward a private arrangement of parenthood appears to support intentional or voluntarist theories of parentage that claim adults obtain parental rights or duties by intending, promising, contracting, or agreeing to be parents. Unfortunately, none of these standard moral devices for controlling rights and duties can extend to controlling parentage.

A *Parenthood by Intention (Simple Voluntarism)*

Some family law scholars support "intentional parenthood," according to which the fact that determines parentage is the intention to be a parent.[84] Aside from rhetorical lapses, no one believes subjective intentions alone are sufficient to create parental duties or rights.[85] Adults must *do* something, like gestate a child or plan donor conception, with the intent to become a parent.[86] Regardless, this focus on intent is a false start. The reasons may seem obvious on reflection, but making them explicit avoids mistakes later.

1 Disambiguating Intentional Parenthood

"Intent" is dangerously ambiguous, as lawyers know. First-year law students are trained to specify the mental state referred to by "intent" and the object of that mental state. Criminal law uses "intent" to refer to an actor's "purpose," which is the "conscious object to engage in conduct of [a certain] nature or to cause such

[83] Sarah Abramowicz, *Contractualizing Custody*, 83 FORDHAM L. REV.67, 80–85 (2014).

[84] Marjorie Maguire Shultz, *Reproductive Technology and Intent-Based Parenthood: An Opportunity for Gender Neutrality*, 1990 WIS. L. REV. 297; Jacobs, *supra* note 4.

[85] *See* Ayelet Blecher-Prigat, *Conceiving Parents*, 41 HARV. WOMEN'S L.J. 119, 136–38, 150–51 (2018) (explaining this ambiguity). For example, Storrow defends an account that he calls "parenthood by pure intention" but concludes "intent should be an element of parental functioning so as to entitle unmarried persons to pursue parenthood by pure intention." Richard F. Storrow, *Parenthood by Pure Intention: Assisted Reproduction and the Functional Approach to Parentage*, 53 HASTINGS L.J. 597, 665 (2001). Jacobs offers an intent theory but gives gestational parents priority to become parents through intent. Jacobs, *supra* note 4.

[86] Blecher-Prigat, *supra* note 85, at 137.

a result."[87] In contrast, a tort is intentional if done with purpose or knowledge.[88] Despite this disagreement, criminal law and tort law assume that intentions are conscious mental states with which we perform discrete acts. Similarly, some family law scholars assume that intentional parenthood must require some moment of purposeful or deliberate choice.[89]

Philosophers study another type of intention: intentions for the future.[90] Michael Bratman calls them "plans." A plan is a present commitment to a course of action that guides many acts over time. For example, a student's intention to be a corporate lawyer guides their course selection and networking. Intentions in this sense must manifest in some acts; otherwise, they remain mere wishes. Plans are distinct from wishes or desires in another way. Plans are constrained by norms of practical rationality.[91] A student can desire to be a lawyer and not be a lawyer, but they intend to be a lawyer only if their actions manifest some consistent commitment. Planning intentions may also be central to joint activities. In a study group, I intend to study and to study with you, and you do the same. When our intentions interlock in this way, each of our intentions commits us to adjust our behavior to facilitate the other's intentions. We now have a shared plan to study together rather than just studying alongside one another.[92]

The ambiguity of "intent" complicates intentional parenthood. Betty, David, and Raymond each desired to conceive and raise a genetic child. Each formed a plan to that effect, which their oral agreement meshed into a shared procreative parenting plan. To facilitate it, they performed many actions with more specific intentions. Acting with the purpose of creating a child, David and Raymond each delivered sperm to Betty. She performed artificial insemination with the same purpose. To facilitate the pregnancy, they together attended obstetrics appointments, arranged a home birth, and paid for medical care. The adults also took steps to effectuate their plan to raise the child. Raymond arranged parental leave. David and Raymond set up a nursery. The threesome posted a pregnancy announcement to embed the child in their social networks. After the birth, Betty and David signed an acknowledgment of parentage with the purpose of establishing their joint legal parenthood. The threesome then began sharing parenting time with the purpose of parenting together.

87 Model Penal Code § 1.13(12), 2.02(a) (Am. Law Inst. 1962).

88 Restatement (Second) of Torts § 8A (Am. Law Inst. 1965).

89 Jacobs, *supra* note 4, at 480–81.

90 Kieran Setiya, *Intention*, *in* The Stanford Encyclopedia of Philosophy (Edward N. Zalta ed., 2018), https://plato.stanford.edu/archives/fall2018/entries/intention/ (last visited Mar. 11, 2024). Criminal and tort law rarely care about future-directed intentions, dismissing them as mere motives behind *mens rea*. Michael T. Rosenberg, *The Continued Relevance of the Irrelevance-of-Motive Maxim*, 57 Duke L. J. 1143 (2007).

91 Michael Bratman, Intention, Plans, and Practical Reason (1987).

92 Michael Bratman, Shared and Institutional Agency: Toward a Planning Theory of Human Practical Organization (2022).

This case illustrates at least five dimensions of ambiguity that an intentional theory must resolve. Which intentional state matters: desires, knowledge, purposes, plans, or agreements? Which intentional content matters: to create a child, raise a child, be a social parent, or be a legal parent? Can the intention be held only by the nonbiological parent, or must it be shared with the gestational or genetic parents, or both? Is the intention formed before conception, at conception, during pregnancy, at birth, or during caregiving? Last, is a subjective intention sufficient, or must it be embodied in particular acts, like signing a contract, procuring ART, or caring for the child?

Fortunately, previous chapters already pruned the list of possibilities. A person is not a parent because they purposefully or knowingly created a child (Chapter 2). Nor is it enough that someone purposely cares for a child (Chapter 3). We can also easily rule out desire as the relevant intentional state. Scholars sometimes argue that the costs of ART reveal the strength of an adult's desire to be a parent,[93] but the desire to conceive or raise a child alone cannot make one a parent. Nor is it necessary. Many adults have children to please their partners. Perhaps this is a bad reason to have a child, but it does not disqualify someone from parenthood. The remaining candidates are the knowledge, purpose, or plan to become a social or legal parent.[94]

Subsection 2 argues that an individual's purpose or plan to be a social or legal parent is insufficient to create parental rights or duties. Purpose is the more demanding intentional state, so if it is insufficient, knowledge is also. Sections B and C argue that two standard ways to create joint future intentions, by promising or agreeing, are also insufficient. Section D considers the possibility that adults can intentionally acquire parentage through a *sui generis* social convention.

2 The Purpose or Plan to Be a Parent Is Not Sufficient for Parentage

Intentional parenthood is most intuitive in ART cases. Birth parents who use fertility services engage in the same objective conduct as surrogates or gamete donors.[95] A married couple may conceive a child when the husband donates sperm at a clinic,

93 *See, e.g.*, Linda S. Anderson, *Adding Players to the Game: Parentage Determinations When Assisted Reproductive Technology Is Used to Create Families*, 62 Ark. L. Rev. 29, 56 (2009); Margalit, *supra* note 4, at 103.

94 Prebirth intentions should not be conflated with parental caregiving, which happens in Nejaime's position that equality requires "crediting parenthood's social dimensions," under which he includes intent, function, and formal family status. NeJaime, *supra* note 30, at 2333–2335, 2338. The biological-social dichotomy is too blunt. Heather Kolinsky identifies still another ambiguity. Cases sometimes refer to presumed marital parents (gestational and spouses) as the presumptively "intended parents." Kolinsky Heather, *The Intended Parent: The Power and Problems Inherent in Designating and Determining Intent in the Context of Parental Rights*, 119 Penn St. L. Rev. 801, 808–12 (2014). The idea seems to be that presumptions reflect common expectations about who expects to raise the child. I avoid this language because it conflates subjective expectations, statistical generalities about expectations, and normative social expectations.

95 Anderson, *supra* note 93, at 53, 56.

the clinic uses his sperm and a donor egg to create an embryo, and the wife carries the fetus to term. It is tempting to think that what distinguishes the husband from a sperm donor and the wife from a surrogate is that the spouses plan to raise the child. Furthermore, Chapters 2 and 4 argued that genetic and gestational parents complete their conditional rights by committing to duties, which sounds like adopting a prospective intention to raise the child. Unfortunately, neither the purpose nor the plan to be a parent can ground parental rights or duties.

In some situations, our intentions are sufficient to alter personal rights and duties. Under subjective theories of consent, my intention to play tackle football transforms other players' duty not to touch me into a privilege to tackle me. This power reflects my innate moral authority over who may touch my body. Parentage cannot have a similar normative basis. No matter how much someone loves a child, they cannot give themselves parental rights or duties simply by adopting a plan to raise the child. Even if the child has no parents, an adult cannot claim parenthood the way one claims unowned property. No one has a personal moral power to create parental rights or duties.

This problem for pure intentional parentage is not unique to parentage. As explained in Chapter 1, no one has a personal moral power to give themselves rights over others unilaterally, because this power to limit others' liberty is inconsistent with moral equality. For similar reasons, no one can have a personal power to give themselves *duties to others* unilaterally. This power may sound innocuous. If I unilaterally give myself new duties to you, it seems that I expanded your liberty. Are you not better off with this resource and claim on me?

Suppose I unilaterally gave myself a duty to deliver you a daily newspaper. You might find the paper's ideology offensive. You might be environmentally conscious. Even if having the paper did increase your welfare and facilitate your plans, you might not want the responsibility that comes with this claim on me. Now, I need your permission before I can take a vacation, and you may not want such authority over my life. This example may sound trivial, but imagine if I declared myself bound to your service. My unilateral power to create duties to you becomes authority over your life. A moral tagalong is no mere annoyance; it is a moral imposition.

Morality has tools that allow agents to deliberately create new personal duties, but those tools require participation by the potential rights-holder. Anything less fails to respect them. It would be inconsistent with the child's status as an equal citizen if adults could acquire parental duties simply by adopting a prospective intention to parent the child.

B *Parenthood by Promise-Making*

Of course, most parentage voluntarists do not believe intentions alone generate parental rights or duties. Instead, they draw analogies with other moral powers. Promising is our most familiar tool for deliberately creating new duties. Philosophers have developed sophisticated theories of promissory morality, some of which seem germane to parenthood.[96] Some parents seem to become parents by making a promise, especially stepparents or adoptive parents. One might hope to interpret the commitment that grounds all parental duties as a kind of promise to raise a child.

I hope to prescind from foundational moral debates by limiting myself to common, even if not universally accepted, features of promissory morality. According to most accounts, promisors and promisees create bilateral duties through some joint exercise of authority over their moral lives. The promisor accepts a duty to the promisee to fulfill the promise given, and the promisee assents to this claim against the promisor (avoiding unwanted moral authority).[97] Little of this standard promissory apparatus applies to parentage.

The first obvious question is, Who is the promisee? I see two options: the child or another adult. This Section considers whether an adult can obtain parental rights or duties by promising the child to serve as their parent. Section C turns to promises among adults.

1 Promises Cannot Ground Parenthood for Infants or Young Children

Promissory duties cannot ground the initial assignment of parenthood for infants. Few birth parents do anything remotely like promising to raise the child. In fact, I believe it is conceptually impossible to make a promise to a fetus, infant, or toddler. Promising is a cooperative speech act. One cannot make a promise to a prelinguistic child any more than one can make a promise to a pet. Even under reliance theories that do not require robust assent from the promisee, the infant or toddler cannot rely on a promise they cannot understand.[98]

Promises are integral to our intimate relationships with young children. By using promises to cede some of their authority back to the child, parents can allow children to make their own decisions and model respect for the child learning to participate in moral life.[99] Promises cannot, however, be the foundation of this parental relationship. Even if an adult promises to parent a young child and the child accepts, the child's assent cannot justify the adult's parental authority. Parental authority is permissible only because children lack sufficient agency for their decisions to command respect (1.II.B.2.a). Many parents will promise to love their

[96] For example, Shiffrin argues the power to create duties by promising is necessary for humans to shape our moral landscape to form relationships. Seana Valentine Shiffrin, *Promising, Intimate Relationships, and Conventionalism*, 117 PHIL. REV. 481 (2008).

[97] *But see* Hallie Liberto, *Promises and the Backward Reach of Uptake*, 55 AM. PHIL. Q. 15 (2018); Shiffrin, *supra* note 96. Shiffrin argues acceptance is unnecessary because a promisee's interest in "avoid[ing] the sometimes charged relation of moral debtor to the promisor" is protected so long as they "have a right (and a low-cost opportunity) to reject the promise or waive performance." *Id.* However, neither solves the problem of unwanted moral authority.

[98] T.H. v. J.R., 84 N.Y.S.3d 676, 685 (N.Y. Fam. Ct. 2018) (noncustodial parent cannot claim reliance by two-year-old).

[99] Nick Leonard, *Promises and All of the People Who Rely on Them*, 54 J. SOC. PHIL. 114 (2023).

children forever, but such promises are acts of reassurance, not the foundation of the moral relationship.

It is tempting to suppose that a parent must at least implicitly promise to raise their child. Given children's deep need for parents, it seems immoral for an adult to take custody of a child without tacitly promising to be a parent indefinitely.[100] A similar temptation to invoke tacit acceptance was discussed in 4.II.A.2. It is tempting to say that anyone who brings a child into their home tacitly accepts parental duties, but tacit consent is a distraction. To protect children's right to a parent, the state must insist that no one take indefinite custody of a child without parental duties, regardless of the adult's intentions. An appeal to tacit promises will replicate this dialectic. Instead of postulating a novel type of tacit promise that requires neither a speech act by the promisor nor assent or reliance by the promisee, we should recognize that morality imposes parental duties on custodial caregivers. Shorn of personification, "imposes" means that no adult may take custody of a child without incurring permanent parental duties. Again, this is a conditional liberty. To justify this condition, we need not appeal to promises or consent. The condition is necessary to protect the child's fundamental right to a parent.

2 Promises Cannot Ground Adoptive Parenthood for Youth

Even if they cannot ground a general theory, promises still seem like an intuitive basis for adopting older children. A youth close to full moral agency can genuinely assent to an adult's promise to be their parent. Moreover, without this promise from the adult, the youth would likely regard the adult as imposing on their life. The youth would maintain emotional distance rather than invest in the relationship. The child's assent and reliance look like traditional aspects of promissory morality. Adoption statutes even have a legal element akin to promissory assent insofar as teenagers must consent to adoption.[101]

Similarities in the initiation of the relationship should not lead us to overlook other critical differences between promissory moral relationships and parenthood. First, promisees have the power to release promisors, but a child has no power to release their adoptive parent. The promisee has a claim to performance but no duty to accept it. A power to waive performance, continuous with the power to assent, is essential to preserve the promisee's authority over their lives.[102] If a youth can accept

[100] Shiffrin claims "a commitment of real magnitude underlies the child–parent relationship, namely that the parent will care for the child indefinitely," which she treats as evidence that parents must be able to make a promise to a newborn without acceptance or expectation-induced reliance. Shiffrin, *supra* note 96, at 510 n.43. I draw the opposite inference: we should not interpret a parent's dedication to a newborn through the promissory tools that competent agents use to arrange mutual relationships.

[101] *E.g.*, TENN. CODE ANN. § 36-1-117(i)(1) (West) (consent required by child over fourteen).

[102] Shiffrin, *supra* note 96. Leonard insists promisees acquire a power to determine how promisors fulfill their promise, especially when promises have competing components. Leonard, *supra* note 99. I am unsure if promisees generally acquire this power, but it does not track parenthood.

an adult's promise, they should also have the power to release the adoptive parent from their promissory parental duties.

Of course, parental release is inconsistent with social and legal norms. A child's rejection does not release an adoptive parent from their responsibility. Nor can a child escape so easily from a parent's authority. That requires legal emancipation. One might try to save the promissory approach by interpreting emancipation as a release, but that would misconstrue emancipation. Once a child has the capacity and is willing to direct their own life, forcing them to remain subject to a parent's authority denies their status as an equal citizen.[103] Emancipation is necessary because parental authority becomes inconsistent with a mature minor's full agency. It is not continuous with a youth's power to assent to parenthood.

Second, promissory duties are content-independent, but parental duties are not. While we often use promises to modify or tailor existing duties, a duty is distinctly promissory when the fact that the agent promised is a primary reason to fulfill it. We can promise to do something we had no other reason to do. For example, I might promise to pick up a stranger's mail. Because we have a reason to fulfill our promises independent of their content, we can make promises to do almost anything. The content of the promise fixes the content of the duty. If I promise to pick up the mail on Mondays for four weeks, the owner cannot blame me when a package gets stolen on Tuesday or in the fifth week.

Parents' personal duties bear no similar separation. Even if adoption begins with a promise, the adoptive parent's reason to care for the child is not because they promised. In the early days of a relationship, the force of their duty might seem promissory in this manner. The morning after an adoption, if you ask the adult why they are making waffles, they might answer, "Because I promised to be this kid's parent." A year later, if this remains a significant part of their reason to fulfill their parental duties, something went wrong. A parent should act from concern for the child. Perhaps the adult only had permission to raise the child because they promised, but that does not mean their parental relationship is distinctively promissory.

Third, this difference affects the *content* of parental duties. Adults cannot use promises to tailor their parental duties, such as promising to be part-time or short-term parents. This is clear in current law. Nevertheless, we must consider whether morality would allow adults to create limited parental duties by making narrower promises to a youth.

Imagine Jerk and Aloof live on a deserted island when a ten-year-old washes ashore. Jerk believes the child is old enough to fend for themselves, so he declares he will help only as beneficence requires. Aloof also refuses to parent the child, but she does promise to share her shelter and food. If that is all Aloof ever does – coldly hand the child food and not lock them out – she violates her moral duties to the child

[103] Floyd v. Abercrombie, 816 So. 2d 1051, 1056 (Ala. Civ. App. 2001).

created by her voluntary undertaking. Anyone who creates a relationship of dependency acquires caregiving duties, as I argued in 4.II.A.3. Aloof could use narrow promises to alter her caregiving duties only if the child were an equal moral agent able to assent to this limitation on the child's needed relationships.

Nevertheless, the hypothetical suggests one way for promises to be relevant to parenthood. Sometimes, we use promises to assume roles that carry moral duties, the weight and content of which are independent of our promises. I might promise the school crossing guard to take her place for ten minutes while she uses the restroom. If I leave after five minutes, I break my promise to the guard, but only an obtuse moral analysis would focus on my promise or the guard. A child might have been gravely hurt! The force of my duty to the children is independent of the weight of my promissory duty to the guard. So is its content. If the guard did not return after twenty minutes, I could leave without breaking my promise, but I may still violate my duty to the children. Neither the guard nor I have the authority to modify crossing guard duties. Indeed, the same duties could arise with no promises. If I found a vest on the ground and donned it to help a few children cross, I might incur a similar duty not to abandon the role. Sometimes, we get stuck holding the door.

Even if we assume a role through a promise, this does not entail that role morality is reducible to or grounded in promissory morality. Some adults may become stepparents or adoptive parents by making a promise to youth, but their resulting parental duties are not promissory in nature.

C *Parenthood by Contract*

Perhaps adults become parents by exchanging promises *with one another*. Not all parenthood can be contractual. That would rule out single parents. It would also create problems for unmarried birth parents who never reach any agreement. Instead, this section explores the possibility that *some* adults contract into parental status with their partners.

American law recognizes many parentage agreements, and many family law scholars advocate expanding adults' power to contract about parenthood.[104] The analogy between parentage agreements and contract law is appealing because they facilitate autonomy in similar ways. The law allows adults to create parental rights and duties without state oversight by manifesting their assent to share parenthood. Such private ordering allows adults to build families of the forms that they value. Holding the adults to their ex ante parenting choice provides assurance so they can make these long-term coparenting plans with less fear of defection, hopefully creating more stable relationships that benefit children.

[104] Yehezkel Margalit, Orrie Levy & John Loike, *The New Frontier of Advanced Reproductive Technology: Reevaluating Modern Legal Parenthood*, 37 Harv. J.L. & Gender 107, 136–39 (2014) (proposing that law should require contracts for multiparent technologies); Abramowicz, *supra* note 83.

These similarities are crucial but limited. As is true across family law, the reasons for and against private ordering must be carefully assessed for each unique context.[105] The law of contracts and parentage agreements have few doctrinal similarities because most moral justifications for contracts do not apply to parenthood. The different justifications affect all the salient moments of legal doctrine, including formation, interpretation, modification, breach, and remedies.

1 Parentage Agreements Are Not Moral Contracts

The first difference lies in the acts that count as exercising the moral or legal power to create contracts and parentage agreements. A promissory exchange theory has long been the leading moral theory of contract law, at least since Charles Fried's *Contract as Promise*.[106] A contract arises when one person promises to do something in exchange for another person doing or promising something.[107] In contrast, most parentage agreements involve no apparent exchange of promises. In most cases, the operative provision is a simple declaration such as "signing this Acknowledgment of Parentage … will establish parentage of our child."[108] Under the preconception agreement statutes, a person becomes a parent by "consenting" to the birth parent's use of assisted reproduction. In implied parentage agreement cases, like de facto parenthood, courts look for evidence of a shared plan to coparent rather than an exchange of promises.[109]

Two exceptions – surrogacy and open adoption – involve explicit promissory exchanges.[110] A surrogate promises to carry the child and waive parental rights; in exchange, a commissioning parent promises to pay compensation.[111] A birth parent promises to waive parental rights; in exchange, an adoptive parent promises ongoing contact.[112] Notably, commissioning and adoptive parents never promise to parent. Adoptive parents must still complete the legal process. The surrogacy contract will have a declaration for the commissioning parents, like an acknowledgment of parentage. Nevertheless, agreements for surrogacy and open adoption often style themselves as "contracts," so it is worth considering whether to take the moniker at face value.

105 Brian H. Bix, Families by Agreement: Navigating Choice, Tradition, and Law 9–27 (2023).

106 Charles Fried, Contract as Promise: A Theory of Contractual Obligation 2 (2015).

107 Richard Craswell, *Contract Law, Default Rules, and the Philosophy of Promising*, 88 Mich. L. Rev. 489, 497 (1989). A competing strand of moral theory attempts to ground contract in reliance induced by the promise. *Id.* at 499–503.

108 *See* forms cited *supra* notes 47, 48, 49.

109 For example, New York's highest court ruled that a nonbiological parent has standing as a "parent" to seek custody if the parties "entered into a pre-conception agreement to conceive and raise a child as co-parents," but the opinion focuses on the parties' conduct during and after the pregnancy without trying to discern ex ante promises. *In re* Brooke S.B. v. Elizabeth A.C.C., 61 N.E.3d 488, 491–92, 500 (N.Y. 2016).

110 E.g., *In re* Baby, 447 S.W.3d 807, 813 (Tenn. 2014).

111 E.g., Johnson v. Calvert, 851 P.2d 776, 782 (Cal. 1993); Rebouché, *supra* note 71, at 1596.

112 Tucker, *supra* note 77, at 2360–61 (describing legal norms and arguing promises should generate a familial right to visitation rather than contractual rights).

Perhaps other parentage agreements could be reinterpreted as implied-in-fact contracts. All parents have informal contracts in a broad sense.[113] Few make detailed promises about how they will raise the child, but many may promise to coparent together. That promise is abstract, but no more so than other valid contracts. A person might contract for nanny services, relying on social norms that define this role. The abstract promise to coparent might be interpreted as a promise to fulfill customary parental duties, which the parties tweak as they raise the child. Construing abstract terms in light of customary norms and past performance is the bread and butter of contract interpretation. Of course, most parentage agreements do not even include an express promise to coparent. Nevertheless, the parties might be acting on implied-in-fact promises. Perhaps they, and any reasonable person, would interpret a declaration of parentage to mean that (1) the partner promises the birth mother to parent the child, and in exchange, (2) the birth mother promises to allow the partner to be a parent. Or perhaps a reasonable person would infer this from any plan to cohabit and raise a child.[114]

This reinterpretation of parentage agreements as implied-in-fact contracts moves us a long way from a traditional theory of contracts as an exchange of promises or consensual duties, and I have doubts about this move.[115] Nevertheless, the contractual model of parentage agreements is flawed for deeper reasons that apply even to an explicit contract to coparent.

2 Parenthood Is Not a Promissory Exchange

Promissory exchanges are incapable of creating *parental* rights and duties. By exchanging promises, the parties alter their bilateral relations with one another. A promisor incurs a duty *to the promisee* because they exercise authority over their

113 Some welfarist contract theorists interpret parenthood as an instance of relational theory of contract. Elizabeth S. Scott & Robert E. Scott, *Parents as Fiduciaries*, 81 Va. L. Rev. 2401 (1995). Descriptive relational contract theory offers an insightful model of the evolution of norms in familial relationships, and normative relational contract theory offers plausible insights about the efficient allocation of authority between child, parent, and state. However, I have found no plausible normative relational account of the acquisition of parenthood.

114 *See* Baker, *supra* note 53, at 31–35.

115 Reinterpreting parentage agreements as implied-in-fact contracts distorts both doctrines. An implied-*in-fact* contract exists only if the parties' conduct (as interpreted by a reasonable person) would clearly demonstrate mutual assent to a promissory exchange, despite their lack of oral or written promises. *See Express Contracts Including Contracts Inferred or Implied in Fact*, 1 Williston on Contracts § 1:5 (4th ed. 2021). Implied-in-fact contracts risk turning ordinary cooperative activities into contracts. People often cooperate without clear expectations about each other's roles, much less acting on an implicitly shared understanding that they have consented to an exchange of legal duties. A parent may enlist a cohabitant to help raise the child, and the cohabitant may agree to help, yet neither party may have any expectation of permanent parental rights or duties. States have good reason for a de facto parent doctrine, but its function is to protect the child's right to a parent, not to enforce implicit exchanges between the adults. Insisting that any voluntary obligation must be contractual unduly flattens the normative landscape.

moral duties when making this promise. A promisee holds the correlative claim *against the promisor* because they assented to the promise. In contrast, the primary purpose of a parentage agreement is to create rights and duties relating to a child. Two people cannot create moral duties *to a third person* by making promises to one another, much less giving themselves rights over others.[116]

Another way to see this problem is to ask, Who would a prospective parent *wrong* if they were to break their promise to be a parent? Consider a broken *post*conception agreement. After conceiving a child with donor sperm, Ann meets Betty, and they fall in love. Several months into the pregnancy, Betty promises to coparent the child, and Ann promises to share parenthood. A week after the birth, Betty panics and moves out. She wrongs Ann by breaking her promise, but Betty has not violated a promissory duty to the child. The newborn did not accept Betty's promise. The child was not induced by the promise to develop relational attachments. The child's life might improve if Betty helps raise them, but that is true of many adults who made no promises, like Ann's parents. Suppose, instead, that Ann realized she did not want to share the child, so she kicked Betty out. Ann broke her promise to Betty but did not violate a duty to the child. Ann could have chosen not to invite Betty to coparent in the first place. The child has no right to demand Ann accept any willing coparent who might improve their life. Even if parentage agreements were contracts, they would not generate rights or duties to the child, who is not a party to the contract.

To salvage the contract analogy, one might argue that the child is a third-party beneficiary of the parentage agreement. When two people enter into a contract for the benefit of a third, that third party can sue to enforce the contract.[117] If Cleo hires Dru to build a house for Eli, then Eli can sue to force them to build the house. Ann and Betty exchanged coparenting promises for the child's benefit, so maybe the child could sue Betty for leaving or Ann for kicking Betty out.

Although intriguing, this analogy cannot explain how adult agreements create parental rights. A third-party-beneficiary contract cannot give the parties rights over the third party. Each person has authority over their own life, which the law leverages to allow parties to give one another claims. Dru can accept a duty to Cleo to build a house for Eli. Cleo can accept a duty to Dru to pay him for building the house for Eli. Neither Cleo nor Dru has a power to create a duty for Eli to accept the house.[118] That is precisely the structure of relations created by a parentage agreement.

116 Merle H. Weiner, A *Parent–Partner Status for American Family Law* 169–79 (2015).

117 *Donee, Creditor, Intended, and Incidental Beneficiaries, Generally*, 13 Williston on Contracts § 37:7 (4th ed. 2021); Restatement (Second) of Contracts § 304 (Am. Law Inst. 1981).

118 A promisor might have independent authority over the third party. If Cleo were Eli's employer, then she might have authority to direct him to accept Dru's assistance. Similarly, Kathy Baker insists that once the initial parental authority "emanates" from gestational labor, then parentage agreements can be treated as consensual transfers of parental entitlements. Baker, *supra* note 53, at 45–47. This model fits the structure of VAPs and preconception agreements, but one cannot assume the initial assignment of parenthood includes a power to transfer or share parenthood via consent. The right to transfer entitlement via ordinary contracts is justified by appeal to personal autonomy. We need a different

Worse, the analogy cannot even capture parental duties. A third-party-beneficiary contract does not itself create any duty to the third party. Admittedly, the Restatement (Second) of Contracts says the contract "creates a duty in the promisor to any intended beneficiary." However, the reporter's commentary infers that the contract creates this duty because the third party can sue to enforce it.[119] This is a non sequitur, as Stephen Smith has argued. Individuals can often sue to enforce duties not owed to them. The better legal interpretation is that a promisor incurs a duty to the third party when they rely on the promise.[120] A beneficiary can enforce the contract only if they rely in a specific and reasonable way on its terms. Moreover, the promisor and promisee can rescind or modify the contract until the third party relies on it.[121]

These doctrinal principles reflect the underlying interpersonal morality. Suppose Cleo and Eli have a falling-out before Eli hears anything about the contract. Cleo no longer has a reason to build a house for Eli, so she can instruct Dru not to build it. Cleo's release eliminates Dru's only reason to build the house, which is to fulfill his promise to Cleo. Eli has no right to the house. He just missed out on this piece of good luck. However, if Eli had heard about the contract and purchased land for the house, Cleo and Dru would have had a reason to build the house (or refund any losses on the land) because they caused Eli to rely to his detriment.[122]

For the above reasons, the exchange of parenting promises among adults cannot directly generate obligations to the child, even on a third-party-beneficiary model. Betty has no duty to parent the child, and Ann has no duty to allow Betty to parent the child. They will incur a duty to the child only after they act on the agreement in ways that cause the child to need them both for care and guidance. Once we recognize the need for reliance, the normative baseline shifts in ways that drift further from a contract model. The child never relies on *the specific terms* of the adult's agreement. Thus, the terms of the adult promises will never fix the relevant baseline to decide what duties the adults owe the child. How, then, can the agreement cause the child to rely in ways that might create duties? As I argued in 4.II.A, each child has a right to parental care and guidance from their custodial caregiver, so whoever rightfully fulfills that role incurs parental duties. In other words, adult contracts generate parental duties only by incorporating political parenthood.

explanation for why the bundle of parental rights includes a private power to share or transfer parenthood. Part III turns to that task.

119 Restatement (Second) of Contracts § 304 (Am. Law Inst. 1981).

120 Stephen A. Smith, *Contracts for the Benefit of Third Parties: In Defence of the Third-Party Rule*, 17 Oxford J. Legal Stud. 643, 648, 655 (1997).

121 Restatement (Second) of Contracts § 311 (Am. Law Inst. 1981).

122 Unfortunately for moral clarity, third-party-beneficiary law conflates duties grounded in contract and tort by awarding damages measured by the third-party's expectations rather than counterfactual harm.

3 Parenthood Is Not Fixed by the Adult's Intentions

The final divide between contracts and parentage agreements concerns the parties' control over the content of their duties. Contractual duties do not merely arise *because* parties consent to an exchange of duties – their consent *determines the content* of the duties.[123] Contract law enforces the parties' ex ante intentions as reflected in their words or conduct. The standard justification for this rule is that it facilitates autonomy. The function of contract law is not to promote specific socially valued activities but to respect the parties' authority to pursue their chosen ends together.[124]

If parentage agreements rested on a contractual foundation, prospective parents could tailor their duties. An adult might enter into part-time agreements to parent only during the evenings and weekends, a limited-duration parenting agreement for only two years, or a conditional parenting agreement for only so long as the adult relationship persists. Adults might agree to weaker duties, such as to care for the child when convenient, or stronger ones, such as to ensure the child wants for nothing its entire life. As discussed in II.B.2, neither prospective nor current parents have legal authority to tailor parenthood. Parentage agreements only allow adults to become parents, full stop. Parents are free to arrange their lives as they wish, but even written custody agreements are not enforceable contracts.[125]

Even if adults can tailor parenthood at the margin, the relationship between parenthood and its tailored terms must be fundamentally different from the relationship between contract defaults and bespoke terms. Contract law starts with an assumption that a contract's terms represent the full extent of parties' relational obligations.[126] Imposing default rules requires special justification. Randy Barnett, for example, argues that default rules must be salient norms known to most parties, so the law can infer that parties intend to be bound by these norms unless they opt out.[127]

Family law cannot assume adults' intentions are the primary determinate of their duties to a child. A parentage agreement is not just an exercise of autonomy among adults. It establishes authority over a child's life. The state cannot be neutral about the content of that arrangement. It must ensure custodial caregivers have obligations and rights sufficient to secure the child's primary goods, including their right to a parent. Parentage agreements are less like an ordinary contract than a contract to fulfill a constitutional office. An individual may promise to fill

123 Gregory Klass, *Promise, Agreement, Contract*, *in* RESEARCH HANDBOOK ON PRIVATE LAW THEORY 39, 40 (Hanoch Dagan & Benjamin C. Zipursky eds., 2020).

124 Jody S. Kraus, *The Correspondence of Contract and Promise*, 109 COLUM. L. REV. 1603, 1617 (2009).

125 *See* Bassett v. Saunders, 835 So. 2d 1198, 1201 (Fla. Dist. Ct. App. 2002).

126 Charles Fried, *The Ambitions of Contract as Promise*, *in* PHILOSOPHICAL FOUNDATIONS OF CONTRACT LAW 17, 37 (Gregory Klass, George Letsas & Prince Saprai eds., 2014).

127 Randy E. Barnett, *The Sound of Silence: Default Rules and Contractual Consent*, 78 VA. L. REV. 821 (1992).

a public office in exchange for a salary. They have official duties only because of their promise, and they wield the office's powers only because they promise to fulfill its duties. However, the power to enter into this "contract" does not rest on their authority to arrange their life. They may enter into this contract only if they meet qualifications fixed by the constitution, and it denies them any power to modify the office's duties or powers. Similarly, even if adults can become parents through agreements, family law determines who can enter into these agreements to be parents and restricts their authority to tailor the default rights of parenthood fixed by the community.[128]

D *Parenthood by a* Sui Generis *Conventional Moral Power*

If contractual ideas related to consent or promise cannot justify the authority to enter into parentage agreements, then perhaps another normative power better fits this private allocation of parental rights and duties. Joseph Millum argues that social conventions expand our moral power to obligate ourselves. An adult can take on the social role of parent the same way one takes on the social role of doctor or fiancé, by performing whatever act society dictates counts as accepting the role. Can parentage law be justified as the rules that society has declared count as exercising a moral power to give ourselves parental obligations?

1 Parenthood via Conventional Act Theory

Like many moral voluntarists, Millum has slightly different concerns than legal academics. As I explained in Chapter 4, one intuition behind stronger forms of voluntarism is that adults cannot complain about parenthood's burdens if they voluntarily accept its duties. However, voluntarism also has the counterintuitive implication that sexual procreators have no duties unless they volunteer. Some voluntarists, like Elizabeth Brake, welcome this conclusion. Others, like Millum, find this bullet too hard to bite. To retain both voluntarism and procreative duties, Millum seeks to expand voluntarism through a clever adaptation of speech act theory.

Millum believes individuals have a standing moral power to obligate themselves to fulfill social roles. Conventional norms specify which acts constitute taking on a social role. Fiancés say, "I do," and physicians complete a white-coat ceremony. Anyone who performs a conventional triggering act with knowledge of its meaning

[128] Margalit argues adults should be able to "contract into" state-defined statuses. MARGALIT, *supra* note 4, at 128. However, a contract metaphor loses most of its value when the state defines the bundle of parental duties and rights and so few foundational principles of contract law apply. In a similar vein, I find Margalit ambiguous about the relation between the status and contract. For instance, only two adults can contract into full parenthood, yet any number can contract for a desired bundle of parent-like obligations and concomitant rights. *Id.* at 163–68, 175.

incurs a moral duty to fulfill the social role.[129] The agent need not intend to adopt these duties. Someone who raises a placard at an auction is obligated to pay, even if they only want to raise the price. Someone who silently accepts an engagement ring is engaged, even if they only want to avoid hurting their partner's feelings. Social norms, not subjective intentions, fix the meaning of the triggering act and its resulting duties.

If communities do have this broad power to define *sui generis* normative conventions, then Millum could unify all the diverse means for acquiring parental duties under a voluntarist banner. Adults acquire parental duties to a child by performing whatever commissive acts their society conventionally regards as assuming parental roles. Conventionalism easily explains adoption and parentage agreements, as well as the presumptions. Marrying a pregnant woman or holding a child out as one's own may be socially understood as expressing acceptance of parental roles.

Millum needs a few more twists to interpret sexual procreation as a speech act. Some commissive acts rely surprisingly little on language. Speech acts often have semantic content distinct from the resulting duties. Fiancés who exchange detailed vows still incur marriage law's default duties. Other commissive acts require little or even no verbal speech. Most American fiancés mark the moment of marriage by saying, "I do," but they could stomp on wine glasses or jump over a broom. A person can get engaged by silently accepting a ring. Millum argues that voluntary sex is conventionally understood as accepting parental duties in this fashion. It does not matter what parties say, if anything, about parenthood. Social conventions demand procreators raise their children, so anyone who engages in heterosexual intercourse knowing about the convention incurs a moral duty to parent any resulting children. Millum's position fits with a common legal argument that anyone who engages in sex "impliedly consents" to parental duties.[130]

2 What Acts Might Count as Acceptance of Parenthood

I would interpret our familial conventions differently than Millum, but his conventionalist account has more revealing difficulties that generate insights into voluntarism. Identifying these limits helps reveal what makes an adequate commissive act and when conventional powers generate genuine moral duties.

First, heterosexual intercourse is a poor candidate for a commissive act. Most commissive acts involve arbitrary conduct accompanied by ceremonial trappings and express commitments. The triggering act is something people have little reason

[129] Millum believes it is sufficient that they should have known the conventional meaning. Joseph Millum, The Moral Foundations of Parenthood 88 (2018). I find a knowledge-based principle more plausible, and all the objections below apply to his negligence condition.

[130] Margalit, *supra* note 4, at 82–83 (sex is an implied agreement to parental duties because the "sexual relationship is indicative of the desire, will, and intention of the parties … to become the legal parents").

to do unless they intend to invoke the convention, such as smashing a champagne bottle or exchanging rings. Ritualistic ceremonies, like a wedding or white-coat ceremony, add solemnity to assure parties' earnestness, create witnesses to attest to the act, and invite group members to reinforce their shared norms. Speeches from participants and officiants surround the act to ensure shared intentions and informed consent. Sex, in contrast, typically occurs in private, and partners rarely make express commitments about parenting. The absence of formalities is especially problematic because of the strong incentives to engage in sex irrespective of parental intentions. Even with strong biological parenting norms, it is implausible to claim that heterosexual intercourse expresses acceptance of parental duties in the same way that slipping on a ring expresses acceptance of an engagement.

Second, even if our community did have such a convention, a moral duty would not arise simply because the sexual partners knew that others would interpret their conduct as acceptance of parental roles and attribute parental duties. What justifies the community imposing parental duties? The account is missing a moral premise.

Some conventional powers are justified via autonomy. A convention can increase agents' range of options by allowing them to bind themselves to predefined duties. Marriage, for example, facilitates family formation by allowing couples to opt into a default bundle of moral rights, duties, and remedies. A "sex-constitutes-parentage" norm cannot be justified in this way. Conventional powers directly facilitate autonomy only if the agents at least intend to bind themselves to something.[131] Fiancés do not need to know the details of civil marriage, but if they exchange vows with no intent to bind themselves, they perform only a rehearsal or a jest. By contrast, most couples have sex without intending to opt into any duties. They may also share a nonstandard understanding of their duties. Both might agree that only one of them will parent the child.

If, like Millum or implied consent legal theorists, one believes that a conventional act creates duties regardless of whether agents intend to bind themselves, the justification of the convention must shift.[132] American contract law made a similar move when transitioning to its objective theory. A promisor is bound by what a reasonable person would interpret them as saying, even if their subjective intent was idiosyncratic. Contract law still expands autonomy by increasing our range of options, but this systemic autonomy benefit comes at the cost of imposing duties on unwilling individuals. The natural justification for this imposition appeals to reliance causation. Speakers should not invoke promissory conventions in ways likely to lead reasonable listeners to believe they are promising when they have no such

[131] Kraus, *supra* note 124.

[132] Millum recognizes this problem but nevertheless denies his conventionalist theory needs reliance to generate duties. MILLUM, *supra* note 129, at 97. His argument, found mostly in a footnote, relies on two examples (auction placards and beer rounds) better explained through shared acceptance of local customs. *Id.* at 98 n.52.

intent. The law can fairly hold speakers liable rather than demand everyone else guard against idiosyncratic nonpromissory promises.[133]

The only people who might rely on the conventional expressive meaning of sexual conduct are the partners themselves. In a culture with biological parenting norms, sexual partners may reasonably interpret one another's choice to have sex as expressing their willingness to fulfill the social duty to raise any unintended children. Suppose Calvin is willing to have sex with Brenda only because he interprets her consent to sex in this manner. Brenda knew about the convention but had no such intention. By causing Calvin to rely on her, Brenda incurs a moral duty to Calvin to help him meet his social duty to raise the child.

However, a reliance-based conventional duty cannot ground parenthood. Brenda incurs a horizontal duty to Calvin because her commissive act caused his reliance. The child, who did not exist yet, did not rely on her speech acts. The child will need a caregiver, but procreators cause this need regardless of any conventions. Moreover, not all sexual procreators will incur horizontal duties to help parent. If Calvin knew that Brenda did not want to raise children, he could not reasonably believe her consent to sex evinced willingness to fulfill social child-rearing duties. When evaluating reliance, shared intent and known context will trump the conventions.

Most importantly, this type of reliance on the convention cannot fully justify either party's moral duty to raise the child. The hypothetical assumes that society attributes duties to Calvin based on genetics. Brenda has a moral duty to help Calvin meet society's expectations, but her duty does not justify society's choice to impose parental duties on Calvin in the first place. Genetic parental duties may be unjust. Individuals can incur a moral duty to help one another bear social obligations, but these personal duties cannot be used to bootstrap a justification for social duties.

The problem is easiest to see with unjust norms but persists even for beneficial conventions. Society must justify imposing duties on anyone who performs the conventional triggering act. For most commissive acts, this is simple because the conduct is arbitrary. Restricting our liberty to shake hands is trivial. It is difficult to justify triggering acts that are meaningful conduct, like sex. A community may use heterosexual intercourse as a trigger for parental duties only if it can justly insist that adults have sex only on the condition that they parent any resulting children. In other words, what Millum depicts as a normative power is better understood as a conditional liberty.

As explained in 4.II.A.2, the challenge for a conditional liberty is to justify the limit on agents' liberty to perform the act. Even if Calvin and Brenda had sex knowing about the biological parenting norm, that choice does not justify society's decision to make parental duties a condition on their liberty to have sex – any more than Frank's choice to walk on the sidewalk justified the social norm that pedestrians may bump one another. Their knowledge only shows they had notice of the social norm. Notice

133 Restatement (Second) of Contracts § 19(2) (Am. Law Inst. 1981).

is one factor that affects whether it is fair to insist agents choose between forgoing sex or incurring parental duties, but this forced choice must also be consistent with basic liberties and justice.[134] A social convention that treats walking on the sidewalk as waiving one's freedom of speech would create no moral duties, even if a pedestrian knew about the convention. The moral heavy lifting is not done by a power (consent, acceptance, willingness, etc.) but by the political justification for restricting agents' liberty.

Courts and scholars should stop stretching to insist that consent to sex somehow "counts as" consent to parental duties.[135] We should admit, as Martha Fineman has long insisted, that the law imposes financial support duties on sexual procreators to privatize our collective obligation to children.[136] The question is whether this is a fair restriction on sexual or procreative liberty, which 3.III.C answered with a heavily qualified maybe. For similar reasons, we should resist interpreting the residential presumption as a case of parentage by commissive act. "Holding oneself out as a parent" is not a speech act that creates parental duties (although it is a speech act for other purposes). Instead, as explained in 4.III, the community has determined that an individual cannot act as if they were a parent for a long time (and legal parents cannot allow them to do so) without creating presumptive duties and rights.

* * *

Individuals cannot acquire parental rights and duties through personal moral powers, including agential powers like intending, moral powers like promising or contracting, or social powers like performing speech acts. Nevertheless, surveying those possibilities refined the puzzle facing parentage agreements. Allowing citizens to allocate parenthood among themselves facilitates familial autonomy, but individuals lack any inherent personal authority to decide who will raise a child or on what terms. Why, then, may any private person have a normative power to determine who gets the authority to shape a child's life? Is the assignment of parenthood an inherently public function that requires state involvement?

III NORMATIVE POWERS IN A POLITICAL CONCEPTION OF PARENTHOOD

The derived liberty argument underlying genetic parents' liberty can justify a similar liberty for nonbiological parents. A community must have a system of law to create a power to commit to parenthood in ways consistent with equal respect for the child, legal parents, and putative parents. Section A defends a liberty right to become

134 In response to a similar worry, Millum insists that the cost of having to either refrain from vaginal sex or have vaginal sex only with partners who commit to abortion is not "substantial enough to undermine voluntariness." MILLUM, *supra* note 129, at 100. That misses the point. Society limits sexual liberty by allocating the cost of child-rearing to procreators. The relevant question is whether this limitation on liberty is just, not whether the cost renders the conduct involuntary.

135 Emily J. Stolzenberg, *Nonconsensual Family Obligations*, 48 BYU L. REV. 625, 653–58 (2022).

136 MARTHA FINEMAN, THE AUTONOMY MYTH: A THEORY OF DEPENDENCY (2004).

a legal parent irrespective of biology. It also wards off two prominent objections to the right to be a parent, most notably that this right justifies child redistribution. Sections B, C, D, and E then describe how the law structures the legal powers necessary for the liberty to pursue nonbiological parenthood. All states must have adoption law, but the law should also maintain various powers to establish parenthood by agreement.

A *The Right to Be a Nonbiological Parent*

Genetic and gestational parents have a derived liberty to raise their biological children. Many reasonable people value biological families, and a community has no legitimate reasons to interfere with its members' procreative parenting projects, provided the community ensures that adults parent adequately and limits the distributive effects of biological parentage. Of course, other reasonable citizens value parenthood irrespective of biological ties. Some heterosexual couples are physically unable to conceive or gestate a child. Many LGBTQ+ adults are in relationships where the partners cannot both have biological ties to the same child. Some adults may have ethical objections to procreation but still want to raise a child. Adults should be able to pursue the families they value so long as they can become parents without denying others equal respect.[137]

Any restrictions on nonbiological parenthood must be justified by public reasons. No legitimate reasons exist for a legal regime of exclusively biological parenthood. The only plausible reason is that children benefit from procreative parenting, but, as was argued in 2.II.C, the value of genetic ties cannot legitimately justify biological parentage rules, much less justify making biology the *sine qua non* of parenthood. Of course, many critics of ART and same-sex parenthood flout the liberal principle of legitimacy. They may openly oppose LGBTQ+ parenthood to prevent children from learning nontraditional ideas about gender and sexuality. Any liberal-egalitarian community must reject such efforts to use coercive power to buttress one vision of the good life.

Such restrictions on family liberty are also a classic method of subordination. Dominant groups maintain social hierarchy by denying others the right to form or maintain families.[138] The United States has long used this strategy against Black families. As oppressors and victims realize, parenthood is both a valued personal

137 Although no American courts have recognized a constitutional right to adopt, Altman argues that a right to adopt can be grounded in children's need for parents and adults' interests in family formation. Scott Altman, A *Right to Adopt and Parental Licensing*, 65 Ariz. L. Rev. 835, 844–45 (2023). While parental rights cannot be grounded directly in individual interests, I consider below whether a similar argument can be made in terms of primary goods.

138 *See, e.g.*, Randall Kennedy, Interracial Intimacies: Sex, Marriage, Identity, and Adoption (2012); Angela Onwuachi-Willig, *A Beautiful Lie: Exploring* Rhinelander v. Rhinelander *as a Formative Lesson on Race, Identity, Marriage, and Family*, 95 Calif. L. Rev. 2393 (2007); R.A. Lenhardt, *Marriage as Black Citizenship*, 66 Hastings L.J. 1317, 1326–35 (2014).

experience and a political responsibility. Raising the next generation is a central way citizens contribute to their community. Being publicly recognized as worthy of raising a family is a crucial social basis of self-respect, a primary good.[139] Biological and nonbiological parents fulfill the same valued functions. As Douglas NeJaime argues, parentage law cannot use biological ties to "undermine commitments to equality based on sexual orientation, gender, and marital status."[140] Justice requires the community to ensure all members have a fair opportunity to fulfill the publicly valued role of parenthood.

To ensure equal familial liberty and equal opportunity to be a parent, the state must create legal mechanisms that allow an adult to become a parent without regard to biological ties. These tools for nonbiological parenthood must be shaped to ensure equal respect for the child and other adults, particularly biological and legal parents. Sections B, C, D, and E describe how parentage agreement law creates this regime.

Before delving into the legal details, I must defuse a reductio threatening the right to be a parent. If a community does not have enough children to adopt or surrogates willing to carry children, then the only way the state can ensure all childless adults can be parents would be by redistributing newborns from their biological parents. Child redistribution sounds like the plot of a dystopian novel. A state that demands birth parents allow other citizens to raise their children co-opts their bodies and family life in the service of others. Previous chapters also blocked the two obvious escape routes from this dystopia. Neither the child nor their birth parents have a basic right to procreative parenting that could trump a claim for redistribution.

Instead of looking for a right that could trump redistribution, I reject the implicit theory of parental rights that generates claims for redistribution. Under an interest theory of rights, individuals have a right to be a parent if child-rearing is so essential to human flourishing that others have a duty to help satisfy this interest in parenthood. The reductio is off and running. Under my account, adults have a derived liberty to pursue nonbiological parenthood. The state may restrict citizens' parenting projects only for public reasons, and no legitimate reasons exist to justify restricting parenthood to biological parents. Individuals have no right to demand the community supply a child to satisfy their interest in child-rearing any more than to demand the community satisfy their interest in art or religion. Rejecting a right to raise some child undercuts most of the impetus for the reductio.

Nevertheless, I also argued that citizens should have an equal opportunity for parenthood regardless of biological ties, so we must consider whether this principle

139 John Rawls, Political Liberalism § VII.6, at 318–19 (2005); John Rawls, A Theory of Justice § 82, at 477 (1999). Because legitimate public reasons for family regulation and recognition go hand in hand, I reject Ristroph and Murray's claim that the desire for family recognition is ideologically suspect, reflecting the legal system's illegitimate "establishment" of favored family forms. *Contra* Alice Ristroph & Melissa Murray, *Disestablishing the Family*, 119 Yale L.J. 1236, 1257–58 (2009).

140 Douglas NeJaime, *The Constitution of Parenthood*, 72 Stan. L. Rev. 261, 335–37 (2020).

of justice requires redistributing parental rights. In a Rawlsian framework, justice concerns the distribution of primary goods that all citizens need as free and equal persons living a full life within a cooperative society. However, Rawls's category of primary goods is heterogeneous.[141] It contains at least three relevant, distinct types of goods: all-purpose resources, basic liberties, and opportunities. Only the first are ever redistributed in any ordinary sense.

Resources like income or housing are useful for pursuing any conception of the good. A community may sustain economic structures that shape its members' lives only if each member receives a fair share of the all-purpose resources generated by those structures. Child-rearing is not an all-purpose means in this sense. Moreover, a state cannot regard authority over children as a resource for adults without denying children's dignity as equal citizens.

The second type, the basic liberties like freedom of expression, are never redistributed. When police prevent protestors from blocking a highway, they are not redistributing liberty from protestors to commuters. The protestors had no liberty to protest in the street in the first place. All citizens are entitled to a system of equal liberties, including speech and movement.[142] No one's claim to expressive liberty can give them unilateral authority to decide where others may travel. Parenting cannot be a basic liberty for similar reasons of equal liberty. No one can have a basic right to authority to control a child's life consistent with treating them as equals.

If child-rearing is a primary good, it falls in the third category: opportunities valued by most but not all conceptions of the good. For example, some citizens regard education as constitutive of a meaningful life, others view it instrumentally, and the rest are indifferent. A representative in Rawls's original position, not knowing whether they will regard specific opportunities as meaningless or indispensable, would reject a state that insists everyone take a fair share of opportunities or neglects institutions necessary to make opportunities possible. Instead, they would select a system of free choice against a "background of diverse opportunities, which opportunities allow the pursuit of a variety of ends."[143] No one has a claim to any specific opportunity, but everyone is entitled to a system that creates opportunities, ensures opportunities are formally open to everyone, and provides everyone with adequate basic means to pursue them.

Child-rearing is an opportunity valued by many, but not all, reasonable citizens. Childless adults do not have a right to parent some child, but they do have a right not

141 Paul Guyer, *Principles of Justice, Primary Goods and Categories of Right: Rawls and Kant*, 23 Kantian Rev. 581, 606–09 (2018). Rawls's list of primary goods included (i) "the basic rights and liberties … required for adequate development and full and informed exercise of the two moral powers"; (ii) "[f]reedom of movement and free choice of occupation against a background of diverse opportunities, which opportunities allow the pursuit of a variety of ends"; (iii) "offices or positions of authority and responsibility"; (iv) "income and wealth"; and (v) the "social bases of self-respect." John Rawls, Justice as Fairness: A Restatement 58–59 (2001).

142 Rawls, *supra* note 141, § 32.2, at 112.

143 *Id.* § 13.2, at 43–44, § 17.2, at 58.

to be legally excluded from parenthood. States must maintain legal tools to enable nonbiological parents to become legal parents consistent with the child's and other parents' rights. Like the right to marry, the right to be a parent is a positive right to laws that give everyone a power to create legal rights and duties necessary to pursue families consistent with the rights of others.[144] Moreover, because child-rearing is a primary good, the state may legitimately dedicate public funding to create parenting opportunities through adoption, IVF, or surrogacy. Infant redistribution is not necessary to ensure a fair equal opportunity to become parents.

Some ethicists would argue that justice *requires* public funding of ART because infertility is a "disease" in the technical sense of a deviation from statistically normal physical functioning that prevents adults from pursuing ends they value.[145] These arguments have limited purchase, at least within a Rawlsian liberal-egalitarian framework. While healthcare is a basic right, the reasons for this right do not apply to fertility treatments.

First, some physical and psychological capabilities are all-purpose means useful for any valuable life. Second, the state must ensure all citizens have the capabilities or accommodations necessary to live as equals in the community, given the society's language, physical spaces, and economic structures. Biological procreation is neither an all-purpose good nor necessary to participate as an equal in our community. Some citizens "deem having genetically related offspring a constitutive element of leading a good life,"[146] but procreation is just one among many such life projects.[147] Public officials cannot legitimately treat procreative projects as more valuable than friendship, artistic creation, or spiritual experience. The state may support citizens' projects only consistent with general principles of distributive justice. Fertility treatments for aspiring parents are more socially productive than plastic surgery for aspiring actors, but both groups can pursue similar projects without draining healthcare resources that other citizens need for *any* valuable project. Justice does not require significant public funding for ART, so long as each citizen receives a just share of all-purpose resources and the law authorizes parentage through ART and rules for nonbiological parenthood.

B *Creating New Parenthood: Adoption*

Adoption law helps meet the community's obligations to ensure children have parents and adults have parenting opportunities. Since it spread across the states, adoption's avowed goal has always been to match orphaned or neglected children

144 Gregg Strauss, *The Positive Right to Marry*, 102 VA. L. REV. 1691 (2016).

145 For discussion, see Emily McTernan, *Should Fertility Treatment Be State Funded?*, 32 J. APP. PHIL. 227 (2015).

146 Justine Burley, *The Price of Eggs: Who Should Bear the Costs of Fertility Treatments?*, *in* THE FUTURE OF HUMAN REPRODUCTION: ETHICS, CHOICE, AND REGULATION 126 (John Harris & Søren Holm eds., 1998).

147 McTernan, *supra* note 145.

with adults willing to meet their need for care and guidance.[148] Unfortunately, agencies and states were also racist, classist, sectarian, xenophobic, and homophobic, so adoption often discriminated against birth families and some adoptive parents. Nevertheless, federal and state reforms have reshaped adoption so that it can, in theory, empower adults to become parents in ways that respect the equal status of children and other adults.[149]

1 Legal Powers Underlying Adoption

As discussed in 2.1, federal constitutional law forced adoption law to protect any adult with a liberty right to raise a child, including legal, presumptive, and biological parents. Although the law now requires consent by legal and biological parents, the label "consent" obscures as much as it reveals. Consent and its effects differ for different actors.

A CONSENT BY BIOLOGICAL PARENTS. Adoption law must ensure biological parents have an opportunity to commit to raising the child, and if they have, a right to veto adoption. When a birth parent consents to infant adoption, they exercise a power to waive their liberty to perform caregiving. This waiver builds on the forfeiture ideas in Chapter 2. Birth parents have a liberty to raise their child or not, which respects the adult's familial autonomy, but their liberty is conditional on prompt commitment to parental duties, which respects the child's right to a parent. Unfortunately, commitment and promptness are vague (scalar) concepts. Some courts draw arbitrary lines, while others struggle with ad hoc judgments. Either approach can interfere with parents' planning and children's stability.

Law should empower biological parents to waive their parental liberty definitively. The waiver procedure must be designed to ensure informed consent and prevent coercion, especially given America's history of mistreating vulnerable birth parents. However, a lengthy veto or recission period would infringe on children's rights by undermining their relationships with their caregivers. It might also infringe on adoptive parents' rights. For the reasons explained in 4.III.B, an adoptive parent acquires a right to continue their parenting project if they obtain custody rightfully and make "a significant and continuing effort . . . to discharge the responsibilities of parenthood."[150] Given the difficulty of aligning these three rights, state procedures for consent to adoption and constitutional decisions will inevitably vary.

148 Gilbert A. Holmes, *Extended Family System in the Black Community: A Child-Centered Model for Adoption Policy*, 68 TEMPLE L. REV. 1649, 1673 (1995).

149 *Id.* at 1675–79 (arguing open adoption contracts are especially valuable to preserve Black extended family systems). I do not meant to imply that foster and adoption law eliminated discrimination or struck the ideal balance between respecting families and protecting children; perhaps states should look for alternatives to adoption that preserve foster children's relationships with their birth parents. Cynthia Godsoe, *Parsing Parenthood*, 17 LEWIS & CLARK L. REV. 113, 160–64 (2013).

150 *In re* Baby Girl Eason, 358 S.E.2d 459, 460 (Ga. 1987).

When a birth parent consents to adoption or relinquishes an infant to an agency, the state also terminates their parental duties. While these birth parents have not discharged or transferred their personal causal duty to the child, the community has sound reasons to treat these actions as terminating their *legal* duties. The threat of ongoing legal duties might encourage birth parents to keep children who they are unable or unwilling to raise. Birth parents may also confuse an ongoing duty to ensure the child receives care with ongoing authority over the child's life. The law should avoid encouraging birth parents to deny a child's right to a parent or interfere with the authority of the adoptive parents.

B CONSENT BY LEGAL PARENTS. An established legal parent has a constitutional right to veto any adoption unless they are unfit or have abandoned the child. When a legal parent consents to adoption, they do more than waive their liberty to parent. They exercise a power to resign from the parental role, abdicating their legal rights and duties.

Two reasons justify this power to resign parenthood. First, it protects parents' equal liberty. Parents have a lengthy and demanding duty to serve another person's ends, which raises concerns about involuntary servitude. Even if an adult deliberately accepts parental duties, subsequent events may make the burden overbearing. A community can allow adults to bind themselves to indefinite parental duties only if it also gives them a power to end the relationship. Second, a resignation power is necessary to protect the child's rights to a parent and to generic primary goods. If a legal parent is no longer willing or able to raise the child, forcing them to remain parents would deprive the child of their right to care and guidance and risk exposing them to neglect or abuse. Allowing resignation gives parents a liberty to cause their child psychological harm, but coerced caregiving would be worse. The law should do more to help parents in crisis, but it must also offer some procedure for unwilling legal parents to resign parenthood without legal punishment and in ways designed to secure the child's right to adequate care.

C CONSENT BY ADOPTIVE PARENTS. It may seem to go without saying, but prospective adoptive parents must also "consent" to parenthood. Their consent, however, is fundamentally different. It is a traditional commissive speech act. Adoptive parents exercise a legal power to create rights and duties for themselves and the child by making a public commitment to the child in a ceremony before a judge.[151] The state must insist that any unrelated adult exercise this power to adopt

[151] Adoption has intriguing similarities with oaths, which are understudied as a distinct moral power. Thaddeus Metz argues that oaths enable us to deliberately form a new relational identity characterized by a relationship of trust and regulated by conventional duties (marriage, physicians), sometimes even without acceptance by the obligee (e.g., president of the United States). Thaddeus Metz, *The Ethics of Swearing: The Implications of Moral Theories for Oath-Breaking in Economic Contexts*, 71 REV. SOC. ECON. 228 (2013). Nevertheless, oaths are express speech acts, so even if they are an

as a condition of taking indefinite sole custody of a child. Without this power, a custodian has no parental duties or rights. Their caregiving can generate a personal duty but not parental duties (4.III.A.4), and allowing anyone to take custody without parental duties denies the child's basic right to a parent (4.IV.A). Adoption vests parental rights in adoptive parents, making them full parents in every sense.[152]

All states should prohibit unregulated transfers of child custody. This practice, sometimes referred to as "child rehoming,"[153] circumvents the procedures for relinquishment and screening (III.B.2.a) necessary to ensure the child has a caregiver willing and able to fulfill the parental role. The informal caregiver lacks legal authority to make crucial decisions to guide the child's life and ensure their basic rights, such as enrolling them in school, consenting to their medical treatment, or obtaining welfare benefits. For similar reasons, child protective services should not pressure parents to place children in indefinite guardianships with unauthorized foster parents.[154] Even if the social workers' goal is to protect the child's extended familial ties, the caregiver's liminal legal status denies the child's right to primary goods – both material goods and a parent.

Rehoming and unauthorized foster care must be distinguished from a parent's power to designate someone to act *in loco parentis* or as a temporary guardian. All states allow parents to transfer physical and legal custody of their child to a temporary guardian for limited purposes and times. Parents need the authority to delegate powers to a daycare or school. Parents in crisis also need the authority to rely on relatives or friends for temporary care. Some parents allow their children to live with relatives for lengthy periods, particularly in Native American communities. A political community

intriguing analog for adoption, VAPs, or preconception agreements, they are a nonstarter for genetic, gestational, marital, residential, or de facto parenthood.

152 Naomi Cahn, *Perfect Substitutes or the Real Thing?*, 52 Duke L.J. 1077, 1125–47 (2002) (identifying intestacy and incest as areas where law struggled to treat adoptive and biological children identically). States must also severely restrict adoption annulment and allow only narrow damages claims for misrepresentations in the adoption process, both of which presuppose adults can condition their parental duties on having a child with certain qualities. Margaret M. Mahoney, *Permanence and Parenthood: The Case for Abolishing the Adoption Annulment Doctrine*, 42 Ind. L. Rev. 639 (2009).

153 Thirteen states criminalize rehoming, and twenty-eight more define circumstances in which parents can transfer temporary guardianship. Abby Holland, Note, *Regulating Unregulated Custody Transfer*, 33 Geo. J. Legal Ethics 591, 601 (2020); Child Welfare Info. Gateway, Unregulated Custody Transfers of Adopted Children, 3 (2022), www.childwelfare.gov/resources/unregulated-custody-transfers-adopted-children/; Jenn Morson, *When Families Un-Adopt a Child*, The Atlantic (2018), www.theatlantic.com/family/archive/2018/11/children-who-have-second-adoptions/575902/ (last visited Mar. 31, 2022).

154 *In re* Interest of Z.J.H., 162 Wis.2d 1002, 1025 (1991) ("contracts of a parent by which a parent attempts to transfer permanently the custody of his child to another are invalid as contrary to public policy"); Josh Gupta-Kagan, *America's Hidden Foster Care System*, 72 Stan. L. Rev. 841 (2020); Lizzie Presser, *"They Took Us Away From Each Other": Lost Inside America's Shadow Foster System*, ProPublica (2021), www.propublica.org/article/they-took-us-away-from-each-other-lost-inside-americas-shadow-foster-system (last visited Mar. 31, 2022).

with the authority to specify children's rights must decide what kinship-caregiving arrangements are consistent with the child's right to a stable caregiver with the duty and authority to guide their lives.

D CHILD'S CONSENT. Some children also have a right to veto adoption. From an infant's perspective *as an equal citizen*, it does not matter whether biological or adoptive parents raise them. Infants have a right to a parent but no right to a specific parent (because genetics, gestation, and causation do not justify correlative duties to parent). Young children will have opinions about their adoption, but because they are still developing the capacity to judge or pursue their own ends, their opinions cannot be determinative. Someone else – the court in adoption or the legal parent in second-parent adoption – must decide on the child's behalf in consultation with the child.

However, once an older child can judge their relationships for themselves, the community should not give anyone parental authority over them without their consent. Even if these minors remain incompetent for most purposes, so they are rightfully subject to state custody via foster care, the state should nevertheless respect their relational decisions. Most states require the child's consent at age fourteen or twelve, while a handful begin as early as ten.[155] The differences arise from factual and moral uncertainty about children's abilities and the inaccuracy of age-based generalizations. Some "jurisdictions explicitly allow courts to dispense with the consent requirement if doing so is in a child's best interests."[156] This vestige of a consultation model is inappropriate for youth capable of judging for themselves. However, perhaps it is a poorly phrased rule meant to allow courts to evaluate each child's capacities individually.

2 Limits on Adoption

The community's duty to ensure that each child has an adequate parent both mandates and circumscribes state regulation of adoptive parents.

A AGENCY SCREENING. A public official (or private agency with delegated authority) must perform ex ante screening to ensure prospective adopters are willing and able to parent the child. Screening must be limited to this narrow function.[157] While adoptive parents will have authority to use their values to guide the child's life, the public standards for qualifying adoptive parents and assigning adoptive children must remain

155 A.B.A. Child Custody and Adoption Pro Bono Project, *Hearing Children's Voices and Interests in Adoption and Guardianship Proceedings*, 41 Fam. L.Q. 365 (2007).

156 *Id.* at 377.

157 Altman argues screening cannot be justified on this ground because our inability to predict abuse and the low base rates for abuse by adoptive parents suggest screening will result in a high false positive rate, rejecting many competent adoptive parents. Altman, *supra* note 137, at 851–55.

constrained by the principle of public reason. Officials who try to shape adoptive families to fit their vision of an ideal family disrespect the adults and the children as citizens entitled to live by their own values.

Unfortunately, child welfare and adoption agencies have long abused – as many still do – this screening authority to discriminate based on class, race, disability, sexual orientation, marital status, and religion. Historically, orphanages engaged in pervasive religious instruction. Adoption authorities insisted on racially homogenous families and deemed children with disabilities unadoptable.[158] Even after the government stopped officially abducting indigenous children for boarding schools or adoption to assimilate them, child welfare agencies removed native children from their families for little or no reason, misconstruing cultural differences as neglect.[159] Child welfare agencies still remove children of color from their families at disproportionate rates, largely because parents receive the blame for poverty.[160]

States and agencies also officially discriminated against adoptive parents based on their beliefs about religion, culture, gender, or sexuality. None of these factors are relevant to whether an adult is qualified to adopt an infant or young child.[161] Agencies act illegitimately when they try to "match" children and adoptive children in ways that mimic biological families.[162] As Dorothy Roberts and others have argued, the state cannot legitimately shape families to match monoracial, heterosexual, gendered family forms.[163] However, for older foster youth who have begun developing their own religious beliefs, cultural ties, gender identity, or sexual orientation, the agencies should seek foster and adoptive parents willing to facilitate these aspects of the child's developing conception of the good.[164] The adoptive parent's obligation, like that of any parent, will be to help the child develop their ability to live by their own judgment.

Should private adoption and foster care agencies be subject to similar public reason limits? Historically, private adoption agencies were de facto public institutions. They held physical custody of children who were wards of the state.

158 Elizabeth Bartholet, *Where Do Black Children Belong? The Politics of Race Matching in Adoption*, 139 U. PA. L. REV. 1163, 1176–78 (1990).

159 Thomas L. Crofoot & Marian S. Harris, *An Indian Child Welfare Perspective on Disproportionality in Child Welfare*, 34 CHILD. & YOUTH SERVS. REV. 1667 (2012); DOROTHY ROBERTS, TORN APART: HOW THE CHILD WELFARE SYSTEM DESTROYS BLACK FAMILIES – AND HOW ABOLITION CAN BUILD A SAFER WORLD 102–05 (2022).

160 ROBERTS, *supra* note 159, at 68–76, 119–21.

161 Alicia L. Fedewa, Whitney W. Black & Soyeon Ahn, *Children and Adolescents with Same-Gender Parents: A Meta-Analytic Approach in Assessing Outcomes*, 11 J. GLBT FAM. STUD. 1 (2015); Benjamin Graham Miller, Stephanie Kors & Jenny Macfie, *No Differences? Meta-Analytic Comparisons of Psychological Adjustment in Children of Gay Fathers and Heterosexual Parents*, 4 PSYCHOL. SEXUAL ORIENTATION & GENDER DIVERSITY 14 (2017).

162 Cahn, *supra* note 152, at 1148–49.

163 ROBERTS, *supra* note 159; Solangel Maldonado, *Discouraging Racial Preferences in Adoptions*, 39 U. C. DAVIS L. REV. 1415 (2005); Jordan Blair Woods, *Religious Exemptions and LGBTQ Child Welfare*, 103 MINN. L. REV. 2343, 2417–18 (2018).

164 Woods, *supra* note 163, at 2411–14.

Contemporary independent contractors often have a similar structure. In *Fulton v. Philadelphia*, for example, Philadelphia assigned children to private charitable foster agencies, which accepted the responsibility to recruit and screen foster parents for each child. The city delegated two public functions: temporary custody of children and the selection and training of foster parents. Having delegated its authority over children, the city may not permit the agency to require foster parents to follow the agency's religious values.

States may still use religious adoption agencies, even ones that represent only people who share their religious beliefs, so long as the agencies do not wield authority over children or have a monopoly on adoption services. Religious agencies' recruitment efforts may skew the pool of adoptive parents toward religious believers, but that does not infringe on the children's rights.[165] A foster child in a community of religious adoptive parents is in the same situation as a child born into a community of religious birth parents. The state must also ensure that enough private agencies exist to cover any adults turned away by religious agencies. If the law requires screening by an agency and religious agencies have an effective monopoly, then the law is giving private persons authority to choose who may adopt. Such domination is inconsistent with equal liberty.

Fostering is a liminal status that raises additional concerns. Foster parents can guide the child's daily life only with some discretion to use their comprehensive values. Yet, the child will eventually return to their legal parents or be placed with adoptive parents. Foster parents should avoid shaping a child's commitments in ways likely to conflict with the guidance of their current or future parents. For example, foster parents may expose a child to religious ideas and experiences to develop their spiritual sensibility, but they should not engage in intensive religious instruction or force children to participate in religious practices. Foster parents must act on limited reasons that stick closer, but not exclusively, to public reasons. Foster agencies, in contrast, should follow a strict ideal of public reason. They exercise delegated public authority over the community's most vulnerable children. A foster agency cannot be allowed to use its authority to push foster children toward a particular conception of the good.

B HONORING PREFERENCES OF BIRTH AND ADOPTIVE PARENTS. In a private placement adoption, birth parents can select adoptive parents by surrendering a child contingent on adoption by a designated person. States are not required to give birth parents this power, but it is a permissible and pragmatic approach.

165 Contrary to the common argument that religious exemptions benefit children, antidiscrimination rules modestly increase the probably of finding foster and adoptive placements and substantially reduce wait times, especially for difficult-to-place children. Netta Barak-Corren, Yoav Kan-Tor & Nelson Tebbe, *Examining the Effects of Antidiscrimination Laws on Children in the Foster Care and Adoption Systems*, 19 J. EMPIRICAL LEGAL STUD. 1003 (2022).

Biological parents have no claim right to dictate who will parent their child. Their liberty right to raise the child – and hence to exercise coercive authority to shape their life – is contingent on fulfilling the child's right to parental care and guidance. A birth parent who places a child for adoption chooses not to accept this obligation.[166] Moreover, the law has little reason to suppose birth parents make the best decisions. Birth parents have no privileged information about what life is best for the child and no special ability to judge the quality of adoptive parents. Any information they have about adoptive parents can be shared with a court. Nevertheless, pragmatic reasons support the statutes that allow birth parents to select adoptive parents. Placing a child for adoption can be a gut-wrenching decision, especially if a birth parent wants to raise the child but cannot do so adequately. Allowing birth parents to choose who raises the child may help them follow through with their judgment that adoption is best for the child.

Does a state deny equal respect to children when it allows birth parents to choose who will raise them? A birth parent's unreviewable decision will shape the child's life. Suppose a birth parent who loves *The Real Housewives of New York* chooses urban socialites over a rural couple. This is a silly reason for choosing parents, but the child has no legitimate objection. If the state's adoption screening concludes that the socialites will provide adequate care, the child receives what they are entitled to as an equal citizen. The child would have no legitimate objection had they been born into a family of socialites, so the child cannot object to being adopted by them.

However, the rural couple might. The birth parent's choice was classist. Other birth parents may select adoptive parents based on race, ethnicity, sexuality, or religion. We cannot simply dismiss these as private preferences outside the law. States criminalized interracial marriage to enforce norms of racial purity, which shaped norms of interracial intimacy that will long outlast the legal doctrine. Welfare agencies also targeted poor, immigrant, Catholic, Native American, and unmarried birth parents to transfer their children to adoptive parents who were middle-class, native, Protestant, white, and married. A public policy that ignores private preferences will perpetuate discriminatory norms created by state actions.

Nevertheless, three differences likely justify restricting antidiscrimination laws to agencies. First, agencies are easy to regulate, but policing the preferences of birth or adoptive parents is costly, intrusive, and counterproductive. Screening individuals for bias may dissuade birth or adoptive parents from pursuing beneficial adoptions. Second, even if an agency's policy and a birth parent's preferences wrong potential adopters in the same way, the agency policy transcends this individual case to affect many adoptive parents and children. This instrumental difference blends into the last, expressive reason. The social meaning of an individual choice is diluted by the agent's conflicting motives and the multitude of decisions by other individuals. In contrast, agencies act through general policies with clear and loud expressive effects.

166 *Contra* Baxter, *supra* note 14, at 914–15.

Even if agency discrimination arises from individual decisions of social workers, the public easily imputes their discrimination to tacit approval by the agency and the state. A state may take measures to reduce discrimination by birth parents, but it must expressly prohibit discrimination by adoption agencies.

The law has principled reasons to hesitate before policing the preferences of prospective adoptive parents. Some adults may want to adopt a child who can be part of their ethnic or racial community, which they define by ideas about biological heritage. Other citizens may believe religious status is heritable. Biological parents may raise their children according to these nonpublic values, so long as they also ensure their children develop an ability to reach their own value judgments. Adoptive parents should have the same liberty.

However, a liberal state cannot actively facilitate these preferences. An agency may not, for example, maintain a website that enables adults to search for adoptive children by race or religion. By facilitating private preferences resting on comprehensive values, the state is shaping adoptive children's lives differently based on nonpublic reasons. Moreover, the state may refuse to honor the preferences of prospective parents that contribute to injustice in adoption. Richard Banks has argued that allowing white adoptive parents to act on racial preferences has systematically harmed Black children.[167] In the United States, equal respect for adoptive children may be impossible so long as prospective parents remain at liberty to adopt based on racial preferences. Accordingly, states may refuse to accommodate prospective parents' preferences for racial matching, as Banks argued, or limit international adoption to steer parents into domestic multiracial adoptions, as Solangel Maldonado has argued.[168]

C OPEN ADOPTION. Scholars like Lisa Tucker argue that birth parents who enter into an open-adoption agreement should have a right to visitation like a noncustodial parent.[169] To evaluate this proposal, it is instructive to consider a more expansive possibility first. The Massachusetts Supreme Court concluded that when a foster child and birth parent have a relationship before the adoption, the court may order postadoption contact even if the adults never agreed to an open adoption.[170] It concluded the benefits of contact in this scenario are sufficiently clear for a court to override the adoptive parent's contrary judgment. Could a state mandate open adoption generally and give all birth parents a right to postadoption contact?

Mandatory open adoption would place a unique limit on the authority of adoptive parents. Nevertheless, it could be legitimate. To ensure children's primary goods,

167 R. Richard Banks, *The Color of Desire: Fulfilling Adoptive Parents' Racial Preferences Through Discriminatory State Action*, 107 YALE L.J. 875 (1997).

168 Maldonado, *supra* note 163.

169 Tucker, *supra* note 77, at 2360–64.

170 *In re* Adoption of Vito, 728 N.E.2d 292, 303 (Mass. 2000).

the community must define the limits of parental discretion. If it concludes that adoptive parents systemically underestimate the benefits to children of an ongoing relationship with their birth parents, the law could limit adoptive parents' authority to deny all contact.[171]

Of course, adoptive parents have sound reasons to oppose open adoption. As Anita Allen explains, adoptive parents want "to have a family of their own," which means "being able, with the usual constraints of law and society, to define the parameters of one's most intimate sphere ... Open adoption practices strike some people as *dictating* the fusion of families and *mandating* specific intimacies."[172] Allen's insight is genuine, but to be more precise, even mandatory open adoption does not mandate familial intimacy. The birth parent is never forced to exercise visitation. The birth parent now gets to decide whether to maintain an intimate relationship with the child and adoptive family. Enforceable visitation rights transfer a small piece of authority over the child's intimate relationships to the birth parent.

This is a general problem with nonparental visitation: an adult with no duty to the child has the authority to decide whether to visit and how to guide the child's life during visitation. I see two options to address this problem. If the nonparent has a presumptive right to visitation, the law must fashion a new quasi-parent fiduciary duty. It will be difficult to reconcile this division of authority with the child's right to relatively unified guidance (1.II.B.2.b). A birth parent must fit their judgments about visitation alongside the adoptive parent's judgments about the rest of the child's life. Yet when they disagree, the birth parent's judgments about narrow visitation decisions would take precedence over the adoptive parent's wider judgments, effectively transferring more authority that calls for a broader duty. Instead, the adults could share authority over this visitation. In cases of disagreement, a public official could make the all-things-considered judgment for the child about whether to maintain the nonparental relationship.

Now consider open-adoption agreements. If birth parents obtain a right to visitation, this private agreement transfers a piece of parental authority over the child. A legislature has legitimate authority to shape the bounds of parenthood, but birth and adoptive parents have no personal authority to revise parental rights and duties contractually (II.C.3). Might the powers behind adoption (III.B.1) justify giving private individuals this limited authority to rearrange parenthood?

The birth parent's power to waive their caregiving liberty does not entail a power to waive conditional upon ongoing visitation. The birth parent wants to retain authority over the child while disowning the duties that make it permissible. By comparison, no one thinks that a birth parent could retain authority over the child's religion. The

[171] Solangel Maldonado, *Permanency v. Biology: Making the Case for Post-Adoption Contact*, 37 Cap. U. L. Rev. 321, 325–29, 332–39 (2008) (describing possible benefits of postadoption contact, especially for transracial adoption); Tucker, *supra* note 77, at 2335–37.

[172] Anita Allen, *Open Adoption Is Not for Everyone*, *in* Adoption Matters: Philosophical and Feminist Essays 47, 60–61 (Sally Haslanger & Charlotte Witt eds., 2005).

adoptive parent's power to commit to parenthood does not include a power to confer a right to visitation. Their core parental duty will be to exercise substitute judgment about what is best for the child. They cannot promise to ignore their future judgment about whether a relationship with a birth parent is good for the child.[173]

Proponents of open adoption may regard this argument as unduly formal. Why not trust the birth and adoptive parents' shared judgment about what is best for their future families? If the birth parent kept the child, the state would have deferred to their judgment. When the adoption is complete, the state will defer to the adoptive parent's judgments. Moreover, states trust separated parents in a similar situation, allowing them to arrange their family life through custody agreements. Why not treat open-adoption contracts like custody agreements?

The custody analogy reveals the limits of the trust argument. Separated parents enter into a custody agreement to plan how they will meet their ongoing parental duties. By contrast, open-adoption contracts reassign authority to a birth parent who has no legal duty to the child. Moreover, even custody agreements are not enforceable in any ordinary sense of the word. The custody order remains open, so either parent can petition for a modification if they believe circumstances have changed. In disputed cases, the custody agreement is not enforceable; it is some evidence of what is good for the child because it reflects the parents' past judgment. Parents are not bound by their past judgments. Ultimately, a court makes a prospective judgment about whether modifying the arrangement is in the best interests of the child.

This model can help us better understand open-adoption agreements, even in states that nominally "enforce" them. When adoptive parents cut off visitation, the birth parent files a petition, and a court decides what ongoing contact – if any – is in the best interests of the child. Neither the adoptive nor the birth parent's judgment is entitled to deference. In effect, the agreement waives parental priority without giving birth parents enforceable visitation rights. The open-adoption contract effectively transfers to a judge the responsibility to make a comprehensive judgment for the child. If a community believes adoptive children benefit sufficiently from contact with their birth parents, then the community can empower adoptive parents to agree to share this portion of their authority with birth parents, subject to judicial power to resolve disagreements about what ongoing contact benefits the child.[174]

173 The problem is with the duty of loyalty, not that unpredictability makes precommitment an irrational strategy to facilitate the child's interests. Abramowicz, *supra* note 83, at 120–21.

174 Thus, I support Laufer-Ukeles's concept of tiered parenthood for shared parental custody but oppose tiers of legal visitation rights for birth parents, relatives, or tertiary caregivers. Pamela Laufer-Ukeles, *The Children of Nonmarriage: Towards a Child-First Family Law*, 40 YALE L. & POL'Y REV. 384, 445 (2021); Laufer-Ukeles, *The Relational Rights of Children*, 48 CONN. L. REV. 741, 762–68, 804–05 (2015); Laufer-Ukeles, *The Case Against Separating the Care from the Caregiver: Reuniting Caregivers' Rights and Children's Rights*, 15 NEV. L.J. 236, 287–89 (2014). Even if visitation will not undermine the primary caregiving relationship, it disrupts the child's right to parental guidance, unless the law creates a novel quasi-parent duty.

C Sharing Parentage after Birth: Second-Parent Adoption and Acknowledgments of Parentage

So far, our concern has been with creating entirely new families, but the law also empowers a presumptive or legal parent and their partner to share parenthood. Subsection 1 clarifies this normative power by analyzing the paradigm case of second-parent adoption. Subsection 2 explains the justification for allowing adults to wield this power at all, while Subsection 3 argues that states should extend this power to allow birth parents and their partners to complete an acknowledgment of parentage without judicial supervision.

1 Second-Parent Adoption as a Joint Normative Power

Orphan adoption, second-parent adoption, and de facto parenthood all create new parent–child relationships, but the doctrines rest on distinct moral relations. Orphan adoption creates a family for a child with no parents. Any biological, presumptive, or legal parents must waive or resign from parenthood. When they waive their parental liberty, they are not exercising authority over the child. But that is precisely what happens in second-parent adoption. The legal parent has authority over the child, which they use to allow another adult to become a second parent.

In that respect, second-parent adoption may sound like de facto parenthood, but these doctrines are also fundamentally different. When a legal parent consents to share caregiving with their partner, the parent transforms their partner's duty not to interfere into a privilege to help raise the child; once the child develops attachments, the legal parent forfeits their authority to withdraw the de facto parent's caregiving privilege (4.III.D). Second-parent adoption involves no such waivers, privileges, or forfeitures. When a legal parent consents to adoption, the parent empowers their partner to become a coequal parent immediately and prospectively by express commitment.

These differences get obscured if one treats stepparent adoption as the paradigm, as did the Uniform Adoption Act (UAA). A legal parent and their spouse may coparent for years before pursuing adoption. The UAA commentary argues that adoption "simply formalizes a de facto parent–child relationship," so "denying the petition to adopt is not likely to alter the existing custodial arrangement."[175] The commentary mistakes a common instance for a paradigm. Stepparent adoption does not require an established custodial relationship. A stepparent can adopt a newborn or toddler after a whirlwind romance with their parent. Even when a child and stepparent have a developed relationship, adoption does more than "formalize" it. It fundamentally and permanently alters de jure relationships. The stepparent becomes a legal parent with duties of support and claims to physical and decisional custody.

[175] UNIF. ADOPTION ACT § 4-100, cmt. (UNIF. LAW COMM'N 1994).

Second-parent adoption involves the joint exercise of two legal powers: the legal parent agrees to share parenthood, and their partner commits to be a parent. One might insist that the parent's approval "waives" their objection to the adoption, but the approval is less like a waiver of a claim against interference than an offer to enter into a contract. The parent's approval confers a new legal power on their partner. Without this approval, the partner is a pure third party with no standing to petition for adoption. With it, the partner's public commitment will alter their legal relation to the child. Second-parent adoption law gives the legal parent and their partner (and sometimes the child) joint power to create parental status.

2 Second-Parent Adoption Justified by Equal Respect

What justifies this joint power to share parenthood? For reasons canvassed in Part II, it cannot rest on familiar powers like intending, promising, or contracting justified by the adults' authority over their own lives. A political conception of parenthood can justify second-parent adoption through a private- and a public-facing argument.

A PROTECTS EQUAL LIBERTY FOR ADULTS. A joint power to share parenthood is an *extension* of the legal parents' familial liberty. A legal parent should be able to share parenthood with a partner so long as this familial arrangement is consistent with equal respect for the child and the partner – as it can be if the adults have a moral power to establish parental rights and duties deliberately and prospectively.

To see why justice demands second-parent adoption, consider the dilemmas facing lesbian and gay families described by Nancy Polikoff.[176] Many same-sex couples chose to raise children despite knowing the nonbiological intended parent could not establish legal parenthood. Informal coparenting created subordinating asymmetries in their relationships. The nonbiological parent rearranged their life to dedicate themselves to raising the child, but the legal parent could always change their mind and take the child at any time. The nonbiological parent's right to maintain the parent–child relationship depended on the legal parent's ongoing good will. The law gave the legal parent authority over their partner's familial liberty.[177] Although the biological parent had legal parental rights, their ability to pursue their desired family was also precarious. They built a family in reliance on support from a nonbiological parent who was at liberty to leave them and the child at any time with no child support. The biological

[176] Nancy D. Polikoff, *This Child Does Have Two Mothers: Redefining Parenthood to Meet the Needs of Children in Lesbian-Mother and Other Nontraditional Families*, 78 Geo. L.J. 459 (1989); Polikoff, *A Mother Should Not Have to Adopt Her Own Child: Parentage Laws for Children of Lesbian Couples in the Twenty-First Century*, 5 Stan. J. C.R. & C.L. 201, 202 (2009).

[177] Courtney G. Joslin, *Autonomy in the Family*, 66 UCLA L. Rev. 912, 949 (2019).

parent's ability to maintain their chosen life for themselves and their child depended on their partner's ongoing goodwill.

Contract theorists call this an "assurance" problem, but the label can be misleading. From a welfarist perspective, the goal is to give parents and partners enough assurance of cooperation to make efficient decisions about coparenting. Contingent facts and nonlegal enforcement mechanisms can solve incentive problems. If an individual can predict their partner will cooperate based on their trustworthiness, self-help enforcement, and reputational incentives, they can decide it is worthwhile to risk defection rather than forgo coparenting. They may accept this risk rationally and voluntarily. Nevertheless, it is still subordinating. Each adult gets decide whether the other can continue the parenting project central to their life. Without legal rights and duties, a legal parent and a de facto parent can pursue a coparenting project only by subjecting themselves to this subordination.

Functional parent doctrines constrain the subordination without eliminating it. If parties must rely on a marital or residential presumption, then the subordination persists for two years until the statute of limitations applies. The de facto parenthood doctrine creates legal rights only after the child forms parental ties. Until then, the parent can revoke their consent to share parenthood, and the de facto parent can walk away.[178] Moreover, the de facto parent must persuade a judge that continued coparenting serves the child's interests. A de facto parent can wrest control from a legal parent only by submitting to the value judgments of judges and psychologists. Furthermore, functional doctrines do not solve the status problem that both parties intended to solve: the child only has one legal parent for all other purposes. If the biological parent is unavailable or passes away, the nonbiological parent will struggle to ensure they maintain their relationship.[179] To avoid a period of subordination, the adults need a shared power to commit to parenthood prospectively.

Parenting contracts would create duties prospectively, but contracts cannot solve this problem. Contracts solve the assurance problem by giving the promisee a right to sue for damages or specific performance, so their specific claim is preserved regardless of whether the promisor performs.[180] Coparenting does not involve discrete rights that can be guaranteed by coerced performance or damages.[181] Moreover, a full coparenting contract would be impermissible for the same reason as a binding open-adoption contract. A legal parent cannot promise to maintain their partner's relationship with the child in the future when the parent decides the

178 Abramowicz, *supra* note 83, at 94–95.

179 Jacobs, *supra* note 5.

180 *See Compensation as Basic Principle of Damages*, 24 WILLISTON ON CONTRACTS § 64:1 (4th ed. 2024); ARTHUR RIPSTEIN, FORCE AND FREEDOM: KANT'S LEGAL AND POLITICAL PHILOSOPHY 82–83, 166 (2010).

181 *But see* Katherine M. Swift, *Parenting Agreements, the Potential Power of Contract, and the Limits of Family Law*, 34 FLA. ST. U. L. REV. 913, 955–56 (2006) (briefly imagining damage regime for parentage contracts); Scott Altman, *A Theory of Child Support*, 17 INT'L J.L. POL'Y & FAM. 173 (2003) (arguing child support may be damages for breach of a duty to the child).

relationship is no longer good for the child. The promise to abdicate their future judgment violates the legal parent's fiduciary duty.

Second-parent adoption solves the assurance problem differently by empowering adults to share parenthood. Both adults commit to share the authority and obligation to meet the child's need for care and guidance. The new parent incurs a support duty and obtains a right to an ongoing relationship.[182] The legal parent can commit not to exclude the nonbiological parent because they both commit to sharing the fiduciary authority to judge what is in the child's best interests. Joint parenthood does not eliminate the possibility of disagreement but allows both parents to face any disagreement as equals. If they cannot agree, the authority to make the necessary substitute judgments transfers to the court, as it does for biological coparents.

Giving adults this joint power to share parenthood is consistent with respect for the child. The legal parent already has authority over the child's household and relationships, which they can use to cohabit or to share caregiving (4.II.B.3). When both adults want to commit to parenthood, legal recognition of their permanent commitment likely facilitates the child's welfare. Children need dependable caregivers and stable relational attachments. Someone who plans to raise the child and is willing to incur legal duties will likely be an adequate parent.[183] The legal parent also has information about the child's needs, the partner's character, their ability to work together to raise the child, and the quality of the child–stepparent relationship. While legal parents sometimes choose their partners poorly, it is unlikely that public officials will make better judgments. Admittedly, the parent of a newborn will have less private information about their partners' parenting ability, but the significance of relational stability for early child development increases the importance of commitment. The law appropriately defers to the judgment of legal parents.

182 An adequate scheme of child support must account for all child-rearing costs, not simply financial outlays, to remove the risk that one coparent will leave their partner with a disproportionate share of primary caregiving. Ayelet Blecher-Prigat, *The Costs of Raising Children: Toward a Theory of Financial Obligations*, 13 THEORETICAL INQUIRIES LAW 179, 199 (2012). Not all aspects of coparenting projects can be preserved, however. Cook argues even full compensation is inadequate because the "extended, pervasive, and profound commitment" between the adults makes their particular relationship essential to the coparenting project. Phillip Cook, *On the Duties of Shared Parenting*, 6 ETHICS & SOC. WELFARE 168, 180 (2012). Financial support is insufficient because the remaining parent did not want to be a well-financed single parent, and arranging a substitute coparent (nanny or relative) is insufficient because their former partner has a right to reject this proposed intimacy. Thus, Cook concludes, each coparent has a (prima facie) juridical duty to continue sharing parenthood releasable only with their partner's consent. Cook's argument illustrates the problem with taking a personal perspective on problems of political morality. Insofar as his argument depends on the form and extent of the cooperation, rather than its substantive end as it must as a Kantian account, the argument would apply to any similar relationships like spouses, business partners, or employees. However, no one can have such a right to indefinite and open-ended authority over another person consistent with equal respect.

183 Swift, *supra* note 181, at 955.

B JUSTIFIED BY CONCERNS OF PUBLIC EQUALITY. Second-parent adoption law also helps ensure citizens' public-facing equality. Without the power to establish legal parenthood, de facto parents face constant challenges to their familial relationships. Third parties may even be legally obligated to ignore the de facto parent's decisions. Only legal parents can enroll a child in school, consent to their medical treatment, or take them out of the country. A power of attorney can limit the practical difficulties but is not recognized for all public purposes. The moments of legal misrecognition will likely be repeated in social contexts, where de facto parents must fight for the respect afforded to legal parents as a matter of course.

Such differential treatment of biological and nonbiological parents carries an implicit public message. The law trusts genetic fathers to raise a child so long as they are willing to commit to parenthood through a paternity acknowledgment or petition. Why deny nonbiological parents a similar formal procedure to commit to shared parenthood, insisting instead that they perform extensive caregiving required to meet a functional test? The only plausible reasons are illegitimate favoritism of genetic heritage (2.II.C) or distrust of the parenting of nonbiological parents. By withholding second-parent adoption, the community implies that the nonbiological parent's public commitment is insufficient for them to be trusted as quality parents. Law should not openly mistrust the agency of nonbiological parents. Avoiding this public expressive insult is another reason for empowering nonbiological parents to deliberately commit to sharing parenthood.

The states should maintain rules for second-parent adoption that empower a legal parent and their partner to commit to shared parenthood prospectively. This joint power enables parents and their partners to coparent in ways that enable their mutual respect, respect the child's rights, and manifest the public equality of nonbiological parents.

3 Voluntary Acknowledgments, Equal Liberty, and Equal Respect

Ten states maintain voluntary acknowledgments of *parentage* that serve as a private equivalent of second-parent adoption. "Acknowledgment" is a misnomer.[184] While a *paternity* acknowledgment provides evidence of genetic parentage that is then binding on the parties,[185] a *parentage* acknowledgment is not evidence of an

184 As a rhetorical trope, the term "acknowledgment" suggests the intended parent was *already* a parent – which begs the question in a way that downplays the significance of this private adoptive power.

185 Although some states treat paternity acknowledgments as binding even if the parties signed knowing its averments were false, that does not entail that the forms are not a way to prove genetic paternity. The legal consequences of a fact are distinct from the procedure for settling the fact and the truth of the underlying fact. Federal law requires states to treat VAPs like a judicial order because Congress wanted to promote legal finality that would facilitate child support collection. Rule of law and instrumental reasons can justify treating evidence as if it established a fact, even if the fact is demonstrably false and the evidence was produced by fraud or collusion. Rules to ensure the finality of orders do not alter the underlying fact.

independently existing fact. This form constitutes the parties' agreement.[186] As discussed in I.B.2, the essence of a parentage acknowledgment is that (1) the gestational parent agrees to share parenthood with her partner and (2) the nonbiological intended parent accepts parenthood. By immediately creating prospective rights and duties for nonbiological parents, parentage acknowledgments avoid the liminal periods in functional parentage or second-parent adoption.[187]

A PARENTAGE ACKNOWLEDGMENTS RESPECT EQUAL DIGNITY OF THE CHILD AND OTHER ADULTS. Because voluntary acknowledgments of parentage allow two private individuals to decide who has parental authority with no public oversight, they seem to run headlong into the objection that sank intentional parenthood (II.A.2). How can the law enable private individuals to decide who else can raise the child without disregarding the child's equal status?

This objection resurrects the apparent dilemma facing all *acquired* private rights discussed in 1.I.B.3. We need a power to acquire rights without others' permission, but no one has any personal authority over others. Recall that positive law is essential to relieve the dilemma. By specifying a scheme of private law that reconciles private liberties and defines how individuals acquire rights, law transforms the unilateral act of private acquisition into an exercise of legitimate public power. For similar reasons, the state can allow adults to acquire parental rights by their own actions if the law defines the power and the resulting rights in ways that ensure equal respect for the child and other adults. Chapters 2 and 4 explain why law can empower genetic and gestational parents to claim parental authority consistent with equal respect. This subsection explains why law can use parentage acknowledgments to empower legal parents to designate an unrelated person as a second parent.

Voluntary acknowledgments of parentage must satisfy the now familiar requirements for all parentage rules. Any such acknowledgment must confer full parental duties to preserve the child's right to a parent. All model forms appropriately make the signatory a parent, full stop.[188] Parties need not use the model forms, but their agreements cannot alter the substantive terms of parenthood fixed by law. For example, adults cannot use a parentage acknowledgment to exceed the number of parents the community has concluded may share parenthood simultaneously. Ideally,

186 One might argue the form is evidence of parties' assent to parenthood, especially if one is also inclined to honor oral agreements. This seems to be the approach taken in the UPA 2017. Article III requires VAPs to be in writing, as required by federal law (UPA 2017 § 302(a)(1)), but Article VII also enforces an oral agreement for assisted reproduction if the party produces clear and convincing evidence of the agreement (UPA 2017 § 704(b)).

187 Jacobs argues the law should move to a fully intentional approach for initial parenthood by demanding "all parents must sign an intentional acknowledgment of parenthood that establishes the maternity and/or paternity of the child." Jacobs, *supra* note 4, at 496–98. Even this is not a fully intentional system, because it presupposes a nonvoluntarist way to identify which adults may sign the form. Jacobs, for example, favors gestation against genetics. *Id.* at 474–77.

188 Katharine K. Baker, *Quacking like a Duck: Functional Parenthood Doctrine and Same-Sex Parents*, 92 CHI.-KENT L. REV. 135, 162 (2017).

forms would facilitate informed consent by describing parental duties of care, guidance, and support. However, intended parents can also commit to shared parenthood in general, as they do in adoption. The acknowledgment of parentage must also be consistent with the rights of other adults. Most other adults will have no basis to object because they have no claim to raise the child themselves, but an acknowledgment cannot bind other biological or presumed parents who have a liberty right to raise the child. A parentage acknowledgment statute may protect other potential parents by requiring adoption in those cases or by empowering biological and presumed parents to submit a simultaneous form waiving parental rights.[189]

Even if voluntary acknowledgments of parentage meet these requirements, private parentage arrangements would still be objectionable if they systematically lead to less adequate parenting. One might think that the formalities of adoption law contribute to successful families. The formal processes encourage deliberation and solemnity. Parents and stepparents might decide carefully because social workers, lawyers, and judges are involved. Adoption hearings also require an express public commitment and invoke social norms to reinforce it, which might improve parenting. In contrast, parties who conclude a parentage declaration in private may act hastily under the influence of childbirth's mix of euphoria, exhaustion, and trepidation, which might increase the rates of regret and family dissolution.

Although theoretically possible, this incentive story is difficult to take seriously as a reason to reject acknowledgments. I am aware of no empirical studies that suggest intended nonbiological parenthood is less stable than other family forms.[190] Some good reasons exist to speculate that parentage acknowledgments will increase family stability compared to the status quo. The intended parents will likely coparent even without it, and their relationships will be less stable. By comparison, genetic fathers who sign paternity acknowledgments at the hospital remain more involved than fathers who establish paternity later through a petition or not at all, even controlling for the quality of the adult relationships.[191]

Last, some may be wary of parentage acknowledgments because they circumvent adoption screening. However, it is essential to choose the comparison class carefully. Parentage acknowledgments enable a birth mother to share parenthood only if the child has no other parent. Accordingly, acknowledgments should be compared to

189 UPA 2017 § 302(b).

190 Courts speculate that an intent test promotes stability by allowing parties to trust in a shared plan. *See* Johnson v. Calvert, 851 P.2d 776, 783 (Cal. 1993). Most lesbian and gay families involve one nonbiological intended parent and are excellent parents. Charlotte J. Patterson, *Parents' Sexual Orientation and Children's Development*, 11 Child Dev. Persp. 45 (2017).

191 Ronald Mincy, Irwin Garfinkel & Lenna Nepomnyaschy, *In-Hospital Paternity Establishment and Father Involvement in Fragile Families*, 67 J. Marriage & Fam. 611 (2005). The paltry rates of genetic father involvement also belie the seriousness of this objection to acknowledgments for nonbiological parents. Only 43 percent of nonresidential genetic fathers see their five-year-old child more than once a month. Marcia J. Carlson, Sara S. McLanahan & Jeanne Brooks-Gunn, *Coparenting and Nonresident Fathers' Involvement with Young Children after a Nonmarital Birth*, 45 Demography 461, 473 (2008).

uncontested second-parent adoptions. Most states do not require evaluations for stepparent adoption, and courts rarely order an investigation. Moreover, as I argued in 3.II.B.2, we cannot assume ex ante screenings are effective. Judges and social workers are imperfect predictors of parenting quality, their biases magnify social discrimination, and their investigations can impede vital bonding processes. Because the law already trusts legal parents to vet stepparents, demanding couples complete an adoption screening is unlikely to improve the quality of their caregiving. On balance, the instrumental concerns likely favor parentage acknowledgments, but this conclusion admittedly rests on speculative empirical comparisons.

B PARENTAGE ACKNOWLEDGMENTS JUSTIFIED TO PROTECT EQUALITY FOR LGBTQ+ CITIZENS. Considerations of political equality for parents tip the balance. LGBTQ+ advocates insist that requiring nonbiological parents to adopt their own children treats them as second-class parents.[192] These equality arguments for parentage acknowledgments have a valid core but must be shorn of two problematic tendencies. First, the assertion that intended nonbiological parents should not have to adopt "their own children" begs the question. That they *should* be parents at birth is precisely what needs to be established. Second, advocates of equality must be careful to avoid disparaging adoptive families. Adoptive parents perform the same valuable function as any parents. Adoption screening, if properly limited and justified, is not intrinsically demeaning.

On the other hand, states should not ignore the history of adoption discrimination. Until the late twentieth century, few American states allowed LGBTQ+ individuals or couples to adopt. Some private adoption agencies still discriminate against LGBTQ+ adults, unmarried couples, and anyone who does not profess their sectarian religious commitments. Although federal law prohibits discrimination based on sex in state contracts with agencies, the regulations seesaw between prohibiting discrimination based on religion or LGBTQ+ status and exempting religious agencies.[193] Even if religious liberty

[192] NeJaime, *supra* note 30, at 2318–19 (arguing that an adoption requirement implies only biological parents are "real parents," denying the "parent–child relationship that already exists in fact" for intended parents). Some scholars also suggest that recognizing preconception agreements but not VAPs discriminates based on race and class because African American and low-income couples are less likely to plan conception medically. Libby Adler, *Inconceivable: Status, Contract, and the Search for a Legal Basis for Gay & Lesbian Parenthood*, 123 Penn St. L. Rev. 1, 37 (2018). I find this argument unconvincing given other differences between preconception planning and VAPs, most notably that only the former involves deliberate creation of a child.

[193] *See* Adrianne M. Spoto, *Fostering Discrimination: Religious Exemption Laws in Child Welfare and the LGBTQ Community*, 96 N.Y.U. L. Rev. 296, 319 (2021). In July 2023, the US Department of Health and Human Services (HHS) proposed a new rule that would prohibit discrimination in foster care based on sexual orientation but would also create an administrative procedure to evaluate requests for religious exemptions under the Religious Freedom Restoration Act. HHS Grants Regulation, 88 FR 44750-01 (July 12, 2023) (describing litigation over the administrations' vacillating rules during the Obama, Trump, and Biden administrations).

requires exemptions for agencies,[194] the state should strive to structure its family law to avoid preserving adoption law's historical heterosexism.

As Nancy Polikoff demonstrated decades ago, states can subordinate lesbian and gay citizens by insisting that all nonbiological parents complete second-parent adoptions.[195] This rule creates a system of parental licensing that applies only to a subclass of parents, one including most gay and lesbian parents.[196] They can pursue parenthood together only by subjecting their homes and characters to the judgment of social workers and judges – the officials historically tasked with officially discriminating against lesbian and gay parents. The public reasonably interprets the selective scrutiny as expressing official skepticism about the quality of parenting by lesbian and gay couples – skepticism that has been proven to be unfounded and recognized as so by all the professional medical associations.[197] Subjecting the procreative projects of same-sex couples to added hurdles – several thousand dollars, bureaucratic frustration, and emotional distress – also exacerbates inequality in familial goods.

To reduce this unfairness, many states extended the marital presumption to lesbian spouses. This reform was also constitutionally required. The marital presumption (or the consent-to-ART statutes) can establish a husband's paternity even if the spouses know he is not the biological father, sometimes over the objection of a known genetic father.[198] States discriminate based on sex if they deny the marital presumption to a nonbiological parent in a marriage of two females. A similar analysis requires parentage acknowledgments for lesbian couples in states that treat paternity acknowledgments as binding even when the parties know the signatory was not the genetic father. The only plausible reason to refuse to extend parentage acknowledgments which bind nonbiological fathers to a lesbian coparent is to support a dual-gender vision of parentage – a rationale that patently violates equal protection.

Does equal protection also require states to extend the marital presumption or parentage acknowledgments to gay male couples?[199] Doctrinally, this limit should survive constitutional review. The statutes do not involve facial discrimination.

194 The US Supreme Court has ducked the issue, for now. Fulton v. City of Philadelphia, 593 U.S. 522, 542 (2021).

195 Polikoff, *supra* note 176, at 526.

196 Two females can arrange IVF so that one is a genetic parent and the other a gestational parent, but they will more often use artificial insemination because it is vastly cheaper and more reliable.

197 Patterson, *supra* note 190; Charlotte J. Patterson, *Children of Lesbian and Gay Parents: Psychology, Law, and Policy*, 64 AM. PSYCHOLOGIST 727 (2009).

198 The marital presumption and consent-to-ART statutes are marriage benefits that cannot be denied same-sex couples without denying them an equal right to marry, following *Obergefell v. Hodges*, 576 U.S. 614 (2015), and *Pavan v. Smith*, 582 U.S. 563 (2017), but it is difficult to predict how courts will apply the right to marry after *Dobbs v. Jackson Women's Health Organization*, 597 U.S. 215 (2022). Accordingly, this analysis focuses not on the right to marry but on discrimination on the basis of sex and gender.

199 NeJaime, *supra* note 30, at 2344–45.

A parentage acknowledgment or marital presumption must begin with the gestational parent, which means they are denied to any mere genetic parents, whether they contributed sperm or eggs. That rule affects more males than females and more gay than straight couples, but a disparate impact alone does not trigger heightened constitutional scrutiny.[200] A challenger might argue that the statutory preference for gestational parents rests on gender stereotypes about natural motherhood,[201] but the rationale for a gestational presumption also offers well-tailored, compelling reasons to limit parentage acknowledgments or the marital presumption to gestational parents (4.III.C). Gestation and labor are taxing physical work, which the state treats as a proxy for prebirth commitment and, thus, presumed parenthood at birth – including authority to share parenthood. Mere genetic parents and nonbiological intended parents have no similar work to do during pregnancy that could justify immediate presumed parental authority.[202]

Although a parentage acknowledgment regime limited to gestational parents is constitutionally permissible, concern for equality may still lead states to allow genetic parents to initiate acknowledgments. A genetic parent who signs an acknowledgment has legally committed themselves to parenthood just as if they had filed a parentage petition, and so should be entrusted with parental authority like the gestational parent. Of course, these parentage acknowledgments implicate the rights of the gestational parent, so the law cannot allow a genetic parent to initiate an acknowledgement of parentage unless the gestational parent waives their parental liberty. A state may empower gestational parents to sign a waiver form to accompany the genetic-based parentage acknowledgment, but any at-birth waiver will raise concerns akin to surrogacy and adoption. Accordingly, a statute that authorizes genetic parents to initiate parentage acknowledgments should include whatever additional protections the community affords for gestational surrogacy, such as regulations during pregnancy, and for genetic surrogacy, such as waiting periods or recission rules (see III.E).

D *Sharing Parentage before Birth: Preconception Agreements*

The law should also empower parties to share parenthood before the birth or conception. All the pieces are in place to understand the role of prebirth agreements.

Many preconception agreements are not agreements in any deep sense that would require a new legal power; they rest on the liberties described in previous chapters. When a gestational parent and a genetic parent (male or female) conceive a plan to conceive a child through assisted reproduction, each has a conditional liberty to raise the child (3.III and 2.III). When they take joint custody, each incurs legal duties and completes their status as legal parents. So long as the second genetic parent

200 Washington v. Davis, 426 U.S. 229 (1976).

201 United States v. Virginia, 518 U.S. 515 (1996).

202 Baker, *supra* note 53, at 47–48.

waived their liberty to raise the child, neither the child nor any other adult has a legitimate objection to these two biological parents sharing parentage.

Perhaps surprisingly, this analysis renders some cases of three parents a humdrum affair. Nothing about the analysis changes if a genetic mother, genetic father, and gestational parent agree to conceive and raise a child together. All three should have a conditional liberty to raise the child. If the community has concluded that three adults can meet a child's right to a parent, the three biological parents should have parental rights and duties. This conclusion need not rely on a special normative power aside from the biological parents' conditional caregiving liberties. The hard cases, as illustrated by the case of Raymond, Samantha, and David, involve preconception agreements with an intended nonbiological parent.

1 Preconception Agreements from Consent to Artificial Insemination

Preconception agreements have a peculiar statutory origin in the consent-to-ART statutes. As explained in previous chapters, these statutes might rest on causal principles (3.I.B) or estoppel principles (4.II.B.3). When a husband induces his wife to conceive a child with donor gametes, or a wife induces her husband to develop parental attachments with a donor-conceived child, either spouse can be estopped from rebutting the marital presumption to protect the other's reasonable reliance.[203] However, these statutes do not simply protect reliance interests retrospectively. The husband obtains parental status at birth before he performs the caregiving that can develop relational attachments. These statutes give married couples the power to create parental rights and duties *prospectively*.

Admittedly, the statutory text aligns poorly with its power-conferring function. The statutes require consent only from the nonbiological parent, often making no mention of the birth mother's agreement. The only thing that the birth mother must do is conceive through assisted reproduction. Her choice to pursue artificial conception is not the type of arbitrary conduct typically used for a commissive act. Nevertheless, the statutes presuppose the wife's consent to share parenthood.[204] It would only make sense to say that a husband consents to his wife's artificial insemination if both spouses agreed upon a shared plan to raise the child together. Legislators likely did not think they needed to mention the wife's consent because dominant gender ideology imagines a responsible birth mother suing an

[203] Katherine Baker surmises that the husband's consent is necessary because the marital presumption changes the husband's parental rights and duties to the nonbiological child. Baker, *supra* note 188, at 171. While an intriguing moral argument, it is difficult to reconcile with the marital presumption law. A husband is a presumed father when his wife lies about contraception or conceives a child in a secret affair, which is equivalent to when she secretly used her husband or donor's sperm for artificial insemination.

[204] Courtney G. Joslin, *Protecting Children(?): Marriage, Gender, and Assisted Reproductive Technology*, 83 S. Cal. L. Rev. 1177, 1254–55 (2009).

irresponsible father, mostly ignoring mothers who do not raise their children or want to exclude responsible fathers.

Interpreted this way, consent-to-ART statutes have the same two legal effects as second-parent adoption and acknowledgment. They (1) confer a legal power on birth mothers who use ART to empower their spouse to become a parent regardless of biology and (2) treat the spouse's consent to assisted reproduction as a commitment to parental duties and rights.

2 Preconception Agreements Justified to Protect Equal Procreative Liberty

The same reasoning behind parentage acknowledgments can justify empowering spouses to share parenthood earlier in the assisted reproduction process. Regardless of parentage law, couples will form shared plans to conceive children with donor gametes. A shared procreative parenting project seems permissible, yet it threatens the spouses with subordination similar to coparenting.

Without a binding preconception agreement, each party remains at liberty to abandon the procreative parenting project during the pregnancy or the child's infancy. The nonbiological parent may decide they no longer want to raise a child, forcing the gestational parent to raise the child on her own. The gestational parent may decide they want to raise the child alone, denying their partner any opportunity to parent. Each party's ability to continue coparenting rests on the other's good will, so they can plan donor conception together only by accepting a relationship of subordination. That subordination will persist until they complete an adoption or acknowledgment, the statute of limitations for rebuttal passes, or the nonbiological parent establishes de facto parenthood.

Although both parties' ends are at risk, the subordination is asymmetrical. The gestational parent has a liberty right to parent based on gestational work (4.III.C) and, in some cases, genetic maternity (2.III). The biological parent's ability to pursue their chosen familial ends is at risk, but their legal liberty to parent is not. The nonbiological parent has no comparable legal liberty to parent. As Jessica Feinberg and Doug NeJaime have argued, this places nonbiological parents "at the mercy" of the gestational parent.[205] The biological parent can veto their parental status entirely. In the language of 1.I.B.3, the familial liberty of the nonbiological parent is subject to the biological parent's choice.

Of course, not all asymmetric authority is morally objectionable. Sometimes it is morally required, as it is partly in this case. Gestational parents must have unilateral authority over reproduction to respect their bodily integrity and reproductive liberty. Only they may decide whether to undergo ART and whether to share this project with their partner. Only they may decide whether to have an abortion or whether to have a Cesarean section. Nonbiological intended parents can only pursue

[205] Feinberg, *supra* note 59, at 1549; NeJaime, *supra* note 30, at 2320.

a procreative parenting project by accepting this subordinate position vis-à-vis the gestational parent.[206]

Nevertheless, the gestational parent's right to bodily integrity does not require inalienable and unilateral authority over a newborn. By empowering a gestational parent and their partner to commit to shared parenthood before conception, the law can enable couples to pursue procreative parenting through donor conception without subordination.[207] Either adult can change their mind about coresidential parenting, but they must still share parental rights and duties.

This coparenting commitment should be binding when the gestational parent becomes pregnant.[208] If the couple breaks up before insemination or implantation leads to pregnancy, then the subsequent fertility treatments are unilateral and not part of a shared procreative parenting project. The gestational parent's ex-partner has no duty or liberty to raise the child.[209] If a couple breaks up after insemination or implantation, the nonbiological intended parent should have a duty to support the gestational parent who undertook this procreative parenting project in reliance on them. The nonbiological parent also has a political duty of support as a causal parent (3.II.A.4).[210] They should also have the liberty to parent vis-à-vis the gestational parent, which is how the agreement rectifies the subordination of nonbiological parents in shared procreative plans.

That parental liberty must also be consistent with the child's right to a parent. Unlike the gestational parent, the nonbiological intended parent has no "natural" way to demonstrate commitment during pregnancy that justifies presumed parentage at birth. When the couple breaks up before the birth, the nonbiological intended parent occupies much the same position as a mere genetic father. States could insist that the nonbiological parent's liberty remain conditional, demanding proof of the commitment through court petitions. However, as we saw in III.B and III.C, the law has other artificial powers. If the preconception agreement is a binding legal commitment to enforceable

206 *See In re* Matter of M.F., 312 Kan. 322, 351 (2020) (explaining parentage agreement must be consistent with gestational parent's state constitutional right to decide whether to take the pregnancy to term). In light of *Dobbs v. Jackson Women's Health*, 597 U.S. 215 (2022), the reasoning of *In re Matter of* M. F. would no longer apply as a matter of federal constitutional law.

207 Joslin's accounts of consent-to-ART statutes relies on appeal to the moral significance of procreation. Joslin, *supra* note 204 ("bringing a child into the world is a profound action"). In contrast, this account need only appeal to the mutual reliance of the parties for the long-term commitment, which will in turn facilitate child welfare.

208 This timing conclusion fits UPA 2017 § 707(a), but is contrary to dicta in some cases. In a postbirth disagreement, the Kansas Supreme Court directed lower courts to focus on whether "each individual [has] made up her mind as of the time of the baby's arrival" because "the crystallization of the parties' individual intents at the time the child enters the world configures the family." *In re Matter of* M.F., 312 Kan. at 352. It explained that concern for stability justified focusing on the intentions at birth rather than subsequent parenting, but the court did not appear to consider whether a family might be configured earlier. Cases that reach the court only after months or years of coparenting should be straightforward custody disputes. *In re* Marriage of Dee J. & Ashlie J., 103 N.E.3d 627, 629 (Ill. App. Ct. 2018) (seven months of caregiving was sufficient).

209 As before, I am setting aside questions about embryo disposition.

210 Shultz, *supra* note 84, at 324 (emphasizing protection of ability to plan for future based on reciprocal expectations).

duties, it satisfies the child's condition on parental rights, so the law should treat the nonbiological intended parent as a presumed parent with a right to shared custody.

This theory justifies two doctrinal expansions. Preconception agreements should not be limited to married couples. The moral asymmetry created by a donor-conceived parenting project is the same regardless of the parents' marital status.[211] States might argue that marriage evinces the spouses' shared intent, but the law can require written agreements to dispel any uncertainty about the shared coparenting plan (or clear and convincing evidence of an oral agreement).[212] The states might also argue that marital commitments increase familial stability or resources, but the law does not require biological coparents to marry, although it would bring the same benefits. States have no sound public reasons to deny nonmarital couples the power to enter preconception agreements.[213] Furthermore, no legitimate reasons justify limiting preconception agreements to romantic partners.[214] The law should stop imagining donor conception as a medical substitute for sexual procreation, which would not ground parenthood in any case. Platonic friends may establish a family by developing a plan to conceive and raise a child together.[215]

The law must limit preconception agreements in ways similar to parentage acknowledgments and adoption to ensure they respect the rights of the child and other adults. States must, for example, limit the number of parties who can sign preconception agreements and void provisions purporting to create tailored parenthood. Perhaps most importantly, any other biological or presumed parent must waive their reproductive and parental liberties. Consequently, equal liberty principles do not entail states must expand preconception agreements to gay male couples. A preconception agreement between a mere genetic parent (male or female) and a nonbiological intended parent implicates the rights of the gestational parent in ways that must be handled through surrogacy law.

E *Arranging Parentage before Birth: Surrogacy*

Surrogacy agreements raise similar problems of asymmetric authority. Commissioning parents plan to form their own family with the child, not to coparent with the gestational parent. They share gametes with her only because she agrees to help them form a family by waiving her parental liberty.[216] If a gestational parent may

211 Jessica Feinberg, *Parent Zero*, 55 U.C. Davis L. Rev. 2271, 2310–11 (2021) (arguing a mutual intent theory of marital preconception agreements statues would extend to nonmarital agreements).

212 Joslin, *supra* note 204, at 1226.

213 L.F. v. Breit, 736 S.E.2d 711, 721–22 (Va. 2013).

214 Feinberg, *supra* note 22, at 824; Storrow, *supra* note 22, at 336–48; Joslin, *supra* note 204, at 1225.

215 Randy Frances Kandel, *Which Came First: The Mother or the Egg? A Kinship Solution to Gestational Surrogacy*, 47 Rutgers L. Rev. 165 (1994).

216 P.M. v. T.B., 907 N.W.2d 522, 537 (Iowa 2018) ("The Ms would not have entrusted their embryos fertilized with P.M.'s sperm to T.B. if they thought she would attempt to raise the resulting child herself.").

change her mind and raise the child, she can use the commissioning parents to pursue her ends. She can force the genetic parent to share parenthood with her and prevent the nonbiological intended parent from becoming a parent through a parentage acknowledgment or adoption.[217] As NeJaime argues, commissioning parents are "at the mercy" of the gestational parent.[218] Of course, a gestational parent is also at the mercy of the commissioning parents, who might later refuse to help her with the pregnancy or deny their responsibility for the child. Binding surrogacy agreements can avoid this subordination.[219]

However, some ethicists argue that the surrogacy project to create a child for others to raise disrespects the child and the surrogate. Such objections often rely on Kant's formula of humanity, which commands us to treat others as ends in themselves, not as mere means to our ends. The parties to a surrogacy agreement create a child to meet the commissioning party's desire to parent and the surrogate's financial needs, which one might argue treats the future child more like an object than a future person.[220] Similarly, others may argue that commissioning parties treat surrogates as objects whose primary value lies in being a means to provide a child.[221] Both objections are unsound as a matter of personal and political morality. The mistake is easier to see among adults, so I will start there.

1 Consistent with Equal Respect for the Surrogate

I begin by explaining why the "use" objection does not apply to surrogacy as a matter of personal morality (i.e., Kant's Doctrine of Virtue), before turning to the legal requirements necessary to maintain political respect for surrogates. The mistakes in both objections are easiest to see if one compares surrogacy to employment.

[217] Feinberg, *supra* note 59, at 1549.

[218] NeJaime, *supra* note 30, at 2320.

[219] One might argue that surrogacy agreements should be binding to protect commissioning parents from harm. They yearn to be parents, and their expectations build throughout the pregnancy, which makes it traumatic if a gestational parent changes their mind. However, this experience seems identical to all prospective infant adoptions, and the harm to prospective adoptive parents does not justify forcing birth parents to complete adoption. I suspect the intuitions about harm in surrogacy cases reflect nonwelfarist expectations based on rights grounded in agreements, causation, and gestation. Moreover, if the goal is to reduce harm, this argument adopts the wrong temporal perspective. While dramatic breakdowns have rhetorical force, welfarists should adopt an ex ante approach that considers the parties' transaction costs ex ante, recognizing that stricter legal enforcement will affect how often parties enter the contracts, their terms, and the parties' expectations.

[220] H. T. Krimmel, *Surrogate Mother Arrangements from the Perspective of the Child*, 9 Logos 97 (1988).

[221] Patrone argues the gestational surrogate violates her duty of self-respect by using her embodied agency as a mere means to financial gain, in the same way that a person denies their own dignity through prostitution or (for Kant) any nonmarital sexual activity. Tatiana Patrone, *Is Paid Surrogacy a Form of Reproductive Prostitution? A Kantian Perspective*, 27 Cambridge Q. Healthcare Ethics 109 (2018). I reject Kant's arguments that anyone who engages in sex for pleasure or payment fails to respect themselves as a rational being because I see no difference between those maxims and the maxims of anyone willing to engage in any physical activity for pleasure or payment.

An employer uses employees to pursue the employer's projects. Fortunately, the Formula of Humanity does not prohibit us from treating others as a means, only treating them as a *mere* means.[222] According to one interpretation, this imperative requires the agent to act only on principles others could accept as rational agents with their own ends.[223] According to another, an agent must act only on principles that treat others as if they had absolute worth rather than only relative worth contingent on the agent's own ends.[224] To avoid running afoul of this principle, an employer must commit to obtaining their employee's consent; to not exploiting background conditions to obtain unfair terms; to not exercising their ongoing authority to overbear the employee's will; and to limiting their directives to leave the employee room to form and pursue their own ends. An employer committed to these limits treats their employee as an agent with value of their own, rather than an object with value only insofar as the employee serves the employer's ends. The employee can accept the employer's intention to use them in this way while still regarding themselves as a rational agent pursuing their own ends through the employment relationship, as opposed to being coerced, exploited, dominated, or manipulated to serve their employer's ends.

Some job categories have relational dynamics that increase the moral risk, such as domestic employees like nannies or nurses. Domination is more likely when employees live at their place of work. The employees' relative economic disadvantage also increases the risk of exploitative terms. When there are familial attachments, manipulation is more likely. An employer may use a nanny's concern for the child to co-opt the nanny's ability to live their own life. Some jobs also cross ordinary norms about bodily autonomy and privacy. A nurse, for instance, must avoid taking advantage of their access to the patient's body, and the patient must avoid asking the nurse to perform services inconsistent with the nurse's sense of bodily autonomy or integrity. Despite these risks, few people suspect employers always treat nannies or nurses as mere means.[225]

If they abide by similar limits, commissioning parents need not treat surrogates as a mere means. They must avoid exploiting the surrogate's financial disadvantage to obtain consent or negotiate unfair terms. That requires walking a fine line, especially in international surrogacy. Commissioning parents must also manage the ongoing relationship. They must avoid manipulating the surrogate by taking advantage of her

[222] Immanuel Kant, *Groundwork of the Metaphysics of Morals*, *in* Practical Philosophy, AK 4:428–31 (Mary J. Gregor ed., 1999).

[223] Samuel Kerstein, *Treating Persons as Means*, *in* The Stanford Encyclopedia of Philosophy (Edward N. Zalta ed., 2019), https://plato.stanford.edu/archives/sum2019/entries/persons-means/ (last visited Apr. 19, 2022).

[224] Patrone, *supra* note 221, at 117.

[225] Stephen Wilkinson, Bodies for Sale: Ethics and Exploitation in the Human Body Trade 176–77 (2004). One might worry that the surrogacy relationship is psychologically likely to lead commissioning parents into disrespectful treatment, which Wilkinson calls the "displacement thesis." *Id.* at 39–40. I doubt any tight empirical connection between surrogacy and disrespectful attitudes, and I also reject the normative premise that a liberal state may legitimately regulate to ensure respect in this sense.

concern for the fetus, for them as intended parents, or for her "contractual" duties. As Rachel Rebouché explains, the risk of manipulation is high because agencies, lawyers, and prenatal counselors align with the interests of commissioning parents.[226] Furthermore, all parties must manage their expectations for ongoing relationships. Surrogacy can generate feelings of intimacy that lead parties to form familial expectations, some of which they may not plan to fulfill or may be unlikely to sustain. Some surrogates develop deep personal ties with the commissioning parents and expect their connection to persist, feeling used when they cut ties after the birth.[227] Surrogacy relationships are a moral minefield, but commissioning parents can navigate it in ways that exhibit due regard for surrogates as agents with their own ends.

Of course, as I argued in Chapter 1, personal respect is insufficient for political respect. Elizabeth Anderson aptly describes the domination created by modern employment.[228] Employers wield indefinite and open-ended authority to direct their employees' actions during a large portion of their lives. Employers' discretion to dismiss at-will employees for any (nondiscriminatory) reason expands their de facto authority to encompass employees' private lives. An employee can be fired for how they spend their leisure time. Even if a virtuous employer intends never to wield this authority improperly, the employee's liberty remains subject to the employer's choice. An employee can escape this domination by quitting, but since employment is the primary mechanism for distributing primary goods in liberal societies, most citizens can escape the authority of one employer only by submitting to another. Anderson surmises that the only way (if that) to reconcile liberal employment with egalitarian commitments is through comprehensive labor regulations with unemployment benefits, worker safety protections, collective bargaining, and employee representation on corporate boards.

Surrogacy raises all the typical concerns of employment that justify a regulatory approach, plus some idiosyncratic ones.[229] First, the law must police surrogacy relations to ensure meaningful consent. States can facilitate informed ex ante consent with mandatory disclosures, psychological counseling, and independent legal counseling. If pregnancy is a transformative experience that one cannot understand beforehand, then informed consent also requires limiting surrogacy to people who have already carried a child, as most statutes do.[230] The state may need other legal mechanisms to reduce exploitation, such as price regulations and unconscionability doctrines.[231] Moreover, a pregnant surrogate cannot simply walk

226 Rebouché, *supra* note 71.

227 Pamela Laufer-Ukeles, *Mothering for Money: Regulating Commercial Intimacy*, 88 Ind. L.J. 1223, 1233 (2013).

228 Elizabeth Anderson, Private Government: How Employers Rule Our Lives (and Why We Don't Talk about It) (2017).

229 Laufer-Ukeles, *supra* note 227, at 1250–56.

230 Wilkinson, *supra* note 225, at 167–69.

231 Yehezkel Margalit, *In Defense of Surrogacy Agreements: A Modern Contract Law Perspective*, 20 Wm. & Mary J. Women & L. 423, 449–50, 463–65 (2013). I agree with many of Margalit's prescriptions, but

away from this employment, not without the physical and emotional risk of abortion, so ensuring ongoing consent is even more difficult.[232]

Second, like all risky work, surrogacy must be regulated to reduce the risk of harm to surrogates. Pregnancy carries ineliminable risk, particularly in the United States. Nevertheless, the maternal mortality rate (32.9 per 100,000)[233] is lower than loggers (91.7), roofers (47), and garbage collectors (33.1).[234] Even normal pregnancy alters the pregnant person's body, but many forms of physical and repetitive employment wear on employees' bodies in ways that liberal-egalitarian societies treat as permissible, at least when workers have public or private insurance. Whether these risks justify prohibition or regulation depends on empirical and normative assessments of the relative risks. States with surrogacy statutes have chosen to manage this risk by require commissioning parents to maintain insurance for the surrogate and their family.

States must also constrain commissioning parents' authority over the surrogates' medical decisions to ensure their bodily integrity. Surrogates must have a *legal* and *effective* right to control medical decisions, including whether to abort, how to give birth, and who will be their provider. States must prohibit contracts that give intended parents legal authority over these matters. However, prohibiting these provisions is likely insufficient for reasons that Rebouché notes.[235] Savvy repeat players like lawyers or agencies lay the groundwork for self-help enforcement. They draft contracts with unenforceable terms to obtain compliance from parties with less legal knowledge. They use negotiation to create relationships and forge expectations that parties feel bound to honor. Agencies also build relationships with medical providers that create a conflict of interest, enabling them to influence medical decisions.[236] The same tools of relational contracting that promote cooperation can also circumvent laws designed to protect vulnerable parties. Perhaps the appropriate response is direct ongoing regulation of the relationship, such as through a licensing body that could enforce a professional ethics code for surrogacy.[237]

The state must also determine whether lifestyle provisions are permissible and how they will be enforced. Anderson argues that the law must prevent employers

the extent of regulation necessary to reconcile surrogacy with respect makes employment a better analogy.

232 Laufer-Ukeles, *supra* note 227, at 1236.

233 Jennifer Mubell, *What's Behind the Spike in U.S. Maternal Mortality*, AM. MED. ASS'N (May 25, 2023), www.ama-assn.org/delivering-care/population-care/what-s-behind-spike-us-maternal-mortality (last visited Jan. 29, 2024).

234 Madison Hoff, *The 14 Deadliest Jobs in America*, BUS. INSIDER, www.businessinsider.com/deadliest-jobs-in-america-bls-2022-12 (last visited Jan. 29, 2024).

235 Rebouché, *supra* note 71, at 1632–35.

236 Pamela Laufer-Ukeles, *The Disembodied Womb: Pregnancy, Informed Consent, and Surrogate Motherhood*, 43 N.C. J. INT'L L. 96, 132–36, 144–45 (2018).

237 Liezl Van Zyl & Ruth Walker, *Beyond Altruistic and Commercial Contract Motherhood: The Professional Model*, 27 BIOETHICS 373 (2013).

from leveraging their legitimate authority to control employees' lives outside work, but the work–life line is fuzzy when the work is pregnancy. Lifestyle provisions often regulate behaviors affecting fetal health, such as substance abuse, air travel, diet, exercise, or bed rest. Surrogacy contracts also include provisions about postbirth behavior, such as contact, handling the child, or breastfeeding.[238] Some of these provisions attempt to address agency problems, on the assumption that a surrogate who plans not to parent has weaker intrinsic incentives to incur burdens that facilitate optimal fetal development. As Hilary Berk explains, others are "emotion work" designed to manage the parties' relationships with one another and the child to help ensure a successful surrogacy.[239]

It is difficult to imagine acceptable remedies for lifestyle provisions. Injunctive relief raises typical servitude objections to specific performance in service contracts. A surrogacy agreement might instead specify liquidated damages.[240] By analogy, the NFL and MLB collective bargaining agreements allow football and baseball teams to include player "bonuses" for workouts, diet, weight loss, and substance abuse.[241] However, a state may refuse to permit deductions or awards for lifestyle provisions in a surrogacy contract because the specified payments suggest the child's value to the intended parents depends on their qualities. Even if these provisions are unenforceable, savvy lawyers and intended parents with social power will include them to control and manage emotions in ways that redefine the social norms of parenthood.[242]

Another set of questions surrounds the social and economic preconditions for rightful surrogacy markets. Some feminists worry that women enter surrogacy arrangements primarily because women lack adequate alternative opportunities to obtain primary goods for themselves or their families due to sex discrimination in law, markets, caregiving, and education. In that context, an open surrogacy market may further entrench gender injustice by reinforcing social norms that treat women as valuable primarily for procreation. A liberal state may choose to deny the force of law to surrogacy contracts that exist because of and contribute to gender injustice, just as it may prohibit prostitution because this work is performed primarily by women due to gender oppression and contributes to persistent gender inequality.[243] On the other hand, surrogacy is a rare practice with a small cultural impact in

[238] Berk, *supra* note 70, at 162–71.

[239] Berk, *supra* note 70.

[240] Rebouché, *supra* note 71, at 1620–23.

[241] Ahiza Garcia, *The Weird Rules in the Fine Print of Sports*, CNN Bus. (2017), https://money.cnn.com/2017/06/30/news/companies/contracts-nba-nfl-mlb-terms-cba/index.html (last visited Apr. 25, 2023).

[242] Berk, *supra* note 70, at 171–74.

[243] Christie Hartley & Lori Watson, Equal Citizenship and Public Reason: A Feminist Political Liberalism (2018). Wilkinson is skeptical of "moral climate" arguments because it is not "moral rocket science" to distinguish respectful forms of regulated surrogacy from disrespectful types of objectification. Wilkinson, *supra* note 225, at 179–81. Consensual encounters are not wrongful, so critics must show surrogates cannot genuinely consent because they were coerced actively or "omissively," by which he means an actor with a duty to help the surrogate conditioned help on

a society that tolerates pervasively gendered social roles. Banning surrogacy removes an employment opportunity for the least advantaged women, for whom surrogacy is a rational economic decision that can be explained without appeal to manipulation or influence.[244] Moreover, the sociological evidence suggests that, in domestic surrogacy in wealthy countries, the surrogate mothers tend not to be poor, uneducated, or from racialized minorities.[245] Perhaps the community should allow potential surrogates to make their own choices.

Reasonable people may come down on either side of this debate. A liberal state may conclude that surrogacy, subject to significant regulation, is consistent with respect for the surrogate and gender equality.

2 Consistent with the Equal Respect for the Child

Despite its intuitive appeal, the "baby selling" objection to surrogacy is difficult to articulate as a valid argument. Commissioning parents and surrogates have a shared plan with two fundamental aspects: (1) create a child and (2) arrange for the commissioning parents to raise the child. Neither is inconsistent with treating the child as a person or equal citizen.

I begin with the second aspect. Surrogacy critics are correct that the state cannot recognize any agreements to sell parental rights.[246] No private person ever has the power to transfer parental rights because no one may wield authority over a child's life without parental duties. Any purported transfer undermines the premise of rightful parental authority. Furthermore, once someone has a duty to parent the child, they violate their duty by "waiving" their parental rights (even if the state must allow them to do so to protect the child). If they resign their parental right to benefit

something she did not want. *Id.* at 173; Stephen Wilkinson, *Exploitation in International Paid Surrogacy Arrangements*, 33 J. APP. PHIL. 125 (2016) (similarly arguing international surrogacy is exploitative only if surrogates lack adequate opportunities because of "acts or omissions of governments"). Wilkinson's argument seems to assume that liberal states may prohibit surrogacy contracts only if they wrong surrogates, but this assumption reduces distributive justice to relational wrongdoing. A liberal-egalitarian state may regulate a category of activities to prevent exploitation, even if some instances of that activity are consensual, respectful, and beneficial to the parties. A social world saturated with racialized associations, pornographic imagery, or surrogacy contracts may affect default attitudes that people bring to interactions in ways that undermine the social basis of self-respect.

244 Kimberly D. Krawiec, *Altruism and Intermediation in the Market for Babies*, 66 WASH. & LEE L. REV. 203 (2009).

245 Laufer-Ukeles, *supra* note 227, at 1234–35.

246 Some courts and scholars try to skirt the baby-selling objection by arguing "payment is owed not for the baby itself, but for the provision of gestational service together with the transfer of" parental rights. Cécile Fabre, *Surrogacy*, *in* THE INTERNATIONAL ENCYCLOPEDIA OF ETHICS 1 (2020). P.M. v. T.B., 907 N.W.2d 522, 536 (Iowa 2018). This move begs the question. Since parenthood is the only permissible basis for custodial authority of a child, payment for parental rights (along with gestational services) is the only thing that "selling a baby" could be.

the recipient, they also violate their fiduciary duty to act in the child's interest. That fiduciary violation would be particularly egregious if done for payment.

However, none of these objections apply to surrogacy. The gestational parent has no duty to raise the child. Their duty as a causal parent is to ensure the child has adequate caregivers, which they fulfill if they reasonably believe the commissioning parents will provide adequate care. Moreover, most surrogacy cases involve no transfer of parental rights.[247] When one commissioning parent is the sperm or egg donor, as is the case in most surrogacy, the mere genetic parent has a conditional liberty to parent the child. The surrogate simply waives her parental liberty and leaves the genetic parent to raise the child. Once the genetic parent accepts parental duties, they become a full parent and should have the power to share parenthood with their partner, the nonbiological commissioning parent (III.D). In a gestational surrogacy arrangement, all the adults are acting within the scope of duties and privileges described already.

What about the first aspect of the agreement? Many ethicists suspect that creating a child for someone else to raise violates the child's dignity as a person, especially if the arrangement involves payment. Chapters 2 and 3 already rejected arguments that adults fail to respect their biological children if they place them for adoption. Might adults disrespect a child by creating the child for the adult's *benefit*?

The commissioning parent(s) plan to create a child to fulfill their desire to experience parenthood.[248] If this desire renders the plan wrongful, then most procreators wrong their children, including heterosexual couples who deliberately conceive through sex. Fortunately, the Formula of Humanity does not prohibit a parent from acting on self-regarding motives, so long as their maxim also treats the child at the same time as an end in themselves.[249] Parents would violate this

[247] Some ethicists argue surrogacy contracts involve no transfer of parental rights *because* they are services contracts. For example, Hanna argues that when a surrogate sells gestational services, the gestational work that would generate parental interests for her instead generates parental interests for the commissioning parents, "in the same way that my employer acquires rights over the products of my labor by paying for my services." Jason Hanna, *Revisiting Child-Based Objections to Commercial Surrogacy*, 24 BIOETHICS 341, 343–45 (2010). *See also* R. Jo Kornegy, *Is Commercial Surrogacy Baby-selling?*, 7 J. APP. PHIL. (1990); WILKINSON, *supra* note 225, at 149; MILLUM, *supra* note 129, at 34. The gestational parent is more like an employee who produces an object they never own than an artisan a contractor who produces an object that they own and then sell. The argument assumes a principle, rejected in 4.II.B.2, that the work of gestation to produce a child generates interests that can justify parental rights in the same way a person can acquire property rights by creating an object. Gestational parents have a conditional liberty to parent because they invested in a procreative parenting project. In any case, an individual cannot transfer their interest in the parenting project. The very idea of transferring interests is incoherent. Nor can an individual transfer the juridical right that protects their interest in parenting. An individual can maintain their conditional liberty to parent only if they accept full parental duties.

[248] Adeline A. Allen, *Surrogacy and Limitations to Freedom of Contract: Toward Being More Fully Human*, 41 HARV. J.L. & PUB. POL'Y 753, 804 (2018) (arguing "surrogacy serves only the commissioning parents").

[249] Stuart Oultram, *Does the Baby-Selling Objection to Commercial Surrogacy Misuse Immanuel Kant?*, *in* ARGUMENTS AND ANALYSIS IN BIOETHICS 177 (Matti Häyry et al. eds., 2010).

imperative if, for example, they procreate because they want a living doll for their amusement. Fortunately, this attitude is rare. Most procreators, including commissioning parents, want to experience parenthood *by* fulfilling their child's needs. That maxim treats children as ends in themselves, even if parenting is simultaneously good for the adult.[250]

Most surrogates act on a similar maxim. The altruistic surrogate plans to conceive a child to help the commissioning parents form a family. She uses the child to benefit the intended parents, but she plans to help the commissioning parents by enabling them to meet the child's needs. Paid surrogates also intend to benefit themselves and their family financially. Financial motives do not align as neatly with the child's well-being, but money and care are not exclusive. Our maxims are often overdetermined. Nannies and teachers can accept their position for wages without treating children as mere means, so long as they also commit to acting in the child's interests. The same can be true of a surrogate. A surrogate with financial motives does not treat the future child as a mere means so long as she also wills to act in ways consistent with the child's well-being.

Critics of surrogacy may suspect this psychological picture is unrealistic. Perhaps financial motivations increase the likelihood that surrogates will take subtle risks that reflect inadequate regard for the future child's interests. Perhaps openly commercial surrogacy markets encourage these careless attitudes, leading to slightly worse outcomes on average. Even if not technically inconsistent, financial motives might crowd out other-regarding motives.

These objections rely on speculation about the relative efficacy of economic, biological, social, legal, and moral incentives. Legislatures must investigate those empirical premises, but I doubt the instrumental argument is sound. Literature reviews suggest that children born through surrogacy have satisfactory perinatal outcomes and normal child psychological development.[251] Sociological literature also casts doubt on the underlying cynicism about the gestational parent's incentives.[252] It This objection also conflicts with the other typical objection to surrogacy that surrogates need protection because they underestimate their attachment to the fetus. Last, Kim Krawiec argues that if criticism of surrogacy rests on this sociological worry that commercial markets will distort our attitudes toward children, then we should also prohibit payments to intermediaries in these markets, like sperm banks and adoption agencies – yet no one is clamoring for those limits.[253]

250 Not all procreative plans are permissible simply because the parents cherish the child. For example, adults who pursue designer babies presuppose a child's value is contingent on traits like their beauty or musical abilities. No child may accept, consistent with self-respect, these parents' maxim that they deserve care only insofar as they have certain traits valued by their parents.

251 Viveca Söderström-Anttila et al., *Surrogacy: Outcomes for Surrogate Mothers, Children and the Resulting Families – a Systematic Review*, 22 Hum. Reprod. Update 260 (2016).

252 Laufer-Ukeles, *supra* note 227, at 1231, 1236–37.

253 Krawiec, *supra* note 244.

Assuming states will at least permit altruistic surrogacy, I see no convincing reason not to treat the prebirth gestational surrogacy commitments as presumptively binding. Some argue that the child is harmed because they lose a relationship with their gestational parent. These harms cannot justify duties for the same reason as genetic harms in Chapter 2. There is no way to explain how the child is harmed without raising nonidentity problems and presupposing nonpublic biological values. If requiring adoption has benefits for the child, it must be because adoption procedures improve parenting quality. I have already rejected similar arguments for parentage acknowledgments. A genetic commissioning parent is entitled to legal parenthood regardless, so this individual can choose whether to cohabit with their partner or pursue second-parent adoption. Rejecting prebirth parenthood merely increases the uncertainty and instability until adoption is complete or the residential presumption attaches.[254]

Furthermore, as Feinberg and NeJaime contend, differential treatment of gestational and genetic parents has expressive meaning. Many states allow (as they should) gestational parents to share parenthood with their partners without public screening through preconception agreements, parentage acknowledgments, or the marital presumption. These states only screen the partners of mere genetic parents. There are no legitimate reasons to doubt the partners of a genetic parent categorically. When one commissioning parent has a genetic tie to the child, demanding that their partner complete adoption burdens the family for little benefit, disrespects the judgment of the genetic parent, and slights the nonbiological parent's ability to commit to parenthood. These are sound public reasons to treat gestational surrogacy agreements as binding when one commissioning parent is a genetic parent.

These arguments do not apply when intended parents commission a surrogate to use egg *and* sperm donors. When the commissioning parents have no liberty to raise this child based on genetics or gestation, they are in an identical position to adoptive parents, subject to the same reasons for screening (III.B.2.a). Advocates may argue that intended parents demonstrate commitment by completing the difficult and expensive surrogacy process, but the same could be said of adults who persevere through infant adoption. Moreover, focusing on commitment puts the cart before the horse. Commissioning parents have a claim to *some* legal tool for nonbiological parenthood, but they are still missing a basis for the liberty to raise *this* child. They cannot claim parental liberties simply because they created the child (2.II.C). Nor can they receive this authority from the biological parents. Gamete donors and gestational parents can waive parental rights but have no authority to assign parenthood to a third party without public oversight (III.B.2.b).

States have legitimate reasons to treat commissioning couples who lack any biological tie to the future child differently. That does not mean the law must adopt this position. Their joint plans involve similar risks of subordination. The

[254] *In re* Paternity of F.T.R., 833 N.W.2d 634, 649–50 (2013); Feinberg, *supra* note 59.

commissioning parents purchased donor embryos to start their own family, which they shared with the surrogate only because she agreed to help them start their family. The surrogate accepted the embryo only because the commissioning parents planned to parent the child. A law could recognize this agreement as binding if the community judges that screening is unnecessary to protect children's right to a parent. If it does, the law must also reconsider its justifications for screening in all infant adoption cases.

CONCLUSION

No one has personal authority to decide who will raise a child. The power to transfer, share, or arrange parentage cannot be justified by the morality of intentions, promises, or contracts. Nevertheless, similar legal powers can be justified from a political perspective. Child-rearing is a primary good valued by many reasonable citizens, and the parental office is part of the basic structure of the political community. All citizens have a right to fair equality of opportunity for parenthood. The community must create legal mechanisms to empower nonbiological parents to pursue parenthood in ways that respect the child's right to a parent and the parental liberty of genetic and gestational parents. Existing parentage agreement law, with interstitial reform, can meet this challenge. Adoption law empowers nonbiological parents to volunteer to raise a child without parents. A gestational parent can also agree to share parenthood through second-parent adoption, voluntary acknowledgments of parentage, or preconception agreements. Finally, the states may reasonably decide to allow a genetic parent, a surrogate, and a nonbiological intended parent to arrange parentage before conception through surrogacy.

6

Parentage Conflicts

Recall the introductory case of Pamela, Eric, Richard, and Alicia. After raising Alicia for fifteen years, Eric discovered that his wife Pamela had conceived Alicia in an affair with her business partner Richard. Eric divorced Pamela and sued Richard for child support. This conflict was one of many occasioned in the last fifty years by the decline of the marital presumption, the rise of genetic paternity, and the expanding number of parentage rules. Yet, American law has not developed a satisfying theory to reconcile cases where parentage rules conflict.

Federal courts have eschewed any effort to resolve conflicting constitutional parentage rights since the Supreme Court's fractured decision about genetic and marital fathers in *Micheal H.*[1] A few states adopted priority rankings for a subset of parentage rules, primarily between marital and genetic parents. A few doctrines align certain grounds, such as the rules for adoption or acknowledgments that require the consent of the birth parents. However, no states have settled the relationship among all their rules, and many, including those that have adopted the UPA 2017, have few priority rules at all. When the inevitable conflicts arise, many statutes direct family courts to choose which parentage rule should apply on a case-by-case basis, considering all the underlying policy concerns. Recent reform efforts would require judges to instead decide which putative parent will best serve the child's interests. Both conflict rules invite a family court judge to rely on empirical speculation and their vision of valuable families.

An alternative approach unfolded over the last four chapters. Each ground of parentage – genetics, causation, caregiving, and agreements – has a justified but limited function in the assignment of political parenthood. After Section I reviews existing law for conflicting parentage claims, Section II concludes the book by reconstructing parentage law based on the lessons of Chapters 2 through 5. By reassembling these pieces, a pluralist theory of parentage law can offer a just and ordered set of rules for handling parentage conflicts with little resort to ad hoc and unguided judicial discretion.

[1] Michael H. v. Gerlad D., 491 U.S. 110 (1989).

I EXISTING LAW ON CONFLICTING PARENTAGE PRESUMPTIONS

American states use three approaches to adjudicate competing parentage claims: (1) categorical rankings among the presumptions, (2) ad hoc application of the principles underlying the presumptions, and (3) a best interests of the child standard. The first two regimes stem from the same provision in the 1973 Uniform Parentage Act. Under § 4(b), if multiple presumed fathers assert competing claims in a timely fashion, "the presumption which on the facts is founded on the weightier considerations of policy and logic controls."[2]

As interpreted by one group of courts, this provision requires judges to articulate categorical rankings among parentage rules. This interpretation fits the legislative history. The drafters borrowed the final preposition ("founded on weightier considerations of policy and logic") from the rule for competing evidentiary presumptions in the 1953 Uniform Rules of Evidence. Commentary explains that when evidentiary presumptions conflict, the court should apply whichever reflects the "preponderance of public policy." If the underlying policies are equally important, the court should appeal directly to first principles.[3] Applying a similar methodology to parentage conflicts, some state courts created categorical rankings of the statutory rules.

A handful retain a strong marital presumption.[4] The Alabama Supreme Court held that children's need for "psychological stability" outweighs the interest of genetic fathers in a relationship, "so that as long as the husband persists in his parental roles, the marital presumption is conclusive."[5] The court extended similar reasoning to nonmarital parents, ruling that genetic evidence should not be admitted to rebut the residential presumption.[6] Other courts chose the opposite categorical ranking. The Tennessee Supreme Court concluded that a proven genetic father has full statutory parental rights, which a presumed father cannot abrogate.[7] Still others treat spouses and cohabitants differently. The Wyoming Supreme Court held that genetics always trumps the holding out presumption, but the marital presumption should trump genetics if it preserves an established familial relationship that serves the child's interests.[8]

2 UPA 1973 § 4(b).

3 Rule 15, 62 HANDBOOK OF THE NATIONAL CONFERENCE OF COMMISSIONERS ON UNIFORM STATE LAWS AND PROCEEDINGS OF THE ANNUAL CONFERENCE MEETING 173 (1953); Rule 301(b), *Presumptions*, 83 HANDBOOK OF THE NATIONAL CONFERENCE OF COMMISSIONERS ON UNIFORM STATE LAWS AND PROCEEDINGS OF THE ANNUAL CONFERENCE MEETING 918 (1974). *See Conflicting Presumptions*, 1 FEDERAL EVIDENCE § 3:12 (4th ed. 2023).

4 Jessica Feinberg, *Restructuring Rebuttal of the Marital Presumption for the Modern Era*, 104 MINN. L. REV. 243 (2019) (identifying six statutes that deny standing to genetic parents).

5 R.D. v. S.S., 309 So. 3d 146, 155 (Ala. Civ. App. 2020). *See ex parte* C.A.P., 683 So. 2d 1010, 1012 (Ala. 1996).

6 *Ex parte* T.J., 89 So. 3d 744, 747 (Ala. 2012).

7 *In re* T.K.Y., 205 S.W.3d 343, 352 (Tenn. 2006).

8 TL *ex rel.* TL v. CS, 975 P.2d 1065, 1068 (Wyo. 1999). Wyoming subsequently adopted the UPA 2002, which its supreme court has interpreted to effectively adopt a conclusive presumption for biological parentage even against marital fathers. Matter of Paternity of AAAE, 471 P.3d 990, 996 (Wyo. 2020)

When interpreted as an invitation to develop categorial rankings, § 4(b) allows each state to choose its own family policies, while still offering determinacy and predictability within each state. However, it is unclear whether state legislatures expected to empower appellate judges to declare their state's family policy. A few legislatures took it upon themselves to rank some presumptions in their statutes. In Nevada and Missouri, genetic evidence creates a "conclusive presumption."[9] No statutes provide a complete ranking of parentage rules. When unranked presumptions conflict, these statutes revert to the weightier policy test.[10]

A second group of courts interpreted the UPA 1973 conflict provision differently. Noting that the uniform act directs a court to weigh presumptions "on the facts," they concluded it requires "an ad hoc determination of the weight attributed to the … competing presumptions"[11] as applied directly to each case in light of all pertinent circumstances.[12] While it is "inescapable that the best interests of the child must be considered," the child's welfare is "not intended to be dispositive."[13] Courts must also consider the adults' plans, their conduct relating to the child, and the work of a gestational mother or functional parent.[14] They must also weigh "the broader sociological and psychological ramifications of its decision," especially potential interference with the stability of bonds among marital or blood relations.[15]

(interpreting WYO. STAT. ANN. § 14-2-817). Other states interpreted the UPA 2002 similarly. Courtney v. Roggy, 302 S.W.3d 141, 146 (Mo. Ct. App. 2009).

9 NEV. REV. STAT. ANN. § 126.051(2) (West 2007); *Courtney*, 302 S.W.3d at 146. California's "conclusive" marital presumption excludes genetic fathers as long as the spouses are cohabiting, CAL. FAM. CODE §§ 7540–44, but court practices are more fluid and allow recognition of multiple presumed parents. June Carbone & Naomi Cahn, *Marriage, Parentage, and Child Support*, 45 FAM. L.Q. 219, 227 (2011).

10 CAL. FAM. CODE § 7612 (West 2020); NEV. REV. STAT. ANN. § 126.051(3) (West 2007); MO. ANN. STAT. § 210.822 (West 2023); Neil S. v. Mary L., 131 Cal. Rptr. 3d 51, 57 (Cal. Ct. App. 2011) (if spouses are not cohabiting, courts apply the "policy and logic" test and give caregiving priority over genetics because the "core considerations are integrity of the family and protection of the child's well-being, which require us to assess the existence and nature of the social relationship between a putative father and child").

11 Kelly v. Cataldo, 488 N.W.2d 822, 826 (Minn. Ct. App. 1992).

12 Doherty v. Leon, 472 P.3d 531, 535 (Ariz. Ct. App. 2020) ("there is no hierarchy among the statutory presumptions").

13 Kelly v. Cataldo, 488 N.W.2d 822, 826 (Minn. Ct. App. 1992). *See also In re* Jesusa V., 85 P.3d 2, 14 (Cal. Ct. App. 4th 2004); Greer *ex rel.* Farbo v. Greer, 324 P.3d 310, 319 (Kan. Ct. App. 2014); ANN M. HARRALAMBIE, 1 HANDLING CHILD CUSTODY, ABUSE, AND ADOPTION CASES § 3:10 (3d ed. 2023) (Natural father's rights when mother is married).

14 *Doherty*, 472 P.3d at 537 (in ruling for same-sex couple over sperm donor, the family court prioritized marital presumption over genetic presumption because public policy favored marriage, the biological and nonmarital mother had "expressed a desire to raise [the child] together," and the nonmarital mother had "always provided a portion of the financial support" and "was the parent with the strongest history with the child").

15 GDK v. State, Dep't of Fam. Servs., 92 P.3d 834, 839 (Wyo. 2004); Kelly v. Cataldo, 488 N.W.2d 822, 826 (Minn. Ct. App. 1992); *In re* Welfare of C.F.N., 923 N.W.2d 325, 333 (Minn. Ct. App. 2018).

Some courts and scholars favor an ad hoc approach because they believe family circumstances are too variable for formal rules to generate fair results.[16] Judges with discretion can reach intuitively correct decisions considering all the facts. On the other hand, relying on multiple, unranked factors and empirical conjecture increases the influence of bias and ideology. Variability among judicial intuitions will also reduce the predictability provided by presumptions. Moreover, it is unclear how judges should balance the welfare of this child and family against the systemic effects of their principles on all children and families.

Whether the UPA 1973 envisioned categorical ranking or ad hoc balancing, the drafters trusted trial or appellate judges to explore and balance the policies underlying the presumptions. In retrospect, this trust seems misplaced. Few courts engage in well-reasoned analysis of their empirical or normative premises.[17] Most assert that children benefit from stability and preserving intact relationships, but I have yet to see any surveying scientific literature on these issues (except in cases discussing the effects of same-sex parenting). Courts consistently conflate stability in legal relationships with stability in the child's residence or caregiver. Most importantly, courts rarely recognize the trade-off between reaching the best result for this child and the systemic effects of a rule or procedure on children and families generally.[18]

Most courts espouse normative premises with little inquiry into the values embodied by state policies or statutes. Courts that favor marriage tend to rely on Justice Scalia's plurality opinion in *Michael H.*[19] This reliance is profoundly misguided. Using his traditionalist methodology for defining fundamental rights, Scalia reasoned that the Constitution protects the parental rights of adulterous biological fathers only if state law treated them as parents consistently throughout American history. Scalia designed this test to disregard recent developments in state law and policy regarding changing family patterns. His explicit purpose was to avoid federal interference with state policy – not to constrain it.[20]

Courts that favor genetic fathers do little better. Some courts assert that genetic fathers have a fundamental right to be legal parents, but they never offer a moral justification for this human right. They can often cite a venerable chain of state precedents, but that chain typically ends in a case dogmatically asserting a natural right. Often, courts rely on precedent cases that never even purport to grapple with

16 *E.g.*, K.E.M. v. P.C.S., 38 A.3d 798, 809 (Pa. 2012). *See Conflicting Presumptions*, 1 FEDERAL EVIDENCE § 3:12 (4th ed. 2023) (discussing paternity presumptions).

17 *See, e.g.*, Atkinson v. Hall, 556 A.2d 651, 653 (Me. 1989) (in an obvious non sequitur, the court inferred that marriage reflected weightier policies than genetics because the common law required proof beyond a reasonable doubt to rebut the marital presumption but the parentage statute required only clear and convincing evidence to rebut the genetic presumption).

18 *See, e.g.*, *ex parte* Presse, 554 So. 2d 406, 412 (Ala. 1989) (blindly quoting a lawyer's unadorned assertion that preservation of marital fatherhood "will be in the child's interest in practically all cases," in a case where the custodial mother had divorced her husband and married the biological father).

19 *Id.* at 414–18.

20 Michael H. v. Gerald D., 491 U.S. 110, 129–30 (1989).

competing presumptions.[21] Other courts favor genetic parents on statutory grounds. Some rely on the 2002 revisions of the UPA, which deleted the earlier provision about weighing presumptions without adding any new rule about how to resolve conflicts. That left only two relevant rules: one that allowed a petitioner to rebut the presumption with genetic evidence, and another that allowed courts to deny petitions for genetic testing on equitable grounds. The drafters assumed timely genetic evidence definitively rebutted the presumptions, and some states interpreted their statutes similarly.[22]

Around the same time, a handful of courts moved in a different direction. They replaced any attempt to balance presumptions with a univocal focus on the interests of this child. The Colorado Supreme Court ruled that when courts estimate the "weightier policy and logic," the "welfare of the child should be paramount."[23] The court worried that paternity findings profoundly affect children's welfare, especially if they have established attachments with a presumed father. Again, the opinion cites no empirical evidence and ignores systemic effects. Nevertheless, its instrumental reasoning remains more persuasive than its statutory reasoning. The court noted that "one of the purposes of the Child's Code [the broader code that includes the UPA] is to secure for each child … care and guidance as will best serve his welfare." It acknowledged that unlike "numerous" other sections of the Child's Code, the Parentage Act never mentions the best interest test. Yet, it never considered why the Parentage Act or its conflict provisions might differ from the other sections. Instead, it declared the legislature "intended the whole paternity proceeding to be about the best interests of the child, and it is, therefore, axiomatic that the trial judge must focus on best interests in resolving competing presumptions." Like so many others, the court conflated a child-centered approach to parentage with the best interest of the child test. Even if parentage law had to be designed exclusively to advance children's interests (it need not), it is not axiomatic that the best way to secure children's welfare is to give a family court judge unbridled discretion to decide what is best for each child based on their estimate of all the relevant facts and values.

21 *In re* T.K.Y., 205 S.W.3d 343, 352 (Tenn. 2006) (citing cases where a biological father opposed infant adoption).

22 Matter of Paternity of AAAE, 471 P.3d 990, 996 (Wyo. 2020); Corey D. v. Travis R., 858 S.E.2d 857, 863 (W. Va. 2021).

23 N.A.H. v. S.L.S., 9 P.3d 354, 364 (Colo. 2000). *See also* Dep't of Soc. Servs. of State *ex rel.* Wright v. Byer, 694 N.W.2d 705 (S.D. 2005) (following N.A.H.). *N.A.H.* cites cases from Arizona, Florida, Kansas, Massachusetts, Minnesota, Montana, Washington, and Wisconsin, although some of these cases adopted a pluralistic approach. Some legal scholars advocated similar approaches. Ilana Hurwitz, *Collaborative Reproduction: Finding the Child in the Maze of Legal Motherhood*, 33 Conn. L. Rev. 127, 172–73 (2000) (advocating courts use a best-interests-of-the-child standard to resolve disputes between candidate mothers in surrogacy cases by considering [1] genetic contribution, [2] preconception intent, [3] gestation as proxies for the person likely to provide the best caregiving, [4] the parent's ability to nurture, [5] the child's need for stability resulting from their initial placement, and [6] the parent's relative ability to help the child deal with identity issues surrounding donor conception).

Nevertheless, the UPA 2017 followed Colorado's approach, and this Act has been adopted in six states. If more than one presumption applies, courts must "adjudicate parentage in the best interests of the child." The act enumerates six factors to guide the best interest analysis: (1) "the age of the child," (2) "the length of time during which each individual assumed the role of parent of the child," (3) "the nature of the relationship between the child and each individual," (4) "the harm to the child," (5) "the basis for each individual's claim to parentage," and (6) "other equitable factors arising from the disruption of the relationship[s]." When one party uses genetics to challenge a presumption, the court must also consider the "facts surrounding the discovery" and any delay in bringing the claim. Using this multifactor standard to resolve parentage conflicts gives trial courts wide discretion subject to little appellate review.

Taken at face value, the UPA 2017 switches topics. Instead of asking which adults have parental duties and rights, it asks which assignment of parenthood will provide this child with the best life. These questions may sometimes overlap, but they are coextensive only if the child is entitled to whichever adult (among those who meet the statutory tests) will facilitate the child's welfare most. I rejected this "best available parent" theory in 1.II.B. Moreover, the best interest standard is necessarily indeterminate in a large share of the relevant cases where the conflict provision is needed. Because of the UPA's statutes of limitations, conflict provision should apply only if a party challenges the presumption before the child turns two or if someone raises a de facto parenthood claim. While toddlers have sufficiently developed relationships for a welfare test to affect the decision, there will often be no legitimate basis for a court to determine whether the infant's life will be better with their gestational, genetic, marital, or residential parent (assuming all are adequate).

Perhaps the UPA 2017's univocal focus on the well-being of this child should not be taken at face value. Although the factors purport to reflect this child's interests, some might encourage courts to consider systemic or adult-centered policies. For instance, a court attentive to "the basis for each individual's claim to parentage" might ask if allowing interventions in this type of case will disrupt other families. Even the factors that relate directly to the welfare of this child, such as the duration or quality of relationships, might leave some space for adult-centered concerns, such as respect for the work of caregivers or gestational parents. The last, catch-all factor seems to direct courts to consider adults' interests. It is difficult to imagine what "equitable factors" will pertain to the child's welfare. Even if the UPA 2017 does not expressly authorize courts to consider systemic policies or adults' interests, the best interest of the child standard often hides contested value judgments behind its patina of univocality and empiricism. I have seen no convincing rationale for using the best-interest standard to adjudicate parentage conflicts except pessimism about any viable alternative.

II CONFLICTING PARENTAGE PRINCIPLES

The viable alternatives were implicit in parentage law all along. The four previous chapters identified a limited, justified role for each ground within a political theory of parentage. With interstitial reform, states can combine these pieces into a system of ordered rules with little recourse to ad hoc judicial decision-making.

After defining the conditions for the rightful acquisition of full parenthood, this part reconstructs the complete puzzle of parentage law. It begins with default rules for the initial assignment of parental liberties and duties, proceeds to rules for prospectively adding new parents, and then considers rules for acquiring parenthood by raising a child. The final section completes the system of parentage law by explaining the role of presumptions and their rebuttal.

A *Acquisition of Full Parenthood*

The reconstruction must start with a precise statement of the conditions for acquiring full parenthood, which are the same regardless of parentage ground. An adult becomes a full legal parent when they satisfy three conditions:

(a) the adult had a liberty to perform custodial caregiving for a child;
(b) the adult voluntarily performed custodial responsibilities of care and guidance for the child; and
(c) the adult fulfilled custodial responsibilities long enough for the child to develop relational attachments.

Once condition (c) is satisfied, the child's political claim against the community to ensure that they have a parent transforms into a claim to this parent (4.III.A), if that claim is consistent with equal respect for the caregiver and other adults. The child's claim respects the caregiver when condition (b) is satisfied. A community may not allow anyone without parental duties to perform indefinite custodial caregiving, but it is fair for law to impose parental duties as a condition of custody only if the adult had a genuine opportunity to decline custody, public assistance prevents parental duties from exacerbating distributive injustice, and law offers some mechanism for resigning the parental relationship (5.III.B.1.b). Last, the parentage assignment respects other adults when condition (a) is satisfied. The adult must have a liberty to perform custodial caregiving, as opposed to a kidnapper with no caregiving liberty or a nanny who has caregiving liberty only subject to others' authority.

When all three conditions are met, the child and the parent each have a claim to a legal relationship and against interference with their relationship. The state respects the child's relational primary goods only if the child has a claim to sustain their established parent–child relationship. The child's political rights justify assigning parental powers and duties to this adult, which the parent holds in a fiduciary sense. The parent acquires their own claim to continue their child-rearing project and preserve the relationship they are building, which the state and other citizens ought to respect (1.I.B.2; 4.III.B). While the parent's and child's rights build only as the relationship develops, the child must have a caregiver with authority immediately, so the law appropriately treats the rightful initiation of custody as the definitive moment.

While substantial, parental rights are weaker than many imagine. A parent's *basic* liberties do not extend to authority over their child's life. For example, the right to freedom of religion cannot justify an adult's religious authority over their child. An adult's only legitimate claim is to be the person who supplies their child's primary goods of caregiving and guidance. The child needs to have their life guided by their parent's personal values, including religious ones, but the law must specify the range of this parental discretion. Only the community has legitimate authority to judge what primary goods every child needs in order to have a valuable childhood and live their own life as an equal citizen within its economic, social, and political structures (1.II.C.1).

B *Initial Parental Liberty: Genetic and Gestational*

Parentage law should begin where childhood begins, with a newborn's biological parents. Gestational and genetic parents have a conditional liberty to perform custodial caregiving. They retain this child-rearing liberty as long as they commit to parenthood and provide the care and guidance that develop parent–child attachments.

1 Genetics and Gestation: Initial Assignment of Parental Liberty

Liberal states cannot legitimately design parentage laws to promote genetic families. Nevertheless, many reasonable citizens value genetic heritage. If this value is consistent with equal respect, citizens should be free to pursue the families they value. To do so, genetic parents need a liberty right to use their genetic code to create children, a liberty right to raise their genetic children, and a claim that no one else create or raise children with their genetic code without their voluntary participation (2.III.A). Because these three rights can be reconciled with equal respect for other adults and the child, citizens have a derived liberty to raise their genetic children.

The rights of genetic parents do not affect most other citizens. An individual has no claim to use others' genetic material to create a child for themselves. Any such claim would violate the principle of equal liberty, sacrificing the ends of genetic parents to promote the familial ends of nonbiological parents.

Reconciling the rights of genetic and gestational parents requires more nuance. Any derived liberty for genetic parents is limited by respect for gestational parents' bodily integrity. Before insemination or embryo transfer, genetic and gestational parents have the same claim to procreative autonomy. Afterward, a genetic parent can no longer have any further claim to control reproduction without violating the gestational parent's right to control her body. Genetic parents cannot claim any right to control a gestational parent's pregnancy (2.III.C.3).

However, neither insemination nor embryo transfer necessarily forfeits or waives a genetic parent's conditional liberty to parent the child. The pregnant person's right to bodily integrity does not entail a claim to exclusive authority over the child. Nor, contrary to prominent scholarly arguments, can the work of gestation or childbirth justify full parental rights at birth that include a right to decide who will raise the child (4.III.B.2). An adult acquires a claim to exclusive authority to shape a child's life once they build a relationship with the child by meeting their need for care and guidance. Only then does the child develop their reciprocal claim to be under this adult's authority (condition (c)). Gestation does not fulfill this political function. A gestational parent's interest in a future relationship with the child is not equivalent to the reciprocal relationship built when an adult decides how to provide a child with a valuable life. However, gestational labor can justify a conditional liberty right to raise the child. If the gestational parent obtained gametes rightfully and wants to raise the child, no one else has the right to insist the gestational parent refrain from their procreative parenting project.

The law must limit child-rearing liberty for biological parents (genetic and gestational) in two ways to ensure equal respect for the child. Their caregiving liberty must be conditional, and the state must maintain distributive mechanisms to offset the parentage lottery.

The state may not allow anyone to deny a child their primary goods, including adequate parental care and guidance. Accordingly, citizens' liberty to raise their biological children must be conditional on a timely commitment to and adequate fulfillment of parental roles (2.III.B.1). If the gestational parent wants to raise the child, the work of gestation and childbirth demonstrates sufficient commitment to future caregiving to satisfy this condition. Accordingly, all states presume the gestational parent is a legal parent unless they expressly waive their parental liberty. States may even allow gestational work to justify a custodial default for gestational parents, especially if they intend to breastfeed the child (4.III.C).[24]

By comparison, genetic parents have little opportunity to demonstrate commitment before the birth. They can assist with the pregnancy by attending medical appointments or providing financial assistance. They can also prepare to raise the child by readying a nursery or taking parenting classes. Accordingly, to sustain their caregiving liberty, genetic parents must either (a) expressly commit to parental duties by signing a parentage acknowledgment or petitioning to establish parentage, or (b) perform parental caregiving with the consent of the genetic-gestational parent. States must have some parentage petition process so that the genetic parent's familial liberty is not subject to the unilateral choice of the gestational parent (4.III.C.1).

[24] With two female parents, a mere genetic mother might also breastfeed by inducing lactation.

The community must also take steps to reconcile a biological parentage regime with equal respect for children. Children are not entitled to the best available parent, any more than the best available school, so a child cannot object to being raised by a genetic parent who provides adequate care. However, children can raise systematic objections if the biological default rule fails to ensure that children reliably receive adequate care. Biological parenting may also entrench intergenerational injustice, especially in the United States, where injustice persistently follows patterns of racial identity that leverage genetic phenotypes. To meet its duty to address these distributive problems, the community might consider licensing, supervising, or supporting parents. Ex ante licensing is unlikely to improve caregiving and is likely to reinforce discrimination based on class, culture, race, or disability. Rather than restricting the parental liberty of already disadvantaged adults, states should supervise all parents lightly and focus public efforts on offering affirmative support (2.III.B.3; 3.III.C).

2 Forfeiture or Waiver of Caregiving Liberty and Parental Duties

Biological parents can forfeit or waive their caregiving liberty. An adult forfeits their conditional liberty to raise a child if their conduct does not demonstrate timely commitment to parental responsibilities or if they prove unwilling or unable to fulfill those responsibilities. Only positive law can specify precisely what actions a parent must perform to demonstrate commitment and when they must do so. Each state will specify its own threshold through some combination of legislation and precedent (2.III.B.1). Similarly, the law must specify what conduct counts as neglect or abandonment sufficient for the forfeiture of parental rights. When a birth parent forfeits their liberty, the child may be adopted without their consent. Abandonment traditionally justifies termination of parental rights, but a state might decide that the value of maintaining existing relationships can justify mandatory open adoption in foster cases (5.III.B.2.c).

The states should also recognize that a child has only one legal parent if one birth parent takes custody and the other never seeks or performs caregiving despite adequate opportunity. Allowing a long-absent biological parent to reassert their child-rearing liberty violates the right of the child and single parent against interference with their relationship. Absent parents may remain a secondary custodian in case of parental death or abandonment. This conclusion requires a revision of state law. Currently, courts will terminate an absent parent's parental rights only if the custodial parent seeks second-parent adoption with a "substitute" parent. This rule illegitimately assumes that all children must have two legal parents, a holdover from discriminatory laws about gendered parenting (2.III.B.1).

Genetic parents should also have a legal power to waive their parental liberty. Their genetic ties do not make them obligated to raise the child. Some scholars believe children are entitled to a life enriched by genetic heritage, but the law can protect this value adequately with a right to know at the age of majority (2.II.C). Most biological parents are also causal parents and, as such, must ensure the child receives adequate care. However, causal parents have no duty to raise the child personally. Gamete donors and birth parents can reasonably trust fertility clinics, adoption agencies, adoptive parents, and the child welfare system to ensure an infant's rights are respected (3.II.B). To facilitate procreative and familial autonomy, the community gives genetic parents (1) a power to waive their claim against another person procreating with their genes and (2) a power to waive their liberty to raise their genetic child. States should maintain procedures for adoption and gamete donation that relieve biological parents of all financial and caregiving responsibilities.

Adoption statutes empower biological parents to waive their parental liberty after the birth (5.III.B.1.a). These statutes must define appropriate protections – like waiting and recission periods – to ensure that waivers by birth parent are informed and not unduly influenced or exploited. Gamete donation agreements empower a genetic parent to waive their claim not to procreate and their conditional parental liberty. Notice that gamete donors never transfer parental duties or rights (2.III.C.2). They never had either. The genetic parents waive their liberty to raise the child, and commitment to parental duties is a condition for parental rights. Once a valid waiver is in place, other adults can obtain a right to use the genetic material for their procreative projects, which gives them a conditional parental liberty that other citizens and the state should respect (5.III.D).

This approach to waiver by genetic parents requires several revisions of existing law. First, law should treat artificial and sexual sperm donation similarly. The state has no legitimate interest in using parental duties to regulate sex. Any lingering worry that sexual procreators will raise false allegations can be addressed by a writing requirement. Second, waivers of parental rights before and after conception should be treated similarly. A biological parent should be able to take on single parenthood voluntarily (2.III.B.1). One birth parent can waive any claim to assistance from their fellow causal parent, and the causal parent can waive their caregiving liberty. Most states already allow a woman to become a sole parent by conceiving at a clinic using an anonymous gamete donor. A child can be adopted by a single parent. A child does not have a claim to be raised by both genetic parents simply because they conceived the child through sex. Adults who conceive through heterosexual intercourse should also be able to arrange parenthood among themselves after conception.[25]

The community may take a different approach to child support. Applying luck-egalitarian principles, officials might conclude that causal parents have a political duty to help the community supply the child with primary goods (3.III.A). Although common in case law, this distributive argument cannot justify the American system that requires procreators to share a percentage of their income

[25] Naomi Cahn, *Perfect Substitutes or the Real Thing?*, 52 DUKE L.J. 1077, 1160–61 (2002) (arguing insistence on dual-parent families fails to recognize not all families replicate sexual families).

with the child (3.III.B). It might justify a European-style approach limited to children's basic needs. Regardless, the states must drastically reform child support to stop exacerbating distributive injustice, such as by imposing unmanageable awards and punitive remedies on impoverished parents. States should also reconsider whether fairness requires relieving some biological parents of the distributive obligation, including victims of statutory rape, gamete theft, and (maybe) deception regarding contraception. The law already takes this political approach to other causal parents, like fertility specialists and gamete donors (3.II.B.4).

3 Parentage by Gestation and Waivers by Gamete Donors

When a gestational parent has no genetic ties with the child, their parental liberties depend on how they obtain the gametes. If they carry a child conceived with donated sperm and eggs, they should have a derived liberty to pursue their procreative parenting project. Recognizing their conditional caregiving liberty does not infringe on the rights of the child, who has only a claim to be raised by some adequate parent (4.III.C). The gamete donors waived their caregiving liberty, and no other adults have any liberty right to raise the child themselves. The gestational parent has a conditional liberty to raise the child and, because of their gestational labor, should be a presumed parent at birth – as they are in all states. When the gestational parent is acting as a surrogate, their rights depend on the parentage agreements discussed below.

C *Adding Parentage by Agreement*

A just community must also maintain avenues to nonbiological parenthood by creating legal tools that empower adults to commit to parental duties. Many citizens value nonbiological families, and the law should enable these citizens to become parents insofar as this liberty is consistent with the rights of the child, the biological parents, and other adults.

1 Full Adoption

States need adoption laws to ensure each child's right to a parent. Adoption also creates opportunities for adults to realize the good of child-rearing without procreation (5.III.B). A child may be adopted into a new family only if anyone with a conditional liberty to raise the child – a legal, presumed, or biological parent – has consented to the adoption or forfeited their liberty through abandonment or neglect. Given the history of adoption abuse, states need procedures to obtain informed consent from birth parents and ensure adoptive parents are willing to fulfill parental obligations. On the other hand, given the history of adoption discrimination, state officials should be wary of using this legitimate authority to facilitate a discriminatory and illegitimate vision of ideal families.

In a just society, adoption opportunities might be rare. Many parents place children for adoption because they feel unable to raise them, often because the United States' inadequate social welfare system means parents bear the brunt of meeting our collective duty to children. The child welfare system exacerbates this injustice in racially oppressive ways by overpolicing families of color and blaming them for poverty-related conduct. I have not attempted to respond to these pervasive injustices in this book. Unless the United States increases financial support for impoverished parents, it is difficult to imagine how we can justly balance the needs of children for adequate caregiving against concerns for systemic racial justice.

2 Second-Parent Adoption and Parentage Acknowledgments

To respect familial liberty, the law should also empower a legal parent and their partner to share parenthood by an express, joint commitment. This is the function of second-parent adoption, acknowledgments of parentage, and preconception agreements. By creating a normative power to generate parental rights prospectively, these laws enable adults to coparent rightfully (5.III.C). They avoid the inevitable period of uncertainty with a functional rule, during which the legal parent has the power to revoke the partner's privilege to continue their parenting project, and the partner has the privilege to leave a now dependent legal parent without support. A legal power to share parenthood is consistent with equal respect for the child. A child needs a relationship with their legal parent, but those relational interests are sufficiently malleable that a legal parent may be trusted to judge whether the child benefits from adding another parent. This decision is an exercise of their parental authority over the child's relational life. If the child has only one legal parent, they should be able to initiate a second-parent adoption. No legitimate reasons exist to restrict this authority based on the sex or marital status of the parent or their partner (5.III.C.2).[26]

Furthermore, all states should have a procedure for parentage acknowledgments around the time of birth (5.III.C.3). Forcing a birth parent and their partner to complete a stepparent adoption for an infant is unnecessary and counterproductive. Screening in stepparent adoptions is typically minimal and ineffective. Intended coparents will usually share coparenting responsibilities even without a formal status, so acknowledgments facilitate and protect infants' relational interests. These statutes also have a salutary expressive effect. They recognize publicly that all citizens have the ability and authority to commit to parenthood without state oversight, treating them as equals in the political institution of the family.

26 Jessica Feinberg, *Parent Zero*, 55 U.C. Davis L. Rev. 2271, 2310–11 (2021).

The handful of parentage acknowledgment statutes, based on the UPA 2017, allow only birth mothers to initiate a parentage acknowledgment. There is no legitimate reason to deny a similar power to genetic parents (5.III.C.3). A gestational parent has presumptive parental authority because gestational work reveals commitment, but a genetic parent who signs an acknowledgment has legally committed themselves to parenthood just as if they had filed a parentage petition. If the gestational parent waives their parental liberty (following whatever additional surrogacy limits the state maintains), the genetic parent should have authority to allow their partner to sign an acknowledgment of parenthood.[27]

Of course, both adoption and acknowledgments must be limited to protect all other legal or putative parents. If a child has two legal parents, both have the authority to veto the addition of any new legal parent; otherwise, one will have unilateral authority over the other's parental liberty. Any biological or presumed parent with a conditional liberty to raise the child has a constitutional right to veto any adoption or acknowledgment. To avoid this problem, the UPA 2017 provides that parentage acknowledgments are valid only if accompanied by a written waiver from any other legal, presumed, or biological parent. These possible parents must give informed consent to their waiver, just as in adoption. The sixty-day recission period provides sufficient protection from duress, and detailed forms would facilitate informed consent.

3 Preconception Agreements

While acknowledgments allow a parent to share parenthood rightfully, prospective parents need the ability to bind themselves earlier to pursue shared procreative plans without subordination. Preconception agreements allow a gestational parent to undertake the burdens of pregnancy without worrying that their partner's support will evaporate, and they allow a nonbiological parent to provide support without the risk that the gestational parent may revoke the permission to parent before they complete an adoption or acknowledgment (5.III.D). No legitimate reasons exist to limit preconception agreements to marital or conjugal couples, any more than adoption or acknowledgments. However, these agreements must include a gestational parent who intends to raise the child. If gestational parents could enter into binding preconception agreements to waive their caregiving liberty, these agreements could circumvent the regulations necessary to reconcile adoption and surrogacy with equal respect for the gestational parent and child (5. III.B.2; 5.III.E).

[27] Douglas NeJaime, *The Nature of Parenthood*, 126 Yale L.J. 2260, 2344–45 (2016).

D *Adding Parents by Caregiving*

Parentage agreements allow parties to coparent rightfully, but many adults raise children without an agreement formally establishing legal parenthood. A community should allow caregivers to develop legal rights through third-party visitation, de facto parenthood, and parentage presumptions, but these doctrines must be carefully circumscribed to reconcile them with parental authority. Properly cabined, these tools can reconcile the parent's authority with the child's psychological well-being and right to stable parental care.

Parents can fulfill their function to provide care and guidance only if they have default authority to decide who develops a relationship with their child. Functional doctrines cannot be reconciled with this authority by insisting, as courts often do, that a legal parent consented to nonparental caregiving (4.III.B.3). Typically, these parents consented to share caregiving, not to share parenthood. A parent must be entitled to seek childcare assistance while they work to support their family. A parent also retains their intimate liberty, including the freedom to choose with whom they live, without risking their parental rights. By default, nonparental caregivers do not have a liberty to parent but only a privilege to care for a child on conditions set by the legal parent.

On the other hand, children develop attachments with long-term caregivers regardless of their legal status. Abruptly terminating the relationship may violate the parent's fiduciary duty (4.II.B.3). Instead of enforcing that duty directly through regulation, states allow visitation petitions from a narrow class of individuals: grandparents, former guardians, or alleged de facto parents. Instead of asking whether the child will benefit from maintaining the relationship – which would substitute the judge's value judgment for the parent's – the court must ask whether the parent's visitation decision fell outside the bounds of reasonable parental judgment. To ensure this deference, states may raise the substantive standard to psychological harm or the evidentiary standard to clear and convincing evidence.

Matters become more complicated when a parent shares responsibility for custody and guidance for a long time. The parent may eventually forfeit their claim to exclusive authority and deference. Forfeiture principles make room for de facto parenthood in two situations: guardianship and cohabitation.

Sometimes, arranging a temporary guardianship is a reasonable exercise of parental authority. A parent facing a health crisis or military deployment should be entitled to entrust their child to relatives or friends without risk of losing their parental rights. The parent–child relationship can be sustained despite such periodic absences, especially with support from the community or extended family. Nevertheless, the absent parent must forfeit their claim to exclusive parenthood at some point (4.III.D). Whether states specify this threshold through de facto parenthood or abandonment, the question is not whether the absent parent waived exclusivity by consenting to share parenthood with the custodian – it is whether the parent forfeited their claim to deference because they have proven unable or unwilling to meet their child's basic needs for care and guidance. If so, the guardian's petition for custody or de facto parenthood must be decided by a court making its own independent judgment about which adult fulfilled parental roles sufficiently to maintain rightful authority over the child.

De facto parenthood can also be permissible when a parent coparents with a relative or cohabitant in the same household. In these cases, the doctrine empowers courts to define, through common law processes, how much caregiving and decision-making parents are permitted to share without forfeiting their claim to exclusive authority (4.III.D). Because parents should be entitled to seek caregiving assistance, I would (tentatively) suggest that caregivers should become parents over the legal parent's objection only if they share approximately equal responsibility for the child's care and guidance. The parent need not expressly agree to share parenthood. De facto parenthood is not merely a tool to cure procedurally defective adoptions (though it can play that role). Nevertheless, the parent must implicitly treat their partner as a coparent. When they hold one another responsible for caregiving, expect to make major decisions together, and treat one another as coparents in interactions with the community, the partner has a privilege to parent the child, satisfying condition (a) of the three conditions for full parenthood listed in II.A. If a child already has two legal parents, each must share parenthood in this manner for their parental rights to be respected.[28] Just as one parent cannot unilaterally authorize second-parent adoption, one cannot unilaterally give their partner a privilege to parent that develops into parenthood. However, if the caregiver does have this liberty right to parent that is in accordance with the rights of the child's parent or parents, once this caregiver fulfills parental responsibilities long enough for the child to build deep bonds, conditions (b) and (c) are also met. The child and partner have acquired a claim to sustain their parental relationship.

E *Presumed Parenthood and Its Rebuttal*

The parentage presumptions track the principles discussed regarding parentage by biology, agreement, and caregiving. The marital and residential presumptions are properly understood as evidentiary presumptions. To understand how they fulfill this function, one must distinguish the facts that trigger a presumption from the facts that trigger a liberty to perform custodial caregiving and full parental duties and rights. These distinctions allow one to conceptualize the presumptions and their rebuttal in a way that aligns existing law with just principles of parentage. A theory of the parentage presumptions must accommodate the multiple bases of parentage for which they are evidence,

[28] Corey D. v. Travis R., 858 S.E.2d 857, 865 (W. Va. 2021).

rather than narrowing them to a single scenario or purpose.[29] The presumption and its rebuttal vary based on the relations among the adults and the timing of the challenge. This analysis begins with heterosexual couples but proceeds to the expanded modern presumptions.

The husband of the gestational parent should remain a presumed parent because, given social norms of marriage, he likely meets all three conditions sufficient for parental rights and duties in II.A.[30] The birth mother's husband is likely (1) to be a genetic parent with conditional liberty to parent the child,[31] (2) to have the genetic-gestational parent's consent to share parenthood, and (3) to have voluntarily performed custodial caregiving after that birth that developed relational attachments grounding the child and parent's right. States traditionally used the presumption to encourage marriage as its preferred family form, but the law must discard this illegitimate purpose, along with express preferences for marital child-rearing and indirect support for the social stigma of illegitimacy.[32] Accordingly, the same three evidentiary inferences are appropriate when a heterosexual man lives with an infant that he holds out as his own child. While cohabitation norms increase uncertainty about the second and third inferences, that uncertainty is reduced once the adults continue to cohabit after the birth.[33] The law should, as it does, treat heterosexual male spouses and cohabitants as parents for all purposes until someone rebuts their parental status in court.

To rebut the presumption, a challenger must contradict the three propositions inferred from marriage or cohabitation that ground parental rights and duties. When a child is conceived by heterosexual intercourse, the gestational, presumed, or alleged parent should be able to rebut a presumption with genetic evidence soon after the birth. A gestational parent may choose not to coparent with a spouse or cohabitant who is not a genetic parent. The partner has a liberty to raise the child only

[29] Feinberg asks courts to choose whether their presumption reflects intent, function, or marriage promotion and revise their rebuttal process to serve that purpose, but she recommends a combination of intent and function similar to my proposals here, with the exception that I seek to integrate them with genetics as well. Feinberg, *supra* note 4, at 260, 297–300. She urges states to dispense with the vestiges of the idea that presumed parenthood rests on inferred genetic paternity, but genetic ties appropriately remain relevant to the initial parentage assignment.

[30] Unlike Nancy Dowd, for example, I would maintain the presumption but allow rebuttal if the spouse did not commit to or perform care. Nancy E. Dowd, *Parentage at Birth: Birthfathers and Social Fatherhood*, 14 Wm. & Mary Bill Rts. J. 909, 928–29 (2006).

[31] Estimates of misattributed paternity hover around 1–2 percent. Maarten H.D. Larmuseau, *Mommy's Baby, Daddy's Maybe: Misattributed Paternity in a Nationwide Blood Group Database*, 291 J. Internal Med. 2 (2022).

[32] Solangel Maldonado, *Illegitimate Harm: Law, Stigma, and Discrimination Against Nonmarital Children*, 63 Fla. L. Rev. 345 (2011).

[33] *Id.* at 387. Maldonado argues that treating marital and nonmarital children equally requires dropping the residence requirement; however, a shared residence (at least overnight visitation) is necessary to infer the adult fulfilled caregiving functions. Although coresidence is not an element of the marital presumption, it can be inferred from marriage, and marital paternity can be rebutted (even after two years) if the spouse is not a biological parent and never lived with the child.

because the law presumes that he is either a genetic parent or has the birth mother's consent. Their relationship triggers the presumption but is not itself an independent ground for a parental liberty. Consent to marry or cohabit is not a binding agreement to coparent an unrelated child.[34] The relationship is also not an independent ground for parental duties. The partner may choose not to be a parent. He has no duty to help the gestational parent raise the child, assuming he did not encourage her to conceive or keep the pregnancy. Moreover, the alleged genetic parent should be able to challenge the presumption. Neither the gestational parent nor their partner has unilateral authority to extinguish the genetic parent's liberty to raise the child.

These facts do not entail the presumptions are unfounded. The automatic presumptions of parentage rest on sound general inferences, while the rebuttal process disproves those general inferences in this specific case.[35] During the child's infancy, genetic evidence should often be sufficient to rebut the marital or residential presumption. The law should probably also, as mentioned above, offer a mechanism for opting out of the marital presumption through an acknowledgment of parentage.[36]

American law mostly complies with these principles. Any involved adults can challenge the parental status of a residential caregiver before they perform enough caregiving to trigger the presumption. Either spouse can seek to rebut the marital presumption before the child turns two, and most states also allow the alleged genetic fathers to challenge it as well. A few states retain a marital presumption that excludes genetic fathers, and a divided US Supreme Court left them in place, but this rule is mistaken as a matter of political morality. Eliminating conclusive presumptions would be less disruptive than it first appears because genetic ties should rebut the presumption only during a child's infancy. A statute of limitations or abandonment principle should prevent most slow-acting genetic parents from challenging a presumed parent.

Unlike in cases of sexual conception between intimate partners, genetic evidence should be irrelevant for rebuttal in two scenarios. First, a gestational parent and their partner may pursue a shared procreative parenting plan using donor

34 *See* Katharine K. Baker, *Bargaining or Biology: The History and Future of Paternity Law and Parental Status*, 14 Cornell J. L. & Pub. Pol'y 1, 47 (2004); Feinberg, *supra* note 26, at 2301.

35 This can mislead some criticism, such as when Feinberg rejects theories that the marital presumption rests on mutual intent or respect for intact families because the presumption applies automatically without inquiry into the spouses' actual intent or the actual stability of their family. Feinberg, *supra* note 26, at 2130, 2315.

36 *Id.* at 2328–30. Carbone and Cahn argue that states should abolish the marital presumption as a proxy for genetics, instead mandating husbands to either submit to paternity testing or sign a VAP waiving testing. June Carbone & Naomi Cahn, *Which Ties Bind? Redefining the Parent–Child Relationship in an Age of Genetic Certainty*, 11 Wm. & Mary Bill Rts. J. 1011, 1066–70 (2002). I support this reform proposal because, as they argue, requiring spouses to make an informed commitment would increase certainty at birth and fairly preclude subsequent denials of responsibility by the father or exclusionary conduct by the mother. However, my goal in this section is to reconstruct existing law, which still recognizes the marital presumption.

gametes. It is preferable to manage these cases with preconception agreements or consent-to-ART statutes, but states without such doctrines should allow couples to rely on the marital or residential presumption and refuse genetic rebuttal. When a female undergoes ART with her partner's participation, the law can infer the adults were acting on a shared plan to coparent. This inference reflects typical expectations and respects principles of equal liberty. As discussed in 5.III.D, reciprocal legal obligations prevent either party from taking advantage of the vulnerability created by a shared plan for procreative parenting. This presumption should apply regardless of the sex of the spouse or cohabitant, as all states to consider the matter have done since *Obergefell v. Hodges*.[37] Of course, these legal duties arise only if the couple had a shared plan. Either party should be able to rebut the presumption soon after the birth with direct or circumstantial evidence they did not plan to coparent when the child was conceived.[38]

Genetic parentage should also not rebut the presumptions in several situations of postconception behavior. Some pregnant persons hide uncertainty about the child's paternity, manipulating their partners into shared parenthood. Other couples openly discuss the uncertainty about paternity and decide to raise the child together regardless. A gestational parent may also have conceived a child with a previous partner or sought donor conception expecting to be a single parent. In all these cases, regardless of the method or circumstances of conception, the gestational parent has allowed their partner to coparent.[39] Once the partner performs enough caregiving for the child to develop attachments, the child develops a right to sustain their parental relationship with the presumed parent, and the presumed parent acquires a right to continue their parental project. Again, these situations can arise regardless of the gender of the nonbiological parent.

Two legal rules protect presumed nonbiological parents. First, most presumptions have a statute of limitations, usually two years. Legislatures should set these limits based on their general estimate of how long it takes for a child to develop attachments that ground their right to this parent. After that point, a presumption should be rebuttable only if the presumed parent certainly did not fulfill the roles that develop this right and duty. Most statutes insist the challenger prove the presumed parent never lived with the child or held themselves out as a parent. This rule

37 576 U.S. 644 (2015). The presumptions cannot simply be extended in a sex-neutral manner because they presuppose the gestational parent has a liberty to parent and share their parenting project. *Contra* NeJaime, *supra* note 27, at 2340–41. Applying the presumption to the spouse or cohabitant of a mere genetic parent would infringe the liberty of the gestational parent and circumvent whatever protections the community deems necessary for surrogacy. *See* 5.III.E.

38 States must avoid conflating procreative parenting plans with postconception coparenting under a single rubric of "intent." Feinberg, *supra* note 4, at 273–74, 278–80.

39 Rather than create distinct presumptions for sexual and nonsexual conception, *id.* at 300–05, we should distinguish the facts that trigger presumptions from the facts that ground caregiving liberties or parental rights and duties, recognizing rebuttal concerns the latter.

protects the parental rights of the child and presumed parent – or it would if courts stopped undermining the time limit with exceptions.

Second, if the child is not yet two years old or the statute has no limitations period, courts may protect presumptive parents with estoppel or de facto parenthood. The former is the more traditional doctrine, but the latter is more accurate for deception or mistake cases.

Suppose a birth mother lied to her husband about his paternity for eighteen months before deciding to cut him out of the child's life. A court might exclude the mother's proffered genetic evidence because allowing her to contradict her prior lies would be unjust to the father. This resort to equitable estoppel is unnecessary and inappropriate. Many courts think estoppel is necessary to maintain a fiction of genetic paternity,[40] but such pretense is unnecessary. Even if admitted, the genetic evidence would prove only that the spouse did not have a liberty to raise the child as a genetic father. It would not rebut the other two presumed facts that are sufficient to ground parental rights and duties: the mother allowed her partner to coparent and the child developed parental attachments. Estoppel also suggests several inappropriate inferences. It implies the court excluded evidence for fairness reasons that demonstrated the spouse is not really a parent. In a similar vein, estoppel suggests that a spouse who did not know the genetic truth should be free to walk away, that a gestational parent who believed her partner was the father could be allowed to rebut, and that the court need not worry when the child already knows the genetic truth.[41]

By contrast, de facto parenthood recognizes the father is a parent with rights and duties. Nevertheless, courts must use this doctrine carefully in rebuttal cases. Legislatures set the time limits for the marital and residential presumption based on their judgment about when children typically develop parental attachments. De facto parenthood supplants their rule with ad hoc judicial judgments about the attachments of a particular child. Both the rule and the standard have specific types of errors and biases.

Estoppel is strictly necessary only when adults start to share parenthood after conception but split before the unrelated adult performs enough caregiving for the child to develop their right to a parent. This claim rests on a razor's edge. The biological parent was not obligated to share parenthood with their partner initially, and they never entered a preconception agreement or parentage acknowledgment that would justify forcing the parent to continue sharing parenthood.

The fairness intuitions behind estoppel have been especially destructive in one salient situation: when a deceived partner wants to renounce parentage. Some courts allow men to disestablish paternity long after the limitations period because it seems unfair to make them remain parents when they were manipulated into their parental commitment. Other courts authorize deceived husbands to sue genetic fathers to

40 Carbone and Cahn, *supra* note 9, at 229.

41 *Id.* at 231.

reimburse the expense of raising a child, as the court permitted in the case of Pamela, Richard, and Eric.[42] These doctrines misunderstand the direction of parental obligations and the sense in which parental duties must be voluntary. Pamela and Richard's fraud wronged Eric, but this conclusion about their horizontal relations does not alter Eric's vertical duties to the child.[43] A presumed father can seek genetic testing of a newborn, after which he may walk away because he has no duty to raise the child. Once someone like Eric raises a child for years, they may not disavow their parental duties or seek compensation for their efforts. The political community may not allow any parent to insist their commitment to the child was conditional on the child's genetic parentage, any more than the child's appearance or abilities.

* * *

To reconstruct a coherent parentage law, we first needed to rebuild the foundation of parenthood. To ensure equal respect for children, the political community must ensure that each child is in the custody of an adult with a duty to provide the care and guidance that each child needs to have a flourishing childhood and develop into a thriving adult. No individual has a personal moral right or duty to exercise this political authority over a child. Nevertheless, raising children is central to many reasonable conceptions of the good life. The community must create legal rules that enable adults to become parents in ways consistent with equal respect for the child, the parents, and other adults.

As American parentage law slowly recognized, no single rule or principle can suffice to ground parenthood. Genetics, causation, caregiving, and agreements all play a role. However, the law cannot accept a tangle of overlapping principles, hiding the conflicts behind judicial discretion. Most of this book refined the existing legal principles of parentage, showing how each piece fulfills a justified yet limited role in a political system of parentage. This final chapter reassembled those pieces into a pluralistic system of rules that can settle most conflicts without recourse to ad hoc judicial judgments. With the guidance of liberal-egalitarian values, states can reconstruct a coherent system of parentage law that enables children and parents to pursue their lives as equal members of the community.

42 D.W. v. R.W., 52 A.3d 1043, 1059 (N.J. 2012).

43 A gestational parent's reasons for misleading their partner affect the horizontal wrongdoing that might justify a tort for paternity deception but cannot alter the nonbiological parent's parental relationship. Susan Ayres, *Paternity Un(Certainty): How the Law Surrounding Paternity Challenges Negatively Impacts Family Relationships and Women's Sexuality*, 20 J. GENDER RACE & JUST. 237, 254–59 (2017).

Index

Printed by Integrated Books International,
United States of America